Realtime Systems

Series editors: Tony Hoare and Richard Bird

Series listing continued at back of book

Realtime Systems

Nimal Nissanke

University of Reading

Prentice Hall

London   New York   Toronto   Sydney   Tokyo   Singapore
Madrid   Mexico City   Munich   Paris

First published 1997 by
Prentice Hall Europe
Campus 400, Maylands Avenue
Hemel Hempstead
Hertfordshire, HP2 7EZ
A division of
Simon & Schuster International Group

Transferred to digital print on demand 2001

Printed in Canada

Library of Congress Cataloging-in-Publication Data

Nissanke, Nimal.
    Realtime systems / Nimal Nissanke.
        p. cm. – (Prentice Hall series in computer
    science)
    Includes bibliographical references and index.
    ISBN 0-13-651274-7
    1. Real-time data processing. I. Title.
    II. Series.
    QA76.54.N58 1997
    004'.33–dc32   96-49195
                                     CIP

British Library Cataloguing in Publication Data

A catalogue record for this book is available from
the British Library

ISBN 0-13-651274-7 (pbk)

---

  2 3 4 5   01 00 99 98

For my loving parents

to whom I owe so much

Contents

Preface

Realtime computing is one of the most demanding and challenging areas in computing. It is also of greatest importance, since realtime software is indispensable to all ultra-reliable and safety critical applications. Realtime systems play an important role in modern life, ranging from domestic appliances to industrial robots, from industrial process control to advanced avionics and from computer games to worldwide stock exchange applications. These applications invariably involve realtime tasks, which often carry significant penalties in terms of cost and loss of life in the event of failure.

The complexity of modern realtime systems requires a deep understanding of the issues involved and the adoption of new approaches to the development of such systems. Recent decades have seen remarkable progress on both these fronts. However, as we begin to conceive more and more complex systems, there are anxieties about current practice, namely about how successfully it is facing the new challenges and whether it is keeping abreast with scientific achievements. This is because some aspects of realtime system design still remain an *ad-hoc* activity and there is a tendency to treat realtime issues as a low level concern. Perhaps, these statements are contentious, but they are intended to highlight a serious problem affecting the profession. It is about technical education and training and, in particular, about the need for translating academic achievements into technical know-how.

The objective of this book is to contribute to this effort with an introduction to the essentials of current know-how. Although its boundary is not very well defined, the body of knowledge relevant to the study of realtime systems encompasses a whole range of topics. There are issues such as clocks, specification, design and modelling of realtime systems, etc., which are exclusive to the study of realtime systems. On the other hand, there are also a number of fairly independent topics having applications outside realtime systems but with a definite realtime dimension. These concern, for example, scheduling, task allocation and fault tolerance, etc. This book attempts to give the reader a deeper understanding over a range of such important topics.

This text promotes an integrated approach to realtime systems design, with an equal emphasis on developing practical skills. This calls for both breadth and depth in its study. Breadth is taken to mean an overall understanding of the subject area. Because of the complexities involved, an appreciation of the system as a whole is paramount in the design of realtime systems. The design for service can no longer be totally separated from the design against failures, and neither can be separated from the design of such features as the user interface. On the other hand, depth is understood in terms of a detailed working knowledge in certain techniques and approaches. Such a detailed understanding not only provides some immediately useful tools in practical problem solving, but also gives a greater appreciation of the complexities involved. This enhances vigilance, a vital quality when dealing with critical applications.

At the same time, the book strives, to a certain extent, to elevate the study of realtime systems to a more rigorous level. This is motivated by the desire to provide a better framework for the study of realtime systems, facilitating a higher level of abstraction and a sharper focus on concepts and issues. Invariably, this framework relies greatly on mathematics – an essential ingredient for transforming any body of technical knowledge into a scientific discipline. The study of realtime systems is undergoing such a transformation and is benefiting greatly from wider practical application of mathematical methods to specification, design, modelling and verification of realtime systems.

The book will also familiarize the reader with some of the recent advances in formal methods – an area in software engineering with significant achievements over recent years. Cross fertilization achieved through this combined study of realtime systems and formal methods is beneficial to both fields in different ways: the field of realtime systems in terms of rigour and the field of formal methods in terms of realistic computer systems for the application of new mathematical techniques.

Some of the topics in this book emerged from a final year option in an undergraduate course in computer science and a module offered on an M.Sc. course at the University of Reading, UK. As a result, the book is suitable for both undergraduate and postgraduate students, but is also aimed at researchers and professionals wishing to improve their understanding of realtime systems. The topics have been selected in such a way that they reflect both current practice and, in certain cases, the state-of-the-art. However, the book does not claim to be a comprehensive treatment of the issues addressed. In this respect, the reader may find Bibliographical Notes in Chapter 1 particularly useful. Below is a brief overview of the book; a summary is also given in Section 1.5 of Chapter 1.

Each chapter deals with a fairly independent topic. Chapter 1 sets the scene with a brief general introduction to the subject matter. Most of the issues raised are dealt with in greater detail in subsequent chapters. Chapter 2 is a discussion about time and individual clocks when taken in isolation. It is a study of theoretical and practical notions of time in the context of realtime systems. Note that the term *realtime* is used here in a system context, whereas the term *real time* is used in a temporal context. Chapter 3 continues this discussion and establishes certain relationships between real time and its clock representations, as well as temporal relations in both these domains separately. It also introduces a clear distinction between states and events and a classification of events. Chapters 4 and 5 introduce Petri Nets as a medium for modelling realtime systems. Chapter 6 takes this discussion further by introducing an extended Petri net framework for the study of both functional and timing aspects of such systems. Chapters 7 and 8 continue the same theme but in CSP and Timed CSP. Chapter 9 outlines an approach for partitioning of realtime software early in the development process. The issues discussed here are taken further in Chapter 10, which deals with the allocation of tasks in a multi-processor system and provides a natural link to the study of scheduling problems in realtime systems. Chapter 11 lays the foundation for this study. Chapters 12, 13 and 14 address specific scheduling problems and are devoted to scheduling in single and multi-processor architectures under static and dynamic environments. Chapter 15 is an introduction to fault tolerance and includes a discussion about errors and faults, recovery mechanisms and the use of redundant software and hardware components. Chapter 16 returns to the theme begun in Chapters 2 and 3 and deals with systems of clocks found in common multi-processor architectures. It also introduces a number of clock synchronization algorithms, which are of significant interest from the point of view of fault tolerance, the topic of the preceding chapter.

Appendix A provides a selection of realistic realtime problems as open ended exercises for exploring the applicability of the ideas presented in this book. Appendix B presents mathematical proofs for selected observations made in a number of chapters. Appendix C contains a brief description of the basic mathematical notation, a substantial part of which is from the Z Notation – a formal specification language used for requirements specification. Appendix D provides a short introduction to the Schema Language, which is also a part of the Z Notation.

The book relies extensively on a number of publications. These have been cited under Bibliographical Notes at the end of each chapter. Usually, these references have not been cited in the main body of the chapters so that the discussion flows without interruption. The exceptions to this are Chapter 15 and Realtime Scenarios in Appendix A, which cite the relevant references at the most appropriate place. The Bibliographical Notes also contain other references for further reading.

Acknowledgements

I wish to express my gratitude to the students who have attended my course on Realtime Systems at the University of Reading. Their critical study of the material presented in this book has been a valuable contribution. I wish to extend special thanks to Ali Abdallah, Francis Cottet, Neil Foggo, John Graham, Ulla Isaksen, Johnson Thomas and Shirley Williams for helpful comments and suggestions on the manuscript; their comments and assistance have improved the text significantly. In particular, I wish to mention Ali Abdallah's considerable insight with regard to the material in the chapters on clocks and CSP. I am also thankful to Mauro Pezze for clarifying certain issues related to the material in Chapter 6. I wish to acknowledge the material provided by Peter Goulden, Neil Robinson, Darren Ryden and Andrew Downton. Their material forms the basis of some of the realtime scenarios given in Appendix A. My thanks go also to independent reviewers for a number of important improvements that they suggested. This book has significantly benefited from the support given to my research by Rockwell Collins (UK) Ltd, which I gratefully acknowledge. I am also very grateful to Jackie Harbor of Prentice Hall for her advice and her role in bringing this book into existence and to Alison Stanford for painstaking editorial work.

I owe a great deal to my family, Machiko, Samaya and Hikaru, for carrying much of the strain of this undertaking. They have been a vital source of support, love and encouragement.

Chapter 1

Introduction

1.1 What are Realtime Systems?

1.1.1 Applications and Defining Characteristics

Realtime systems are commonplace: controlling domestic appliances such as washing machines and central heating systems; serving as gate keepers and cashiers at car parks; and even catching speeding motorists. Obviously, there are other more sophisticated applications. Some typical ones are:

- flight control in avionics;
- air traffic control;
- process control in industrial plants, laboratory experiments and nuclear power stations;
- remote exploration of such environments as underwater, outer space and high risk or contaminated areas;
- robotics;
- patient monitoring;
- command and control in defence industry;
- virtual reality, opening a new era in human computer interaction.

Such applications may employ a variety of technologies such as radio, radar, sonar, laser and computer vision. With the rapid growth of capabilities of modern computers, realtime systems are being placed in control of many such applications of increasing complexity and economic and social importance.

The nature of computing underlying these systems may vary, ranging from complex numerical computations, as in radar and in particle physics, to relatively simple computations over extensive amounts of data, as in image processing. The time scales may also vary from application to application, and may be measured, for example, in milli-seconds (10^{-3} s) or μseconds (10^{-6} s). The most characteristic feature of these systems, however, is not the operational time scale, but

1

the emphasis placed on real time in defining the required system behaviour. Thus, realtime computing does not necessarily imply fast computing, but, rather, it guarantees the timely response of the system to external events.

1.1.2   Hard and Soft Realtime Systems

The correct behaviour of non-realtime systems is founded on the *logical correctness* of the result. By contrast, realtime systems require both the logical correctness of the result and its *timing correctness*. The definition of logical correctness, also referred to as functional correctness, is itself not unique and depends on how a system is viewed abstractly. As discussed below, in systems exhibiting purely sequential behaviour the logical correctness is often expressed in terms of correct inputs and outputs, whereas in systems involving concurrency it is defined in terms of correct patterns of behaviour or order of events and communications. In this sense, timing correctness may be viewed as an extension to logical correctness that includes a unique new dimension, namely, real time. However, there are virtues in viewing the two notions of correctness as separate issues, both for theoretical and practical reasons. This is because reasoning about time and the measurement of time differs fundamentally from reasoning about other physical and abstract quantities.

The two notions of correctness may also be traded off against each other. The result is two broad categories of realtime systems: *hard realtime systems* and *soft realtime systems*. In hard realtime systems, timing correctness is critically important and may not be sacrificed for other gains. In the case of certain hard realtime systems, especially realtime safety critical systems, timing correctness may be so important that criteria on logical correctness may sometimes be relaxed in favour of achieving timing correctness. A typical example is an auto-pilot on an aircraft, the failure of which to check the altitude at prescribed times may have catastrophic consequences. In such circumstances a result of poorer quality, but on time, may be preferable to a late if highly accurate result.

In soft realtime systems timing correctness is important but not critical. An occasional failure to observe it should not result in serious consequences. Soft realtime tasks are performed as fast as possible, or as timely as possible, but are not constrained by absolute deadlines, and their timing correctness may be sacrificed under special circumstances such as peak demands on the processor or the communication medium. By contrast, no such timing requirements are associated with non-realtime tasks, although they can be subjected to other performance related requirements.

The discussion of correctness of realtime behaviour is continued in Section 1.2.3.

1.1.3 Time and Event Driven Systems

Another classification of realtime systems, having a particular relevance at the implementation level, is based on events and clock times and distinguishes between *event-triggered* or *interrupt-driven* architectures and *time-triggered* architectures respectively. Despite the conceptual differences between them, the two kinds of architecture often co-exist in many real life applications. Interrupt-driven systems respond to external events by first detecting interrupts (signals) raised by an interrupt mechanism and then generating the appropriate control signal or action dynamically.

Time-triggered architectures operate in accordance with clock times as shown by an integrated independent clock or as determined appropriately from the readings of a system of clocks. The former concerns uni-processor architectures and the latter centralized and distributed multi-processor architectures. Time-triggered architectures basically operate by treating regular clock pulses as a special interrupt signal, leading to the regular polling of possible points of interaction. As the logical clock reading reaches certain predefined values, an appropriate action is selected for execution from a lookup table.

Both types of architecture are common in practical applications and have merits and drawbacks. It can be argued that it is easier to reason about time-triggered systems since the assumptions underlying their design are more explicit and specific. They are also considered robust on the grounds of tightly controlled interfaces between subsystems and independent functioning of subsystems based on local clocks. On the other hand, interrupt-driven systems could be an efficient mechanism for responding to external events. This depends on a low frequency of interrupts, requiring as a result a low interrupt service rate.

1.1.4 Structure of Realtime Systems

Most realtime computer systems are parts of other systems, including larger computer systems. The final effect of the computer system would be through mechanical or other systems interacting with the environment. A realtime system may therefore be viewed as consisting of the *controlling system*, usually a computer, and the *controlled system*, which in turn consists of *sensors* and *activators*. The system receives information about the environment from sensors and affects the environment by means of activators. Some activators may not necessarily act on the environment, but, instead, may simply adapt to changes in the environment in a passive manner, for example by controlling the system exposure to the environment or by activating additional sensors. Sensors are operated by the effect of light, heat, pressure, radar and other forms of energy in the outside environment, and take the form of pressure gauges, thermometers, microphones, hydrophones, receivers and video cameras. The sensors may produce analog or discrete data. Activators may affect the environment through discharging similar forms of energy to the environment in a controlled manner and may take the form of mechanical devices, heaters, displays, switches, transmitters, etc.

The system interaction with the environment may be both periodic and sporadic. This results from the fact that every realtime system necessarily consists of a monitoring component and a reactive component. Realtime systems not possessing both these components in some form are rare and are of limited purpose. An example of a realtime system that is dedicated primarily to monitoring is a seismograph, an instrument intended for detecting and recording ground motions due to earthquakes in real time. In general, the monitoring subsystem is intended for sampling the environment and, therefore, may function basically in a highly regular predictable manner. The reactive subsystem, on the other hand, may be called into action sporadically upon detection of irregularities or excessive deviations in the controlled or observed environment by the monitoring subsystem. In this sense even a seismograph has a reactive component.

1.1.5   Embedded Realtime Systems

A system is a collection of components working in parallel, each with a specialized functionality that is designed to deliver a specific service. In delivering this service, the components interact with each other through exchange of information and through sharing of resources, potentially influencing each other's behaviour. The degree of this interaction may vary in extent and form (space) as well as in frequency and regularity (time). Obviously, realtime systems incorporate both these dimensions to varying extents.

All systems invariably interact with the environment, encompassing both operators and users. The nature of service provided by a system may be better understood by partitioning the environment into two subenvironments: an *active environment* comprising, for example, operators that intervene in the system behaviour for operational purposes, and a *passive environment* comprising, for example, users who are interested only in the service provided and the ambient environment which has no interest at all in the existence of the system. The active environment communicates with the system through an interactive computer control interface, whereas other users communicate with it through an interactive user interface.

Certain systems may not involve an active environment. These are often referred to as *embedded systems* and are typically mobile. An example is modern fully automated space probes. There are, however, other more common embedded systems, especially if a system is viewed as a hierarchy of nested subsystems. Any such subsystem may be seen as a system in its own right while treating its exterior as its execution environment. Naturally, such systems exhibit the characteristics of embedded systems since no direct operator intervention is possible and the functionality has to be supported fully from within.

1.2 Abstraction of Realtime Systems

Any computation necessarily involves real time. This does not mean, however, that it is necessary to consider real time in its full complexity. As in any scientific activity, abstraction has a definite purpose and is intended to produce abstractions (theories or abstract artefacts) and appropriate models for describing and understanding some aspects of the reality relevant to a given problem. The success of abstraction depends on the meaning of the word 'appropriate' – a word that often escapes a proper initial description and yet enters subsequent judgements in quite categorical terms concerning what is a good abstraction and what is a poor abstraction. This indicates the difficulties in putting abstraction into practice. Abstraction should be neither too vague nor too detailed in relation to the problem in hand. This applies especially when dealing with real time because, unlike all other metrics of measurement, real time is extremely complex and often confusing.

Note the distinction made here between the terminology: '*real time*' and '*realtime*'; the term *real time* is used in a temporal context, whereas *realtime* is used in a system context.

1.2.1 Forms of Abstraction

The simplest form of abstraction of real time reduces it to an ordering, possibly a partial ordering, of events in real time according to their temporal precedence. The precedence relation may sometimes be implicit, as in the case of *inputs* and *outputs*, where it is taken for granted that outputs follow inputs. Systems that are based on the notions of *input* and *output* are referred to as *transformational systems*. Their specification may be given as an input–output relation. Conformity of the actual behaviour with the specified input–output relation is understood as logically correct behaviour. One implication of this view is that the computations concerned terminate; otherwise the correctness has to be treated as contributing only to a partial understanding.

In situations where the real time events may not be seen simply as inputs and outputs, but as more general complex patterns of interactions of the system with its environment, the temporal precedence relation is explicitly recognized, if not explicitly stated. Systems founded on events and interactions correspond to what are referred to as *reactive systems*. Since the interactions are typically non-terminating, the correctness has to be investigated by using more elaborate models than those employed in transformational systems.

Further down on the ladder of abstraction comes some explicit notion of real time. As evident from the variety of timed and untimed systems of temporal logic aimed at the study of realtime systems or dedicated to the study of time in general, the choice of abstractions of *real time* is quite wide. Three major forms of abstraction are founded on the following: (a) an explicit notion of clock time, (b) an implicit notion of real time through time intervals, relations between them and through durations and (c) a qualitative notion of real time through modalities of time (as exemplified by words such as *some time* and *always*). These abstractions are useful for different purposes, especially for the purpose of reasoning about different aspects of the system. The representation of real time appropriate for a particular realtime system needs to be chosen on the basis of the attributes of real time which are most relevant to the study of the particular system.

1.2.2   Modelling Frameworks

There are many frameworks for modelling realtime systems. Among them are temporal logic, timed extensions of Petri nets, timed extensions of Communicating Sequential Processes (CSP), Real-Time Logic (RTL) and Duration Calculus. Although they serve similar purposes, these frameworks have different capabilities. In relation to modelling frameworks, this book limits its study to Petri nets and CSP only.

Petri nets have proved to be a versatile tool for the study of computer systems, incorporating different architectures and covering a range of diverse applications. A major attraction of the theory of Petri nets has been the underlying mathematical foundation and its graphical language, enabling visualization and, in certain cases, simulation. Thus, the greatest strength of Petri nets is their analytical and modelling capability. However, a well-known weakness of Petri nets is that the framework does not handle large problems well. The inherent simplicity of the basic idea is soon lost even with problems of moderate size. Although the problem is particularly noticeable in the case of Petri nets, it is however wrong to single out Petri nets in this respect. The scalability of many new approaches to industrial problems is a major concern. There is a growing realization that complexity of models is not always a problem of the language, but often reflects the size and complexities of the application. A part of the answer to this lies in the provision of tools with some degree of automation. With adequate tool support, Petri nets could be a valuable tool in the design and analysis of computer systems. An additional factor in their favour is the significant amount of research already devoted to their theory. For dealing with realtime systems, Petri nets have been extended in several ways. Some of these attempts have been considerably influenced by the applications they were originally intended for, but any shortcomings are being redressed by current research.

CSP and Timed CSP provide an alternative approach. Although compared to Petri nets they are of more recent origin; both CSP and Timed CSP have secured a promising place among the formal languages, having a major impact on realtime systems design. CSP is designed for the study of concurrency, a pattern of behaviour emanating from abstraction when real time is suppressed in the quantitative sense. Timed CSP restores real time in an explicit form, providing in the process a number of logically related models to view both concurrency and realtime behaviour. An advantage of using CSP is that it provides a formal language enabling both specification and formal proof, thus facilitating rigourous validation and verification of systems.

1.2.3 Correctness of Realtime Systems

Section 1.1.2 made a distinction between *logical correctness* and *timing correctness*. Both these notions are important, and, as mentioned there, the weight attached to each depends on the nature of the application, that is, whether it is a hard realtime application or a soft realtime application. *Timeliness* or timing correctness – the property that describes whether a system meets its timing constraints fully – is what characterizes hard realtime systems. Timeliness depends ultimately on the timing requirements of the application and very little can be said about it in general terms. Apart from such application specific properties, there are several global temporal properties having a crucial bearing on timing correctness. This section concentrates on these properties.

As pointed out in Section 1.2.1, the study of a particular realtime system requires the adoption of an appropriate theoretical framework with adequate capabilities for dealing with real time or temporal properties of interest as well as other spatial properties. A formal description of the system expressed in the chosen framework, along with everything entailed by the description within the framework, constitutes a *theory* of the system. One can visualize possible behaviours of the system as implied by the theory by referring to various *models* envisaged by the theory. Although they are distinct categories, theories and models are related and are complementary to each other.

As a consequence of abstraction, a theory of a system may omit certain aspects of real time. Two basic ways in which theories view real time aspects of systems is to consciously concentrate on the qualitative aspects of time or to consider both qualitative and quantitative aspects, usually with some bias towards one or the other. Qualitative study of realtime systems invariably leads us to temporal properties such as *liveness, fairness, eventuality* and *safety*. These properties concentrate on the occurrence, or the frequency of occurrence, of individual events. Liveness is a temporal property that guarantees the eventual occurrence of events whereas fairness guarantees their occurrence sufficiently frequently. It is impossible to quantify 'sufficient frequency' since there is no quantitative notion of time in a purely qualitative study. This concerns both liveness and fairness and, thus, both notions are free from any explicit timing constraints governing when an event may occur or how frequently. It is clear that eventuality is a property which concerns both liveness and fairness and precludes the introduction of events or transitions that will never take place.

By contrast, the notion of *safety* in qualitative studies of temporal properties guarantees the non-occurrence of certain events or their relegation to a very low probability of occurrence. Safety thus seems to be contradicting what is implied by eventuality, but this concept is explained by Lamport, the author of some of these terms, using the phrase that '*something bad never happens*'. The intention is that certain events will not take place under certain global conditions. Thus, safety introduces a certain context dependence for events to occur.

It is important to note that the notion of *safety* here is to be understood as a notion that counters the notion of progress conveyed by *liveness*. This notion of safety differs from another frequent use of the term in the computer science literature – the notion of safety that applies to *safety critical systems* where it concerns prevention of risks to human life or property. The two notions are not necessarily identical. For example, certain safety requirements in safety critical systems may forbid a certain action while requiring, at the same time, that another action is undertaken in order to avert a high risk situation. On the other hand, there are circumstances when certain system needs come under both categories of safety requirement.

The need for fairness arises in abstractions that allow *non-determinism*. Non-determinism is a theoretical concept introduced for a number of reasons. Firstly, it is a recognition that the environment is independent of the system and is outside its control; therefore, the system must be prepared to cope with all possible environmental actions. Even in cases where environmental behaviour is eventually deterministic, the relevant information may be lacking at high level design stages. Secondly, non-determinism is a means of leaving greater implementation freedom deliberately and preventing premature commitments to particular design choices at the early stages of formulation. Obviously, all non-deterministic behaviours are eventually resolved and eliminated by specific design decisions. The idea is to make the application insensitive to such decisions at the user requirements level and to make sure that the user does not rely on features that have not been requested as part of the requirements.

It is important to realize that the temporal properties can be formally reasoned about theoretically, typically in frameworks founded on temporal logic and concurrency. Concurrency is an abstraction of real time behaviour where the system is viewed as a set of sequential processes executing simultaneously certain atomic (non-divisible) actions and potentially interacting with each other. The abstraction relies on the assumption that each process has its own processor and executes its own program. It also usually ignores the speed of execution due to the absence of any absolute notion of real time.

Two key notions underlying the models used in the study of concurrent systems are *maximal parallelism* and *interleaving models*. Maximal parallelism assumes that events occur as soon as they are enabled. In the absence of a quantitative notion of time, the phrase 'as soon as' means here that the occurrence of enabled events is not inhibited by other constraints such as lack of resources. Thus, maximal parallelism relies implicitly on the availability of sufficient computing power, which in the extreme case may mean a separate processor for every process with the appropriate capabilities. As a result, concurrency occurs in the most general sense, whereby the events are ordered only partially. That is, there can be events which neither precede nor follow each other and, thus, they occur simultaneously and independently.

This generality is broken down by the introduction of the notion of *interleaving* – a total order on events or a sequence of events. If each interleaving is interpreted as a record made by an independent observer, there are circumstances when all observers must agree and, in particular, when interleaving expresses a cause–effect relationship. And there are circumstances when the observers may differ as in the case of distributed systems. Certain subsequences of the interleaving may express other requirements such as mutual exclusion.

1.3   Design and Implementation Issues

Once system behaviour is properly understood, attention may be directed towards implementation issues, shifting emphasis from an understanding of behaviour to how to resource it efficiently and cost effectively. Despite the conceptual difference between the two, there is no sharp demarcation between these activities. They often overlap and iterations between them during the design process are quite common.

The design of realtime systems requires the accommodation of diverse task constraints. The determination of these constraints requires first a good understanding of the problem and then an optimal solution to a number of closely related high level subproblems, namely, problem decomposition at systems level, identification of tasks, determination of system architecture, allocation of tasks to processors, scheduling of tasks under timing, resource and other constraints, etc.

1.3.1   Constraints on System Behaviour

The demand for processing on any realtime system may fluctuate significantly over time. This is because even periodic tasks last over finite lengths of time and the processor may have to attend to a large number of both periodic and sporadic tasks over any given length of time. Furthermore, these tasks have strict timing constraints such as deadlines. In addition, there is a spatial dimension. Most realtime systems have to operate with scarce resources. This is especially so in embedded systems, where, although the computing resources may become not so critical with the increasing miniaturization of computers, there are different peripheral, power supply and other ancillary resources which are almost as important as the central processor for their functioning. Access to such resources may be subject to various forms of constraint ranging from mutual exclusion to simultaneity. Realtime tasks may further have precedence constraints affecting their order of execution imposed by the processing requirements of the application. There may also be placement constraints on tasks either for security reasons or for fault tolerance.

1.3.2   Architectural Concerns

Realtime systems may be implemented on different hardware architectures. The choice of hardware is ideally made depending on the problem, but with the growing tendency towards greater distribution of both system functionality and information, realtime systems are increasingly implemented as distributed systems. Common distributed systems aim at the effective use of resources through load sharing, and the general homogeneity of the processors makes them less sensitive to failure. In distributed realtime systems the distribution may be motivated by the need for fault tolerance and, in this context, much tighter resource limitations may make the provision of required resilience against failures an extremely difficult task.

1.3.3   Resource Allocation

Optimum use of available resources is a major concern in realtime systems. It is closely related to the granularity of computational tasks, timing requirements of the application, processor capabilities, resource limitations and the underlying communication network. The task granularity could determine, to a large extent, the overall communication requirements of the application, as well as the processing and performance requirements. The smaller the task granularity, the greater is the risk of increasing communication costs through indiscriminate allocation of tasks to processors. On the other hand, the greater the task granularity, the greater is the risk of creating processing bottlenecks because of processor overloading. Thus, there can be direct communication costs and indirect costs. In this connection, initial problem decomposition, as well as the grouping of computational activities into tasks in the subsequent design process, have a crucial bearing on optimum resource utilization. This requires careful balancing of merits and penalties in such design decisions.

This kind of optimization may be managed differently at different stages. In the early design phases, when the knowledge about the actual hardware architecture is limited, this may be done in the form of software partitioning, which addresses how best to organize computational activities. Note that software partitioning is an activity which, although it does not refer to the actual hardware support, may have implications for it. Later, when the actual hardware support is known, it may be brought to the forefront of resource utilization considerations by a more elaborate task allocation process. Task allocation can take into account detailed hardware features, thus enabling a more realistic assessment of costs and more specific means to improve resource utilization.

It is clear that the outcome of software partitioning and task allocation is a spatial distribution of tasks. The next requirement is to order them in time for execution on the allocated processors in such a way that the externally specified timing constraints are all satisfied. This activity is known as scheduling. Despite the wealth of published results and important achievements, scheduling is also one of the hardest problems in computing. As a result, there are no general solutions. However, there are significant practical achievements in a number of areas, namely, in static and dynamic scheduling, uni-processor and multi-processor scheduling and, to a lesser extent, in distributed scheduling.

1.3.4   Critical Realtime Systems

The primary concern of conventional design is to make sure that the system, or the product, functions correctly, assuming that everything supporting the functioning of that system also works correctly. However, there are many applications where such confidence in ideal behaviour could be badly misplaced. There can be failures in the infrastructure supporting the system and in the environment surrounding it. It could be a power failure or electro-magnetic interference. It could also be an internal failure due to poor design or a design error. Even with best endeavours, modern computer systems are too complex for their correctness to be guaranteed. Under such circumstances, as in all other branches of engineering, there must be safeguards against such failures that ensure the ability of the system to continue to deliver the service expected of it fully or partially or, in the worst case, to guarantee the safety of any human life involved, the environment and the system itself.

Reliability and safety are some of the additional key attributes that specify stringent design criteria applicable to ultra-critical realtime systems over and beyond the usual functional requirements. In practical terms, reliability and, to a significant extent, safety are achieved through fault tolerance, which is a collection of highly specialized measures such as recovery mechanisms and redundancies intended to assure its attainment. These redundancies come in different forms. They may include, to name a few approaches, redundancies in hardware, redundancies in software, and employment of diverse tools and diverse methodologies during the development process. The intention is to mask any errors, to provide spare resources to cope with failures and to limit reliance on too narrow a technological base.

1.4   Future Prospects

System design that observes the required timing and other constraints can in general be quite complex, requiring highly specialized tools and languages for their specification, analysis, modelling and verification. Rigorous approaches to these are active research areas at present and, therefore, are at the experimental stage of development with respect to their practical application. Equally, the effectiveness of less formal pragmatic approaches in current use is not widely known. However, practically viable rigorous approaches are emerging and this will enable the attainment of quality and a high degree of confidence. At the same time, attention is being paid to the integration of both rigorous and other widely used pragmatic approaches, aiming at versatile and effective use of both tools and human expertise.

1.5   Organization of this Book

Figure 1.1 provides a broad overview as to how various chapters relate to some of the important issues raised in this chapter. Chapters 2 and 3 are dedicated to a discussion about real time and clocks. This aims at a mathematical abstraction of clocks, an understanding of how representations of time by clocks relate to true real time and an understanding of different notions of time in the realtime context. This study treats time in an explicit form. As noted in Section 1.2.1, there are other approaches such as temporal logic and duration calculus treating time differently. In this respect, some guidance on suitable literature may be found under the bibliographical notes in the next section and in the chapters concerned.

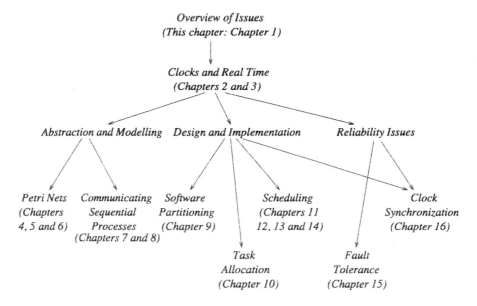

Figure 1.1 Organization of chapters

Chapters 4–8 introduce two specific frameworks for modelling and reasoning about realtime systems. The framework proposed in Chapter 4 is based on Petri nets. There have been a number of attempts to extend Petri nets to deal with time. Chapters 5 and 6 deal with one particular such approach, capable of dealing with both the functional and timing aspects of such systems. In this connection, Chapter 5 introduces a simple time augmentation to Petri nets, with emphasis on modelling realtime systems. A more complete study of the general approach is given in Chapter 6. It must be emphasized that the approach is based on ongoing research and, therefore, is subject to further development. Chapters 7 and 8 provide an alternative approach in CSP and Timed CSP. Both Petri nets and CSP enable reasoning about concepts such as *safety, liveness, non-determinism* and *deadlock* in more practical and precise terms.

Chapters 9 and 10 on software partitioning and task allocation open the discussion about the efficient use of resources. Software partitioning addresses how best to organize computational activities without particular reference to the actual hardware support. The latter is taken into account in Chapter 10 on task allocation. This chapter proposes a general framework for considering the actual architectural features and suggests algorithms for allocating tasks with an optimal interprocessor communication cost.

Chapters 11–14 are devoted to scheduling. Chapter 11 is a general statement of the problem in the multi-processor context. Attention is drawn to a small number of results, the choice between competing techniques being made from considerations of both practical value and the desired coverage of topics. Chapter 12 presents two well-known algorithms in uni-processor scheduling: rate monotonic (static) scheduling and deadline driven (dynamic) scheduling. Chapters 13 and 14 deal with the multi-processor case, the former with static scheduling and the latter with dynamic scheduling. Despite the intractability of the general problem, scheduling is an area with significant achievements. In this respect, the treatment of scheduling is far from comprehensive and many significant contributions have been left out.

Chapter 15 is devoted to fault tolerance, a topic of extreme importance in the design of ultra-critical systems. It is a field in its own right with a wealth of accumulated knowledge. The aim here is to expose the reader to the issues involved and some well-known approaches. This chapter provides a broad understanding of the subject in a form that facilitates further study.

The final chapter, Chapter 16, returns to the theme of clocks, but with respect to systems of clocks found in multi-processor architectures, including distributed systems. As well as being a challenging problem in realtime computing, synchronization of nodal clocks in such architectures is a highly relevant practical problem. Lack of clock synchronization is a well-documented cause of many failures in vital realtime systems, often with severe cost penalties. This requires clock synchronization to be a fault tolerant activity in critical applications, making the study of clocks from this perspective an ideal vehicle for illustrating fault tolerance. In this respect, the chapter has a natural link with the previous chapter and introduces a number of important algorithms used in clock synchronization.

One of the main pedagogic handicaps in teaching realtime systems is the lack of access to the requirements of typical real life applications. This is partially addressed in Appendix A by providing a selection of open ended realistic realtime problems. As mentioned there, these exercises may serve a variety of purposes and may be easily related to material covered in this book.

Detailed proofs for selected observations in several chapters may be found in Appendix B. Appendices C and D concern part of the mathematical notation used in the text.

1.6   Bibliographical Notes

Books devoted to realtime systems differ considerably in scope. Levi and Agrawala [92] present a fairly general treatment of the subject covering also such issues as realtime operating systems, communications and task allocation. Burns and Wellings [18] place emphasis on programming aspects. Motus and Rodd [103] propose an approach based on communicating processes for modelling realtime systems. Books such as Calvez [19], Edwards [41] and Pyle *et al.* [121] illustrate the application of pragmatic approaches such as structured design to designing realtime systems and the life cycle model of software development. Bennett [13] deals with both design and implementation issues with particular reference to realtime control systems. Tsai *et al.* [160] discuss verification and debugging of distributed realtime systems through monitoring at run-time. The series of books [43, 52, 53, 76, 122, 141, 143, 164, 163, 166] dedicated to realtime systems covers a whole range of separate issues both from the theoretical and practical points of view.

The references listed under Kavi [72], Son [151] and Stankovic and Ramamritham [157] are good sources of important research contributions to the field and include a number of seminal works. The current trends are perhaps best reflected in the proceedings of the annual IEEE symposia on realtime systems [129]. Another source of recent developments is the the *Journal of Real-Time Systems* [71].

Some representative formal approaches to specification and design of realtime systems may be found in [34, 47, 57, 61, 70, 66, 114, 21, 22, 128, 138, 166, 165]. Works such as those by Davies [34], Hooman [34, 61], Reed [131] and Schneider [142] treat realtime systems as communicating sequential processes; the work by Jahanian and Mok [66] is founded on predicate logic and Presburger arithmetic, while Galton [47] and Ostroff [114] are founded on temporal logic. Chaochen, Hoare and Ravn [21], Chaochen, Ravn and Hansen [22] and Ravn, Rischel and Hansen [128] propose Duration Calculus for the specification and verification of realtime systems, an approach which considers real time implicitly through durations of states.

A stimulating discussion about real time and the implications of different abstractions of real time in relation to realtime systems may be found in an article by Kurki-Suonio [84].

Chapter 2

Clocks

This chapter introduces a precise definition for clocks used in practice and contrasts them against clocks exhibiting ideal behaviour. The notation and the terminology introduced in this chapter are used later when dealing with clocks and metrics of time used in realtime systems.

2.1 Introduction

Time is a concept of unrivalled practical significance entering everything we experience. This special status is acquiring even greater significance with the technological revolution taking place today, transferring more and more crucial aspects of our life to man-made machines. The result is the creation of artificial environments, or independent complex systems, interacting with users, the natural environment and one another supposedly in a predictable and well-understood manner. In many cases, certain fundamental aspects of the correctness of this interaction is judged with respect to time.

The development of such systems therefore has to be founded on a proper understanding of time: its representation, measurement and how to reason about time. Our discussion of time is guided by these practical considerations.

The concept of time has been a subject of intense philosophical debate, reaching even greater heights with the achievements of relativistic physics. Our concern here is the representation of *Newtonian time*, with further adjectives 'scientific' and 'technical' emphasizing the limitation of our discussion to technological applications and terrestrial time. Thus, it deliberately avoids any discussion of philosophical issues on time and concentrates on a mathematical understanding of time suitable for formalizing clocks.

2.1.1 Set Theoretic and Process View of Time

In connection with possible mathematical representations, time may be seen as

- a metric consisting of, among other things, a 'set' of time values;
- a continuously evolving unique 'process'.

These should be seen as complementary means, each helping us to understand different aspects of time, the former in relation to measurements of time and the latter in relation to temporal references to events.

Let us make a distinction between time in an objective sense, often referred to in the related literature as *Galilean time*, and time as understood with respect to representations on actual clocks. The former corresponds with the 'true real time' and we may think of it only in highly abstract terms. In terms of its definition, the closest we may get to is that it is an ordered set of all definite and distinct historical events in our bounded space. Unfortunately, this statement will not withstand close scrutiny due to the 'circularity' of the definition of time with respect to itself. However, the important thing is its independence from clock representations, and in order to highlight this we use the term *real time* or *objective time* for the time in this unique objective sense, and the term *clock time* or *concrete time* for the possible representations of time using clocks.

For obvious reasons, both these sets of time values are expected to be totally ordered sets by some relation '$\leq$' and, with it, we take on board its other variant and extensions '$<$', '$>$' and '$\geq$' inspired by number theory. For any two time values t_1, t_2, the predicate $t_1 < t_2$ means that 'time t_1 precedes time t_2'. We also assume that these sets are equipped with operators appropriate for addition '$+$' and subtraction '$-$' of time values and lengths of time.

The notion of a continuously evolving process allows the capture of certain characteristic aspects of time. Again, this is a simplistic view. We propose that time as a process consists of a certain marker, called '*current time*', and designate the current time in the informal sense, continuously taking values of the real time or the appropriate concrete representation.

2.1.2 Dense versus Sparse Time

Sets of time values may be seen as either dense or sparse. Within our framework, this is an issue which concerns essentially the possible representations of real time, that is, clock time. In the case of clock time, the choice between these two options is restricted because of the distinctions to be made between clock time and real time.

A dense set is a set equipped with an ordering such as '$<$' so that between any two elements in the set there is always a third element. Common examples of dense sets are the sets of rational numbers $\mathbb{Q}$ and real numbers $\mathbb{R}$. However, there is a distinction between $\mathbb{Q}$ and $\mathbb{R}$; $\mathbb{Q}$ is countable and $\mathbb{R}$ is not. $\mathbb{Q}$ is countable because all its elements may be put into a one–to–one correspondence with the elements in N. The sets of natural numbers N and integers ℤ are, on the other hand, sparse sets.

The use of a dense time metric may be justified in situations where the times of occurrence of any pair of events can be arbitrarily close to each other. Some typical realtime scenarios where a dense time metric may be appropriate are:

(a) distributed systems with local nodal clocks, where it is practically impossible to achieve perfect synchronization of clocks; see Chapter 16;

(b) asynchronous systems where, by definition, events may occur at arbitrary times;

(c) systems exhibiting analog behaviour which, by definition, applies to continuous domains of values.

The areas of applicability of sparse time metric follow conversely from the above and are as follows:

(a) uni-processor and centralized systems with a single clock or a master clock – again see Chapter 16;

(b) synchronous systems where events occur at arbitrary times, but in a coordinated manner;

(c) systems exhibiting totally discrete behaviour.

2.1.3   Real Time

Let us denote by $\tilde{\Theta}$ the *real time* (objective time) as a set of 'time values'. One may characterize it as uncountable (non-denumerable) and dense and, as mentioned earlier, to be totally ordered by relations such as $\leq$ and $\geq$. Thus, any pair of time values taken from $\tilde{\Theta}$ are comparable by means of the precedence relation $\leq$. The latter property is equivalent to '*linearity*' of time. In some cases, it may be appropriate to insist that $\tilde{\Theta}$ does not contain greatest or least elements, or the converse with respect to either or both of them. These mathematical concepts correspond to the assumption, or the exclusion, of starting/ending points in history. For most practical purposes, it is useful to view $\tilde{\Theta}$ as $\mathbb{R}^+$, which is the set of non-negative real numbers.

In the process view of real time, no values of current time are ever repeated. Also, strictly speaking, no agent may either control *current time* or observe its progress directly. However, this situation may not be placed beyond our sight forever; it may become imperative to adopt at some stage an independently specified superior clock, at least as an approximation to real time.

Considering the practical nature of our discipline, let us introduce a formal designator (a *free variable*)

NOW : $\tilde{\Theta}$

for current time, and assume that it is made available to us. The nature of this variable is quite unique. Firstly, it never assumes a value it has assumed before and always assumes a greater value than its previous values; and secondly, no one has any control over it. The first feature agrees with our intuitive understanding of time as a continuously evolving process without repeating history in the absolute sense. Thus, NOW is a variable with a full awareness of its own history. Without the notion of a 'historical' trace, this behaviour cannot be expressed formally, but let us be content with this informal, nevertheless clear, understanding.

Formalization of clocks here is based on *right-open* (*left-closed*) time intervals in $\tilde{\Theta}$, that is, intervals which include the left end (starting point) but exclude the right end. More details on right-open intervals and other possible representations are given in Section 3.1 of Chapter 3.

2.1.4   Clock Time

As mentioned earlier, *clock time* (concrete time) corresponds with the representations of time as shown on clocks. Unlike real time, the underlying set consists of discretized 'time values'. We use the notation $\mathbb{T}$ for referring to the set of time values used in any given representation of clock time. Let us associate with $\mathbb{T}$ a granularity and a total ordering relation $\leq$. As will be seen later, the actual behaviour of clocks inevitably differs from the desired behaviour. In order to distinguish between these two behaviours, let us introduce two notions of granularity: *actual* (at post-implementation stages) or *target* (at design stages) granularity and *calibrated* granularity.

The term *actual* or *target* granularity, denoted here by Δ, refers to a length of time between two elements in $\tilde{\Theta}$ defining the actual or desired separation in real time between pairs of consecutive values in $\mathbb{T}$. Ideally, Δ should be a constant and our discussion in Sections 2.2–2.4 adopts this as a premise. Despite the distinction made between design and post-implementation stages through the terms *actual* and *target* granularities, let us simplify the terminology by adopting a single term, namely, *actual* granularity, for both of them.

On the other hand, a given clock measures the 'distances' between pairs of elements in $\mathbb{T}$ in integral multiples of some ∇, which is a unit of measurement for 'counting' time in $\mathbb{T}$. Because of its relationship with the actual granularity Δ in measuring time, ∇ is referred to here as *calibrated granularity*.

More formally, clock time may be viewed as a quadruple

$$(\mathbb{T}, zero, next, \nabla)$$

where $\mathbb{T}$ is the set of clock time values, *zero* is a distinguished element in $\mathbb{T}$, *next* is an injective (one–to–one) function on $\mathbb{T}$ and $\nabla \in \mathbb{R}^+$. The need for ∇ being in $\mathbb{R}^+$ should become clear shortly. Informally, *next* is analogous to the successor function on $\mathbb{N}$. For example, $next(t)$ returns the value immediately after t in $\mathbb{T}$. Clearly, the relation $\leq$ may be inferred from *next*. Values of $\mathbb{T}$ are thus of the form *zero*,

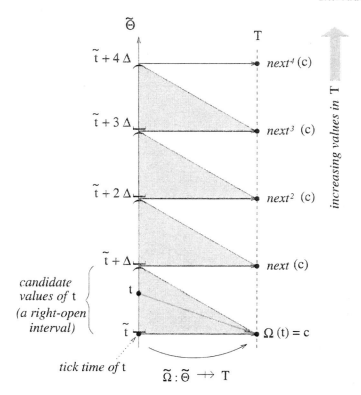

Figure 2.1 Metrics of real time and clock time

$next(zero)$, $next(next(zero))$, etc., or, alternatively, $zero$, $next(zero)$, $next^2(zero)$, $next^3(zero)$, etc. Let *prev* (for 'previous') be the inverse function of *next*. With the function *next* in place, it is possible to define, as appropriate, other required operators and relations such as '+', '−' and '≤'. The relationship between the two metrics $\tilde{\Theta}$ and $\mathbb{T}$ is illustrated in Figure 2.1.

It is clear that, whatever the representation of clock time values, $\mathbb{T}$ is closely related (isomorphic) to $\mathbb{N}$. In this connection, let us introduce a function *measure*

$$measure : \mathbb{T} \to \mathbb{N}$$

and define it such that for any $c \in \mathbb{T}$

$$
\begin{aligned}
measure(zero) &= 0 \\
measure(next(c)) &= 1 + measure(c)
\end{aligned}
$$

The 'distance' between a pair of elements c_1 and c_2 in $\mathbb{T}$ may be defined as

$$\| (c_1, c_2) \| = \nabla \times | \, measure(c_1) - measure(c_2) \, |$$

where $| \, n \, |$ denotes the absolute value of the number n.

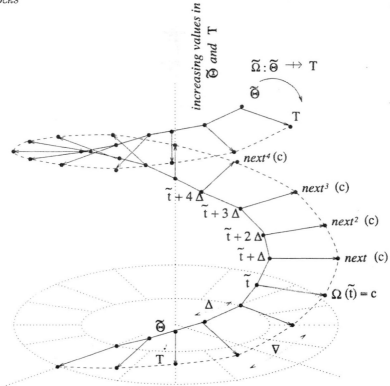

Figure 2.2 Representation of real time and clock time as a 'helix'

Thus, ∇ provides us with a way to relate 'measurements' of time in the representation $\mathbb{T}$ to $\mathbb{R}^+$. This suggests that, in order to relate $\mathbb{T}$ to $\tilde{\Theta}$, what is required is the ability to relate $\tilde{\Theta}$ to $\mathbb{R}^+$. This can be achieved by relating Δ to $\mathbb{R}^+$. Note that in the special case of adopting $\mathbb{R}^+$ for $\tilde{\Theta}$, $\Delta \in \mathbb{R}^+$.

The properties of *next* and *prev* which are of immediate relevance to us are:

Observation 2.1 For values of t and s in the domain of the functions *next*, *prev* : $\mathbb{T} \rightarrowtail \mathbb{T}$

$$t < next(t)$$
$$prev(t) < t$$
$$prev = next^{-1}$$

The functions *next* and *prev* are also related to ∇ and two relationships relevant here are as follows:

Observation 2.2 For values of t in the domain of the functions *next* and *prev*

$$\| (next(t), t) \| = \nabla$$
$$\| (prev(t), t) \| = \nabla$$

As a process, clock time exhibits a clear distinction as compared with real time: it may be controlled, observed and even the values may be repeatable in rudimentary representations.

Having made the distinctions between $\tilde{\Theta}$ and $\mathbb{T}$ and between Δ and ∇, the most general form of the relationship between the two metrics of time may be visualized as shown in Figure 2.2. We treat the quadruple $(\mathbb{T}, zero, next, \nabla)$, as well as other functions such as $\| \cdots \|$ establishing how far apart two points are in clock time, as a metric and often refer to it also as $\mathbb{T}$. Any ambiguity in the usage of $\mathbb{T}$ should be clear from the context.

2.2   Ideal Clocks – A Mathematical Definition

2.2.1   Clock Mechanism

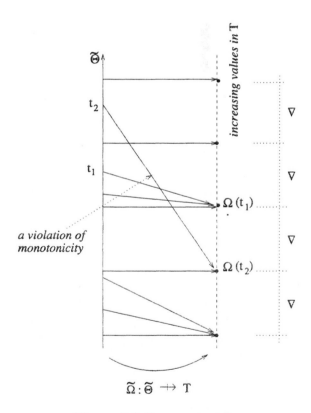

Figure 2.3 On monotonicity

The essence of a clock is its ability to map real time to an appropriate representation and, thus, this may be viewed as a function from $\tilde{\Theta}$ to $\mathbb{T}$, namely,

$$\tilde{\Omega} : \tilde{\Theta} \rightarrowtail \mathbb{T}$$

The function $\tilde{\Omega}$ is partial because of the desire to leave freedom for the clock to be non-operable for certain time values. Given a specific value t of real time for which $\tilde{\Omega}$ is defined, its representation is found by function application, $\tilde{\Omega}(t)$ or, alternatively, $\tilde{\Omega}t$. However, in addition to being a function, a clock must possess some further properties. The first property is expressed in the following observation:

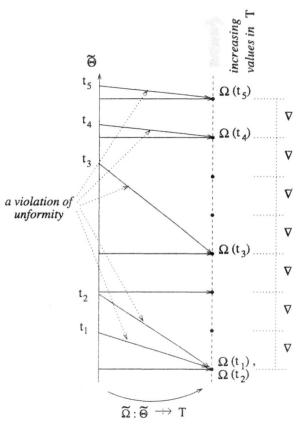

Figure 2.4 On uniformity

Observation 2.3 Representation of time must progress, or at least not regress, with time.

$$\forall\, t_1, t_2 : \tilde{\Theta} \; \bullet \; (t_2 > t_1 \Rightarrow \tilde{\Omega}t_2 \geq \tilde{\Omega}t_1) \; \wedge \; (\tilde{\Omega}t_2 > \tilde{\Omega}t_1 \Rightarrow t_2 > t_1)$$

The above concerns the *monotonicity* of the representation. In other words, representation of any two distinct time values of real time must be in the same relation as the real times themselves, or at least, must be equal; see Figure 2.3. The converse of the first implication in Observation 2.3 holds except for the equality.

The second property concerns the *uniformity*. It needs further clarification due to the discretized nature of $\mathbb{T}$. This is because uniformity may be observed only to the accuracy of difference between adjacent representation values; see Figure 2.4.

> **Observation 2.4** Progression of temporal representation must be 'uniform' relative to real time.

$$\forall\, t_1, t_2, t_3, t_4 : \tilde{\Theta} \bullet\ t_2 - t_1 = t_4 - t_3 \Rightarrow$$
$$\left(\|\,(\tilde{\Omega} t_2, \tilde{\Omega} t_1)\,\| - \|\,(\tilde{\Omega} t_4, \tilde{\Omega} t_3)\,\|\right) \in \{-\nabla, 0, +\nabla\}$$

where ∇ denotes the calibrated granularity of time in $\mathbb{T}$.

The above is a reasonable requirement provided that ∇ is a granularity in the true sense of the word.

> **Observation 2.5** *Calibrated granularity* ∇ is the smallest 'non-zero' measure of time that can be made in $\mathbb{T}$.

$$\exists\, t_1, t_2 : \tilde{\Theta} \bullet\ \|\,(\tilde{\Omega} t_2, \tilde{\Omega} t_1)\,\| = \nabla$$

Our treatment of clocks relies implicitly on the above observation.

The understanding gained so far does not refer to cases when the clock may fail to show the 'time'. No clock, however, covers the whole of eternity, and all have a finite life span. A clock must be expected to tell the 'right' time for all values of real time since its 'birth', or the latest 'reset', so it is fair to have a lower bound on values of $\tilde{\Theta}$ defining $\tilde{\Omega}$. The situation at the end of the useful life of a clock may be easily dealt with, since it then ceases to be a clock. The following observation expresses this requirement on clocks.

> **Observation 2.6** The function $\tilde{\Omega}$ is a partial function in the following sense:

$$\exists\, t_0 : \tilde{\Theta} \bullet\ \mathrm{dom}\ \tilde{\Omega} = \{\, t : \tilde{\Theta} \mid t \geq t_0\,\}$$

Furthermore, in order to ensure that clocks make progress with passage of real time and thus avoid trivial solutions to $\tilde{\Omega}$, let us require the following to be true:

> **Observation 2.7** Clocks must make progress at least every Δ units in real time, Δ being the actual clock granularity.

$$\forall\, t : \tilde{\Theta} \bullet\ t \in \mathrm{dom}\ \tilde{\Omega} \Rightarrow \tilde{\Omega}(t + \Delta) > \tilde{\Omega}(t)$$

If required, a less stringent alternative requirement to the above is the following:

Observation 2.8 Clocks must make progress.

$$\forall t : \tilde{\Theta} \bullet t \in \operatorname{dom} \tilde{\Omega} \Rightarrow \exists t' : \tilde{\Theta} \bullet t' > t \land \tilde{\Omega}(t') > \tilde{\Omega}(t)$$

It is clear that the above two properties concern the *liveness* of clocks.

Let us adopt the terminology '*clock function*' when referring to any function $\tilde{\Omega}$ satisfying Observations 2.3, 2.4, 2.6 and, as appropriate, 2.7 or 2.8. The same applies to alternative substitute definitions to be introduced later for $\tilde{\Omega}$.

Some further properties which may be considered for $\tilde{\Omega}$ are:

(i) When $\mathbb{T} \subset \tilde{\Theta}$, it may be required that

$$\forall t : \tilde{\Theta} \bullet t \in \mathbb{T} \Rightarrow t = \tilde{\Omega}(t)$$

(ii) When $\mathbb{T}$ and $\tilde{\Theta}$ are disjoint or $\mathbb{T} \subset \tilde{\Theta}$, it may be appropriate to consider a partial surjective function for $\tilde{\Omega}$. This may be appropriate if each value in $\mathbb{T}$ must correspond to some value in real time $\tilde{\Theta}$.

A clock is characterized by showing a clock time for the current time. Denoting this as DISPLAY-TIME, an ideal clock may be seen as a pair:

$$\text{IDEALCLOCK} = (\tilde{\Omega}, \text{ DISPLAY-TIME})$$

The two elements of the above pair are related to each other through the following requirement.

Observation 2.9 The current time of an ideal clock must satisfy the following:

$$\text{NOW} \in \operatorname{dom} \tilde{\Omega} \Rightarrow \text{DISPLAY-TIME} = \tilde{\Omega}(\text{NOW})$$

2.2.2   Clock Advancement

The clock works by continuous internal transitions governed by the independent progress of time or, in our formalization, the value of the free variable NOW. These transitions may take place as often as necessary.

Observation 2.10 The internal transitions of an ideal clock are subject to the following real time constraints:

(a) The display must show the right clock representation of real time after every clock transition.

(b) Successive internal transitions must be separated by an arbitrarily small but 'non-zero' interval ε of real time $\tilde{\Theta}$ such that $\varepsilon \ll \Delta$.

(c) For each clock tick there is a unique contemporaneous update of the display, and vice versa.

The above observation determines how the display time is to be updated.

2.3   A Mathematical Definition in Z

It is more convenient to present the results of the above discussion in the Schema Language of the formal specification language Z; see Spivey [152]. This section is a restatement in Z of our discussion so far and may be skipped by the reader not familiar with Z. A basic introduction to the Schema Language may be found in Appendix D.

2.3.1   Definition for an Ideal Clock

The understanding gained above may be summarized in a schema named *ClockWork* consisting of the formulae stated as observations and taken for granted (as axioms).

For simplicity, this section views $\mathbb{R}^+$ as $\tilde{\Theta}$ and $\mathbb{T} \subseteq \mathbb{N}$. Given that Δ and ∇ are lengths of 'time' as measured in $\tilde{\Theta}$ and $\mathbb{N}$ respectively, *ClockWork* may be defined as

---
ClockWork

$\tilde{\Omega} : \tilde{\Theta} \nrightarrow \mathbb{T}$

$\forall t_1, t_2 : \tilde{\Theta} \bullet (t_2 > t_1 \Rightarrow \tilde{\Omega} t_2 \geq \tilde{\Omega} t_1) \wedge (\tilde{\Omega} t_2 > \tilde{\Omega} t_1 \Rightarrow t_2 > t_1)$ (i)

$\forall t_1, t_2, t_3, t_4 : \tilde{\Theta} \bullet t_2 - t_1 = t_4 - t_3 \Rightarrow$

$\qquad \left(\| (\tilde{\Omega} t_2, \tilde{\Omega} t_1) \| - \| (\tilde{\Omega} t_4, \tilde{\Omega} t_3) \| \right) \in \{-\nabla, 0, +\nabla\}$ (ii)

$\exists t_0 : \tilde{\Theta} \bullet \text{dom } \tilde{\Omega} = \{t : \tilde{\Theta} \mid t \geq t_0\}$ (iii)

$\forall t : \tilde{\Theta} \bullet t \in \text{dom } \tilde{\Omega} \Rightarrow \tilde{\Omega}(t + \Delta) > \tilde{\Omega}(t)$ (iv)

Note that $\mathbb{T}$ is considered to be closed under addition with respect to ∇. The predicates (i)–(iv) in the above schema axiomatize the requirements on the monotonicity, uniformity, partiality and liveness of $\tilde{\Omega}$ presented earlier as Observations 2.3, 2.4, 2.6 and 2.7 respectively.

The display of the clock showing the current time may be incorporated as

---
IdealClock

ClockWork

DISPLAY-TIME : $\mathbb{T}$

NOW $\in$ dom $\tilde{\Omega}$ $\Rightarrow$ DISPLAY-TIME $= \tilde{\Omega}$ NOW
---

which includes the identifier DISPLAY-TIME showing the current time in the chosen clock representation.

2.3.2   Clock Advancement

Initialization and resetting of the clock are omitted here for brevity and as no other clock utilities are considered, the behaviour of the clock may be described in terms of changes in its state with clock advancements.

The working of the clock has already been explained in Section 2.2.2. The clock works by continuous internal transitions governed by the independent progress of time or, in our formalization, the value of the free variable NOW. We formalize this by considering an arbitrarily small separation (a strictly positive offset) ε of real time $\tilde{\Theta}$ between successive transitions.

The ticking of the clock may be formalized using a binary valued type:

TICK ::= Tick | Silent

Informally, Tick corresponds to emitting a signal signifying the update of display, and Silent to a nil output in the case of no change. Clock transitions may now be formalized as

---

ClockAdvance ——————————————————

$IdealClock, IdealClock'$

$out! : \text{TICK}$

——————————————————

$\text{DISPLAY-TIME}' = \tilde{\Omega}(\text{NOW} + \varepsilon)$

$\text{DISPLAY-TIME} \neq \text{DISPLAY-TIME}' \Leftrightarrow out! = \text{Tick}$

$\tilde{\Omega}' = \tilde{\Omega}$

---

where each component decorated with a single quote (eg. *IdealClock'*) denotes the value of the corresponding component after the clock advancement. The component *out!* signifies an output.

2.4   Clock Tick Times

This section introduces a *clock tick function* ω pairing the earliest real time value, referred to as *tick time*, and its associated clock value. In this connection, let $\tilde{t}$ denote the tick time (in real time) of the clock reading current at the real time t; see Figure 2.1.

> Definition: For a given real time value $t \in \text{dom } \tilde{\Omega}$, its *clock tick time* $\tilde{t}$ may be defined as
>
> $$\tilde{t} \stackrel{def}{=} min \left\{ x \mid x \in \text{dom } \tilde{\Omega} \ \wedge \ \tilde{\Omega}(x) = \tilde{\Omega}(t) \right\}$$

where *min* is a function returning the smallest element in its operand set of real time values. The function *min* may not be defined for arbitrary sets of real time values. However, it is defined for right-open intervals of time mentioned in Section 2.1.3 and introduced in Section 3.1.1 of Chapter 3.

Clock tick function ω may then be defined using $\tilde{t}s$ as

$$\omega \stackrel{def}{=} \left\{ (\tilde{t}, \tilde{\Omega}(t)) \bullet t : \ominus \mid t \in \text{dom } \tilde{\Omega} \right\}$$

Obviously, clock tick function is a subset of the corresponding clock function and has the following general definition:

Definition: The *clock tick function* ω may be defined in terms of $\tilde{\Omega}$ as

$$\omega \stackrel{def}{=} \left\{ (x, \tilde{\Omega}(t)) \bullet t, x : \ominus \mid t \in \text{dom } \tilde{\Omega} \wedge x = min\left(\left(\tilde{\Omega}^{-1} \circ \tilde{\Omega} \right) (\{t\}) \right) \right\}$$

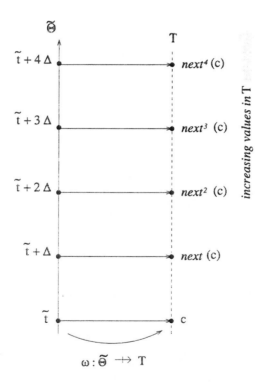

Figure 2.5 Clock tick function ω

It may be noted that ω is an injective function. Figure 2.5 illustrates the clock tick function for $\tilde{\Omega}$ shown in Figure 2.1. The following is an alternative definition for $\tilde{t}$ based on ω:

Observation 2.11 Clock tick time of $t \in$ dom $\tilde{\Omega}$

$$\tilde{t} = \omega^{-1}(\tilde{\Omega}(t))$$

It is thus obvious that tick times are parametrized by the chosen clock function $\tilde{\Omega}$.
   There are some interesting relationships linking clock tick times with values of both real time and clock time. Note that these are based on Observations 2.3, 2.4, 2.6 and 2.7. It is clear that the values of $\tilde{t}$s constitute a discrete domain and that, from the above definition of ω and the observations mentioned, $t + \Delta$ is also a tick time for a given tick time t.

Observation 2.12 Tick times are the real time values for which ω is defined. For any given $t \in \tilde{\Theta}$, t is related to its tick time $\tilde{t}$ as

$$t \in \text{dom } \omega \Rightarrow t = \tilde{t}$$

One of the relationships between arbitrary values of real time and their corresponding tick times is expressed in the following.

Observation 2.13 The relationship between real time values and their tick times. For every $t \in$ dom $\tilde{\Omega}$

$$\tilde{t} \le t < \tilde{t} + \Delta$$

The following concerns real time values with coincident clock times.

Observation 2.14 As a consequence of the above, for any given t_1 and t_2 in $\tilde{\Theta}$ such that $t_1 \in$ dom $\tilde{\Omega}$ and $t_2 \in$ dom $\tilde{\Omega}$,

$$\tilde{\Omega} t_1 = \tilde{\Omega} t_2 \vdash \tilde{t}_1 \le t_2 < \tilde{t}_1 + \Delta$$

where $\Gamma \vdash \phi$ states that the formula ϕ is *provable* from the formulae Γ. The above helps us to reason about the translation of '=' from $\mathbb{T}$ to $\tilde{\Theta}$.
   Another observation about real time values with coincident clock times is the following:

Observation 2.15 Given any t_1 and t_2 in $\tilde{\Theta}$ such that $t_1 \in$ dom $\tilde{\Omega}$ and $t_2 \in$ dom $\tilde{\Omega}$,

$$\tilde{\Omega} t_1 = \tilde{\Omega} t_2 \vdash 0 \le |t_2 - t_1| < \Delta$$

Note that the above relies on the following definition:

Definition: Absolute difference between t_1 and t_2 in $\tilde{\Theta}$ is denoted by:

$$
\begin{aligned}
|t_2 - t_1| &= t_2 - t_1 && \text{if } t_2 \ge t_1 \\
&= t_1 - t_2 && \text{if } t_2 \le t_1
\end{aligned}
$$

It follows from Observation 2.15 that any event which appears to be an 'instantaneous' event in clock time may be in fact a 'durative' event in real time occurring in an interval smaller than the actual clock granularity; see Sections 3.1 and 3.6.4 of Chapter 3.

An observation about the ordering of clock time values and real time values is the following:

> **Observation 2.16** Given any t_1 and t_2 in $\tilde{\Theta}$ such that $t_1 \in$ dom $\tilde{\Omega}$ and $t_2 \in$ dom $\tilde{\Omega}$,
>
> $$\tilde{\Omega}t_1 < \tilde{\Omega}t_2 \vdash t_1 < \tilde{t_2}$$

The above helps us in reasoning about the relation $<$ as it applies to time in $\bar{\Theta}$. The proofs of some the above relationships are given in Section B.1 of Appendix B.

2.5   Standard Metrics of Time

Let us now turn our attention to more pragmatic aspects of time and clocks. The applicability of the metrics of time discussed below to realtime systems is dependent on how active an application is in time and its geographical (spatial) scale. The following is a classification of metrics and standards in general use.

(i) Astronomical Time Metric

This metric is based on celestial observations. Its relevance lies in the use of conventional calendars in our ordinary life.

(ii) External Standard Physical Time

This metric is based on devices exploiting the periodicity of physical oscillations in pendulums, crystals and subatomic particles. It is the latter two that have relevance in modern technology, because of their unrivalled accuracy and absence of mechanical components vulnerable to wear and tear.

The above two metrics are not identical, and the latter is often forced, from time to time, to make appropriate but minute corrections to keep in phase with astronomical time. International agencies such as Universal Time Coordinated based in Paris are entrusted with the maintenance of the standard metric of the external standard physical time.

Considering that the external standard physical time has a much finer granularity and accuracy than the clocks under consideration and that it represents practically the closest representation to real time, it is time to adopt the external standard physical time as a sufficiently close approximation to real time. With this in mind, let Θ refer to the most superior form of external standard physical time available.

Furthermore, let us continue to use the variable NOW, but ranging over Θ, for referring to the current time in the metric Θ. That is,

NOW : Θ .

Ambiguity in its usage may be resolved from the context.

Certain applications may require an awareness of the following variations in time:

- Geographic variations

  These are governed by international conventions and conform to what is known under Geographic Time Zones.

- Seasonal variations

  These are covered by national conventions and amount to switching times by fixed amounts on agreed (unsteady) dates of the year.

2.6   Time in Realtime Systems

2.6.1   Clocks in Realtime Systems

There are three notions of clocks used in realtime systems,

1. Physical Clock

   This corresponds to the actual physical device measuring time. From the point of view of our discussion, the important aspects of the physical clock are its reading and the rate of progress of its clock time (i.e. the clock rate) with respect to the external standard physical time.

2. Logical Clock

   This is a software implementation based on the physical clock aimed at avoiding direct intervention with the latter. Basically the logical clock enables the reading of the physical clock with a predefined offset to counter against any discrepancy in time. Resetting the clock simply amounts to a change of this offset. Also, the logical clock is assumed to have the same clock rate as the physical clock.

3. Fault Tolerant Clock

   Applications, which are based on distributed architectures and are designed to function 'normally' despite any possible nodal clock failures, incorporate what is called a *fault tolerant clock*. A fault tolerant clock is essentially a high level abstraction of a system of clocks. As an abstract clock, it is 'insensitive' to failures of a certain number of individual clocks of the underlying system. This is the subject of Chapter 16.

2.6.2 Time Metrics used in Distributed Systems

Distributed realtime systems usually assume the existence of an independent chronoscopic external reference time, referred to simply as the *external reference time*. There are several additional notions of time:

(i) Internal Physical Time

This is the nodal approximation of a given processor to the external reference time.

(ii) Local (Physical) Time

This corresponds to the reading of the local physical clock.

(iii) Logical Time

An adjusted value of the physical clock reading above and used as the local time base.

(iv) Approximate Global Time

This corresponds with the nodal approximation to a common time base among the processors constituting the distributed system. This is achieved through internal synchronization of time.

(v) External Reference Time

This is the metric adopted as the final reference for reasoning about the behaviour of the whole system. It fulfils this role only by being superior to all other metrics listed above in (i)–(iv). The most eligible for this is the external standard physical time.

2.7 Real Clocks

2.7.1 'Correct' Clocks

No real clock displays the ideal behaviour described in Section 2.2. Furthermore, practically and theoretically speaking, there is no way of establishing the agreement between any two clocks, no matter how accurate they may be. This is because of the communication delays caused by all sorts of circumstances in practice, and even if most such delays are overcome, there remains, in theory, one delay that may not be overcome, that is, the time taken by the communication signal itself. Therefore, when dealing with clocks, the notion of absolute correctness must be abandoned.

The notion of a *'correct'* or *'good'* clock is, therefore, a relative and approximate notion, and is judged by the following criterion:

$$1 - \rho \le \frac{\delta_{measured}}{\delta_{specified}} \le 1 + \rho$$

where ρ is the permitted deviation of clock rate from the external reference time; see Figure 2.6. The value of ρ depends on the application, but typically is of the order $\rho \simeq 10^{-5}$; and the symbol δ above with appropriate subscripts denotes the measured and specified difference in clock reading over a given interval of time. Often, a lower bound of $\frac{1}{1-\rho}$ is used in the above inequality, but for small values of ρ, the difference is insignificant.

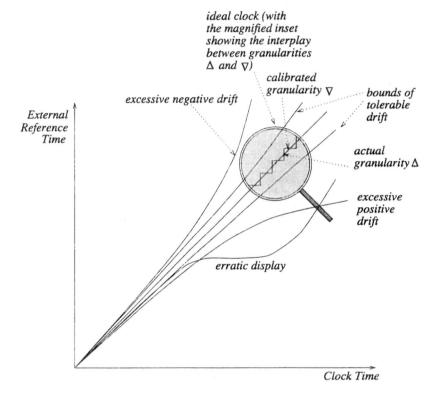

Figure 2.6 Behaviour of real clocks

The above sense of 'correctness' amounts to a relaxation of the axiom on uniformity in the definition given for the ideal clock introduced in Section 2.2 and to its replacement by the following:

$$1 - \rho \leq \tfrac{\Delta}{\nabla} \times \tfrac{\|(\Omega(t_1),\, \Omega(t_2))\|}{t_1 - t_2} \leq 1 + \rho$$

Ω being a new clock function capable of accounting for the essential features of 'real clocks'. The factor $\tfrac{\Delta}{\nabla}$ in the above is a recognition of the need to consider the relationship between the actual granularity Δ (in Θ) and calibrated granularity ∇ (in $\mathbb{T}$). The above assumes that t_1, t_2, Δ are all in $\mathbb{R}^+$. Note that $\tfrac{\Delta}{\nabla}$ is a conversion rate for relating time measured in $\mathbb{T}$ to external reference time Θ. When expressed in a single unit of measurement, $\tfrac{\Delta}{\nabla}$ must ideally be close to unity. In general,

Δ varies with real time and, therefore, may not be a constant. In many practical situations, the adoption of a constant Δ is a reasonable approximation to the actual behaviour. Clock rates over longer periods of time may be related to $\frac{\Delta}{\nabla}$ by using an average value of Δ. In this case, the condition $\frac{\Delta}{\nabla} < 1$ signifies fast clocks and $\frac{\Delta}{\nabla} > 1$ slow clocks.

Unless stated or implied otherwise, henceforth the clock function Ω will refer to the clock showing the external reference time. Similarly, Ω_i will refer to nodal logical clocks, i being an appropriate clock index. As a simplification let us assume in chapters other than Chapter 16, without much loss of generality, that $\frac{\Delta}{\nabla}$ is unity.

The new clock function Ω differs from $\tilde{\Omega}$ given in Section 2.2 in using the most superior discretized time metric available, that is, the external standard physical time Θ instead of $\tilde{\Theta}$. Thus,

$$\Omega : \Theta \twoheadrightarrow \mathbb{T}$$

Other properties considered in $\tilde{\Omega}$ have also to be revised. The property of monotonicity stated as Observation 2.3 is retained, while the property of uniformity, Observation 2.4, is replaced in accordance with the discussion above and the liveness requirement with that given under Observation 2.8. Note that the formulae for these properties need to be written in terms of Ω and Θ.

Furthermore, as will be discussed later, clocks may violate the above-mentioned observations during the 'synchronization period' of an ensemble of clocks (see Chapter 16). It might therefore become necessary to relax the monotonicity requirement even in between successive synchronizations in order to spread out, if necessary, the clock corrections over a longer period. Other aspects of the definition remain the same as in Section 2.2.

2.7.2   Idealization of Correct Real Clocks   .

This section revises the definition in Z given in Section 2.3 along the lines of our discussion above. In view of our discussion in the previous subsection, the definition of *ClockWork* for real clocks becomes,

---
ClockWork
$\Omega : \Theta \twoheadrightarrow \mathbb{T}$

$\rho : \mathbb{R}$

$\forall\, t_1, t_2 : \Theta \;\bullet\; (t_2 > t_1 \Rightarrow \Omega t_2 \geq \Omega t_1) \;\wedge\; (\Omega t_2 > \Omega t_1 \Rightarrow t_2 > t_1)$

$\forall\, t_1, t_2 : \Theta \;\bullet\; \left(1 - \rho \leq \frac{\Delta}{\nabla} \times \frac{\|\Omega(t_1) - \Omega(t_2)\|}{t_1 - t_2} \leq 1 + \rho\right)$

$\exists\, t_0 : \Theta \;\bullet\; \mathrm{dom}\; \Omega = \{t : \Theta \mid t \geq t_0\}$

$\forall\, t : \Theta \;\bullet\; t \in \mathrm{dom}\; \Omega \Rightarrow \exists\, t' : \tilde{\Theta} \;\bullet\; t' > t \wedge \Omega(t') > \Omega(t)$

2.7.3   Measurement of Small Time Intervals

The contribution of granularity to the accuracy has practical relevance only in relation to small time intervals. In the measurement of such intervals the following relations apply. For this, consider an interval in external reference time Θ, which is punctuated by the start time e_s and end time e_t of an event e; see Figure 2.7.

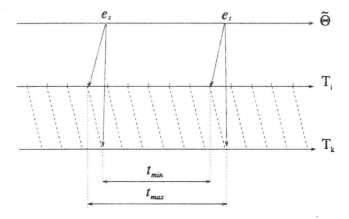

Figure 2.7 The effect of clock skew on measurements

Note that $\mathbb{T}_i$ and $\mathbb{T}_k$ denote the clock metrics used at nodes i and k respectively. The same event e may be recorded with respect to the two separate clocks and the duration δt of the event may vary between the following extremes:

$$\frac{\Delta_g}{\nabla_g \times (1+|\rho_g|)} \left(\| \left(\Omega_k(e_t), \Omega_i(e_s) \right) \| - 2\nabla_g \right) \leq \delta t \leq$$
$$\frac{\Delta_g}{\nabla_g \times (1-|\rho_g|)} \left(\| \left(\Omega_k(e_t), \Omega_i(e_s) \right) \| + 2\nabla_g \right)$$

where ρ_g denotes the clock drift of the clock system as a whole, assumed uniform as a simplification. The same applies to Δ_g and ∇_g.

2.8   Bibliographical Notes

One may find fascinating, and useful from our perspective, general discussions about time in literature; among them Coveney and Highfield [29], Gale [45], Kuhn [83], Lucas [96], Newton–Smith [106] and Whitrow [169]. A more technical exposition of time in relation to computing may be found in Gabbay *et al.* [44]. The technical issues raised here in relation to realtime applications may be found in Kopetz and Ochsenreiter [80, 81] and Lamport [86]. Another relevant contribution is Corsetti *et al.* [28]. A broader view of both the philosophical and technical issues related to our discussion may be found in Hoogeboom and Halang [60] and Koymans [82]. Abadi and Lamport [1] raise some interesting issues, among them certain problems associated with the use of a variable such as NOW for the current time.

A brief introduction to the mathematical notation used here is given in Appendices C and D. However, the reader is advised to consult Spivey [152] for a more comprehensive description.

2.9 Exercises

1. The mathematical definition given in Section 2.2 dealing with ideal clock behaviour considered four properties, namely, monotonicity, uniformity, liveness and partiality. Discuss the implications and any other desirable properties for dealing with clocks where the representation metric $\mathbb{T}$ is:

   (a) a subset of the type $\tilde{\Theta}$;

   (b) a finite set (e.g. 24 hour clock).

   If appropriate, suggest how the above situations may be dealt with formally and incorporate your solution in the formalization of clocks in Section 2.2.

Chapter 3

Clocks and Real Time

States, events and actions necessarily involve real time. Their non-realtime abstraction reduces timing aspects to some form of ordering of states and events. This ordering corresponds with the manner in which states prevail (obtain) over real time or events occur in real time. Obviously, this view may be inadequate in the study of certain realtime systems. This chapter is about how real time may be accounted for in situations where the time of occurrence of events, or the times over which states obtain, matter.

3.1 Points and Intervals of Time

An appropriate representation of time is a crucial element in any formalization of realtime systems. A primary concern here is the appropriateness of using 'points in a time axis' explicitly for reasoning about temporal properties. Two immediate issues raised by this standpoint are the continuity and instantaneity of time, having profound ramifications on our understanding of change. These can be both pragmatic and philosophical. For example, is instantaneity just a matter of perception arising from the limitations of our senses or instruments in detecting the occurrence of certain events? Alternatively, are there some events which are truly instantaneous, that is, taking no time at all?

In non-realtime computations it is common to think of events as instantaneous events. In this context, the events are merely state transformations or state transitions and are simply convenient abstractions. However, instantaneity is a difficult concept in realtime applications. Firstly, instantaneity signifies the existence of atomic events in the true sense. Furthermore, even if such events exist their occurrence may not be pinned down to a particular instant in real time. Therefore, it is generally impractical to adopt points in real time for referring to occurrences of events. This suggests the appropriateness of intervals of real time instead.

Secondly, there is a more fundamental difficulty with instantaneity. This is

36

because events bring about changes in state, for example as in the case of turning off a light, instantaneity may potentially admit the prevalence of contradictory states at certain instants. In such situations, there can be a logical difficulty not only in understanding the state of affairs at such an instant, but also in dealing with the resulting global inconsistency in the theory describing the system.

On the other hand, there can be justifications for instantaneous events. The literature on realtime systems often resolves various difficulties encountered in formal treatments of events by restricting them to certain well-understood and convenient classes. Two of these important classes are durative (prolonged) events and instantaneous events. As indicated earlier, the occurrence of instantaneous events takes no time at all, while the durative events do take time. Because of the difficulties encountered in dealing with instantaneity, instantaneous events are often assigned a subordinate role by using them as markers for the beginning and end of the durative events. Obviously, this does not provide for a solution since we are still left with the question as to the nature of the state at the beginning or the end of a durative event.

Thus, despite the fact that the existence of atomic instantaneous events is arguable in computational practice, they are conceivable in theory. Because of the inherent difficulty in establishing what this actually means and as an effective way of dealing with conflicting states at certain instants, let us restrict the use of intervals of real time to what are referred to as *right-open intervals*, that is, contiguous stretches of time from the starting marker inclusively but strictly up to the end marker (see below).

3.1.1   A Notation for Intervals of Time

We list below some widely used notation for *bounded* intervals of time. The notation is applicable to both continuous and discrete domains of time. Note that t_1 and t_2 are, respectively, the start and end points of the intervals such that $t_1 \leq t_2$.

$(t_1, \ t_2)$ –   An *open* interval consisting of all time values from t_1 to t_2 exclusive of both t_1 and t_2.

$[t_1, \ t_2)$ –   A *right-open* (left-closed) interval consisting of all time values from t_1 to t_2, including t_1 but excluding t_2.

$(t_1, \ t_2]$ –   A *left-open* (right-closed) interval consisting of all time values from t_1 to t_2, excluding t_1 but including t_2.

$[t_1, \ t_2]$ –   A *closed* interval consisting of all time values from t_1 to t_2 inclusively.

Note that some of the notation has other applications, namely, $[t_1, \ t_2]$ for denoting a sequence consisting of two elements (time values), and $(t_1, \ t_2)$ for denoting an ordered pair of elements. The following are *unbounded* intervals of time:

(t, ∞) –   A *left-open* unbounded interval consisting of all time values from t to infinity but excluding t.

$[t, \infty)$ –   An unbounded interval consisting of all time values from t to infinity including t.

Another notation used occasionally is $\langle t_1, t_2 \rangle$, where no distinction is made between open or closed ends of time intervals.

3.2   Intervals in Real Time

As has already been indicated, the set of real numbers $\mathbb{R}$ serves as an ideal representation for real time. Let Γ denote the set of all possible right-open intervals in this representation. Thus,

$$\Gamma : \mathbb{P}(\mathbb{P}\,\mathbb{R})$$
$$\Gamma \stackrel{def}{=} \{[t_1, t_2) \bullet t_1, t_2 : \mathbb{R}\}$$

where $\mathbb{P}$ denotes the power set of the set concerned and

$$[t_1, t_2) = \{t \bullet t : \mathbb{R} \mid t_1 \leq t < t_2\}$$

As above, analogous definitions for time intervals (t_1, t_2), $(t_1, t_2]$ and $[t_1, t_2]$ may also be given. As a further example, $[t_1, t_2]$ may be defined as

$$[t_1, t_2] = \{t \bullet t : \mathbb{R} \mid t_1 \leq t \leq t_2\}$$

Note that the above definition of Γ excludes unbounded intervals as its elements. Given a right-open interval θ of the form $[t_1, t_2)$, let us refer to its lower (left) end t_1 as $left(\theta)$ and to its other (right) end t_2 as $right(\theta)$. Their formal definitions are obvious. Given an interval θ with extremities t_1 and t_2, the length of θ is given by $length(\theta) = t_2 - t_1$ for $t_2 > t_1$, and zero otherwise.

Let us introduce a function *cl* giving the closed version of any given fully or semi-open interval. For example, it may be defined for right-open intervals as

$$cl\ [t_1, t_2) = [t_1, t_2]$$

When dealing with the evolution of a particular system or the history of one of its particular aspects, it is important to be able to refer to certain subsets of Γ such that each such subset contains only totally disjoint intervals of time. The intention is to associate such subsets with states and events as a way of defining their meaning, that is, for specifying intervals over which a given state obtains or a given event occurs. The set of these subsets $\mathbb{O}$ may be defined as

$$\mathbb{O} \subset \mathbb{P}\,\Gamma$$
$$\mathbb{O} = \{\theta : \mathbb{P}\,\Gamma \mid \forall x, y \in \Gamma \bullet x \neq y \wedge x \in \theta \wedge y \in \theta \Rightarrow cl\ x \cap cl\ y = \varnothing\}$$

EXAMPLE

Given a set h of time intervals such that $h \in \mathbb{O}$ and $h = \{\theta_1, \theta_2, \theta_3, \cdots \theta_n\}$, h may be viewed as a sequence of right-open time intervals as shown in Figure 3.1.

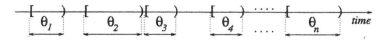

Figure 3.1 A disjoint set of right-open intervals

When dealing with events, it is natural to expect that all desirable events terminate. In order to ensure this, let us consider a certain subset $\mathbb{O}_f$ of $\mathbb{O}$ such that each element of $\mathbb{O}_f$ consists of a finite number of disjoint right-open intervals. Thus,

$$\mathbb{O}_f = \{\theta \in \mathbb{O} \mid card(\theta) \in \mathbb{N}\}$$

where $card(\theta)$ denotes the cardinality of θ.

3.3 Intervals in Clock Time

Let us examine the relationship between right-open intervals Γ in real time and the corresponding intervals Γ_c measured with reference to clock time. In doing so, let us base our discussion here on Observations 2.3, 2.4, 2.7 and 2.6 of Chapter 2 and, therefore, the results established in Section 2.4 remain applicable.

An interval θ in real time is measured as an interval θ_c in a given clock representation. One would expect θ_c to be determined as

$$\theta_c = \tilde{\Omega}(\!|\ \theta\ |\!)$$

The nature of the relationship between θ and θ_c with respect to the end points in intervals may be investigated in detail as follows:

$$
\begin{array}{lll}
t \in [t_1,\ t_2) & \Leftrightarrow\ t_1 \le t \wedge t < t_2 & \text{def. of } (\_,\_) \\
 & \Rightarrow\ \tilde{\Omega}t_1 \le \tilde{\Omega}t \wedge \tilde{\Omega}t \le \tilde{\Omega}t_2 & \text{monotonicity of } \tilde{\Omega} \\
 & \Leftrightarrow\ \tilde{\Omega}t \in [\tilde{\Omega}t_1, \tilde{\Omega}t_2] & \text{def. of } [\_,\_]
\end{array}
$$

Thus, for any time value within a right-open interval $[t_1,\ t_2)$ of real time, its clock representation would lie in the corresponding closed interval of concrete time, that is, in $[\tilde{\Omega}t_1, \tilde{\Omega}t_2]$. It may be observed further that

$$
\begin{array}{ll}
t \in [t_1,\ t_2) \Rightarrow \tilde{\Omega}t \in [\tilde{\Omega}t_1, \tilde{\Omega}t_2) & \text{if } t_2 \in \text{dom } \omega, \text{ and} \\
t \in [t_1,\ t_2) \Rightarrow \tilde{\Omega}t \in [\tilde{\Omega}t_1, \tilde{\Omega}(t_2 + \Delta)) & \text{if } t_2 \notin \text{dom } \omega
\end{array}
$$

According to the above, the interval in clock time corresponding to any right-open interval in real time may be given either as a right-open interval or as a closed interval. For the purpose of uniform treatment of intervals in clock time, let us consider all intervals in clock time also only in the right-open form.

Given such an interval $\theta_c = [t_{1c}, t_{2c})$, let us refer to its left end t_{1c} as $left(\theta_c)$ and to its right end t_{2c} as $left(\theta_c)$. Their formal definitions are obvious. Given an interval $\theta_c = [t_{1c}, t_{2c})$, both t_{1c} and t_{2c} being finite, the length of θ_c is given by $length(\theta_c) = t_{2c} - t_{1c}$.

> **Observation 3.1** Functions *left* and *right* from Γ to Θ may be related to functions *left* and *right* from Γ_c to $\mathbb{T}$ as follows:
>
> $$\tilde{\Omega}(left(\theta)) = left(\tilde{\Omega}(\!\mid \theta \mid\!))$$
> $$\tilde{\Omega}(right(\theta)) = right(\tilde{\Omega}(\!\mid \theta \mid\!)) \quad \text{if } right(\theta) \in \text{dom } \omega$$
> $$= prev(right(\tilde{\Omega}(\!\mid \theta \mid\!))) \quad \text{if } right(\theta) \notin \text{dom } \omega$$

See page 19 for the definition of *prev*. The above equalities may be used as *interval projection laws*.

Let us now examine what it means in real time for a particular clock time to be within a certain interval of clock time, that is, $\tilde{\Omega}t \in [\tilde{\Omega}t_1, \tilde{\Omega}t_2)$. One of the consequences is that

$$\tilde{\Omega}t \in [\tilde{\Omega}t_1, \tilde{\Omega}t_2) \Rightarrow t \in [\tilde{t}_1, \tilde{t}_2)$$

a proof for which is given in Section B.2 of Appendix B under Observation 3.2.

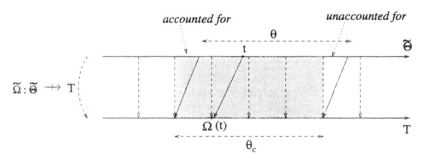

Figure 3.2 Clock representation of time intervals

Thus, for any clock value within a right-open interval of clock time, the corresponding real time would lie in a right-open interval of real time, obtained, for example, as $[\tilde{t}_1, \tilde{t}_2)$ using the appropriate clock tick times corresponding to t_1 and t_2 in real time. It follows from the above that certain real time values just outside the left end of a right-open interval may seem to appear inside its measured clock interval while certain real time values just inside the right end of an open interval may seem to appear outside the measured clock interval; see Figure 3.2.

Observation 3.2 In summary, the following relationships hold between intervals of real time and their clock representations:

$$t \in [t_1, \, t_2) \;\; \Rightarrow \;\; \tilde{\Omega}t \in [\tilde{\Omega}t_1, \tilde{\Omega}t_2) \qquad\qquad \text{if } t_2 \in \text{dom } \omega$$
$$t \in [t_1, \, t_2) \;\; \Rightarrow \;\; \tilde{\Omega}t \in [\tilde{\Omega}t_1, \tilde{\Omega}(t_2 + \Delta)) \quad\;\; \text{if } t_2 \notin \text{dom } \omega$$
$$\tilde{\Omega}t \in [\tilde{\Omega}t_1, \tilde{\Omega}t_2) \;\; \Rightarrow \;\; t \in [\tilde{t}_1, \tilde{t}_2)$$

3.4   Relationships between Time Intervals

3.4.1   Relationships between Intervals in Real Time

Potentially an infinite number of events may occur in any given interval. What distinguishes one event from another is the physical content, that is, what actually takes place when the events occur. Formalization of the physical content of events is the subject of Section 3.6. In the realtime context, physical aspects of events take the form of intertask constraints expressing all kinds of dependencies among events. An obvious example here is the resource dependency of tasks. Despite the importance attached to the physical content of such events, the concern of this section is how to reason about the intervals of their occurrence.

At a purely temporal level, such dependencies between events reduce to relationships between intervals. In this connection, there is a certain well-known set of relevant relationships between intervals. These originate from a system of temporal logic due to Allen [4]. Using the concept of time interval introduced earlier, the temporal relations introduced by Allen may defined as follows:

before, equal, meets, overlaps, during, starts, finishes $: \Gamma \leftrightarrow \Gamma$

Given any $\theta, \theta' : \Gamma$

$$
\begin{aligned}
\theta \ before \ \theta' \; &\overset{def}{\Leftrightarrow} \; right(\theta) < left(\theta') \\
\theta \ equal \ \theta' \; &\overset{def}{\Leftrightarrow} \; \theta = \theta' \\
\theta \ meets \ \theta' \; &\overset{def}{\Leftrightarrow} \; right(\theta) = left(\theta') \\
\theta \ overlaps \ \theta' \; &\overset{def}{\Leftrightarrow} \; left(\theta) < left(\theta') < right(\theta) < right(\theta') \vee \\
& \qquad\quad\; left(\theta') < left(\theta) < right(\theta') < right(\theta) \\
\theta \ during \ \theta' \; &\overset{def}{\Leftrightarrow} \; left(\theta') < left(\theta) \wedge right(\theta) < right(\theta') \\
\theta \ starts \ \theta' \; &\overset{def}{\Leftrightarrow} \; left(\theta) = left(\theta') \wedge right(\theta) < right(\theta') \\
\theta \ finishes \ \theta' \; &\overset{def}{\Leftrightarrow} \; right(\theta) = right(\theta') \wedge left(\theta') < left(\theta)
\end{aligned}
$$

A notation in common usage for *before* is

$$\theta < \theta' \overset{def}{\Leftrightarrow} \theta \ before \ \theta'$$

It may be noted that

before	is transitive.
during	is a partial order on Γ.
equal	is an equivalence relation on Γ.
overlaps	is non-transitive, irreflexive but symmetrical.

It may be further observed that

$$\theta \text{ overlaps } \theta' \iff \theta \cap \theta' \neq \varnothing \wedge \theta \neq \theta'$$

Allen's other non-primitive predicates then follow immediately from above without any change. For example,

$$in : \Gamma \leftrightarrow \Gamma$$
$$\theta \text{ in } \theta' \iff \theta \text{ during } \theta' \vee \theta \text{ starts } \theta' \vee \theta \text{ finishes } \theta'$$

3.4.2   Relationships between Intervals in Clock Time

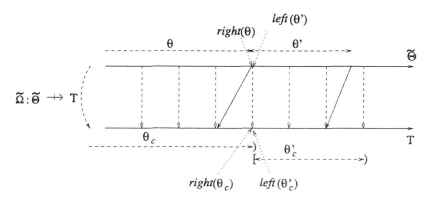

Figure 3.3 The case of $right(\theta)$ and $left(\theta')$ being a tick time

Let us first distinguish the above relations on time intervals in real time and in clock time by using the subscript c for relations in clock time and reserving un-subscribed version to relations in real time. For example, $before_c$ and $meets_c$ are relations on intervals in clock time, whereas $before$ and $meets$ are relations on intervals in real time. This is in line with with our earlier notation θ_c for clock representation of an interval θ in real time. Note also that $before_c$, $equal_c$, $meets_c$, etc., are relations on Γ_c.

Except for $meets_c$, all other relations on Γ_c are analogous to those given in Section 3.4.1. Given any $\theta_c, \theta_c' : \Gamma_c$, the relation $meets_c$ on Γ_c can be defined as

$$\theta_c \text{ meets}_c \theta_c' \stackrel{def}{\iff} right(\theta_c) = left(\theta_c') \vee prev(right(\theta_c)) = left(\theta_c')$$

The situations covered by the above are illustrated on Figures 3.3 and 3.4.

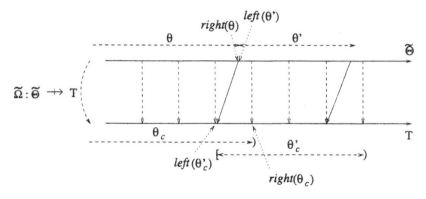

Figure 3.4 The case of $right(\theta)$ and $left(\theta')$ not being a tick time

3.5   Correspondence between Real Time and Clock Time Temporal Relations

First, let us introduce a relation $\approx$ from Γ to Γ_c:

$$\forall \theta : \Gamma; \; \theta_c : \Gamma_c \;\bullet\; \theta \approx \theta_c \Leftrightarrow \theta_c = \tilde{\Omega}(\!| \theta |\!)$$

Observation 3.1 introduced in Section 3.3 holds for any $\theta \approx \theta_c$.

Now let us examine the correspondence between Allen's temporal relations on Γ and Γ_c. Although, except for the pair *meets* and *meets$_c$*, the temporal relations in real time and a given clock representations are identical in form, they do not necessarily mean the same for a given pair of intervals. Understanding the interrelationship between these two categories is essential for predicting possible implications of observations made in one metric with respect to the other. For example, what is the significance with respect to real time if two intervals measured as θ_c and θ'_c in the clock representation are related to each other through θ_c *meets$_c$* θ'_c? This section presents some of these correspondences, leaving their formal justifications to Section B.2 of Appendix B.

The significance of *before* and *before$_c$*

An examination of what is meant by θ *before* θ' in Γ_c and θ_c *before$_c$* θ'_c in Γ leads us to the following observations:

Observation 3.3

θ *before* $\theta' \vdash \theta_c$ *before$_c$* $\theta'_c \vee \theta_c$ *meets$_c$* θ'_c

Observation 3.4

$\theta \approx \theta_c, \theta' \approx \theta'_c, \theta_c$ *before$_c$* $\theta'_c \vdash \theta$ *before* θ'

The significance of *equal* and *equal*$_c$

It may be shown that

Observation 3.5

$$\theta \; equal \; \theta' \Rightarrow \theta_c \; equal_c \; \theta'_c$$

On the other hand, $\theta_c \; equal_c \; \theta'_c$ may correspond to two right-open intervals $\theta \approx \theta_c$ and $\theta' \approx \theta'_c$ in Γ such that θ and θ' relate to each other in a variety of ways involving the relations *before*, *starts*, *finish*, *during* and *overlaps*. Appendix B does not include a proof for the above because of the large number of possible combinations.

The significance of *meets* and *meets*$_c$

Again, it may be shown that

Observation 3.6

$$\theta \; meets \; \theta' \Rightarrow \theta_c \; meets_c \; \theta'_c$$

However, the significance of $\theta_c \; meets_c \; \theta'_c$ in Γ_c is more complex. In order to reduce the number of possible relationships between θ and θ' in Γ, the following simplifying assumption is adopted:

$$left(\theta) < left(\theta') \wedge right(\theta) < right(\theta')$$

leading to

Observation 3.7

$$
\begin{aligned}
\theta \approx \theta_c, \theta' \approx \theta'_c, \\
left(\theta) < left(\theta'), right(\theta) < right(\theta'), \\
\theta_c \; meets_c \; \theta'_c \quad \vdash \quad \theta \; before \; \theta' \vee \theta \; meets \; \theta' \vee \\
\theta \; overlaps \; \theta'
\end{aligned}
$$

3.6   Application of Temporal Intervals

Our representation of real time so far has had no physical content. The intervals were void of any physical processes or their properties, consideration of which leads us to *states* and *events*.

3.6.1 States and Events

Since it is a primitive notion, the definition of the term *state* involves a certain degree of circularity. Broadly speaking, it characterizes the condition of a system at a given instant in time or over a given interval of time. Even a basic device such as a switch is a complex system when viewed in sufficient detail. However, the most essential feature of a switch is that it is either on or off. This high level view, which is usually the user's point of view, results in two possible states of the switch. Thus, the state of any system is an abstraction of reality in which some of its selected features relevant to a given stage in problem solving remain unchanged over the interval of time concerned. It does not necessarily mean that every feature in the system remains unchanged over the given interval.

The *events* are again an abstraction of a reality that characterizes the practically significant changes in state. A related term consists of the *actions* which are events brought about by agents.

It is important to appreciate that, while they share certain things in common, there are certain fundamental distinctions between states and events. Through a detailed study in the *Logic of Aspect*, Galton [46] shows that these two notions belong to two different logical categories, based not on any difference in their role with respect to the notion of change, but on how we choose to represent change through them. More specifically, states and events are alternative means of describing change; states describing states of change and events describing change of state. Some of the differences between the nature of states and events are detailed below.

States *obtain* at a *moment* or over a range of moments. States are *homogeneous* and *dissective*, that is, if a state obtains during an interval then the same state obtains at every moment in that interval and during every subinterval. Since they obtain during every subinterval, it is ambiguous to speak of the duration of a state without reference to a specific interval. States can be characterized by *propositions* and, therefore, are *negatable*. It is meaningful to talk of a proposition representing a certain state *not* being true. In contrast, events *occur* over an *interval*, which may be infinitesimal. Events are *unitary* and are *inhomogeneous*. If an event is split up into subevents, then each subevent is not the same as the original event. Not being associated with propositions, events cannot be negated. Non-occurrence of an event is not its negation.

3.6.2 Describing States

As mentioned above a state may be described by a proposition. Since a proposition is the meaning of any sentence which is either true or false, propositions may describe all kinds of states. For example, the occurrence of an event may be captured through a 'state' in which the event has taken place, is taking place or will have taken place. This is the notion of state referred to in Galton [46]. For example, the sentences

```
Front gate has been opened.
Front gate is open.
```

report two different kinds of state. The first sentence in our example above reports an 'irrevocable' state of historical affairs resulting from the occurrence of an event. It is a sentence within the exclusive scope of event logic. The state reported in the second sentence is perhaps closer to that used in computer science. Both kinds of states may be described by means of propositions in the same manner.

Given a state s described using a proposition p, the notation p_t may be used to mean that the state s obtains at time t. For example, if p denotes the proposition that the front gate is open, $p_{9:30pm}$ means that the front gate remained opened at 9:30 pm. Temporal indexing of propositions in this manner leads us to chronological logic – a subject beyond the scope of our study here. Given any set of disjoint right-open intervals $\theta \in \mathbb{O}$, we may state that s obtains at all intervals in θ as p_θ. By definition,

$$p_\theta \stackrel{def}{\Leftrightarrow} \forall x : \Gamma; \ t : \mathbb{R} \bullet x \in \theta \wedge t \in x \Rightarrow p_t$$

The customary notion of state in computer science is, however, that of a 'state of a system' identified by means of a set of 'state variables'. Such a state is associated with a specific 'assignment of values' to these state variables. Thus, the notion of state in computing is usually described by predicates. When dealing with realtime systems, the assignment of the same values to state variables at different times may be regarded as representing the same state.

In order to describe a given state in computing, it is necessary to discover a suitable set of state variables or attribute names. For example, in the case of the event involving the opening of the gate, one can identify an appropriate time dependent angle α measured, for example, in degrees such that,

State	Informal meaning
$\alpha(t) = 90°$	The gate is open at time t,
$\alpha(t) = 0°$	The gate is closed at time t.

It is clear that α must be a function of time and let us assume it to be a continuous differentiable partial function,

$$\alpha : \Theta \twoheadrightarrow Angle$$
$$\text{ran } \alpha = \{x \mid 0° \le x \le 90°\}$$

where *Angle* is a suitable type of values for measuring angles. Then the states and the events discussed earlier may be associated with

State	Informal meaning
$\overset{t}{\exists}\, t \bullet \dot{\alpha}(t) = \omega \wedge t < \text{NOW}$	The gate was opening.
$\dot{\alpha}(\text{NOW}) = \omega$	The gate is opening.
$\overset{t}{\exists}\, t \bullet \dot{\alpha}(t) = \omega \wedge t > \text{NOW}$	The gate will be opening.
$\overset{t}{\exists}\, t \bullet \dot{\alpha}(t) = -\omega \wedge t < \text{NOW}$	The gate was closing.
$\dot{\alpha}(\text{NOW}) = -\omega$	The gate is closing.
$\overset{t}{\exists}\, t \bullet \dot{\alpha}(t) = -\omega \wedge t > \text{NOW}$	The gate will be closing.

where $\overset{t}{\exists}$ is an existential quantifier qualifying only temporal variables and $\dot{\alpha}(t)$ is the time derivative of $\alpha(t)$. ω is strictly positive and is a constant in situations where the speed of closure may be assumed to be uniform. The meaning of the expressions on the left hand side in the above corresponds to the notion of state as commonly understood in computer science because it identifies a common state variable taking a specific value in different states. The sentences on the right hand side, on the other hand, correspond to states of affairs as represented by propositions.

3.6.3 The Notion of Event Radical

We outline in this section an approach to formalizing events. The most fundamental concept here is the notion of *event radical* due to Galton's *Logic of Aspect* [46]. It serves as the means for overcoming the limitation of tense logic, namely, the inability of tense logic to deal with sentences reporting events. Note that tense logic is a logical system intended for reasoning about sentences involving tense: *past, present* and *future*. The limitation in tense logic results from the fact that it restricts itself to sentences reporting states only. Being a propositional logic with propositions describing only individual states of affairs in isolation, tense logic lacks the means for dealing with changes in states and thus is not equipped to deal with events, which involve more than one state. The source of this difficulty lies in the following. Consider first the following three sentences:

```
The gate was open.
The gate is open.
The gate will be open.                                           (A)
```

reporting the same state of affairs in three different temporal contexts with respect to tense. Tense logic permits the expression of all three associated propositions as

$P\,p$

p

$F\,p$

respectively, where P and F are two tense logical operators standing for the past and future tenses. [Note that tense logic has two further operators: Hp denoting that p has always been true in the past and Gp denoting that p will always be true in the future.] By contrast, although each has a tense and both refer to the same event in different temporal contexts, there is no way of expressing the following two sentences in tense logic:

> The gate has been opened.
> The gate will have been opened.   (B)

This is because there is not a more primitive proposition p which may refer to the same event in the present tense, allowing the formation of Pp and Fp corresponding to the above sentences. Note that the sentence 'the gate is being opened' is not suitable because its past tense is 'the gate was being opened'. The common denominator of such pairs of sentences referring to events is not a proposition but a tenseless entity of a new category, referred to as an *event radical*. In terms of natural language grammar, event radicals may be associated with verbs in the infinitival form. In the formal language, this association may be continued conceptually for distinguishing them from other entities. Notationally, event radicals are shown by the following style of typeset:

> GATE-OPEN .

The above is the event radical embedded in the sentences (B). Event radicals are not themselves events. The events are brought into discourse by two primitive operators: *Perf* for *perfective operator* and *Pros* for *prospective operator*. The two operators allow expression of the sentences in (B) as

> *Perf* GATE-OPEN ,
> *Pros* GATE-OPEN .   ·

It is to be noted that the two operators *Perf* and *Pros* have no analogs of H and G in tense logic. Once an event is reported using either of these operators, the resulting sentences may be freely manipulated in both tense logic and event logic.

Note, for example, that *Perf* GATE-OPEN is a proposition implicitly indexed by a designator for the time NOW. We may generalize this by adopting the notation *Perf*$_t$ GATE-OPEN meaning that the event of opening the gate has already occurred at time t. Note that this means that the state reported by this sentence is true at time t and not necessarily that the event has actually occurred at time t.

The time of occurrence of events may be specified only in relation to intervals. Given an arbitrary durative event radical E and a set of disjoint right-open intervals $\theta \in \mathbb{O}_f$, a predicate Occ_θ E may be used to mean that the event described by the event radical E occurs within every interval in θ. The operator Occ may be defined as

$$Occ_\theta \text{ E} \overset{def}{\Leftrightarrow} \forall x : \Gamma \bullet x \in \theta \Rightarrow Pros_{left(x)} \text{ E} \land Perf_{right(x)} \text{ E}$$

The use of the set $\mathbb{O}_f$ is for ensuring the termination of all instances of any given event. Note that E in the above must not be an event radical of a momentary event (discussed below).

3.6.4 Classes of Events

The above is a superficial introduction to event logic, but with a slightly extended notation. Event logic is conceptually a rich formalism with different classes of events with precise and well understood logical properties. We give an overview of this by a brief informal discussion of event classes.

- *Durative and Punctual Events*:

  Durative events are basically those which take time to occur and their progression may be characterized by an appropriate proposition. Punctual events, on the other hand, are a kind of *instantaneous events* and cannot be caught in the act of happening. As one attempts to pinpoint the time of occurrence of any given punctual event, one realizes that it is either yet to occur or has just taken place.

- *Momentary Events*:

  Momentary events form the other type of *instantaneous* event. They have the peculiar property of having a proposition that describes a state for the instant when the event occurs. Therefore, such an event is not punctual since at that moment it has neither occurred nor is it yet to occur and, thus, can be caught in the act of happening. Galton gives an example of a momentary event as the event of a ball thrown up into the air reaching the peak of the projectile before falling down again.

- *Telic and Atelic Events*:

  A *telic* event is an event which must complete in order for it to have occurred. An example of a telic event is GATE-OPENS-HALF-WAY. Depending on the informal requirements, the gate must open exactly half way, or not less than half way, for this event to have occurred.

  An *atelic* event is an event where there is no notion of completion. An example of such an event is GATE-OPENS-A-LITTLE. It does not matter how much the gate should open for this event to have happened; the event would have taken place with the slightest opening of the gate.

- *Once-only and Repeatable Events*:

  An event that only has a unique occurrence or no occurrence is called a *once-only event*. Events that can occur more than once are called *repeatable events.* Repeatable events can be made into once-only events by giving them a numerical subscript to identify individual occurrences or instances.

- *The Senses of the Progressive*:

    Durative events may be in progress in a number of different senses. Event logic has a special operator *Prog* which returns a state for a given event radical meaning informally that the event concerned is in progress. Formally, however, there are four ways of interpreting *Prog E* for a given event *E*, namely:

    (i) *Narrow Sense* – Once started, an event of this class continues to be in progression at every moment until completion of the event. If such an event is in progression at any moment then the event must be actually taking place at that moment.

    (ii) *Broad Sense* – Once started, an event of this class may not necessarily be in progression at every moment between its start and completion times. In particular, the event may admit temporary interruptions, or 'preemptions' in the computer science terminology, but still the event is considered in progress.

    (iii) *Open Sense* – The event concerned may or may not complete. If it does not complete then it could not have occurred although it was in progress.

    (iv) *Closed Sense* – The event concerned is committed to completion.

The above notions of events are presented here in order to indicate the richness of event logic. It is important to realize that the above and other characteristics of events may be captured formally and, therefore, the framework allows reasoning about a wide variety of real-life situations formally.

3.7   Bibliographical Notes

The notion of right-open intervals used in this chapter is based on that on open intervals suggested by Maibaum [98]. The source of event logic outlined in this chapter is due to Galton [46]. The reader is referred to it for a comprehensive treatment, although a less detailed but sufficient coverage may be found in Nissanke [108]. There are other sources such as Kuhn [83] dealing with the nature of different events in relation to tense. A full account of chronological logic mentioned in Section 3.6.2 may be found in Rescher [134]. Accounts such as those by Alur and Henzinger [5] and Koymans [82] deal with, among other issues, different temporal structures applicable to realtime systems.

Chapter 4

Petri Nets – An Introduction

The aim of this chapter is a brief overview of Petri net theory for the purpose of discussion of its realtime extensions in Chapters 5 and 6. This chapter may be omitted by those who are familiar with the general Petri net theory.

4.1 Basic Concepts

Petri nets provide for a mathematical approach to modelling and analysis of systems, with a convenient, effective and highly intuitive graphical language for their visualization. Petri nets are applicable to a wide class of systems, among them:

- those involving concurrency, synchronization and non-determinism;
- those based on different architectures such as multi-processor systems and distributed systems; and
- those characterized by deterministic, stochastic and other underlying mathematical models.

Petri nets cover a range of diverse applications, including communication protocols, computer networks, manufacturing systems, industrial process control and data flow computing. Similarly, they have been widely used in the study of behavioural properties as well as in areas such as simulations, performance evaluation and fault tolerance.

4.1.1 Petri Nets as Graphs

A Petri net is a *bipartite graph*, which is a graph consisting of two distinct sets of *nodes* or *vertices* and a set of *arcs* between pairs of nodes. The nodes in each arc are drawn one each from the two sets. The two sets of nodes are called *places* and *transitions* and are denoted conventionally by P and T respectively. These sets are non-empty, finite and are of distinct kinds and, thus, are also disjoint. The elements of P and T are denoted by p_i and t_j, i and j being appropriate indices. In graphical presentation of Petri nets, places are shown by 'circles' ○ and transitions by 'bars' | drawn at any inclination.

There are two kinds of *arc* in Petri nets, namely *input arcs* and *output arcs*. As sets, they are denoted by i and o respectively:

$i \subseteq P \times T$ –   The elements in i correspond to arcs from places to transitions; these places are referred to as *inputs* of the transitions concerned.

$o \subseteq T \times P$ –   The elements in o correspond to arcs from transitions to places; these places are referred to as *outputs* of the transitions concerned.

It is clear from the above that other kinds of arcs, such as arcs from places to places, are not permitted. Note also that arcs between pairs of vertices are directed. Thus, an arc corresponding to a pair (p_i, t_k) is different from that corresponding to (t_k, p_i). Obviously, in graphical displays of nets the directions of arcs are shown by arrows.

Petri nets differ from conventional graphs by having, in general, multiple arcs (or *bags* of arcs) between some pairs of places and transitions. Multiplicity of arcs may be seen alternatively as a *weight* attached to a single arc and, therefore, arc weights can be represented as a function

$$W : ((P \times T) \cup (T \times P)) \twoheadrightarrow \mathbf{N}$$

such that

$$\text{dom } W = i \cup o$$

Petri nets occasionally use special kinds of arcs known as *inhibitor arcs*. Inhibitor arcs are permitted from (input) places to transitions only and, thus, do not point to output places. The inhibitor arcs are distinguished in the graphical notation by a small circle in place of the usual arrow head. They are particularly convenient in modelling, but could adversely affect clarity and comprehensibility.

4.1.2   Marking Function

Being models of some real-life systems, Petri nets are supposed to evolve over time, and this evolution may be captured by means of the following:

(i) a 'time invariant' part of the Petri net with five components,

$$(P, T, i, o, W)$$

These components are time invariant in the sense that they remain fixed in the evolution of a Petri net.

(ii) a 'time variant' *marking function*, M, which captures the evolution of the net in time.

Marking is a mapping (a function)

$$M : P \rightarrow \mathbb{N}$$

and effectively associates a number of *tokens* with each place. Any reference to the marking function is meaningless without mentioning its initial value, denoted conventionally by M_0. In general, M_i refers to a specific value of the marking function, i being an appropriate numerical index.

Thus, Petri nets consist of both a time invariant static component and a time varying component. As a consequence, each Petri net as a whole consists of six distinct components, namely,

$$\text{PN} = (P, T, i, o, W, M)$$

4.2   Modelling Systems

4.2.1   On Representation of Systems

As a tool used for modelling systems, the components of Petri nets represent different aspects of the system. Let us examine here the correspondence between Petri nets and systems. This correspondence is presented here through a comparison of features of Petri nets and systems. [The symbol ' $\rightsquigarrow$ ' links model constituents or their behaviour with those of the system.]

The model		*The system*
Places	$\rightsquigarrow$	Potential conditions of the system. Mathematically, these conditions may be stated as predicates.
Transitions	$\rightsquigarrow$	Potential events in the system. These are elementary events in the sense that their internal composition is to be ignored at the level of abstraction of the given net.
Input Arcs	$\rightsquigarrow$	Input arcs to transitions, relating events with the pre conditions (prerequisites) for their occurrence.
Output Arcs	$\rightsquigarrow$	Output arcs from transitions, relating events with their post-conditions – conditions brought about by their occurrence.

Tokens	⤳	Presence of an appropriate number of tokens in an input place signifies 'fulfillment' (or 'readiness') of the condition attached to the place necessary for the occurrence of the event associated with the given place.
Firing or Execution	⤳	Firing (or execution) of a transition signifies the occurrence of its associated event.
Marking	⤳	Currently prevailing system state.
Initial Marking	⤳	The initial system state.
Change of Marking	⤳	A transformation of the system state.

4.2.2   Model of Execution

The evolution of Petri nets is captured by an ordering of the net states as represented by the marking function. Each change of the net state is brought about by the *firing* or *execution* of a transition. The discipline of transition firing is based on the notion of *enabledness* of transitions. A transition t is said to be *enabled* if and only if both following conditions are true:

(a) Every input place p, other than those in inhibitor arcs incident on t, has at least $W((p, t))$ tokens, that is, the weight of the arc from p to t.
(b) Every input place p, from where there is in an inhibitor arc incident on t, has no tokens. In other words, an inhibitor arc treats the negation of the condition attached to its input place as the enabling condition of the relevant transition.

A transition t is said to be *disabled* if it is not enabled.

The firing of transitions alters the value of the marking function and, thus, the state of the net. Firing of transitions and changes in the net obey the following rules:

(i) Only enabled transitions may fire.
(ii) As a transition t fires, $W((p_i, t))$ tokens are removed from each input p_i of the transition t, and $W((p_o, t))$ tokens are deposited at each output p_o of the transition t. The value of the marking function elsewhere is unaltered.
(iii) Firing is instantaneous and complete with respect to rule (ii) above. Firing is also non-deterministic in the case of a choice with more than one concurrently enabled transition. That is, any of the enabled transitions may fire and the transition which is to be fired is chosen arbitrarily. [Strictly speaking, one cannot speak of 'instantaneity' since there is no notion of time.]

4.2.3 Complex System Features

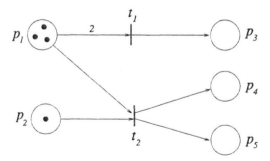

Figure 4.1 Two concurrent transitions

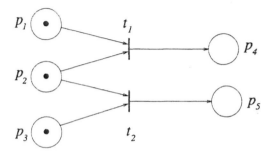

Figure 4.2 Two transitions in conflict

Petri nets are a highly versatile tool. They allow the modelling of complex architectural and behavioural features, such as concurrency and decision points. Some of them are outlined below.

Concurrency	–	Two transitions are said to be *concurrent* if and only if they are both enabled and, further, each may be executed in any order without disabling the other by its execution (see Figure 4.1).
Conflict	–	Two transitions are said to be in *conflict* if they are both enabled, but firing of any one of them immediately disables the other by its execution (see Figure 4.2). The place causing the conflict is said to be a *decision point*.
Symmetric Confusion	–	A special form of conflict, where the concurrency of transitions is affected by the firing of a third transition. In the example given in Figure 4.3, concurrency of t_1 and t_3 is affected by the firing of t_2.

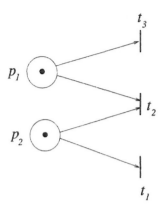

Figure 4.3 Symmetric confusion

Asymmetric   –   Another special form of conflict, where a conflict between
Confusion   two transitions t_2 and t_3 is brought about by firing of a
                         concurrent partner t_1 (see Figure 4.4).

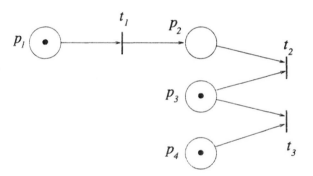

Figure 4.4 Asymmetric confusion

4.2.4   Types of Petri Net

The nature of the marking function enables the identification of several classes of
Petri nets:

- *Condition-event Nets*
  In these nets, each place contains at most one token and the presence of the
  token corresponds to a condition. The conditions may be seen as propositions
  which may take one of the truth values: true or false.

- *Place-transition Nets*

  In these nets, places may contain multiple tokens, the presence of tokens corresponding to a condition and the number of tokens to some capacity or a counter.

- *Predicate-event Nets*

  These nets generalize the above two classes of nets further by allowing particular objects or individuals as tokens. In this case, each condition may be seen as a predicate written with respect to these objects and taking a truth value. The so-called *coloured nets* form a special case of these nets.

4.3   Illustrative Examples

The diagrams cited in this section illustrate some applications of Petri nets, especially in relation to certain characteristic features shared by many diverse systems.

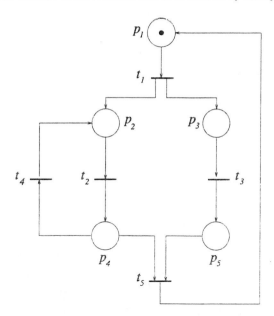

Figure 4.5 A net with potential concurrency and conflicts

Figure 4.5 shows a net, the design of which includes features such as concurrency and conflicts outlined in Section 4.2.3. The next three diagrams show how the behaviours intended by these features come about in the evolution of the net. In particular, Figure 4.6 shows two concurrent transitions subsequent to firing of the transition t_1. If t_2, one of these concurrent transitions, fires it results in the state shown in Figure 4.7, where the transition t_3 causes asymmetrical confusion with respect to transitions t_4 and t_5. On the other hand, transition t_4 is a concurrent

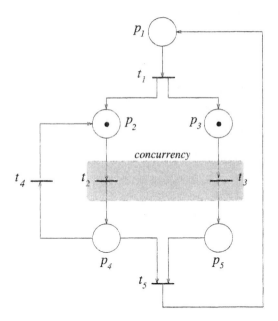

Figure 4.6 A state showing concurrency

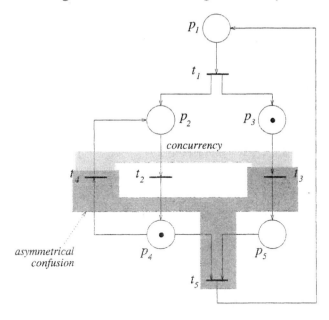

Figure 4.7 A state showing concurrency and asymmetrical confusion

transition with t_3 and causes no asymmetrical confusion with respect to t_3. If t_3 chooses to fire in this state, it will result in the state shown in Figure 4.8, where

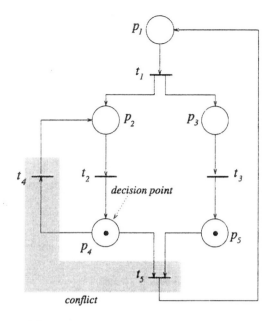

Figure 4.8 A state showing a conflict

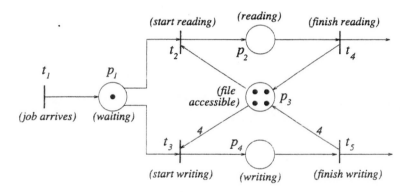

Figure 4.9 Four readers and a writer

transitions t_4 and t_5 are already in conflict.

Figures 4.9 and 4.10 are self-explanatory and may be found in the recommended literature devoted to the subject and, therefore, they are not discussed here in detail. Figure 4.9 models a file access control protocol allowing up to four concurrent readers in read-only mode or a single writer accessing the file in exclusive read and write mode. Figure 4.10 is a model of a communication protocol between two processors. Communications take place between the two processors asynchronously through two independent buffers modelled by places p_2 and p_7. Any new data may be written to either buffer, but only when its previously held data has been read.

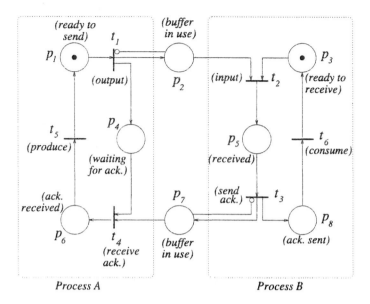

Figure 4.10 A communication protocol

4.4   Properties of Petri Nets

Given any formal notation intended for specification and modelling of systems, it is legitimate to question the properties of models envisaged by it. The kind of properties of interest in Petri nets belong to two categories: those which depend on the structure of the net and those which depend on the initial marking and on the net evolution. This section concerns only the latter, dealing essentially with dynamic properties.

Definition: *Reachability*

A marking M_n is said to be *reachable* from an initial marking M_0 if and only if either $n = 0$ or there exists a sequence of firing $s = \langle t_1, t_2, \cdots, t_n \rangle$ altering the value of the marking function respectively from M_0 to M_1, from M_1 to M_2, $\cdots$, and finally from M_{n-1} to M_n.

The relevance of reachability in the realtime context is obvious. The state corresponding to the marking addressed by reachability may be one of the states not permitted or undesirable for *safety* reasons. The set of all possible markings reachable from M_0 in a given Petri net N is denoted by $R(N, M_0)$.

Two important kinds of nets for dealing with nets where places represent data storage facilities such as buffers and the tokens the relevant data items are the so-called *bounded nets* and *safe nets*. These are related and are defined as

Definition: *Boundedness* and *Safe Nets*

(a) *k-Boundedness*

A PN is said to be *k-bounded* for some given $k \in \mathbb{N}$ if $M(p) \leq k$ for every marking $M \in R(M_0)$ and for every $p \in P$.

(b) *Boundedness*

A PN is said to be *bounded* if there exists a $k \in \mathbb{N}$ such that the net is k-bounded.

(c) *Safe Petri Net*

A PN is said to be *safe* if the net is 1-bounded.

In other words, the number of tokens in each and every place in a k-bounded net never exceeds k for any marking reachable from the initial marking M_0, k being a finite number. By contrast, boundedness is a general notion which relies on some unspecified but a finite number.

Liveness signifies the absence of deadlock in the net, irrespective of the chosen sequence of firing.

Definition: *Liveness*

A PN is said to be *live* if for every marking M reachable from the initial marking M_0 it is possible eventually to fire every transition in the net in some marking M' which is reachable from M.

Although it is a highly desirable property, establishing whether a given system possesses liveness is not always feasible. In such situations, a notion of limited liveness may be acceptable or the only possibility, and in this connection other less stringent criteria on liveness may offer a more practical solution.

Definition: *Persistence*

A PN is said to be *persistent* if for every pair of enabled transitions firing of one does not disable the other.

It is clear from the discussion in Section 4.2.3 that persistence is closely related to conflict free nets.

Fairness is a notion which qualitatively characterizes the extent of potential activity in a net. Among the different notions of fairness are the following.

Definition: *Fairness*

(a) Mutual fairness between transitions.

A pair of transitions is said to be *bounded-fair* if there is an upper bound on the number of executions of either transition while the other is not being executed.

(b) Global fairness in firing sequences.

A firing sequence s is said to be *globally fair* if every transition appears in s infinitely often.

(c) Global fairness in nets.

A net is said to be *globally fair* if every firing sequence starting from M_0 is globally fair.

The other kinds of properties, mentioned earlier that depend on the structure of the net are known as static properties and can be established by studying the net topology. Some examples of such properties are the existence of a live initial marking and whether a given marking is reachable from any other marking.

4.5   Bibliographical Notes

The reader may find the references due to Agerwala [3], Murata [105], Peterson [119, 120], Reisig [133] and Reutenauer [135] to be good introductions to the general theory of Petri nets. The references in Murtata [105] and Peterson [119] are relatively brief and simple introductions and are adequate as further reading prior to the study of the next two chapters. Murtata [105] in particular is a good source of examples illustrating, among others, the net properties discussed in the previous section. A detailed discussion of condition-event nets, place-transition nets and predicate-event nets mentioned in Section 4.2.4 may be found in Reisig [133].

4.6   Exercises

Exercises given at the end of the next chapter serve as the exercises for both chapters. Obviously, timing aspects have to be ignored when attempting them as part of the exercises for this chapter.

Timed Petri Nets

Timing aspects of realtime systems are an important consideration in their modelling, analysis and performance evaluation. The general Petri net theory cannot cope with these important aspects since it lacks an appropriate notion of time.

This chapter is an introduction to a particular temporal extension to the Petri net theory, as a framework for modelling of realtime systems. The approach presented forms a part of a more general framework covered in greater detail in the next chapter.

5.1 Time Augmentation of Petri Nets

5.1.1 Different Approaches

There are several approaches to augmenting Petri nets with time; the following is a brief outline.

(1) *Associating Time with Transitions*

Merlin and Farber [100] and Ramchandani [124] advocate an approach whereby a computation time (execution time, or a delay) c_i is associated with each transition t_i. Alternatively, a time interval $\langle c_{min}, c_{max} \rangle$ may be associated with t_i in order to allow some variation of c_i within the interval.

Firing of an event is interpreted as a durative (prolonged) event, lasting c_i time units from the time of event initiation.

(2) *Associating Time with Places*

Alternatively, following Coolahan and Roussopoulos [27], a computation time c_i may be associated with each place p_i.

In this approach, firing of a transition signifies the instantaneous event of starting the execution of processes attached to its output places, and the continuation of each process for the next c_i time units, c_i being the time associated with the relevant output place p_i. Tokens become 'ready' only upon the termination of all processes thus invoked.

(3) *Time Basic Nets* (TBN)

This is a more general approach, which offers the capabilities of both the above and more. It involves the following:

(a) Associating certain relative time values, referred to in the literature as *time offsets*, with each transition as its time parameters.

(b) *Time-stamping* of tokens for determining the enabling times of transitions.

(c) Associating an interval of clock times with each transition, giving the permitted, or the mandatory firing times of transitions. This interval is defined as a function of time stamps on tokens at input places and time offsets mentioned in (a) above.

5.1.2   A Preliminary Evaluation

Before undertaking a detailed study of approach (3), let us make a comparative evaluation of the basic features of the other two. The less favourable features explain in part the reasons for our choice of (3) for the detailed study.

(i) Although they can be effective in specific areas, approaches (1) and (2) are not versatile enough across applications as a general tool.

(ii) Approach (2) retains two main features of the classical Petri net theory, namely,

- 'instantaneous' nature of firing; and
- system state as represented by the marking function.

(iii) Execution of a transition in approach (2) amounts to triggering one or more processes attached to its output places. This, however, contravenes the spirit of the classical Petri net theory with respect to instantaneous updating of the marking function.

(iv) The consequences of disabling of once enabled transitions in approach (2), caused by the execution of other transitions, is not clear.

(v) The execution of a transition in approach (1) corresponds to execution of a single process in real time, and this may be argued as contravening the features in (ii) above. There can also be potential ambiguities associated with the firing of multiply enabled transitions, namely, whether a multiply enabled transition may fire within the permitted interval time independently of its other firings or whether the possible firings should be separated from each other by the permitted interval.

(vi) In both approaches, the determination of 'executability' of transitions requires global knowledge about the net.

(vii) As will be seen shortly, the enabling time of transitions does depend on the arrival time of tokens at input places, and this dependency does not appear explicitly in either approach.

Let us restrict ourselves to a detailed study of the third approach.

5.2 Time Basic Nets (TBN)

5.2.1 Basic Concepts

In this approach, tokens are *time-stamped*; a time stamp being a record carried by each token of the firing time of the transition which created it. Associated with time stamps is a function *time*. Given a place p, $time(p)$ gives the value of the time stamp of the token at place p, assuming that there is only one time stamp of the tokens at p. *Time* is a partial function

$$time : \ P \nrightarrow \mathbb{T}$$

and is defined only at places where there are tokens. Therefore,

$$\text{dom } time = \text{dom}(M \rhd 1..\,)$$

It is possible to define the function *time* so that it gives the time stamp of a given token at a given place, thus enabling a proper treatment of multiple tokens at any place with different time stamps. This will be addressed in the next chapter. Unless otherwise stated, we therefore assume that *time* is a function from places to clock time. Because of its link with tokens, the value of the function *time* is updated, analogous to the marking function, each time a transition fires.

The permitted firing times of transitions are given in terms of a *time condition*, which is a set of clock time values or <u>absolute time</u> values. In this chapter let us assume that this set forms a contiguous stretch of time. The time condition of any transition is defined in terms of the time stamps of its input places and certain temporal parameters associated with the transition. These temporal parameters are referred to as *time offsets* and are usually specified as lengths of time, that is, <u>relative times</u>. Note that time offsets are fixed parameters of transitions and do not change with time. The function which determines the time condition has to be 'customized' for each and every individual transition. The time condition of a given transition is obtained by applying the function *time* to time stamps of input places of the transition and its time offsets. Note that conventionally time offsets are not listed among the arguments of the function *time*. Thus, the time condition varies with changes to the state of the net.

5.2.2   Enabling of Transitions

A transition is said to be *enabled* if and only if the following hold:

(a) Each input place contains the necessary number of tokens. If inhibitor arcs are being used, then the input places connected with them must be empty. This condition is identical to that of untimed Petri nets.

(b) There are time values in its *time condition* which are greater than, or equal to, the largest time stamp on the input tokens.
This condition requires all the tokens to arrive at the input places before the 'expiry time' of the transition enabling, if the transition concerned is to fire within its time condition.

5.2.3   Firing Period

Identified with each enabled transition is an *enabling tuple*, which is a set of time-stamped tokens at its respective input places. An enabling tuple of a transition t must contain $W((p, t))$ tokens at every input place p, that is, the weight of *normal arcs* from p to t, (p, t) not being an inhibitor arc. Given an enabling tuple, *enabling time* is the latest time stamped on the tokens in the enabling tuple.

The *firing period* of a transition is then defined as the clock time interval whose values are drawn from the time condition of the transition concerned, but are greater than or equal to its enabling time. It follows from this definition that the firing period may not be equal to the time condition in certain circumstances, especially if the expression of the time condition does not involve all the input places of the transition concerned.

5.2.4   Model of Execution

The execution of transitions obeys the following rules:

(i) Only enabled transitions may fire. The firing of a given transition must take place at some time in its *firing period*.

(ii) As a transition t fires, the *enabling tuple* is removed from the input places of t.
This is in line with the rules of untimed Petri nets, but differs in that the choice of tokens to be removed could, in general, depend on their time stamps. This is an issue to be considered if the function *time* takes into account not only the places but also the possibility of different time stamps of the tokens at any given place.

(iii) Firing of a transition delivers to its outputs the appropriate number of tokens, time-stamped with its firing time and according to the arc weight following the rules of untimed Petri nets.

(iv) The other rules in untimed Petri nets remain applicable.

5.3 Illustrative Examples

This section presents a few basic (and hypothetical) examples illustrating the application of TBN to modelling realtime systems. The notation used for time intervals in these examples is as given in Section 3.1.1 of Chapter 3.

5.3.1 A Part of an Auto-pilot

Informal Description:

> The system is basically an automatic override for pilot action, which is invoked in the event of undue delays on the part of the pilot in controlling the aircraft. The delays may be either due to:
>
> (i) pilot failing to choose the manual control as the flight approaches the landing site, or
>
> (ii) pilot failing to adjust the manual control subsequently at the required intervals.
>
> The timing constraints are as follows. In the case of (i), the pilot has to exercise his or her choice of manual control within the t_{sel} time units after entering the landing radius, and in the case of (ii), the adjustments must be made after a minimum separation time of t_{adj}^{min} time units from the previous adjustment. The auto-pilot takes over the control of the aircraft a maximum of t_{adj}^{max} time units after the latest adjustment, but only if the monitoring system observes any excessive deviation from the landing approach.

The untimed Petri net model of the system is as shown in the Figure 5.1 and the role of its transitions and places is described below.

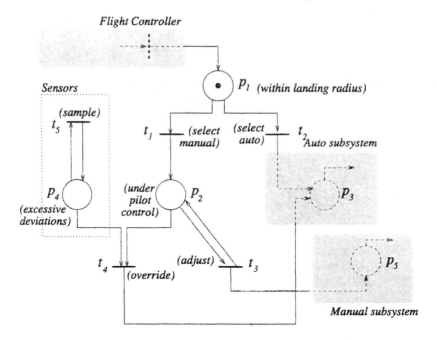

Figure 5.1 A part of an auto-pilot

	Places			Transitions	
Id.	Description		Id.	Description	
p_1	Flight is within landing radius		t_1	Select manual operation	
p_2	Flight is under pilot control		t_2	Invoke automatic operation	
p_3	Flight is under automatic control		t_3	Adjust manual operation	
p_4	Flight deviates excessively from landing approach		t_4	Invoke automatic override	
p_5	(Some output place within manual subsystem)		t_5	Process sensor data (timing not covered)	

The following table presents TBN timing aspects required in extending the above to a timed model of the system. The untimed net, together with the timing specification given below, is considered a timed model of the system.

Transition	Time offsets	Input places	Time condition
t_1	t_{sel}	p_1	$(time(p_1),\ time(p_1) + t_{sel}]$
t_2	t_{sel}	p_1	$(time(p_1) + t_{sel},\ \infty)$
t_3	$t_{adj}^{min},\ t_{adj}^{max}$	p_2	$(time(p_2) + t_{adj}^{min},\ time(p_2) + t_{adj}^{max})$
t_4	t_{adj}^{max}	$p_2,\ p_4$	$[time(p_2) + t_{adj}^{max},\ \infty)$,
			if $time(p_4) > time(p_2)$
		$\emptyset$,	otherwise

5.3.2 A Process Control System

Informal Description:

> The production of a certain product requires from T_1 to T_2 time
> units of total processing time. The processing commences within
> T_3 time units from the delivery of the raw material for the
> product. If the processing is not begun before this time limit,
> the site should discard the raw material and be ready to accept
> new deliveries. Because of the sensitivity to ambient conditions,
> the processors involved in the production are vulnerable to
> failure and, therefore, an additional processor is kept as
> standby. If a processor fails in the middle of its operation,
> it is immediately replaced by the standby processor, but
> incurring an unspecified delay. On termination of processing,
> the processors become available for the next cycle in T_4 time
> units.

As a simplification, let us assume that only up to one processor failure is envisaged
in any cycle of operation. Let us also ignore the aspects related to supply of new
standby processors.

The untimed Petri net model of the system is as shown in Figure 5.2. Its transitions and places signify the following.

Places		Transitions	
Id.	Description	Id.	Description
p_1	Raw material has been delivered	t_1	Start processing
p_2	Processors are available	t_2	Finish processing
p_3	A processor is ready	t_3	Discard raw material
p_4	Processing is taking place	t_4	Processor fails
p_5	Processing has started	t_5	Replace processor
p_6	Processing has started or processor has failed	t_6	Deliver raw material
p_7	Processor has failed		

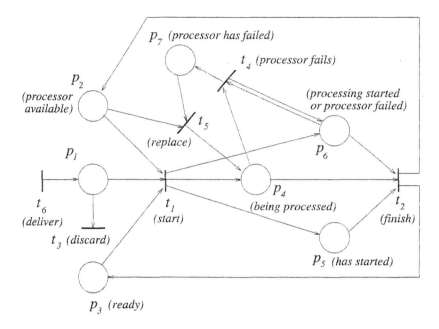

Figure 5.2 Representation of process control system

The places p_4, p_5 and p_6 are introduced specifically for capturing timing requirements. Note that the places p_5 and p_6 are not required in an untimed net; see Section 5.6 for a general justification for this. The use of these three places is such that,

$$time(p_4) \quad - \quad \text{denotes the time of processor replacement,}$$
$$time(p_5) \quad - \quad \text{denotes the start time of processing,}$$
$$time(p_6) \quad - \quad \text{denotes the time of processor failure,}$$

all three time values being clock times. The following table presents timing aspects in TBN for extending the above to a timed model of the system:

Transi-tion	Time offsets	Input places	Time condition
t_1	T_3, T_4	p_1, p_2, p_3	$[time(p_3) + T_4, \ time(p_1) + T_3)$
t_2	T_1, T_2	p_4, p_5, p_6	$[T_0 + T_1, \ T_0 + T_2]$
			where $T_0 = time(p_4) + time(p_5) - time(p_6)$
t_3	T_3	p_1	$[time(p_1) + T_3, \ \infty]$
t_4	T_1	p_4, p_6	$[time(p_4), \ time(p_4) + T_1)$, if $time(p_4) = time(p_6)$
			$\emptyset$, \qquad\qquad\qquad\qquad\qquad otherwise
t_5	$-$	p_2, p_7	$(time(p_7), \ \infty)$

In order to illustrate the working of the above net, consider the following specific scenario, where

$$T_1 = 8, \quad T_2 = 10, \quad T_3 = 3 \quad \text{and} \quad T_4 = 3 \quad \text{time units.}$$

The initial marking is implicit in the State 1, which is outlined below.

State 1: After firing of t_6 at clock time 2; see Figure 5.3:

$time(p_1)$ = 2 (in clock time);

$time(p_2)$ = 0 on one token 1 and on the other token (note that this is an exception to our definition of *time* as a function from places to clock time.);

$time(p_3)$ = 0.

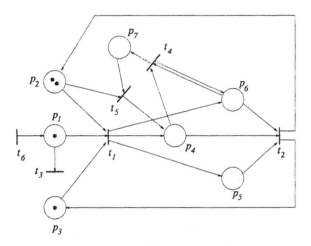

Figure 5.3 Process control system: State 1

Enabled transitions	Time conditions (clock time intervals)
t_1	$[0 + 3, 2 + 3) = [3, 5)$
t_3	$[2 + 3, \infty) = [5, \infty)$

State 2: After firing of t_1 at clock time 4; see Figure 5.4:

$$time(p_2) = 1, time(p_4) = time(p_5) = time(p_6) = 4$$

Enabled transitions	Time conditions (clock time intervals)
t_2	$[4 + 8, 4 + 10] = [12, 14]$
t_4	$[4, 4 + 8) = [4, 12)$

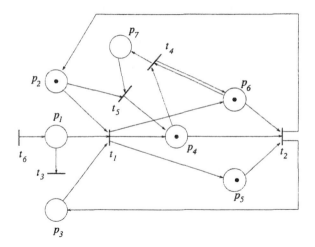

Figure 5.4 Process control system: State 2

State 3: After firing of t_4 at clock time 7; see Figure 5.5:

$$
\begin{aligned}
time(p_2) &= 1; \\
time(p_5) &= 4; \\
time(p_6) &= 7; \\
time(p_7) &= 7.
\end{aligned}
$$

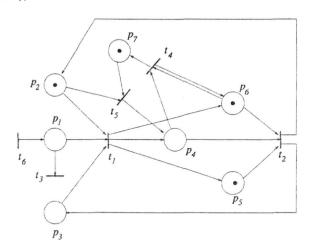

Figure 5.5 Process control system: State 3

Enabled transition	Time condition (clock time intervals)
t_5	$(7, \infty)$

State 4: After firing of t_5 at clock time 13; see Figure 5.6:

$$time(p_4) = 13;$$
$$time(p_5) = 4;$$
$$time(p_6) = 7.$$

Note that,

$$T_0 = time(p_4) + time(p_5) - time(p_6) = 13 + 4 - 7 = 10$$

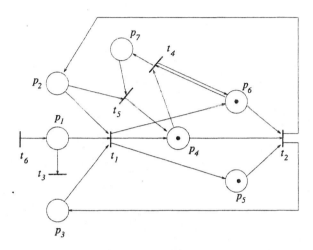

Figure 5.6 Process control system: State 4

Enabled transition	Time condition (clock time intervals)
t_2	$[10 + 8, 10 + 10] = [18, 20]$
t_4	$\varnothing$

State 5: After firing of t_2 at clock time 19; see Figure 5.7:

$$time(p_2) = time(p_3) = 19$$

No transitions are enabled in this state. The plant is thus ready for the next cycle of operation.

5.3.3 Telephone

The system considered here is an ordinary telephone equipment, with reference to its behaviour under user interaction in the calling-out mode. We do not give

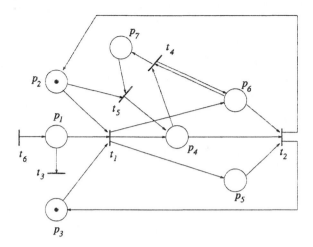

Figure 5.7 Process control system: State 5

an informal description of the system here and rely on our everyday experience in characterising its behaviour. The example is inspired by the work due to Dasarathy [33]. It illustrates the application of timed Petri nets to specification, design and modelling. A more detailed model of the same but without considering time may be found in Section 7.17 of Chapter 7 in CSP. Chapter 8 presents a few selected extensions to it in timed CSP.

Figure 5.8 is intended to serve as the specification, indicating that the purpose is to support a medium of conversation between the two arbitrary users: *caller* and *callee*. The timing aspects of the specification for making a telephone call may be given as below.

Transition	Offsets	Inputs	Time condition
lift1	δt	(not) ringing,	$\{t \mid 0 \le t - time(willing_{caller}) \le \delta t\}$,
caller		on hook, willing	$time(on\ hook_{caller}) \le$ $time(willing_{caller})$
lift2 callee	δt	ringing, on hook, willing	$\{t \mid 0 \le t - time(willing_{callee}) \le \delta t\}$, $time(on\ hook_{caller}) \le time(willing_{callee})$ $time(willing_{callee}) \ge$ $time(ringing_{callee})$, $time(willing_{caller}) + \Delta T \ge$ $time(ringing_{callee})$

First, a few remarks about the notation. Instead of the symbols such as p_i and t_i used earlier when referring to places and transitions, here we use words

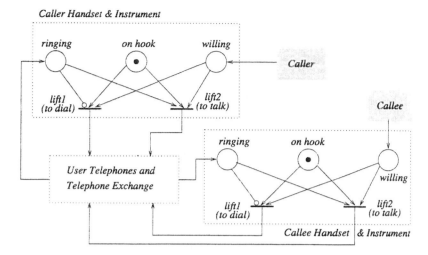

Figure 5.8 Telephone equipment: a high level view

such as *on hook$_{caller}$* as identifiers for places and transitions. Thus, for example, *time(on hook$_{caller}$)* refers to the time of the latest termination of a call by the *caller*, and *time(willing$_{caller}$)* to the time of initiation of the call by the *caller*. Note that transitions with input arcs labelled by '$< n$' are assumed to remove up to n tokens at the relevant input places when they fire.

ΔT and δt are system parameters. ΔT is the specified time for establishing the connection between the *caller* and *callee* and δt – the specified time for instrument response from the moment the handset is taken off the hook. As an example, consider the time condition attached to the *callee's* instrument, according to which the instrument must respond within δt time units after the handset is taken off the hook, but after the instrument has started ringing. The *callee's* instrument must ring within ΔT time units after the *caller* has taken the handset off the hook from the instrument. Obviously, these timing requirements are insufficient and incomplete, and have to be refined in the design stage.

The design involves the discovery and the modelling of the internal structure of the instrument such that the resulting system exhibits the above behaviour. It must also introduce corrective measures as appropriate for dealing with the deviations from the above state of affairs. The structure of the *caller's* instrument is shown Figure 5.9 in some detail.

The timing specification for just one of the transitions and its complementary transitions for exception handling is given below. The primary transition concerns the dialling of individual digits while the transitions dealing with the exceptions concern the cut-off facility taking effect on the first dialling delay, or the user decision to hang up the handset. Let us continue to use subscripted δts to denote an appropriate specification of tolerance on instrument response time or user intervention following the latest event or action. Thus, δt_1 above refers to the total

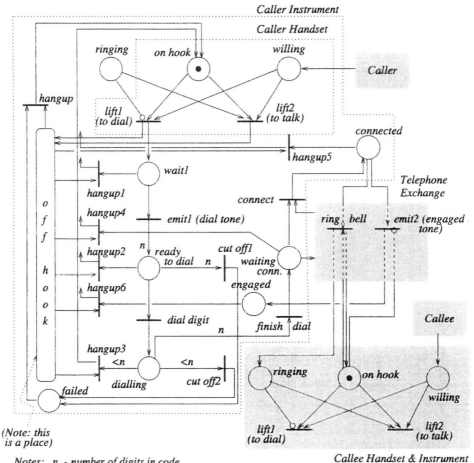

Figure 5.9 Telephone equipment: a detailed view

time allowed for dialling n digits. Although not considered here, it may also be appropriate to constrain the time permitted between successive dialling of digits.

Transition	Offsets	Inputs	Time condition
dial digit	δt_1	ready to dial	$\{t \mid t - time(ready^*) \leq \delta t_1\}$
cut off	δt_1	ready to dial	$\{t \mid t - time(ready^*) > \delta t_1\}$
hangup2	δt_1	ready to dial	$\{t \mid t - time(ready^*) \geq 0\}$

[* Note that *ready** is an abbreviation for the place *ready to dial*.]

5.4   Semantically Specialized Transitions

Transitions may be given semantic attributes characterizing their expected behaviour further. In this connection, let us introduce two semantic notions.

(i) *Semantically Weak Time Transitions*

These transitions may not be forced to fire within the permitted firing period. What is required by weak time semantics is that the firing time satisfies the firing period if the transition chooses to fire.

This may be regarded as a property, characterizing transitions lying on the system interface requiring the participation of the environment, with the exceptions of, perhaps, sensors and actuators.

(ii) *Semantically Strong Time Transitions*

Once enabled, and continue to remain so, these transitions must fire at some time within the permitted firing period.

Such transitions are situated typically in the system interior, and include, for example, reactive transitions lying behind the system interface and other overriding facilities.

EXAMPLE

1. Flight Control System

   The transitions t_1 and t_3 in the auto-pilot discussed in Section 5.3.1 may be given weak time semantics, and t_2 and t_4 – strong time semantics.

2. Telephone

   The desired behaviour of the telephone discussed in Section 5.3.3 may be further clarified by attaching, as appropriate, the above semantic notions with each transition. In this particular case, *cut off* may be characterized by strong semantics in order to signify that it must fire within its time condition, whereas *dial digit* and *hangup2* by weak semantics in order to signify user freedom on his or her choices.

5.5   TBN and Other Timed Petri Nets

The relationship between TBN and approach (1) in Section 5.1.1 to time augmentation of Petri nets is fairly straightforward. Section 5.6 outlines how the timing expressed in one can be translated to the other. Let us confine ourselves here to establishing the link with approach (2) mentioned in Section 5.1.1. Let:

t_{min}^p — The minimum time taken by a token to become 'ready' since arrival at the place p.

t_{max}^p — The maximum 'life time' of a token since arrival at the place p.

Approach (ii) may associate, in general, a pair of time values (t_{min}^p, t_{max}^p) with a place p, meaning that a process attached to the place p may last from t_{min}^p to t_{max}^p time units. A typical use of timing in this approach is illustrated in Figure 5.10.

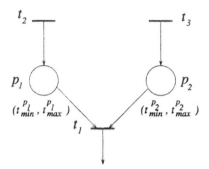

Figure 5.10 A timed net with place attached timing

Timing requirements of the above form attached to places p_1 and p_2 may be translated as a time condition in TBN on the transition t_1. This time condition becomes

$$(max(t_{min}^{p_1} + time(p_1) .. t_{min}^{p_2} + time(p_2)),$$
$$min(t_{max}^{p_1} + time(p_1) .. t_{max}^{p_2} + time(p_2)))$$

where

$min(s)$ — A function returning the minimum value in the set s.

$max(s)$ — A function returning the maximum value in the set s.

$t_1 .. t_2$ — The set containing all time values from t_1 to t_2.

On the other hand, the timing requirements expressed in TBN may be translated back to approach (ii) by dropping the time-stamping of tokens, but the resulting requirements are not unique.

5.6   Representation of Process Durations

Let a transition t have the time offsets t_{min} and t_{max}, leading to a time condition written with respect to an input place p_1 as

$$(t_{min} + time(p_1), t_{max} + time(p_1))$$

Suppose also that there is a need to attach a delay (a computation time) to t with a pair of time values (lower and upper bounds)

$$(d_{min}, \; d_{max})$$

signifying the duration of the delay. Such requirements on durations may be translated as an extension to the net with an additional transition t_{new} and an additional place p_{new} as shown in Figure 5.11, and by associating the time condition

$$(d_{min} + time(p_{new}), \; d_{max} + time(p_{new}))$$

with t_{new}. In Section 5.3.2 on the example of a process control system, we have already seen a practical application of this approach to capturing process durations, as well as other more complex dynamic timing characteristics. The places p_4, p_5 and p_6 in Figure 5.2 have been introduced especially for this purpose.

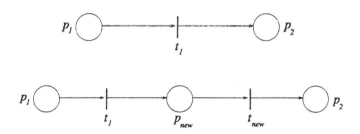

Figure 5.11 Representing durations

5.7 Bibliographical Notes

This chapter is based on the approach due to Ghezzi *et al.* [48] to time augmentation of Petri nets. The next chapter discusses a more general approach proposed by the same authors for the study of time critical systems. The other approaches mentioned are given in Coolahan and Roussopoulos [27], Merlin and Farber [100] and Ramchandani [124]. The reader may also find relevant the references given under Berthomieu and Diaz [14], Diaz [144], Bucci and Vicario [17] and Jensen [68, 69].

5.8 Exercises

1. Complete the time augmentation of the example on telephone in Section 5.3.3. Assume as appropriate arbitrary time values such as $T_5, \; T_6, \; \cdots, \; T_i$, etc., for time offsets of the transitions.

2. Construct a timed Petri net model of the lights at a '*Pelican*' style pedestrian crossing found on urban roads.

The following is a brief description of such a system of lights. These crossings are operated by two coordinated sets of light systems. One of them is an ordinary set of traffic lights intended for motorists, but with the amber light flashing before the lights change over to green. These lights operate in cycles and display the colours in the order: green $\rightarrow$ continuous amber $\rightarrow$ red $\rightarrow$ flashing amber $\rightarrow$ green. The other set of lights is intended for pedestrians and displays alternately a 'green man' and a 'red man'. The display of the 'green man' goes through two phases; a longer non-flashing phase followed by a shorter flashing phase before the lights change over to the 'red man'. The display of the 'red man' on pedestrian lights lasts through exactly the period from the onset of the green light in traffic lights to the end of the continuous display of the amber light. The periods of flashing of the 'green man' and the amber traffic light are also the same. No two lights are to be displayed together at any time in either set when taken in isolation.

Assume as a simplification that the crossing is not pedestrian controlled and that the lights are operated continuously in approximately fixed cycles. Although they may not be observable by the human eye, there can be small gaps in the display of lights in either set and, as a further simplification, assume, if necessary, a uniform non-negative maximum gap of T_0 between all displays.

Timing parameters of the display of lights are as follows.

Phase	*Duration of display*
green on traffic light	T_1
red on traffic light	T_2
continuous amber on traffic light	T_3
flashing amber on traffic light	T_4
continuous 'green man' on pedestrian light	T_5
flashing 'green man' on pedestrian light	T_6
'red man' on pedestrian light	T_7

3. Construct a timed Petri net model of a railway crossing found across minor roads outside towns. Such crossings normally consist of a pair of gates and two traffic lights: red and green. Some of the requirements are implicit in the timing requirements below. The reader is invited to fill in any missing detail as appropriate.

Allow for small temporal gaps in the display of the two lights, with no overlaps at all between the displays. However, there can be temporal gaps and overlaps between the display of lights and the operation of the gates. The representation of these gaps and overlaps in the model must correspond to the normal road safety requirements. As a simplification, assume a uniform maximum time value of $\pm T_0$ for all such gaps and overlaps.

The following symbols denote some unspecified timing parameters of the lights and the gates.

Phase	*Duration/time*
green on traffic light	T_1
red on traffic light	T_2
gate is open	T_3
gate is being closed	T_4
gate is closed	T_5
gate is being opened	T_6
advance warning on train arrival	T_7
minimum time between train crossing and gate opening	T_8
maximum time between train crossing and gate opening	T_9

4. Produce a timed Petri net model for the following system.

   A simple communication service consists of two identical communication stations interconnected by means of a certain medium. The communication medium is capable of dealing with only one transmission at a time. Therefore, stations can not transmit and receive messages at the same time and do not accept more than one message for transmission at any time. Occasionally, the medium may fail to deliver its current message and the failures are detected by timeouts. In case of a failure to deliver, the sending station re-tries the transmission as many times as necessary in the above manner until the receipt of an acknowledgement of successful delivery from the recipient. Each failure is treated as a fresh request.

   Once a message is available for transmission, it is transmitted by the sending station within T_1 time units, unless the transmission is blocked by a current transmission. The messages are of a certain fixed length and, therefore, requires T_2–T_3 time units from the start time of transmission for delivery. Exceeding this limit signifies a failure in transmission. The receiving station acknowledges successful deliveries within T_4 time units, upon which the sending station discards the message within another T_5 time units.

5. Produce a timed Petri net model for the following.

   A safety critical application consists of a sensor monitoring a certain physical process and an actuator for controlling its characteristics by regulating the flow of a coolant depending on the sensor data. Although it is not the overriding objective, economical use of the coolant is an important concern in this application. The sensor samples the state of the process at regular intervals at a frequency of f Hz. When the system is functioning normally, the flow of coolant is increased or decreased by a certain amount, guided by the values read from the sensor. If necessary, the controlling system issues a control signal to the actuator within T_1 time units of receiving data from the sensor and the actuator obeys the instruction within T_2 time units. The sensor may, however, occasionally fail and the failure is detected by the controlling system through the irregularity of the sensor output. In this case, the control system abandons the objective of economizing the coolant and starts providing the process with a predefined uniform flow of the coolant within T_3 time units of the detection to ensure safety. From then on the system makes no further use of the data provided by the sensor. Under its normal functioning mode the actuator regulates the flow as required. In the event of an actuator failure, that is, when the actuator fails to obey an instruction issued by the controlling system within the permitted time, the controller simply shuts the system down within T_4 time units to ensure safety. Other timing parameters may be introduced as necessary.

6. Produce a timed Petri net for the realtime locking system given in Section 8.11.2 of Chapter 8 on Timed CSP.

Chapter 6

Environment-Relationship Nets

Environment-relationship nets (ERN) are intended for the specification, modelling and analysis of time critical systems. These nets provide for a single coherent framework for the study of both the functional and timing aspects of such systems. The capability for dealing with these two categories of requirement within the same framework is highly desirable, especially when it is unrealistic or too cumbersome to treat them separately. Furthermore, ERN provides for a unified framework supporting a range of different specialized nets intended for different purposes. For example, Time Basic Nets (TBN), discussed in the previous chapter, can be seen as a particular kind of ERN designed for dealing only with timing aspects. A major benefit of this unifying role is that ERN can serve as a foundation for building other kinds of net and as a reference framework for their formal description. ERN is also amenable as a framework for refinement of nets, both for achieving rigour in verification of designs and for better management of complexity.

6.1 Structure and Evolution of Environment-Relationship Nets

Environment-relationship nets (ERN) are founded on some new concepts: *environments*, *actions* and an extended notion of transitions. Let us begin with an introduction to these concepts.

6.1.1 Environments

The *environments* enable the modelling of states of different entities in a given application such as resources and agents. Following common practice, they can be represented abstractly as mappings from an appropriate set of variables to their possible values. Given a set of identifiers VAR and a set of values VAL, the set of all possible environments ENV may be defined as the set of all partial functions from VAR to VAL. That is,

$$\text{ENV} \stackrel{def}{=} \text{VAR} \nrightarrow \text{VAL}$$

6.1.2   Actions

Actions bring about changes in the state of a given system. Our intention is to model such changes via environments. The environments allow the flexibility for different agents or components in a system to have different abstractions of the environment and to perceive, if necessary, the states of different objects differently.

For a given transition, the actions are fixed according to the required functionality of the application. Actions are denoted by α, subscripts identifying the transition to which the given action applies. An action α is represented as a relation from ENV^k to ENV^h:

$$\alpha \in \text{ENV}^k \leftrightarrow \text{ENV}^h$$

where k and h are two natural number parameters to be introduced shortly. Note that, for a set S, S^n denotes the n-fold Cartesian product of S on itself. Obviously, the representation of an action α as a relation is the most general case, and corresponds to a non-deterministic action. In contrast, the special case of a deterministic action α may be represented as a partial function

$$\alpha \in \text{ENV}^k \nrightarrow \text{ENV}^h$$

Given an action α, its pre-environment *preenv* and post-environment *postenv* are defined as

$$
\begin{aligned}
preenv &= \text{dom } \alpha \\
postenv &= \text{ran } \alpha
\end{aligned}
$$

An action α is essentially a specification and consists potentially of a large number of specific action instances. Given that a specific pair $(preenv_1, postenv_1)$ is an element of some action α, the pair may be regarded as an abstract representation of a specific instance of the given action α.

6.1.3   Transitions in ERN

This section introduces an extended notion of transitions. This is motivated by the desire to incorporate within this extended notion two ordered sets, one for input places (*preset*) and the other for output places (*postset*), and to associate an action α with each transition. Related to the action are the sets *preenv* and *postenv* of ordered sets (tuples) of environments. Let us view a transition in ERN as a tuple t_{EXT}:

$$t_{\text{EXT}} = (k, h, preset, postset, \alpha, preenv, postenv)$$

where $\alpha, preenv, postenv$ are as defined in Section 6.1.2 above, while others are as defined below.

k and h	–	The arity of tuples *preset* and *postset* respectively (the number of elements in each tuple). Note that $0 \le k \le \#P$ and $0 \le h \le \#P$.
preset *postset*	–	The input and output places of a given transition are represented as two tuples *preset* and *postset*. In order to represent the absence of a *preset* or a *postset* for a given transition, a distinguished value NULL is used. In the case of a singleton tuple (a tuple with just one element), let us simply write the identifier of the place concerned in place of *preset* or *postset*. Note that

$$\begin{aligned} preset \notin P^k &\Rightarrow preset = \text{NULL} \\ postset \notin P^h &\Rightarrow postset = \text{NULL} \end{aligned}$$

$$\begin{aligned} preset = \text{NULL} &\Rightarrow \neg\, \exists\, n \in \mathbb{N} \bullet preset \in P^n \\ postset = \text{NULL} &\Rightarrow \neg\, \exists\, n \in \mathbb{N} \bullet postset \in P^n \end{aligned}$$

where, as usual, P^n denotes the n-fold Cartesian product of P.

Figure 6.1 illustrates how *preset* and *postset* of a given ERN represent input and output places in the corresponding PN. Note that repetition of a place in either of these pairs accounts for the weight of the corresponding arc in PN.

The detachment of the environments, and hence also the actions, from the net structure is how ERN derives its flexibility, but this is achieved at the expense of some additional complexity. This is seen in the relationship between the tuples *preset* and *postset* on the one hand, and *preenv* and *postenv* on the other. Note that these are not totally independent of each other. The tuple *preenv*, for example, contains the environment tuples the action α expects in the places in *preset*. The order of elements in tuples determines the correspondence between the respective places and environments. Figure 6.1 shows how different combinations of certain specific environments (tokens in PN), denoted by c_1, c_2, c_3, etc., at places make the elements of *preevnv* and *postenv*. As a result, the arities of the tuples *preset* and *preenv* must be equal. The same applies to *postset* and *postenv*. The environments making the elements of *preevnv* and *postenv* cannot be arbitrary, but must conform with the specification of the action α associated with the given transition t. For example, according to the elements of *preenv* and *postset* given in Figure 6.1, either $((c_1, c_3, c_6, c_4), (c_7, c_8, c_9, c_{10}))$ or $((c_2, c_3, c_5, c_4), (c_7, c_8, c_9, c_{10}))$ must be an element

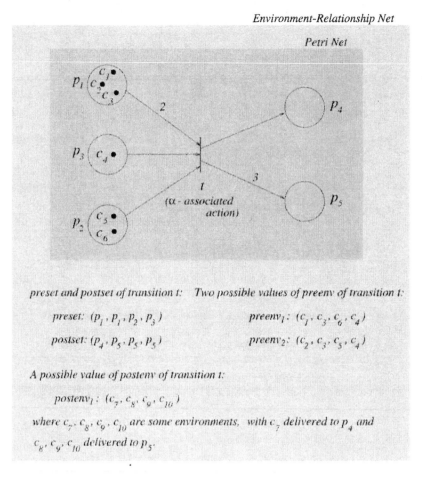

Environment-Relationship Net

Petri Net

preset and postset of transition t: *Two possible values of preenv of transition t:*

   preset: (p_1, p_1, p_2, p_3) *preenv$_1$:* (c_1, c_3, c_6, c_4)

   postset: (p_4, p_5, p_5, p_5) *preenv$_2$:* (c_2, c_3, c_5, c_4)

A possible value of postenv of transition t:

   postenv$_1$: (c_7, c_8, c_9, c_{10})

   where c_7, c_8, c_9, c_{10} are some environments, with c_7 delivered to p_4 and
   c_8, c_9, c_{10} delivered to p_5.

Figure 6.1 Presets and postsets of ERN and inputs and outputs of PN

of α. An alternative to the representation based on tuples here would have been
to adopt sets of places and sets of environment sets and to provide an appropriate
mapping between the two.

Pre and post environments are defined only for non-null *presets* or *postsets* and,
therefore,

$$preset \neq \text{NULL} \quad \Rightarrow \quad preenv \in \text{ENV}^k$$
$$postset \neq \text{NULL} \quad \Rightarrow \quad postenv \in \text{ENV}^h$$

Let us introduce two useful predicates in relation to elements in tuples. Given
any tuple s of some arity n, the elements of which are drawn from some set S,
and a number i, the notation 'e in s at i' is intended to mean that the element e
appears at the ith position in the tuple s, and 'e in s' to mean that the element e
appears somewhere in the tuple s. That is,

$$e \underline{\text{ in }} s \text{ at } i \overset{def}{\Leftrightarrow} \exists n \in \mathbb{N}; \ e_1, e_2, \cdots, e_n \in S \bullet i \in 1 .. n \land$$
$$s = (e_1, e_2, \cdots, e_n) \land e = e_i$$

$$e \underline{\text{ in }} s \quad \overset{def}{\Leftrightarrow} \exists i \in \mathbb{N} \bullet e \underline{\text{ in }} s \text{ at } i$$

The intended usage of these predicates is such that S is a set of places or environments. For example, according to Figure 6.1, both predicates '$c_6 \underline{\text{ in }} preenv_1$ at 3' and '$c_8 \underline{\text{ in }} postenv_1$' are true and the predicate '$c_9 \underline{\text{ in }} preenv_1$ at 2' is false.

Multiplicity of a given environment in *preenv* with reference to a given place in *preset* is not permitted. The reason for this lies in the relationship between ERN and PN. An environment in ERN corresponds to a single token in PN and ERN takes the multiplicity of tokens in PN into account by means of different environments. Thus a given environment may contribute to a transition once only. For this reason

$$\forall p_i, p_j \in P \land e_i, e_j \in \text{ENV} \bullet 1 \leq i \leq k \land 1 \leq j \leq k \land$$
$$p_i \underline{\text{ in }} preset \text{ at } i \land p_j \underline{\text{ in }} preset \text{ at } j \land e_i \underline{\text{ in }} preenv \text{ at } i \land$$
$$e_j \underline{\text{ in }} preenv \text{ at } j \Rightarrow (p_i = p_j \Rightarrow e_i \neq e_j)$$

k being the arity of *preset* and *preenv* as introduced in t_{EXT}. An analogous requirement applies to *postenv* and *postset*. In relation to the example in Figure 6.1, the above requires that c_1, c_2, c_3 are distinct environments. The same applies to the environments c_8, c_9, c_{10}. Note also that transitions with empty *presets* and *postsets* are meaningless; they are excluded by the assertion that

$$preset \neq \text{NULL} \lor postset \neq \text{NULL}$$

6.1.4   Definition of ERN

An *environment-relationship net* (ERN) may be seen as a tuple:

$$\text{ERN} = (P, T, T_{\text{ERN}}, \text{VAR}, \text{VAL}, \text{ENV}, M_{\text{ERN}})$$

where the elements P, T are as in PN discussed in Section 4.1 of Chapter 4, whereas VAR, VAL and ENV are as defined in Sections 6.1.1. The remaining elements of ERN are introduced below:

T_{ERN} –   A set of transitions in the extended sense introduced in Section 6.1.3. Although each has a totally different internal structure and, therefore, T_{ERN} is a collection of heterogeneous entities, let us continue to use, for convenience, the set notation for describing it. Since each element in T_{ERN} has the internal structure of t_{EXT}, the corresponding extended definition for each transition in T may be generated with appropriate subscripts. Thus,

$$T_{\text{ERN}} = \{(k_t, h_t, preset_t, postset_t, \alpha_t, preenv_t, postenv_t) \mid t \in T\}$$

M_{ERN} — M_{ERN} denotes the marking 'function', obtained by replacing the notion of *tokens* in PN with that of *environments*. Thus, M_{ERN} differs in character from the marking function M in PN. Firstly, since no distinctions are made in M among tokens, it was sufficient in PN to keep a count of tokens at places. By contrast, M_{ERN} permits the introduction of 'environment tokens' carrying different kinds of information. Secondly, as a consequence of the latter possibility and because of the need for considering multiple environments at a place, M_{ERN} becomes a relation of the form

$$M_{\mathrm{ERN}} : P \leftrightarrow \mathrm{ENV}$$

Note that the weighting function W in ERN is implicit in the above definition. As mentioned earlier, occurrence of a given place in the *preset*, or in the *postset*, of a transition more than once and occurrence of different environments in the positions corresponding to the given place amounts to multiple arcs in PN.

6.1.5   Manipulation of the Marking Relation

For convenience, let us introduce a number of operators for manipulating the marking relation M_{ERN}. The first operation is to generate the environments represented by the tokens in a selected number of places (given as a tuple) in the marking relation as a set of tuples of environments. Given a tuple of places p-*tuple*, this set of environment tuples, $M_{\mathrm{ERN}} \langle\!\langle p\text{-}tuple \rangle\!\rangle$, is defined as

$$M_{\mathrm{ERN}} \langle\!\langle p\text{-}tuple \rangle\!\rangle \stackrel{def}{=} (M_{\mathrm{ERN}} (\!\langle \{p_1\} \rangle\!)) \times (M_{\mathrm{ERN}} (\!\langle \{p_2\} \rangle\!)) \times \cdots \times (M_{\mathrm{ERN}} (\!\langle \{p_k\} \rangle\!))$$

where

$$p\text{-}tuple = (p_1, p_2, \cdots, p_k)$$

where, for example, $M_{\mathrm{ERN}} (\!\langle \{p_i\} \rangle\!)$ denotes the relational image of the marking relation M_{ERN} through the singleton set $\{p_i\}$. The above permits any given environment at a particular place to participate in more than one environment tuple. Two other operators $\backslash\!\backslash$ and $+\!\!+$ are introduced for removing and adding respectively a set of environments from the marking relation. The environments concerned are given as a tuple e-*tuple*, associated implicitly with a tuple of places p-*tuple* of identical arity:

$$M_{\mathrm{ERN}} \backslash\!\backslash\ e\text{-}tuple \stackrel{def}{=} M_{\mathrm{ERN}} - \{(p_1, e_1), (p_2, e_2), \cdots, (p_k, e_k)\}$$
$$M_{\mathrm{ERN}} +\!\!+\ e\text{-}tuple \stackrel{def}{=} M_{\mathrm{ERN}} \cup \{(p_1, e_1), (p_2, e_2), \cdots, (p_k, e_k)\}$$

where

$$p\text{-}tuple = (p_1, p_2, \cdots, p_k)$$
$$e\text{-}tuple = (e_1, e_2, \cdots, e_k)$$

The intended usage of these operators is such that, in the case of the operator $\|$, *p–tuple* is the *preset* of the transition concerned, and in the case of $+\!\!\!+$, *p–tuple* is its *postset*.

6.1.6   The Model of Execution

A transition t in ERN is said to be *enabled* in a marking M_{ERN} if and only if either its *preset* is empty or there are environments in the *preset* as required by *preenv* of the action attached to t. Let us state this more clearly by employing the predicate $enabled(t, M_{\text{ERN}})$. It may be defined as

$$enabled(t, M_{\text{ERN}}) \stackrel{def}{\Leftrightarrow} preset_t = \text{NULL} \vee (preenv_t \cap M_{\text{ERN}} \langle\!\langle preset_t \rangle\!\rangle \neq \varnothing)$$

Firing of the transition t is a triple:

$$(enab, t, prod)$$

such that

$$
\begin{aligned}
enab &\in (preenv_t \cap M_{\text{ERN}} \langle\!\langle preset_t \rangle\!\rangle) \\
(enab, prod) &\in \alpha_t
\end{aligned}
$$

in the case of non-null values. Note that $(enab, prod)$ corresponds to an instance of the action α_t. It is clear that *enab* stands for the input tuple that *enables* the particular instance of the action, and *prod* for the output tuple *produced* as a result of its execution. Given a firing of the form $(enab, t, prod)$, let

$$
\begin{aligned}
transition((enab, t, prod)) &= t \\
pre\text{–}tuple((enab, t, prod)) &= enab \\
post\text{–}tuple((enab, t, prod)) &= prod
\end{aligned}
$$

As in PN, the firing of transitions is instantaneous and takes place completely. As a result of the firing the marking relation is updated, in this case, by removing the environments in *enab* attached to places in $preset_t$ and adding the environments in *prod* to places in $postset_t$. Thus, the new value of the marking relation, M_{ERN}', after the execution of the action is determined as

$$
\begin{aligned}
M_{\text{ERN}}' &= (M_{\text{ERN}} \| enab) +\!\!\!+ prod, & \text{if } preset_t \neq \text{NULL} \wedge postset_t \neq \text{NULL} \\
M_{\text{ERN}}' &= M_{\text{ERN}} \| enab, & \text{if } preset_t \neq \text{NULL} \wedge postset_t = \text{NULL} \\
M_{\text{ERN}}' &= M_{\text{ERN}} +\!\!\!+ prod, & \text{if } preset_t = \text{NULL} \wedge postset_t \neq \text{NULL}
\end{aligned}
$$

6.1.7   An Illustrative Example

The following is a small example illustrating in detail the concepts introduced in this section.

EXAMPLE

Consider the PN shown in Figure 6.2 with $T = \{t\}$ and $P = \{p_1, p_2, p_3\}$. In extending it to an ERN, let VAR and VAL be

$$\begin{aligned} \text{VAR} &= \{a, b\} \\ \text{VAL} &= \{0, 1, 2\} \end{aligned}$$

This results in the following set of possible environments:

$$\begin{aligned} \text{ENV} = \ & \{\varnothing, \{(a,0)\}, \{(a,1)\}, \{(a,2)\}, \{(b,0)\}, \{(b,1)\}, \{(b,2)\} \\ & \{(a,0), (b,0)\}, \{(a,0), (b,1)\}, \{(a,0), (b,2)\}, \\ & \{(a,1), (b,0)\}, \{(a,1), (b,1)\}, \{(a,1), (b,2)\}, \\ & \{(a,2), (b,0)\}, \{(a,2), (b,1)\}, \{(a,2), (b,2)\}\} \end{aligned}$$

Let us consider an action for the transition t defined as follows:

$$\begin{aligned} \alpha_t = \ & \{((e_1, e_2), e_3) \mid \{e_1, e_2, e_3\} \subseteq \text{ENV} \wedge e_1(a) = e_2(a) \wedge \\ & e_1(b) < e_2(b) \wedge e_1(a) = e_3(a) \wedge \\ & e_1(b) + e_2(b) \le 2 \Rightarrow e_1(b) \le e_3(b) \le e_1(b) + e_2(b)\} \end{aligned}$$

Each action instance in α above consists of two input environments and one output environment. Note how an action *predicate* is used to define α_t, instead of a lengthy enumeration of elements. The symbols e_1, e_2, e_3 are bound (dummy) variables and have no significance outside the definition of α_t. By enumerating the elements in the above set, *preenv* may be found as

$$\begin{aligned} preenv_t = \ & \text{dom } \alpha_t \\ = \ & \{(\{(a,0), (b,0)\}, \{(a,0), (b,1)\}), (\{(a,0), (b,0)\}, \{(a,0), (b,2)\}), \\ & (\{(a,0), (b,1)\}, \{(a,0), (b,2)\}), (\{(a,1), (b,0)\}, \{(a,1), (b,1)\}), \\ & (\{(a,1), (b,0)\}, \{(a,1), (b,2)\}), (\{(a,1), (b,1)\}, \{(a,1), (b,2)\}), \\ & (\{(a,2), (b,0)\}, \{(a,2), (b,1)\}), (\{(a,2), (b,0)\}, \{(a,2), (b,2)\}), \\ & (\{(a,2), (b,1)\}, \{(a,2), (b,2)\})\} \end{aligned}$$

The set *postenv* may be worked out in a similar manner. With the above, the transition t may be given an extended representation as

$$t_{\text{EXT}} = (2, 1, (p_1, p_2), p_3, \alpha_t, preenv_t, postenv_t)$$

and the net as a whole:

$$\text{ERN} = (T, P, \{t_{\text{EXT}}\}, \text{VAR}, \text{VAL}, \text{VAR}, M_{\text{ERN}})$$

According to Figure 6.2, the initial marking has the form

$$M_{\text{ERN}} = \{(p_1, c_1), (p_2, c_2), (p_2, c_3)\}$$

where c_1, c_2 and c_3 denote the following specific environments:

$$
\begin{aligned}
c_1 &= \{(a, 0), (b, 1)\} \\
c_2 &= \{(a, 0), (b, 2)\} \\
c_3 &= \{(a, 0), (b, 1)\}
\end{aligned}
$$

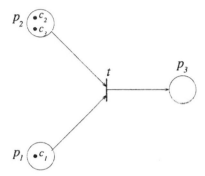

Figure 6.2 An example of an ERN

The environment tuples in the *preset* of t_{EXT} according to the above value of the marking relation are

$$
\begin{aligned}
M_{\text{ERN}} \langle preset_t \rangle &= (M_{\text{ERN}} \langle \{p_1\} \rangle) \times (M_{\text{ERN}} \langle \{p_2\} \rangle) \\
&= \{c_1\} \times \{c_2, c_3\} \\
&= \{\{(a,0), (b,1)\}\} \times \{\{(a,0), (b,2)\}, \{(a,0), (b,1)\}\} \\
&= \{(\{(a,0), (b,1)\}, \{(a,0), (b,2)\}), \\
&\qquad\qquad (\{(a,0), (b,1)\}, \{(a,0), (b,1)\})\}
\end{aligned}
$$

It does not necessarily follow from the presence of the above environment tuples in $M_{\text{ERN}} \langle preset_t \rangle$ that the transition t_{EXT} is enabled. This is because these environment tuples need to be in *preenv* as well. This requires that

$$preenv_t \cap M_{\text{ERN}} \langle preset_t \rangle = \{(\{(a,0), (b,1)\}, \{(a,0), (b,2)\})\} \neq \varnothing$$

Thus, the transition t_{EXT} is enabled. Note that only one environment at p_2 is eligible to participate in an enabling environment tuple. Any firing can produce an environment c at p_3 with a value of $c(b)$ between 0 and 2, since the antecedent of the implication involving $e_3(b)$ in the definition given earlier for α_t is false. The firing

$$((\{(a,0), (b,1)\}, \{(a,0), (b,2)\}), t, \{(a,0), (b,2)\})$$

corresponds to a permitted instance of the action α_t and results in the new value of marking relation $M_{\text{ERN}}{}'$ given below:

$$
\begin{aligned}
M_{\text{ERN}}{}' &= (M_{\text{ERN}} \setminus\setminus (\{\{(a,0),(b,1)\},\{(a,0),(b,2)\}\})) + \{(a,0),(b,2)\} \\
&= (\{(p_1,c_1),(p_2,c_2),(p_2,c_3)\} \setminus\setminus (\{\{(a,0),(b,1)\},\{(a,0),(b,2)\}\})) + \\
&\qquad\qquad\qquad\qquad\qquad\qquad\qquad\qquad\qquad\qquad \{(a,0),(b,2)\} \\
&= \{(p_2,c_3)\} + \{(a,0),(b,2)\} \\
&= \{(p_2,\{(a,0),(b,1)\}),(p_3,\{(a,0),(b,2)\})\}
\end{aligned}
$$

6.2   Properties of Environment-Relationship Nets

Our interest here is in properties of ERN which are analogous to those discussed in Section 4.4 of Chapter 4.

Definition: *Reachability*

A marking $M_{\text{ERN},n}$ is said to be *reachable* from an initial marking $M_{\text{ERN},0}$ if and only if either $n = 0$ or for every $1 \leq i \leq n$ there exists a sequence of firing

$$\langle (enab_1, t_1, prod_1), (enab_2, t_2, prod_2), \cdots,$$
$$(enab_i, t_i, prod_i)\rangle$$

such that

$$enab_i \in preenv_{t_i} \cap M_{\text{ERN},i-1}\langle preset_{t_i}\rangle$$

and the firing of t_i produces the marking $M_{\text{ERN},i}$.

The notions of k-boundedness and general boundedness introduced in Section 4.4 of Chapter 4 for PN remain applicable to ERN. However, their direct application can be in general meaningless. This is because, compared to tokens in PN, the environments in ERN have an extended role. An environment present at a place signifies not only the availability of some data for some computation, but also its validity in a temporal sense. In this respect, the environment may contain information on the expiry time of data. However, it is possible that the application does not consume all such data, leaving open the possible accumulation of *expired* environments in certain places. Such environments are referred to as *dead environments*, with the obvious choice of *live environments* for other environments. This leads to another relevant notion of boundedness, namely *weak boundedness*, for ERN.

Definition: *Weak Boundedness*

An ERN N is said to be *k-weakly bounded* for some given $k \in \mathbb{N}$ if and only if, for every $p \in P$ and for every marking $M_{\text{ERN}} \in R(N, M_{\text{ERN},0})$,

$$\#\{e \mid e \in M_{\mathrm{ERN}}(\!\mid \{p\} \mid\!) \wedge (\exists\, t \in T;\ e\text{-}tuple \in \mathrm{ENV}^{k_t} \bullet p \text{ in } preset_t \wedge$$
$$e \text{ in } e\text{-}tuple \wedge e\text{-}tuple \in preenv_t \cap M_{\mathrm{ERN}}(\!\mid preset_t \mid\!))\} \leq k$$

The net N is said to be *weakly bounded* if there exists a $k \in \mathbb{N}$ such that the net is k-weakly bounded.

In other words, an ERN N is k-weakly bounded if and only if the number of live environments in each and every place P and every marking M_{ERN} reachable from $M_{\mathrm{ERN},0}$ does not exceed k, k being a finite number. It is important to realize that the constitution of the set of environment tuples *preenv* appearing in the above definition is not fixed and varies with the evolution of the net. This enables the consideration of only the live environments in weak boundedness.

The notions of dead and live environments lead to three different kinds of *liveness*: *transition liveness* in the same sense as that in PN, the *net liveness* in the sense that at least one transition is always executable and the *environment liveness* which excludes dead environments from the net. These are introduced below.

Definition: *Transition Liveness*

A ERN N is said to be *transition live* if and only if for every marking M_{ERN} reachable from the initial marking $M_{\mathrm{ERN},0}$ and every transition t in N there is some marking M_{ERN}' reachable from M_{ERN} such that t is enabled in M_{ERN}'.

Thus, the notion of transition liveness remains the same as in the case of PN.

Definition: *Net Liveness*

An ERN N is said to be *net live* if and only if for every marking M_{ERN} reachable from the initial marking $M_{\mathrm{ERN},0}$ at least one transition in N is enabled in M_{ERN}.

The third notion of liveness in ERN is

Definition: *Environment Liveness*

An ERN N is said to be *environment live* if and only if, for every place $p \in P$, marking $M_{\mathrm{ERN}} \in R(N, M_{\mathrm{ERN},0})$ and environment $e \in M_{\mathrm{ERN}}(\!\mid \{p\} \mid\!)$, there exists a transition $t \in T$, an environment tuple $e\text{-}tuple \in \mathrm{ENV}^{k_t}$ and a marking $M_{\mathrm{ERN}}' \in R(N, M_{\mathrm{ERN},0})$ reachable from M_{ERN} such that

$$e \text{ in } e\text{-}tuple \wedge e\text{-}tuple \in preenv_t \cap M_{\mathrm{ERN}}'(\!\mid preset_t \mid\!)$$

In other words, an ERN N is environment live if and only if every environment appearing in any marking relation M_{ERN} reachable from the initial marking enables some transition in a marking $M_{\mathrm{ERN}}' \in R(N, M_{\mathrm{ERN},0})$ reachable from M_{ERN}.

The property of *persistence* and *conflict free nets* are analogous to those discussed under ordinary Petri nets.

6.3   Time Environment-Relationship Nets

Time environment-relationship nets (TERN) are a special case of ERN and are derived from ERN by incorporating in each environment a distinguished variable κ ranging over an appropriate metric of time $\mathbb{T}$. Informally, κ corresponds to the time stamp of the environment concerned. Each time stamp is produced by the action creating the environment and its value is equal to the time of creation of the environment. Thus,

$$\kappa \quad \in \quad \text{VAR}$$
$$\text{ENV} \quad \overset{def}{=} \quad \{f \in \text{VAR} \nrightarrow \text{VAL} \cup \mathbb{T} \mid \kappa \in \text{dom } f \wedge f(\kappa) \in \mathbb{T}\}$$

As a consequence, we have for every action α that

$$\forall (enab, prod) \in \alpha; \; e \in \text{ENV} \bullet e \text{ in } enab \vee e \text{ in } prod \Rightarrow \kappa \in \text{dom } e$$

Given any environment $e \in \text{ENV}$ and an environment tuple $tuple \in \text{ENV}^n$ for some $n \in \mathbb{N}$, the functions *env-time*, *min-time* and *max-time* may be defined as follows:

$$
\begin{aligned}
env\text{-}time(e) &= e(\kappa) \\
min\text{-}time(tuple) &= min\{x \bullet x \in \mathbb{T}; \; e \in \text{ENV} \mid e \text{ in } tuple \wedge x = e(\kappa)\} \\
max\text{-}time(tuple) &= max\{x \bullet x \in \mathbb{T}; \; e \in \text{ENV} \mid e \text{ in } tuple \wedge x = e(\kappa)\}
\end{aligned}
$$

The above functions extract, respectively, the time stamp of the environment e and the earliest and the latest time stamp in any of the environments in *tuple*.

The special status of the variable κ is accompanied by certain rules or *axioms* that we expect the variable κ, the environments, the actions and the evolution of the net to comply with. These are as follows:

Axiom 1 Consistency

> Given the execution of an instance a of the action associated with a transition t,
>
> $$a = (enab, t, prod)$$
>
> the value of κ in each environment appearing in *prod* must have the same value. This value is known as the *firing time* of the action instance a and is denoted by *fire-time(a)*. Thus, the *consistency* requires that
>
> $$fire\text{-}time(a) = min\text{-}time(prod) = max\text{-}time(prod)$$
>
> When *prod* is a singleton tuple, following our convention of writing its element instead of the tuple, we have
>
> $$fire\text{-}time(a) = prod(\kappa)$$

Thus, the set of environment tuples *postenv* has an important role to play as a carrier of time stamps. As a consequence, even a transition without an output place must be assigned a *postenv*, albeit a dummy environment containing just κ, in order to specify its firing time. This explains the use of the implication in

$$postset \neq \text{NULL} \Rightarrow postenv \in \text{ENV}^h$$

on page 86 instead of an equivalence.

Axiom 2 Local Monotonicity

The value of κ in every environment produced as a result of the execution of an action instance

$$a = (enab, t, prod)$$

cannot be less than the value of κ in every environment in *enab* removed by that action. Let us refer to *max-time(enab)* as the *enabling time* of the action instance a and use the notation *enab-time(a)* for it. Obviously,

$$enab\text{-}time(a) = max\text{-}time(enab)$$

Then the requirement expressed in *local monotonicity* may be stated as

$$fire\text{-}time(a) \geq enab\text{-}time(a)$$

Axiom 3 Sequence Monotonicity

The firing times of a sequence of action instances s should be monotonically increasing, and in any case, should not be decreasing. That is, given a sequence such as

$$s = \langle a_1, a_2, \cdots, a_i, \cdots, a_j, \cdots \rangle$$

the following holds:

$$\forall i, j \in \mathbb{N}_1 \bullet a_i, a_j \in \text{ran } s \wedge i < j \Rightarrow fire\text{-}time(a_i) \leq fire\text{-}time(a_j)$$

Such a firing sequence is said to be *time ordered*.

Although the observation of these three axioms is desirable, it is not absolutely necessary to insist on the enforcement of all three at the same time. A closer examination should reveal that it is quite adequate to insist on Axioms 1 and 2 only, since the resulting firing sequences are *equivalent* in a certain sense to those satisfying Axiom 3. This notion of equivalence is based on the following equivalence relation on firing sequences:

Definition: *Equivalent Firing Sequences*

Two firing sequences s and s' are said to be *equivalent* to each other with respect to an initial marking $M_{\text{TERN},0}$ of the net concerned if and only if s and s' are permutations of each other. The notation $s \approx s'$ means that s and s' are equivalent to each other in this sense.

This leads to the following observation:

Observation 6.1 Given a TERN satisfying Axioms 1 and 2 for every firing sequence s with an initial marking $M_{\text{TERN},0}$ there is a time ordered firing sequence s' such that $s \approx s'$.

The above may be proved by induction. Given that s is a firing sequence observed in a net satisfying Axioms 1 and 2, it is required to show that there is always another time ordered firing sequence s' such that $s \approx s'$. The proof is as follows:

Base Case: Let s consist of a single firing. In this case $s \approx s$ trivially.

Inductive Step: Let

$$s = \langle a_1, a_2, \cdots, a_n, a_{n+1} \rangle$$

where

$$a_n = (enab_n, t_n, prod_n)$$
$$a_{n+1} = (enab_{n+1}, t_{n+1}, prod_{n+1})$$

Consider first the front end of the sequence s as given by

$$r = \langle a_1, a_2, \cdots, a_n \rangle$$

Assume as the induction hypothesis that there is a time ordered firing sequence r' such that $r \approx r'$. This permits us to treat r itself as time ordered. In this case, we have

$$fire\text{-}time(a_n) > fire\text{-}time(a_{n+1}) \qquad \qquad (i)$$

as otherwise s should be already time ordered. Since by virtue of induction hypothesis r is time ordered, it is possible to produce from s, by a series of successive swaps of the last element of s, a time ordered firing sequence s' which is equivalent to s. This is permissible, provided that there is no environment produced by the predecessor of a pair being swapped that is intended for consumption by its successor. In the event that there is such an environment, such a swap should not be permissible. Let us apply this requirement to the last two firings in s. An analogous case may be made for any swap in the interior of s by considering the appropriate subsequences of s.

Let us prove that Axioms 1 and 2 warrant such swaps. Our strategy is a proof by contradiction, where it is assumed as a hypothesis that the firing a_{n+1} consumes an environment e produced by the firing a_n. The details of our reasoning are as follows:

1. e in $enab_{n+1}$ the above assumption
2. e in $prod_n$ as above
3. $enab\text{-}time(a_{n+1}) \geq env\text{-}time(e)$ from 1; definitions of $enab\text{-}time$ and $env\text{-}time$
4. $fire\text{-}time(a_n) = env\text{-}time(e)$ from 2; Axiom 1 and def. of $env\text{-}time$
5. $fire\text{-}time(a_{n+1}) \geq enab\text{-}time(a_{n+1})$ Axiom 2 applied to a_{n+1}
6. $fire\text{-}time(a_{n+1}) \geq env\text{-}time(e)$ from 3, 5; transitivity of $\geq$
7. $fire\text{-}time(a_{n+1}) \geq fire\text{-}time(a_n)$ from 4, 6; equality

The conclusion drawn in line (7) above contradicts (i) stated earlier and, therefore, the hypothesis according to which the firing a_{n+1} consumes an environment e produced by the firing a_n cannot be justified when the two Axioms 1 and 2 are in force. This concludes the proof of Observation 6.1.

As a consequence, each firing sequence in a net satisfying only Axioms 1 and 2 belongs to an equivalence class of a time-ordered firing sequence as required by Axiom 3. This justifies placing reliance only on Axioms 1 and 2.

A consequence of time ordering firing sequences is that the firing time of every action in every firing sequence s commencing from the initial marking $M_{\text{TERN},0}$ never decreases. That is, given a sequence such as

$$s = \langle a_1, a_2, \cdots, a_i \rangle$$

the following must hold:

$$fire\text{-}time(a_i) \geq max\{x \bullet x \in \mathbb{T};\ e \in \text{ENV} \mid e \in \text{ran } M_{\text{TERN},i-1} \wedge x = e(\kappa)\}$$

where for $j > 0$ the marking $M_{\text{TERN},j}$ is produced by the firing a_j. In other words, as firings take place the time stamps of newly produced environments must always exceed or remain equal to the the highest time stamp of the current marking. If the above is adopted, as a consequence of Axioms 1 and 2, we then have global monotonicity of the net as a whole. However, this requires global knowledge about the net, which contravenes one of the main tenets of Petri nets. Therefore, the above should not be regarded as the means for achieving time ordering, but as a criterion on its correctness. It could be met by ensuring equal time stamps in the initial marking, monotonicity of clocks, agreement of clocks if relevant, and compliance with Axioms 1 and 2.

EXAMPLE

Let us model the process control system considered in Section 5.3.2 of Chapter 5 in TERN.

The identifiers and descriptions of transitions and places are retained as in the original example. However, TERN permits the adoption of a simpler Petri net as a model of the system. It is as shown in Figure 6.3. Let us use the following variables:

st –   the start time of processing.
fl –   the time of processor failure.
rp –   the time of processor replacement.
pr –   the processor identifier.

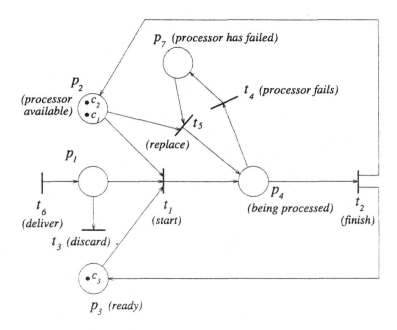

Figure 6.3 Process control system

Let VAR, VAL and the variables concerned be

$$\begin{aligned}
\text{VAR} &= \{\kappa, st, rp, fl, pr\} \\
\text{VAL} &= \mathbb{T} \cup \text{PID} \\
\kappa &: \mathbb{T} \\
st, fl, rp &: \mathbb{T} \\
pr &: \text{PID}
\end{aligned}$$

where PID is a set of processor identifiers with just two values

PID ::= **processor1** | **processor2**

Taking into account the types of variable the set of all possible environments may be defined as

$$\text{ENV} = (\{\kappa, st, rp, fl\} \times \text{T}) \cup (\{pr\} \times \text{PID})$$

Letting *preset_i* and *postset_i* be, respectively, the *preset* and the *postset* associated with the transition t_i, *presets* and the *postsets* of all transitions may be listed as

$preset_1$	$=$	(p_1, p_2, p_3)	$postset_1 = p_4$
$preset_2$	$=$	p_4	$postset_2 = (p_2, p_3)$
$preset_3$	$=$	p_1	$postset_3 = \text{NULL}$
$preset_4$	$=$	p_4	$postset_4 = p_7$
$preset_5$	$=$	(p_2, p_7)	$postset_5 = p_4$
$preset_6$	$=$	NULL	$postset_6 = p_1$

The actions $\alpha_i, i \in 1..6$, associated respectively with the transitions $t_i, i \in 1..6$, may be defined as follows. As in the previous example, the symbols e_1, e_2, e_3, etc., are bound variables, used for defining the permitted instances of each of the actions α_i:

$$\alpha_1 = \{((e_1, e_2, e_3), e_4) \mid e_1(\kappa) < e_4(\kappa) \le e_1(\kappa) + T_3 \wedge e_4(\kappa) > e_3(\kappa) + T_4 \wedge \\ e_4(st) = e_4(fl) = e_4(rp) = e_4(\kappa) \wedge e_4(pr) = e_2(pr)\}$$

$$\alpha_2 = \{(e_4, (e_2, e_3)) \mid T_0 + T_1 \ge e_2(\kappa) \ge T_0 + T_2 \wedge e_2(pr) = e_4(pr)\}$$
$$\text{where}$$
$$T_0 = e_4(st) + e_4(rp) - e_4(fl)$$

$$\alpha_3 = \{(e_1, e_3) \mid e_3(\kappa) > e_1(\kappa) + T_3\}$$

$$\alpha_4 = \{(e_4, e_5) \mid e_4(\kappa) < e_5(\kappa) < e_4(\kappa) + T_1 \wedge e_5(fl) = e_5(\kappa) \wedge \\ e_5(st) = e_4(st) \wedge e_5(pr) = e_4(pr)\}$$

$$\alpha_5 = \{((e_2, e_4), e_5) \mid e_5(\kappa) > e_4(\kappa) \wedge e_5(rp) = e_5(\kappa) \wedge \\ e_5(fl) = e_4(fl) \wedge e_5(st) = e_4(st)) \wedge e_5(pr) = e_2(pr)\}$$

$$\alpha_6 = \{(e_3, e_1)\}$$
$$\text{where}$$

$$e_1, e_2, \cdots, e_5 \in \text{ENV} \qquad \text{(bound variables)}$$
$$\text{dom } e_1 = \{\kappa\}$$
$$\text{dom } e_2 = \{\kappa, pr\}$$
$$\text{dom } e_3 = \{\kappa\}$$
$$\text{dom } e_4 = \{\kappa, pr, st, fl, rp\}$$
$$\text{dom } e_5 = \text{dom } e_4$$

The definition of the actions relies on Axioms 1 and 2, but certain timing constraints have been made explicit. The above specification of α_1 requires the availability of just one of the processors when the processing begins, with the choice of the processor left open. Note also that α_3 illustrates the need for a dummy environment containing just κ for $postenv_{t_3}$. A suitable initial marking would be

$$M_{\text{TERN},0} = \{(p_2, c_1), (p_2, c_2), (p_3, c_3)\}$$

where

$$\begin{aligned}
c_i &\in \text{ENV} && \text{for } i = 1, 3 \\
dom \ c_i &= \{\kappa, pr\} && \text{for } i = 1, 2 \\
dom \ c_3 &= \{\kappa\} \\
c_1(pr) &\neq c_2(pr)
\end{aligned}$$

It is clear from the above example that, compared to TBN models, TERN models can embody more information with a simpler net.

6.4   Strong and Weak Semantics

The practical examples in Section 5.4 of Chapter 5 illustrate the need to characterize the execution order of transitions in time in different ways. The interpretation given there suggested the ordering of transitions in such a way that certain transitions exercise priority over other transitions with respect to the order of execution when they are simultaneously enabled. This section attempts a precise characterization of the semantics of this ordering.

In this connection, let us present two different approaches. The first approach, given in Section 6.4.1, is based on a semantic characterization of firing sequences. Further details may found in the literature cited in the bibliographical notes in Section 6.6. The second approach, proposed in Section 6.4.2, is based on a semantic characterization that centres around transitions and follows the discussion in Section 5.4.

6.4.1   Firing Sequence Based Semantics

Given a transition t and an environment tuple *enab*, the set of possible firing times of t when it is enabled by *enab* is given by

$$\begin{aligned}
act\text{-}time(t, enab) \ = \ &\{x \bullet x \in \mathbb{T}; \ prod \in \text{ENV}^{h_t} \ | \\
&(enab, prod) \in \alpha_t \wedge x = fire\text{-}time(enab, t, prod)\}
\end{aligned}$$

Let us refer to the elements in the set $act\text{-}time(t, enab)$ as the *action times* of α_t under the enabling environment tuple *enab*. In general, the action times may in effect constitute a number of intervals of time. Thus, in TERN we drop the assumption made in the study of TBN that firing times constitute a contiguous stretch of time. If it exists, the end of the last of these intervals plays the role of a *deadline* for the firing of an instance of α_t in that state. This notion of deadline, denoted here as $exp\text{-}time(t, enab)$, may be defined as

$$exp\text{-}time(t, enab) \stackrel{def}{=} \begin{cases} max(act\text{-}time(t, enab)), & \text{if the last interval of} \\ & \text{time in } act\text{-}time(\cdots) \\ & \text{is finite;} \\ \infty, & \text{otherwise.} \end{cases}$$

This approach is based on the following notion of strong firing sequences:

Definition: *Strong Firing Sequence*

Let s be an arbitrary time ordered firing sequence in TERN N

$$s = \langle a_1, a_2, \cdots, a_n \rangle$$

and $M_{\text{TERN},i}$ be a marking reachable from the initial marking $M_{\text{TERN},0}$ and produced by the firing a_i such that $0 \leq i < n$. The firing sequence s is said to be a *strong firing sequence* if and only if the following axiom is satisfied:

Axiom 4 For every $0 \leq i < n$ and for every transition t enabled in $M_{\text{TERN},i}$ by any *enab*, the latest expiry time of the action α_t must be greater than or equal to the firing time of the firing a_{i+1}.

$$\forall i \in \mathbb{N}; \ t \in T \bullet 0 \leq i < n \Rightarrow \forall \ enab \in \text{ENV}^{k_t} \bullet$$
$$(enab \in (preenv_t \cap M_{\text{TERN},i} \langle\!\langle preset_t \rangle\!\rangle) \Rightarrow$$
$$fire\text{-}time(a_{i+1}) \leq exp\text{-}time(t, enab)))$$

Note that Axiom 4 is not specific about the (i+1)th transition to fire. However, since only enabled transitions may fire, it must obviously be an enabled transition. What Axiom 4 requires is that some enabled transition fires within the closest of all expiry times in a given marking. As a consequence, in the event of more than one enabled transition, this model of strong time semantics retains the characteristic non-determinism of Petri nets with respect to the choice of the transition to fire.

This approach enforces a time model known as the *strong time model* by forcing all enabled transitions to fire. This rests on the following axiom:

Axiom 5 All firing sequences are strong firing sequences

and leads to what is referred to as *strong* TERN *nets*.

Definition: *Strong* TERN *Nets*

A strong TERN net is a TERN which satisfies Axioms 1, 2 and 5.

The approach refers to the models discussed in Section 6.3 as *weak time models*. Given a weak TERN, it is possible to construct a strong TERN by extending the former with a new place ARB and including it in both the *preset* and the *postset* of every transition. The place ARB is designed to consist of just one environment with variables, in addition to κ, for keeping a record of the time stamps of all other places of the corresponding weak TERN. The behaviour expected through strong time semantics is achieved by defining the actions of the strong TERN in terms of environments in ordinary places and ARB so that each firing occurs at a time not exceeding the minimum of the maximum possible firing times of the corresponding weak TERN. The place ARB thus plays the role of a global coordinator. In practice, however, it is unnecessary to extend the net in this manner. It is simply a matter of interpretation of a given net as a strong time model.

EXAMPLE

Let us construct a strong TERN for the net shown in Figure 6.4.

Weak TERN

As a weak time model, the TERN shown in Figure 6.4 requires some additional information. In this connection, let VAL $= \mathbb{T}$ and VAR $= \{\kappa\}$, where by convention $\kappa : \mathbb{T}$. The *preset* and the *postset* associated with each of the transitions $t_i, i \in 1..4$, are:

$$
\begin{array}{llll}
preset_1 &=& p_1 \qquad\qquad & postset_1 &=& p_3 \\
preset_2 &=& p_2 & postset_2 &=& p_4 \\
preset_3 &=& p_3 & postset_3 &=& p_5 \\
preset_4 &=& p_4 & postset_4 &=& p_5
\end{array}
$$

The actions $\alpha_i, i \in 1..4$, associated, respectively, with the transitions $t_i, i \in 1..4$, are:

$$
\begin{array}{rcl}
\alpha_1 &=& \{(e_1, e_2) \mid e_1(\kappa) \leq e_2(\kappa)\} \\
\alpha_2 &=& \alpha_1 \\
\alpha_3 &=& \{(e_1, e_2) \mid e_1(\kappa) + 10 \leq e_2(\kappa) < e_1(\kappa) + 15\} \\
\alpha_4 &=& \{(e_1, e_2) \mid e_1(\kappa) + 3 \leq e_2(\kappa) < e_1(\kappa) + 6\}
\end{array}
$$

$$
\text{where}
$$

$$
\begin{array}{ll}
e_1, e_2 \in \text{ENV} & \text{(bound variables)} \\
\text{dom } e_1 = \text{dom } e_2 = \{\kappa\}
\end{array}
$$

The initial marking being considered is

$$
M_{\text{ERN},0} = \{(p_1, c_1), (p_2, c_2)\}
$$

where $c_1, c_2 \in$ ENV and represent specific environments.

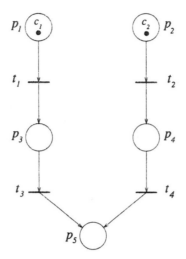

Figure 6.4 An example of a weak time net

Strong TERN

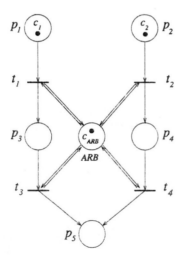

Figure 6.5 A strong time net for the example

Let us construct a strong time model for the net considered above. Its extended topology is shown in Figure 6.5. Let us also extend the set VAR as

$$\text{VAR} = \{\kappa\} \cup \{p_i\text{-}time \mid i \in 1 .. 5\}$$

where

$$p_i\text{-}time : \mathbb{T}; \; i \in 1 .. 5$$

With the addition of the place ARB for enforcing strong time semantics, the *preset* and the *postset* associated with the transitions become

$$
\begin{aligned}
preset_1 &= (p_1, \text{ARB}) & postset_1 &= (p_3, \text{ARB}) \\
preset_2 &= (p_2, \text{ARB}) & postset_2 &= (p_4, \text{ARB}) \\
preset_3 &= (p_3, \text{ARB}) & postset_3 &= (p_5, \text{ARB}) \\
preset_4 &= (p_4, \text{ARB}) & postset_4 &= (p_5, \text{ARB})
\end{aligned}
$$

The following illustrates the extension of the actions:

$$
\begin{aligned}
\alpha_1 = \{&((e_1, e_{\text{ARB}}), (e_2, e'_{\text{ARB}})) \mid max\{e_1(\kappa), e_{\text{ARB}}(\kappa)\} \le e_2(\kappa) \le \\
& e_{\text{ARB}}(p_4\text{-}time) + 6 \wedge \\
& e'_{\text{ARB}} = e_{\text{ARB}} \oplus \{\kappa \mapsto e_2(\kappa), p_1\text{-}time \mapsto \infty, p_3\text{-}time \mapsto e_2(\kappa)\}\}
\end{aligned}
$$

$$
\begin{aligned}
\alpha_2 = \{&((e_1, e_{\text{ARB}}), (e_2, e'_{\text{ARB}})) \mid max\{e_1(\kappa), e_{\text{ARB}}(\kappa)\} \le e_2(\kappa) \le \\
& e_{\text{ARB}}(p_3\text{-}time) + 15 \wedge \\
& e'_{\text{ARB}} = e_{\text{ARB}} \oplus \{\kappa \mapsto e_2(\kappa), p_2\text{-}time \mapsto \infty, p_4\text{-}time \mapsto e_2(\kappa)\}\}
\end{aligned}
$$

$$
\begin{aligned}
\alpha_3 = \{&((e_1, e_{\text{ARB}}), (e_2, e'_{\text{ARB}})) \mid max\{e_1(\kappa) + 10, e_{\text{ARB}}(\kappa)\} \le e_2(\kappa) < \\
& min\{e_1(\kappa) + 15, e_{\text{ARB}}(p_4\text{-}time) + 6\} \\
& e'_{\text{ARB}} = e_{\text{ARB}} \oplus \{\kappa \mapsto e_2(\kappa), p_3\text{-}time \mapsto \infty, p_5\text{-}time \mapsto e_2(\kappa)\}\}
\end{aligned}
$$

$$
\begin{aligned}
\alpha_4 = \{&((e_1, e_{\text{ARB}}), (e_2, e'_{\text{ARB}})) \mid max\{e_1(\kappa) + 3, e_{\text{ARB}}(\kappa)\} \le e_2(\kappa) < \\
& min\{e_1(\kappa) + 6, e_{\text{ARB}}(p_3\text{-}time) + 15\} \\
& e'_{\text{ARB}} = e_{\text{ARB}} \oplus \{\kappa \mapsto e_2(\kappa), p_4\text{-}time \mapsto \infty, p_5\text{-}time \mapsto e_2(\kappa)\}\}
\end{aligned}
$$

$$
\begin{aligned}
\text{where} \quad & e_1, e_2, e_{\text{ARB}}, e'_{\text{ARB}} \in \text{ENV} \\
& \text{dom } e_1 = \text{dom } e_2 = \{\kappa\} \\
& \text{dom } e_{\text{ARB}} = \text{dom } e'_{\text{ARB}} = \text{VAR}
\end{aligned}
$$

where $\oplus$ is the relational overriding operator. For example, the extension of the action α_1 is based on the markings shown in Figure 6.6. The initial marking to be considered is

$$
M_{\text{ERN},0} = \{(p_1, c_1), (p_2, c_2), (\text{ARB}, c_{\text{ARB}})\}
$$

where

$$
\begin{aligned}
& c_1, c_2, c_{\text{ARB}} \in \text{ENV} \\
& \text{dom } c_1 = \text{dom } c_2 = \{\kappa\} \\
& \text{dom } c_{\text{ARB}} = \text{VAR}
\end{aligned}
$$

and

$$
\begin{aligned}
& c_{\text{ARB}}(p_1\text{-}time) = c_{\text{ARB}}(p_2\text{-}time) = 0 \\
& c_{\text{ARB}}(p_3\text{-}time) = c_{\text{ARB}}(p_4\text{-}time) = c_{\text{ARB}}(p_5\text{-}time) = \infty
\end{aligned}
$$

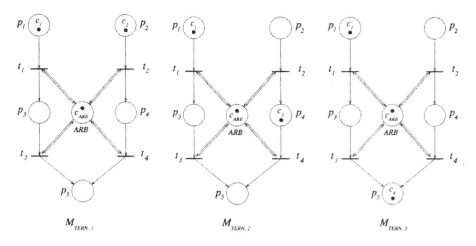

Figure 6.6 Markings enabling the transition t_1

6.4.2 Transition Based Semantics

As mentioned earlier, the semantics in this approach are based on individual transitions rather than firing sequences. Given a transition $t \in T_{\text{TERN}}$ and a marking
M_{TERN}, the set of possible firing times of t in the state corresponding to M_{TERN} is
given by

$$
act\text{-}time(t, M_{\text{TERN}}) = \{x \bullet x \in \mathbb{T}; \ enab \in \text{ENV}^{k_t}; \ prod \in \text{ENV}^{h_t} \mid \\
(enab, prod) \in \alpha_t \wedge \\
enab \in (preenv_t \cap M_{\text{TERN}} \langle preset_t \rangle \wedge \\
x = fire\text{-}time(enab, t, prod)\}
$$

The set $act\text{-}time(t, M_{\text{TERN}})$ represents here the *action times* of α_t under the marking
M_{TERN}. Following our discussion in the previous section, the *deadline* of α_t in that
state may be defined as

$$
exp\text{-}time(t, M_{\text{TERN}}) \stackrel{def}{=} \begin{cases} max(act\text{-}time(t, M_{\text{TERN}})), & \text{if the last interval of} \\ & \text{time in } act\text{-}time(\cdots) \\ & \text{is finite;} \\ \infty, & \text{otherwise.} \end{cases}
$$

It is convenient to have an analogous definition that applies to a set of transitions
ts such that $ts \subseteq T$ and $ts \neq \varnothing$. It may be defined as

$$
exp\text{-}time_{set}(ts, M_{\text{TERN}}) \stackrel{def}{=} \\
min\{x \bullet x \in \mathbb{T}; \ t \in T \mid t \in ts \wedge x = exp\text{-}time(t, M_{\text{TERN}})\}
$$

In this approach let the transitions T of any given net be partitioned into two
disjoint sets: *weak* and *strong*. This partitioning is application dependent and in

a typical application both these two sets are expected to be non-empty. Let the membership in the sets be characterized by two predicates: $weak(t)$ and $strong(t)$ with the obvious meanings as they apply to a transition t.

Definition: *Strong and Weak Time Transitions*

Let s be an arbitrary time ordered firing sequence in TERN N:

$$s = \langle a_1, a_2, \cdots, a_n \rangle$$

and let each of the markings $M_{\text{TERN},i}, 0 \leq i < n$ be reachable from the initial marking $M_{\text{TERN},0}$ and produced by the firing a_i. Then the behaviour of strong and weak time transitions may be characterized by the following two axioms:

Axiom 6(a) Enabled strong time transitions enjoy higher priority over enabled weak time transitions with respect to the execution time:

$$\forall i \in \mathbb{N};\ t_1, t_2 \in T \bullet 0 \leq i < n \wedge strong(t_1) \wedge weak(t_2) \wedge$$
$$enabled(t_1, M_{\text{TERN},i}) \wedge enabled(t_2, M_{\text{TERN},i}) \Rightarrow$$
$$transition(a_{i+1}) \neq t_2$$

Axiom 6(b) In the case of a single enabled strong time transition, it fires before the expiry of its deadline $exp\text{-}time(t, M_{\text{TERN},i})$. In the general case of a set of enabled strong time transitions ts, then one of them fires before the expiry of $exp\text{-}time_{set}(t, M_{\text{TERN},i})$:

$$\forall i \in \mathbb{N};\ ts \in \mathbb{P}\, T \bullet 0 \leq i < n \wedge ts \neq \varnothing \wedge$$
$$ts = \{t \mid strong(t) \wedge enabled(t, M_{\text{TERN},i})\} \Rightarrow$$
$$fire\text{-}time(a_{i+1}) \leq exp\text{-}time_{set}(ts, M_{\text{TERN},i})$$

According to Axiom 6(a), in every state having both strong and weak time transitions enabled in the sense of the meaning in $enabled(t, M_{\text{TERN},i})$, the enabled weak time transitions are 'effectively inhibited' from firing in the current state. This situation will persist in the subsequent firings until a state where none of the strong time transitions are enabled.

Note that according to Axiom 6(b), some transition fires within the closest expiry time of all the enabled strong transitions. If this were not the case, then it would lead to the anomaly that some strong time transitions would be permitted to miss their expiry time in favour of a strong time transition with a longer expiry time. This contradicts the very notion of strong time semantics. Furthermore, it amounts to disabling an already enabled transition with no change in the marking relation at all. It also prevents according all strong time transitions the same status. Axiom 6(b) has the effect of adopting a single latest expiry time for all enabled strong time transitions, its value being equal to that of the transition with the closest expiry time. On the other hand, non-determinism in the choice of the transition to fire next remains unchanged.

EXAMPLE

Let us consider the net in Figure 6.7 as a TERN. Let

$$\text{VAR} = \{\kappa\}$$
$$\text{VAL} = \mathbb{N}$$

where $\mathbb{N}$, the set of natural numbers, represents $\mathbb{T}$. The initial marking has the form

$$M_{\text{TERN},0} = \{(p_1, c_1), (p_1, c_2), (p_2, c_3), (p_2, c_4)\}$$

where the c_is for $i = 1, 2, 3, 4$ denote the following specific environments:

$$c_1 = \{\kappa \mapsto 1\} \qquad\qquad c_3 = \{\kappa \mapsto 3\}$$
$$c_2 = \{\kappa \mapsto 8\} \qquad\qquad c_4 = \{\kappa \mapsto 1\}$$

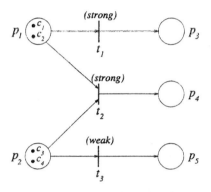

Figure 6.7 A TERN with both strong and weak transitions

Presets and *postsets* associated with the transition t_i, $i = 1, 2, 3$ are

$$\begin{array}{ll} preset_1 = p_1 & postset_1 = p_3 \\ preset_2 = (p_1, p_2) & postset_2 = p_4 \\ preset_3 = p_2 & postset_3 = p_5 \end{array}$$

Consider the actions α_i for $i = 1, 2, 3$ attached to each of the transitions t_i:

$$\alpha_1 = \{(e_1, e_2) \mid e_1(\kappa) < e_2(\kappa) \le e_1(\kappa) + 3\}$$

$$\alpha_2 = \{((e_1, e_2), e_3) \mid (2 < e_1(\kappa) + e_2(\kappa) \le 5) \land$$
$$(e_2(\kappa) < e_3(\kappa) \le e_1(\kappa) + 4 \lor e_1(\kappa) + 6 < e_3(\kappa) \le e_2(\kappa) + 7)\}$$

$$\alpha_3 = \{(e_1, e_2) \mid e_1(\kappa) < 3 \land e_1(\kappa) < e_2(\kappa) \le e_1(\kappa) + 12\}$$
$$\text{where}$$
$$e_1, e_2, e_3 \in \text{ENV}$$
$$\text{dom } e_1 = \text{dom } e_2 = \text{dom } e_3 = \{\kappa\}$$

All three transitions are enabled in the initial marking $M_{\text{TERN},0}$. Their action times are given by

$$act\text{-}time(t_1, M_{\text{TERN},0}) = \{x \bullet x \in \mathbb{N};\ e \in \text{ENV}\ |$$
$$(c_1(\kappa) < e(\kappa) \le c_1(\kappa) + 3 \wedge x = fire\text{-}time(c_1, t_1, e)) \vee$$
$$(c_2(\kappa) < e(\kappa) \le c_2(\kappa) + 3 \wedge x = fire\text{-}time(c_2, t_1, e))\}$$
$$= \{x \bullet x \in \mathbb{N}\ |\ c_1(\kappa) < x \le c_1(\kappa) + 3) \vee c_2(\kappa) < x \le c_2(\kappa) + 3\}$$
$$= \{x \bullet x \in \mathbb{N}\ |\ 1 < x \le 4 \vee 8 < x \le 11\}$$

$$act\text{-}time(t_2, M_{\text{TERN},0}) = \{x \bullet x \in \mathbb{N};\ e \in \text{ENV}\ |\ (c_3(\kappa) < e(\kappa) \le c_1(\kappa) + 4 \vee$$
$$c_1(\kappa) + 6 < e(\kappa) \le c_3(\kappa) + 7) \wedge x = fire\text{-}time((c_1, c_3), t_2, e)\}$$
$$= \{x \bullet x \in \mathbb{N}\ |\ (c_3(\kappa) < x \le c_1(\kappa) + 4 \vee c_1(\kappa) + 6 < x \le c_3(\kappa) + 7\}$$
$$= \{x \bullet x \in \mathbb{N}\ |\ 3 < x \le 5 \vee 7 < x \le 10\}$$

$$act\text{-}time(t_3, M_{\text{TERN},0}) = \{x \bullet x \in \mathbb{N};\ e \in \text{ENV}\ |$$
$$c_4(\kappa) < e(\kappa) \le c_4(\kappa) + 12 \wedge x = fire\text{-}time(c_4, t_3, e)\}$$
$$= \{x \bullet x \in \mathbb{N}\ |\ c_4(\kappa) < x \le c_4(\kappa) + 12\}$$
$$= \{x \bullet x \in \mathbb{N}\ |\ 1 < x \le 13\}$$

Axiom 6(a) forbids the firing of the transition t_3 in the initial marking since it is a weak time transition. The other two enabled transitions t_1 and t_2 are strong time transitions and, therefore, are accorded precedence over t_3. They have a closest expiry time of

$$exp\text{-}time_{set}(\{t_1, t_2\}, M_{\text{TERN},0}) = min\{10, 11\} = 10$$

and one of them must fire within that time, but with each obeying its own set of permitted action times. Note that these sets do not form contiguous intervals of time and contain certain exclusion times.

The transition t_1 is free to fire within the left open interval $(1, 4]$ and, if it fires within this interval, it has to rely on the environment c_1 at p_1. In the resulting marking, t_2 will be disabled while t_3 will be unaffected, paving the way for t_3 to fire if it chooses to fire. On the other hand, if t_2 fires first, then t_1 will remain enabled in the subsequent marking but is restricted to fire some time over the left open interval $(8, 11]$. The transition t_3 can fire only after t_1 fires but may do so up to and including the 13th time unit.

6.5   Relationship with PN and TBN

As was mentioned at the outset, the TBN nets are a special class of TERN. The relationship between the two is best described by outlining the derivation of TBN, as well as PN, from TERN.

The ability to switch between different kinds of net in the manner indicated below is significant from two related perspectives. Firstly, it offers the scope for refinements of nets, enabling gradual introduction of additional details and consideration of additional complexities in an orderly manner. An advantage of this is the possibility for systematic verification of designs. Secondly, it allows the reduction of nets into simpler forms either for convenience in reasoning or in order to focus attention on a chosen aspect of the system.

6.5.1 Classical Petri Nets

This section briefly outlines the definition of the major constituents of PN in terms of TERN. The input arcs in PN may be defined in terms of *presets*:

$$i = \{(p, t) \mid p \in P \land t \in T \land p \text{ in } preset_t\}$$

The set of output arcs o may be defined analogously using the postsets. The weighting function W in PN may be defined likewise as a multi-set using predicates as in set comprehension:

$$W = [\![(p, t) \mid p \in P \land t \in T \land p \text{ in } preset_t]\!] \uplus$$
$$[\![(t, p) \mid p \in P \land t \in T \land p \text{ in } postset_t]\!]$$

Note that multi-sets are a special kind of set permitting multiple occurrences of its elements and $\uplus$ denotes the union of multi-sets. The marking relation M in PN may be defined in terms of M_{TERN} as

$$M = \{(p, n) \mid p \in P \land n \in \mathbb{N} \land n = \#(\{p\} \lhd M_{\text{TERN}})\}$$

6.5.2 Time Basic Nets

The aim of this section is not so much to suggest how a net can be transformed from TERN to TBN, or vice versa, but is an appreciation of the relationship between the two. In general, such a transformation is difficult. This is because the information relevant to the structure of possible 'equivalent' TBN versions is typically embedded in the definition of TERN environments, and its extraction may involve some reasoning about the constitution of environments.

The definition of net topology and net state in TBN in terms of TERN is identical to that of PN introduced in the previous subsection. Here we relate environments and actions of TERN with time conditions of TBN.

Let us restrict the environments in TERN to contain just one variable, namely κ. In other words, the 'environments' in TBN contain no variables for carrying either temporal or state information about the net. Thus, the environments in TBN carry just the transition firing times. Either by restricting the number of tokens in each place to one token or by an appropriate definition of a function, the time stamp of any token at a place may be obtained using a function from places to $\mathbb{T}$. This function has been referred to in Chapter 5 as *time*. For example, the function *time* may be defined as

$$time(p) = max\{x \bullet x : \mathbb{T}; \ e : \text{ENV} \mid (p, e) \in M_{\text{TERN}} \wedge x = e(\kappa)\}$$

for every $p \in P$.

Provided that the corresponding nets in TBN and TERN have the same topology, the time condition in TBN may be derived from actions in TERN. Let actions in TERN have the following general form:

$$\alpha_{\text{TERN},t} = \{(preenv, postenv) \mid pred(e_1, e_2, \cdots, e_k, e_1', e_2', \cdots, e_h')\}$$

where

$$preenv = (e_1, e_2, \cdots, e_k)$$
$$postenv = (e_1', e_2', \cdots, e_h')$$

where *pred* is a predicate involving potentially all environments appearing in *preenv* and *postenv* of the transition t. Let us outline informally a transformation of $\alpha_{\text{TERN},t}$ to the corresponding time condition $\alpha_{\text{TBN},t}$ in the following paragraphs.

The tokens in TBN may be thought of as environments in TERN. Let these 'token environments' in TBN corresponding to each environment e_i or e_i' in TERN be denoted by $\tilde{e}_i$ and $\tilde{e}_i'$ respectively. It is clear that, for example,

$$\tilde{e} \stackrel{def}{=} \{\kappa\} \lhd e$$

An expression of the form $\tilde{e}(\kappa)$ thus gives the time stamp of the corresponding token in TBN. Let $\widetilde{pred}$ be the predicate obtained from *pred* by

(a) replacing <u>first</u> its every prime predicate (i.e. those not containing the propositional connectives $\neg$, $\wedge$, $\vee$, $\Rightarrow$ and $\Leftrightarrow$) containing any term involving state variables (i.e. variables other than κ) with the truth value true,

(b) replacing <u>then</u> remaining environments e with the corresponding $\tilde{e}$.

This amounts to ignoring any state dependent temporal properties of the net. The time condition $\alpha_{\text{TBN},t}$ applicable to transition t in TBN may then be derived as

$$\alpha_{\text{TBN},t} = \{x \bullet x : \mathbb{T} \mid \widetilde{pred}[\tilde{e}_1(\kappa)\backslash time(p_1), \tilde{e}_2(\kappa)\backslash time(p_2), \cdots,$$
$$\tilde{e}_k(\kappa)\backslash time(p_k), \tilde{e}_1'(\kappa)\backslash x, \tilde{e}_2'(\kappa)\backslash x, \cdots, \tilde{e}_h'(\kappa)\backslash x]\}$$

where

$$preset_t = (p_1, p_2, \cdots, p_k)$$
$$preenv_t = (e_1, e_2, \cdots, e_k)$$
$$postenv_t = (e_1', e_2', \cdots, e_h')$$

where, for a predicate Q, the expression $Q[a_1\backslash b_1, a_2\backslash b_2, \cdots, a_n\backslash b_n]$ is identical to that obtained from Q by replacing every term a_i systematically with the corresponding term b_i for $i \in 1 \ldots n$.

EXAMPLE

Let us return to the example on page 98 on the process control system modelled in TERN, and derive the definition for $\alpha_{\text{TBN},1}$ from $\alpha_{\text{TERN},1}$ for the transition t_1.

$$pred_{\alpha_{\text{TERN},1}} = \begin{aligned}[t] &e_1(\kappa) < e_4(\kappa) \le e_1(\kappa) + T_3 \wedge e_4(\kappa) > e_3(\kappa) + T_4 \wedge \\ &e_4(st) = e_4(fl) = e_4(rp) = e_4(\kappa) \wedge e_4(pr) = e_2(pr) \\ &\text{from def. of } \alpha_{\text{TERN},1} \end{aligned}$$

$$\widetilde{pred}_{\alpha_{\text{TERN},1}} = \begin{aligned}[t] &\tilde{e}_1(\kappa) < \tilde{e}_4(\kappa) \le \tilde{e}_1(\kappa) + T_3 \wedge \tilde{e}_4(\kappa) > \tilde{e}_3(\kappa) + T_4 \wedge \\ &\text{true} \wedge \text{true} \end{aligned}$$

replacement of prime predicates containing state variables with true, and then every e with corresponding $\tilde{e}$

$$= \tilde{e}_1(\kappa) < \tilde{e}_4(\kappa) \le \tilde{e}_1(\kappa) + T_3 \wedge \tilde{e}_4(\kappa) > \tilde{e}_3(\kappa) + T_4$$

simplification

$$\alpha_{\text{TBN},1} = \begin{aligned}[t] &\{x \mid (\tilde{e}_1(\kappa) < \tilde{e}_4(\kappa) \le \tilde{e}_1(\kappa) + T_3 \wedge \tilde{e}_4(\kappa) > \tilde{e}_3(\kappa) + T_4) \\ &\qquad [\tilde{e}_1(\kappa) \backslash time(p_1), \tilde{e}_3(\kappa) \backslash time(p_3), \tilde{e}_4(\kappa) \backslash x]\} \\ &\text{def. of } \alpha_{\text{TBN},1} \end{aligned}$$

$$= \{x \mid time(p_1) < x \le time(p_1) + T_3 \wedge x > time(p_3) + T_4\}$$

substitution

Despite the difference in the nets of the examples concerned, namely, the TBN in Section 5.3.2 of Chapter 5 and the TERN on page 98, it is instructive to compare the time condition of the original example in TBN with the one derived above as $\alpha_{\text{TBN},1}$.

In summary, *preset* and *postset* of transitions in TERN correspond to inputs and outputs of transitions and the weighting function in PN and TBN. The environments in TERN are an extended notion of tokens in PN and TBN. In addition to timestamps carried by tokens in TBN, environments in TERN are capable of carrying other information. Predicates defining actions in TERN incorporate, among others, the time conditions of transitions in TBN.

6.6　Bibliographical Notes

This chapter is largely based on the approach due to Ghezzi *et al.* [49]. A notable exception is Section 6.4.2, which deals with an alternative approach to strong and weak time semantics. Other relevant literature may be found under the bibliographical notes of the previous chapter.

6.7　Exercises

Attempt the exercises given in Section 5.8 of the previous chapter in TERN, taking into account the following modifications or additional requirements. The exercise numbering remains unchanged.

1. The TERN model of the telephone instrument is able to pass the actual number dialled to the telephone exchange.
2. The crossing is pedestrian controlled. Pedestrians make requests by pressing a button and the system responds to such requests within T_8 time units, but allows at least T_9 time units for any approaching vehicles to clear the crossing safely. Obviously, $T_9 < T_8$.
3. The duration of the period when the gate should remain closed for road users and the lights should remain red can be set by the operator. In other words, the relevant timing values are not fixed system parameters.
4. In the case of failures in message deliveries, the number of re-trials by the sending station is limited to a predefined maximum.
5. The safety critical system is able to determine the required flow of the coolant as a function of the sensor reading. Sensor failures are detected when the values obtained from the sensor lie outside a predefined range.
6. The specification of the realtime locking system is to be changed so that it is operated not by a physical key but by an internally verifiable coded digital key.

Chapter 7

An Overview of CSP

The behaviour of most realtime systems may be characterized by continuous unfolding of a potentially non-terminating sequence of events. As mentioned in Sections 1.1.2 and 1.2.3 of Chapter 1, the correctness of such systems involves, in addition to the logical correctness of any output produced, a range of other issues, including the form of interaction between different components, in other words, concurrency. The theory of Communicating Sequential Processes (CSP) due to Hoare [59] is intended for the study of concurrent systems, and its augmentation with timed models for the study of general realtime systems. This chapter introduces the core of the CSP notation and demonstrates how it can be used to model concurrent systems. In the development process of any realtime system, it may be appropriate to address first the concurrent behaviour of different components, ignoring time, and then to consider the timing aspects of those components where it matters. Thus, even on its own, CSP still has a strong relevance to the study of realtime systems. This is not surprising since concurrency is an outcome of abstraction at a higher level than the realtime behaviour. Furthermore, any development work in CSP may benefit from its closeness to occam, a programming language implementing a subset of CSP.

Another important aim of our study of CSP here is to lay the foundation for an introduction to timed CSP – the topic of the next chapter.

7.1 About Process Abstraction

CSP is a theoretical framework founded on two distinct types of basic object: events and processes. *Events* are primitive entities and, therefore, are not decomposable. By contrast, *processes*, the most fundamental category of objects in CSP, are complex entities which can be constructed and analyzed using simpler processes. In the final analysis, all processes are constructed from events and a few primitive processes. The behaviour of a process describes the evolution of a system in time

113

and, in particular, how it interacts with its subsystems and the environment. It is often convenient to treat a given system and its subsystems in a uniform manner. In this respect, the behaviour of both systems and subsystems may be viewed in terms of their interaction with an 'extended' environment which includes, alongside the user, a part of the larger system where the system under study is placed. In the case of a totally embedded subsystem, its extended environment consists simply of the immediate surroundings of the subsystem within the overall system. A discussion along these lines may be found in Section 1.1.5 of Chapter 1.

The interactive part of the behaviour of a system can be expressed in terms of events common to the system and its environment. This interaction may be represented through the observable events, or the common points of cooperation between the system and its environment. This view corresponds with what is called *synchronous* behaviour. The non-interactive part of the behaviour of a system concerns its private events, including internal events.

CSP is founded on a number of process composition operators. Each of these operators forms, from its operand processes, a new process exhibiting a distinct behaviour pattern. These process manipulations obey well-understood rules and algebraic laws, and hence the reference to CSP in some literature as a *process algebra*. The algebraic laws facilitate the transformation of processes from one form to other equivalent forms. The theory of CSP is formulated in such a way that the behaviour of the new process can be determined exactly from an understanding of its simpler constituent processes. In other words, the theory is founded on what is called *compositional semantics*.

7.2   Events

CSP regards all events, including communication events, to be non-decomposable or *atomic*. Since there is no notion of quantifiable time in CSP, no durations are associated with events and, in this sense, events are often referred to as being 'instantaneous'. An example is the event *tick* of a clock (see Figure 7.1(a)). Events are identified by means of labels. It is customary to assume that all events relevant to a given application are drawn from a type Σ.

Event labels may be given certain naming conventions in order to reflect their association with, for example, specific processes. These are purely syntactic conventions. In relation to communication events, a convention in common usage is

$c.v$

which denotes the event communicating the value v, or the value of a variable v, over a channel c. Here, no distinction is made between whether v is an input or an output. In situations where such a distinction is desirable, the following convention is used:

$$in?x \quad \text{and} \quad out!y$$

The above denote respectively an input of some object as the value of a variable x over a channel *in* and an output of a specific data item y over the channel *out* (see Figure 7.1(b)).

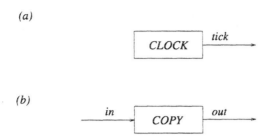

Figure 7.1 Examples of event labels

EXAMPLE

Let us consider a simple mail tool as a detailed running example. The primary purpose of this tool is to receive and store the mail for its user and enable the user to view and send messages. The user interacts with the tool by means of a menu driven interface. As a first step towards defining the events relevant to this example, let us introduce a generic type:

$$[Message]$$

for denoting the set of all possible messages. The elements of Σ may be defined as

$$\Sigma \overset{def}{=} \{open,\ close,\ next,\ previous,\ delete,\ bleep\} \cup$$
$$\{arrive.m \mid m \in Message\} \cup \{dispatch.m \mid m \in Message\} \cup$$
$$\{send.m \mid m \in Message\}$$

Informally, these are intended as labels for the following events:

open	–	Opening the mail tool.
close	–	Closing the mail tool.
next	–	Requesting the display of the next item in the mail bag.
previous	–	Requesting the display of the previous item in the mail bag.
delete	–	Requesting the deletion of the currently displayed item of the mail bag.

bleep	–	Emission of a bleep, signalling the occurrence of other events such as the arrival of a new message.
arrive.m	–	Communication (arrival) of a message m through channel *arrive*.
send.m	–	A user request made through channel *send* for sending a message m.
dispatch.m	–	System dispatching a message m through channel *dispatch*. In relation to *dispatch*, let us use a function *pack* on *Message*, so that $pack(m)$ denotes a modified version of the message m. For example, $pack(m)$ may contain, in addition to m, other information such as a time stamp of the request time and sender's details.

Further events will be introduced later as necessary.

7.2.1   Process Identifiers and Process Alphabets

A process *alphabet* is an explicitly stated set of events that a given process may engage in. Given a process P, its alphabet is denoted by αP. For example, with reference to the processes in Figure 7.1:

$$\alpha\text{CLOCK} = \{tick\}$$
$$\alpha\text{COPY} = \{in?m \mid m \in Data\} \cup \{out!m \mid m \in Data\}$$

EXAMPLE

Returning to our running example, consider the following as the names of some processes in the mail tool:

MAIL-TOOL, MAIL-BAG, DISPATCHER, ICON, INTERFACE

Conventionally, strings of characters written in upper case denote processes. The above are names of processes with the following informally stated functionalities:

MAIL-TOOL	–	The mail tool as a whole.
MAIL-BAG	–	A process for manipulating messages currently held in the mail tool.
DISPATCHER	–	A process for dispatching messages originated by its user.
INTERFACE	–	The user interface process within the mail tool.
ICON	–	A process allowing the invocation of the process INTERFACE by the user.

One may further identify the alphabets of the above processes as

αMAIL-TOOL $=$ Σ

αMAIL-BAG $=$ $\{open,\ next,\ previous,\ delete,\ close\}\cup$
$\{arrive.m\mid m\in \text{ran}\ \ pack\}$

αDISPATCHER $=$ $\{send.m\mid m\in \text{dom}\ \ pack\}\cup$
$\{dispatch.m\mid m\in \text{ran}\ \ pack\}$

αINTERFACE $=$ $\{next,\ previous,\ delete,\ close\}\cup$
$\{send.m\mid m\in \text{dom}\ \ pack\}$

αICON $=$ $\{open\}\cup \alpha$INTERFACE

7.3   Basic Deterministic Processes

First, let us introduce a very special process. In CSP, STOP is a non-decomposable primitive process which never engages in any event of its alphabet. The alphabet applicable to STOP is important and is indicated as a subscript. For example, $\text{STOP}_{\alpha P}$ has the same alphabet as that of the process P.

Given a process, its pattern of behaviour may be extended by prefixing an event as its first event and, thus, creates a new process. The simplest event prefixing has the form

$a \to P$

which denotes the process which is prepared to engage in the event a first, after which it behaves as the process P. For example,

$a \to b \to \text{STOP}$

describes a process which engages in a first, then in b and then stops.

The notation is applicable to processes making multiple offers. Its most general version is the multiple choice operator, which has the form,

$$x : \{x_1, x_2, \cdots, x_n\} \to P(x) \quad \overset{def}{=} \quad \begin{array}{l} x_1 \to P(x_1) \\ \mid x_2 \to P(x_2) \\ \quad\vdots \\ \mid x_n \to P(x_n) \end{array}$$

where x is variable denoting a multiple choice and ranging over the specific choices $x_1, x_2, \cdots, x_n$. The outcome in each case would depend on the choice x_i exercised and, therefore, it is a function of x_i. Such processes are called *deterministic*, since the choice of events on offer, if any, is determined by the environment. Note that ' $\mid$ ' is not a process composition operator, but a delimiter of choices. A consequence of the above definition is the following:

Observation 7.1 On symmetry of choice.

$$(a \to P \mid b \to Q) = (b \to Q \mid a \to P)$$

The above process offers a *choice* of two events a and b to the environment, and then, depending on the outcome, leads, respectively, to processes P and Q.

EXAMPLE

In our running example, some process definitions relevant to the mail tool may be introduced as

ICON	=	*open* → INTERFACE
INTERFACE	=	*next* → INTERFACE
		| *previous* → INTERFACE
		| *delete* → INTERFACE
		| *send.m* → INTERFACE
		| *close* → ICON
DISPATCHER	=	*send.m* → *dispatch.pack*(*m*) → DISPATCHER

The processes ICON and INTERFACE are parts of the user interface. The events of INTERFACE are intended to trigger an underlying process, which provides the required service. Thus, the two processes ICON and INTERFACE are a model of a simple menu system. The process ICON allows opening the underlying process providing the service and, once opened, it offers through INTERFACE a number of further choices. The process DISPATCHER, on the other hand, models an input/output mechanism involving a stimulus *send.m* and an action *dispatch.pack*(*m*), where *pack* is the function defined on page 116.

7.4 Recursion

The definitions of the processes ICON, INTERFACE and DISPATCHER given above are examples of recursive processes. The equation

$$P = F(P)$$

defines a unique process, if every occurrence of P on the right hand side is *guarded* (prefixed) by an event. When the function F is guarded, the notation

$$\mu X \bullet P$$

denotes the unique process defined by $P = F(P)$.

EXAMPLE

As an example, an alternative definition for DISPATCHER is the following:

$$\text{DISPATCHER} \;=\; \mu\,X \bullet send.m \to dispatch.pack(m) \to X$$

which is identical in behaviour to the definition given earlier. Often recursive processes are embedded in other processes. This is illustrated in the following process REQ-DISPATCHER – a dispatcher, which works on request and can be invoked with the event *start* and terminated with the event *finish*. In between these two events, it accepts and dispatches any number of messages:

$$
\begin{aligned}
\text{REQ-DISPATCHER} \quad &= \quad start \to \text{REQ-DISPATCHER-AUX}\\
\text{REQ-DISPATCHER-AUX} \;&= \quad \mu\,X \bullet send.m \to dispatch.pack(m) \to X\\
&\qquad\; \mid finish \to \text{REQ-DISPATCHER}
\end{aligned}
$$

It can be seen that the right hand side of REQ-DISPATCHER-AUX offers an event which terminates the recursion introduced by the μ operator and transfers control to another recursive process. The above is an example of mutual recursion.

7.5   Processes with Internal States

Being a framework dedicated to the study of patterns of behaviour of processes on the basis of events and their possible interactions, CSP does not facilitate the consideration of complex process states. However, CSP processes may capture state information to a limited extent.

EXAMPLE

As an example, the process corresponding to the user reviewing his mail bag may be modelled by means of two separate state variables: *seen* and *rest*. Mathematically, both are sequences of messages. The variable *seen* represents the messages already seen by the user in the current session, while the variable *rest* represents the messages yet to be seen by the user. The two sequences when appended together correspond to the whole mail bag which is denoted by *lot*. Thus,

$$seen,\ rest,\ lot : \text{seq } Message$$

and, where appropriate,

$$seen \frown rest = lot$$

Implicit in this representation is that the message being displayed is the last item in *seen*, if it is non-empty. These sequences may then be regarded as a representation of the state of the mail bag. Note that the following uses some of the notation introduced in Section 7.13.

The following models the state changes of the mail bag brought about by the various events:

$$\text{MAIL-BAG} \quad = \quad \text{MAIL-BAG}'_{\langle\rangle} \tag{i}$$

$$\text{MAIL-BAG}'_{\langle\rangle} \quad = \quad open \rightarrow \text{BAG}_{\langle\rangle,\langle\rangle}$$

$$\mid arrive.m \rightarrow \text{MAIL-BAG}'_{\langle m\rangle} \tag{ii}$$

$$\text{MAIL-BAG}'_{l:lot} \quad = \quad open \rightarrow \text{BAG}_{\langle l\rangle,\ lot}$$

$$\mid arrive.x \rightarrow \text{MAIL-BAG}'_{l:lot^\frown\langle x\rangle} \tag{iii}$$

$$\text{BAG}_{\langle\rangle,\ \langle\rangle} \quad = \quad arrive.x \rightarrow \text{BAG}_{\langle\rangle,\ \langle x\rangle} \tag{iv}$$

$$\text{BAG}_{\langle\rangle,\ r:rest} \quad = \quad arrive.x \rightarrow \text{BAG}_{\langle\rangle,\ r:rest^\frown\langle x\rangle}$$

$$\mid next \rightarrow \text{BAG}_{\langle r\rangle,\ rest}$$

$$\mid close \rightarrow \text{MAIL-BAG}'_{r:rest} \tag{v}$$

$$\text{BAG}_{seen^\frown\langle s\rangle,\ \langle\rangle} \quad = \quad arrive.x \rightarrow \text{BAG}_{seen^\frown\langle s\rangle,\ \langle x\rangle}$$

$$\mid previous \rightarrow \text{BAG}_{seen,\ \langle s\rangle}$$

$$\mid delete \rightarrow \text{BAG}_{seen,\ \langle\rangle}$$

$$\mid close \rightarrow \text{MAIL-BAG}'_{seen^\frown\langle s\rangle} \tag{vi}$$

$$\text{BAG}_{seen^\frown\langle s\rangle,\ r:rest} \quad = \quad arrive.x \rightarrow \text{BAG}_{seen^\frown\langle s\rangle,\ r:rest^\frown\langle x\rangle}$$

$$\mid next \rightarrow \text{BAG}_{seen^\frown\langle s\rangle^\frown\langle r\rangle,\ rest}$$

$$\mid previous \rightarrow \text{BAG}_{seen,\ s:r:rest}$$

$$\mid delete \rightarrow \text{BAG}_{seen,\ r:rest}$$

$$\mid close \rightarrow \text{MAIL-BAG}'_{seen^\frown\langle s\rangle^\frown r:rest} \tag{vii}$$

According to (i) in the above definition for MAIL-BAG, the initial state of the mail bag is empty. In order to manipulate messages in the mail bag, the process MAIL-BAG must engage in the event *open*. An unopened mail bag can only be opened, although it is able to store any incoming messages. This is expressed in (ii) and (iii), which also describe how the content of the mail bag is partitioned into *seen* and *rest* when the mail bag is opened. In the most general state of the opened mail bag, described by (vii), the mail bag may be requested to show the next and the previous messages by the events *next* and *previous* respectively. Here, the mail bag may also be requested to delete the currently displayed message. The definitions (iv), (v) and (vi) are special cases of (vii) but with reduced functionality because of the particular states. The mail bag is able to accept incoming messages uninterrupted in all its possible states. Note how the events such as *next*, *delete*, etc., actually affect the state of the process MAIL-BAG, whereas the definition INTERFACE given earlier does not involve such state changes simply because it has no notion of a state to start with.

7.6 Parallel Composition

As mentioned in Section 7.3, complex processes may be constructed by composition of simpler processes. This is the first of three sections that discuss the CSP operators which allow this. Let us begin with the parallel composition operator. The notation

$$P \parallel Q$$

denotes a new process formed by the *parallel composition* of the operand processes P and Q such that the behaviour of the new process is synchronized with respect to the events in the intersection of the alphabets of P and Q. Given that both P and Q are deterministic processes in the sense that their behaviour is fully determined by the choices made by the environment (in the same sense as that mentioned on page 117), the process $P \parallel Q$ is also a deterministic process.

The operator $\parallel$ is defined in the following manner. Firstly,

$$\alpha(P \parallel Q) = \alpha A \cup \alpha B$$

and secondly,

$$(x : A \to P(x)) \parallel (y : B \to Q(y)) \stackrel{def}{=} z : C \to (P'(z) \parallel Q'(z))$$

where

$$C \quad = \quad (A \cap B) \cup (A - \alpha Q) \cup (B - \alpha P)$$

$$
\begin{aligned}
P'(z) \quad &= \quad P(z) &&\text{if } z \in A \\
&= \quad x : A \to P(x) &&\text{if } z \notin A \\
Q'(z) \quad &= \quad Q(z) &&\text{if } z \in B \\
&= \quad y : B \to P(y) &&\text{if } z \notin B
\end{aligned}
$$

In the case of two simple processes P and Q with $\alpha P = \{a, c, d\}$ and $\alpha Q = \{b, c, d\}$, the above definition leads to the following process unfolding:

$$
\begin{aligned}
(c \to P) \parallel (c \to Q) \quad &= \quad c \to (P \parallel Q) \\
(a \to P) \parallel (c \to Q) \quad &= \quad a \to (P \parallel (c \to Q)) \\
(c \to P) \parallel (b \to Q) \quad &= \quad b \to ((c \to P) \parallel Q) \\
(a \to P) \parallel (b \to Q) \quad &= \quad a \to (P \parallel (b \to Q)) \\
&= \quad \mid b \to ((a \to P) \parallel Q) \\
(c \to P) \parallel (d \to Q) \quad &= \quad \text{STOP}
\end{aligned}
$$

The following properties of the operator $\parallel$ follow from its general definition:

Observation 7.2 Properties of the operator $\parallel$.

$$
\begin{aligned}
P \parallel Q \quad &= \quad Q \parallel P &&\text{(commutativity)} \\
P \parallel (Q \parallel R) \quad &= \quad (P \parallel Q) \parallel R &&\text{(associativity)}
\end{aligned}
$$

Observation 7.3 Interaction with STOP.

$$P \parallel \text{STOP}_{\alpha P} = \text{STOP}_{\alpha P}$$

where the process SKIP is as defined in Section 7.8.2.

Observation 7.4 A property of the operator $\parallel$ applicable to deterministic processes.

$$P \parallel P = P \qquad \text{(idempotency)}$$

The restriction of the above property to deterministic processes is considered in the next section.

EXAMPLE

The use of the operator $\parallel$ may be illustrated by defining the mail tool process as

$$\text{MAIL-TOOL} = \text{MAIL-BAG} \parallel \text{ICON} \parallel \text{DISPATCHER}$$

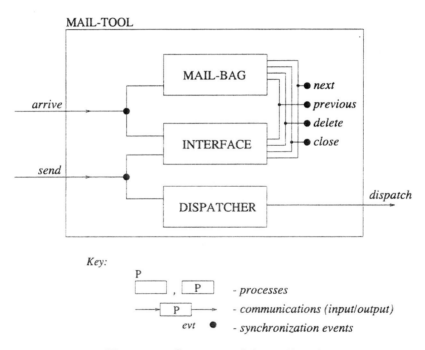

Figure 7.2 Structure of the mail tool

Figure 7.2 illustrates diagrammatically the process MAIL-TOOL when the process INTERFACE is operational. The processes INTERFACE (set off by ICON) and DISPATCHER have to cooperate on the events of the form *send.m*, whereas MAIL-BAG is independent of this communication event.

7.7 Non-determinism

The significance of non-determinism in computing has already being outlined in Section 1.2.3 of Chapter 1. The discussion here concentrates on how to model such behaviour in CSP.

7.7.1 Internal Choice

Two processes may be composed to form a new process using the *internal choice* operator $\sqcap$. The process

$$P \sqcap Q$$

is characterized by the fact that the environment cannot influence the choice between the processes P and Q. The process $P \sqcap Q$ behaves either as P or as Q. The choice between them is made internally and, therefore, it is not possible to predict which one of the processes P and Q may emerge from $P \sqcap Q$.

Observation 7.5 Properties of the operator $\sqcap$.

The operator $\sqcap$ is idempotent, commutative and associative.

All CSP operators, except recursion, distribute through non-determinism. Hence,

Observation 7.6 Distributive properties.

$$P \odot (Q \sqcap R) \;=\; (P \odot Q) \sqcap (P \odot R)$$

where $\odot$ is any CSP operator other than the recursion operator μ.

The inapplicability of the above observation to the recursion operator μ is clear from the following:

$$\mu x \bullet ((a \to x) \sqcap (b \to x)) \neq (\mu x \bullet (a \to x)) \sqcap (\mu x \bullet (b \to x)) \qquad (A)$$

where $a \neq b$, This is because the recursion on the left hand side of (A) may keep offering as and bs in any combination and in any order. By contrast, the choice offered by the process on the right hand side of (A) is settled once and for all, once it is exercised for the first time.

A particular case of Observation 7.6 is the following:

Observation 7.7 A distributive property.

$$P \parallel (Q \sqcap R) \;=\; (P \parallel Q) \sqcap (P \parallel R)$$

Thus, the parallel composition of a process with another process, which contains an internally determined choice, may itself be expressed as a process with an internally determined choice and vice versa. Here is another special case of Observation 7.6.

Observation 7.8 Distributivity of event prefix through $\sqcap$.

$$x \to (P \sqcap Q) = (x \to P) \sqcap (x \to Q)$$

Thus, according to the above, it is immaterial whether to offer an event first and then lead to an internally determined choice or to lead to an internally determined choice immediately, but with the given event as its first offer.

Let us examine the reason for restricting Observation 7.4 given in the previous section to deterministic processes. As a counter example for illustrating this point, consider the parallel composition of a non-deterministic process:

$$a \to P \sqcap b \to P$$

with itself as shown in the following:

$$
\begin{aligned}
(a \to P \sqcap b \to P) &\parallel (a \to P \sqcap b \to P) \\
&= (a \to P \parallel a \to P) \sqcap (b \to P \parallel b \to P) \sqcap (a \to P \parallel b \to P) \sqcap \\
&\qquad\qquad\qquad\qquad\qquad\qquad\qquad\qquad (b \to P \parallel a \to P)
\end{aligned}
$$

$$\text{Repeated application of Observation 7.7}$$

$$= (a \to P) \sqcap (b \to P) \sqcap \text{STOP} \sqcap \text{STOP}$$

$$\text{Observations 7.3 and 7.4}$$

$$= (a \to P) \sqcap (b \to P) \sqcap \text{STOP}$$

$$\text{Observation 7.5}$$

It is clear from the above that idempotency of parallel composition operator does not hold for non-deterministic processes.

EXAMPLE

Returning to our example, the following may be considered as a substitute for MAIL–BAG:

$$\text{MAIL–BAG} \quad = \quad \text{MAIL–BAG}'_{\langle\rangle} \sqcap \text{MAIL–BAG}''_{\langle\rangle,\ \langle\rangle}$$

where the processes $\text{MAIL–BAG}'_{lot}$ and $\text{MAIL–BAG}''_{old,\ new}$ are alternative definitions for the mail bag. The former is identical to that introduced in Section 7.5. The process $\text{MAIL–BAG}''_{old,new}$ is expected to behave as indicated in

$$
\begin{aligned}
\text{MAIL–BAG} \quad &= \quad \text{MAIL–BAG}'_{\langle\rangle} \sqcap \text{MAIL–BAG}''_{\langle\rangle,\ \langle\rangle} \\
\text{MAIL–BAG}''_{old,\ x:new} \quad &= \quad open \to \text{BAG}''_{old\ ^\frown \langle x\rangle,\ new} \\
&\quad\ |\ arrive.m \to \text{MAIL–BAG}''_{old,\ x:new\ ^\frown \langle m\rangle} \\
&\quad\ |\ \ldots\ldots
\end{aligned}
$$

The state variables *old* and *new* in the above denote two non-empty sets of messages corresponding, respectively, to messages which have been previously seen by the user and those which are yet to be seen. Obviously, the above definition of MAIL-BAG$''_{old,new}$ has to be supplemented, as appropriate, with other additional definitions for other specific states.

An important feature of the above definition of MAIL-BAG is that it allows two possible implementations: MAIL-BAG$'_{lot}$ displaying the oldest message in *lot* on invocation of MAIL-BAG, and MAIL-BAG$''_{old,new}$ displaying the oldest message in *new*. The choice between MAIL-BAG$'_{lot}$ and MAIL-BAG$''_{old,new}$ is non-deterministic, or is determined internally. This form of non-determinism prevails until the invocation of the process concerned for the first time, but its subsequent behaviour is fully predictable. In this particular case, however, the non-determinism continues to exist, from the user's perspective, until after the second message is seen for the first time by the user, i.e. when the set *old* ceases to be empty for the first time.

7.7.2   External Choice

Two processes may be composed to form a new process using the *external choice* operator $\Box$. It has the general form

$$P \Box Q$$

The operator $\Box$ is also called the *general* or *deterministic choice* operator. The operator $\Box$ is defined in the following manner:

$$(x : A \to P(x)) \Box (y : B \to Q(y)) \overset{def}{=} z : C \to R(z)$$

where

$$
\begin{aligned}
R(z) &= P(z) & \text{if } z \in A - B \\
&= Q(z) & \text{if } z \in B - A \\
&= P(z) \sqcap Q(z) & \text{if } z \in A \cap B
\end{aligned}
$$

Thus, if the first events offered by P and Q are disjoint, then the new process behaves according to ordinary *choice* ' $|$ ', otherwise according to the *internal choice* operator $\sqcap$. A particular case of the above is

$$
\begin{aligned}
(a \to P) \Box (b \to Q) &= (a \to P \mid b \to Q), & \text{if } a \neq b \\
&= a \to (P \sqcap Q), & \text{otherwise}
\end{aligned}
$$

The operator $\Box$ also shares the properties of $\|$ and $\sqcap$ mentioned earlier.

Observation 7.9 Properties of the operator $\Box$.

The operator $\Box$ is idempotent, commutative and associative.

Furthermore, the following properties hold:

Observation 7.10 Interaction with STOP.

$$P \mathbin{\Box} \text{STOP} = P$$

Observation 7.11 Distributive properties.

$$P \parallel (Q \mathbin{\Box} R) = (P \parallel Q) \mathbin{\Box} (P \parallel R)$$
$$P \mathbin{\Pi} (Q \mathbin{\Box} R) = (P \mathbin{\Pi} Q) \mathbin{\Box} (P \mathbin{\Pi} R)$$

Another distributive property is that which follows from Observation 7.6, namely,

$$P \mathbin{\Box} (Q \mathbin{\Pi} R) = (P \mathbin{\Box} Q) \mathbin{\Pi} (P \mathbin{\Box} R)$$

EXAMPLE

As an example of external choice, consider a very simple mail tool defined as

$$\text{MAIL} = \text{SERVICE1}_{\langle\rangle} \mathbin{\Box} \text{SERVICE2}_{\langle\rangle}$$

where

$$\text{SERVICE1}_{lot} = \quad arrive.m \to bleep \to \text{SERVICE1}_{lot \frown \langle m \rangle}$$
$$| \; print?identity(m) \to \quad (\text{if } \langle m \rangle \text{ in } lot$$
$$\text{then}(lp!m \to \text{SERVICE1}_{lot \setminus \langle m \rangle})$$
$$\text{else SERVICE1}_{lot})$$

and

$$\text{SERVICE2}_{x:lot} = \quad arrive.m \to \text{SERVICE2}_{x:lot \frown \langle m \rangle}$$
$$| \; show?identity(m) \to \quad (\text{if } \langle m \rangle \text{ in } x : lot$$
$$\text{then } (display!m \to \text{SERVICE2}_{x:lot})$$
$$\text{else } (bleep \to \text{SERVICE2}_{x:lot})$$
$$| \; delete \to \text{SERVICE2}_{lot}$$

In the above, *identity* is a one-to-one function with *identity*(m) denoting an appropriate identification of the message m. The identifiers *print, show, lp* and *display* are, respectively, communication channels for print and display requests, linking the process with a printer unit and a display unit.

Following the interpretation given above for $\Box$, it may be verified that the process MAIL corresponds to an amalgamation of the services offered by SERVICE1 and SERVICE2. It supports all the services which are exclusive to SERVICE1 or exclusive to SERVICE2 with no change. In the case of any service common to both but implemented differently, the choice about the actual service supported on MAIL is made non-deterministically. This applies to receiving a message as signified by the event *arrive.m*. An important distinction, however, is that the user may come across a different implementation of the service when receiving messages at different times; sometimes the user may hear a *bleep* and at other times they may not. Thus, an alternative but an identical definition for MAIL would be the following.

$$\text{MAIL} = \text{MAIL}'_{\langle\rangle}$$

$$\text{MAIL}'_{x:lot} = \textit{arrive.m} \rightarrow (\textit{bleep} \rightarrow \text{MAIL}'_{x:lot^\frown\langle m\rangle}$$

$$\sqcap$$

$$\text{MAIL}'_{x:lot^\frown\langle m\rangle})$$

$$| \; \textit{print?id}(m) \rightarrow (\text{if } \langle m\rangle \text{ in } x:lot$$
$$\text{then}(\textit{out!m} \rightarrow \text{MAIL}'_{x:lot\backslash\langle m\rangle})$$
$$\text{else } \text{MAIL}'_{x:lot})$$

$$| \; \textit{show?id}(m) \rightarrow (\text{if } \langle m\rangle \text{ in } x:lot$$
$$\text{then}(\textit{display!m} \rightarrow \text{MAIL}'_{x:lot})$$
$$\text{else } (\textit{bleep} \rightarrow \text{MAIL}'_{x:lot})$$

$$| \; \textit{delete} \rightarrow \text{MAIL}'_{lot}$$

7.8 Other Process Composition Operators

7.8.1 Interleaving Parallel Operator

The process constructed using *interleaving parallel* operator ||| is intended for asynchronous parallel composition of processes. Given the processes P and Q, their interleaved composition is denoted by

$$P \;|||\; Q$$

The operator is defined as

$$(x:A \rightarrow P(x)) \;|||\; (y:B \rightarrow Q(y)) = x \rightarrow (P(x) \;|||\; (y:B \rightarrow Q(y)))$$
$$\square$$
$$y \rightarrow ((x:A \rightarrow P(x)) \;|||\; Q(y))$$

It follows from the above that the operator ||| has the following properties:

Observation 7.12 Properties of the operator |||.

The operator ||| is commutative and associative.

Observation 7.13 Interaction with STOP.

$$P \;|||\; \text{STOP}_{\alpha P} = P$$

7.8.2   ! quential Composition

First, let us introduce the process SKIP, which does nothing but successfully terminates. Successful termination of any process is indicated by the special event denoted by $\checkmark$ (read as 'tick'), which can occur only as its last event.

Sequential composition of the process P followed by process Q is given by

$$P \,;\, Q$$

This process behaves as P and, if the latter successfully terminates, then it behaves as Q, with the simultaneous occurrence of the last event of P, which is a $\checkmark$, and the first event of Q. The following is a property of the operator ' ; ' :

Observation 7.14 Associativity of the operator ' ; ' .

Sequential composition is associative.

7.9   Interrupts

The most general form of interrupt in CSP is akin to sequential composition, but differs from the latter in that it neither requires nor depends on the successful termination of the leading process. This kind of interrupt is shown as

$$P \,\hat{}\, Q$$

which denotes a process that behaves as P up to the occurrence of the first event of Q and then behaves as Q regardless of the extent of P's progress.

Analogous to sequential composition, the interrupt operator $\hat{}$ has the following property:

Observation 7.15 Associativity of the operator ' $\hat{}$ ' .

The interrupt operator $\hat{}$ is associative.

A special version of the above operator is a *catastrophe*, which is denoted by $P \,\overset{\cdot}{;}\, Q$. Its definition relies on a special, usually a unique, event $\frac{\cdot}{7}$ not belonging to αP. Its meaning is perhaps best described as given below as a special case of the general interrupt given above:

$$P \,\overset{\cdot}{;}\, Q \overset{def}{=} P \,\hat{}\, (\tfrac{\cdot}{7} \to Q)$$

According to the above, the first occurrence of the event $\frac{\cdot}{7}$ transfers control from P to Q. A typical example is the event corresponding to a system shutdown.

EXAMPLE

As an example, imagine a mail tool supported on a server which is subject to frequent arbitrary shutdowns without much advanced notice to the user. In such an environment, a utility such as a mail tool must be robust and should not affect the messages held within the tool. In this case, one option is to control all user interactions by mandatory closing of the tool. The following process, which uses the symbol $\frac{1}{2}$ to denote a system shutdown:

$$
\begin{aligned}
\text{ICON} &= open \rightarrow \text{INTERFACE } \hat{\imath} \text{ HOLD} \\
\text{HOLD} &= release \rightarrow \text{ICON}
\end{aligned}
$$

where $\alpha\text{HOLD} = \{release\} \cup \alpha\text{ICON}$, is designed to accommodate such a requirement. If the event $\frac{1}{2}$ occurs, then the process INTERFACE is interrupted and completely withdrawn until the event *release* occurs, when access to the mail tool is restored.

7.10   Event Hiding

It was mentioned in Section 7.1 that the non-interactive behaviour of a system may include internal events, which may be ignored at higher levels of abstraction. This may be done in CSP explicitly in the following manner:

$P \backslash A$

The above denotes a process which does not require the cooperation of its environment on the events in the set A. In the process P the events in A occur on becoming available and are invisible to the environment. Such events do not appear in the trace of $P \backslash A$; see Section 7.13 for the term *trace*.

EXAMPLE

As an example, it is possible to define the process DISPATCHER, the continuously functioning dispatcher, by hiding the events *start* and *finish* in the process REQ-DISPATCHER given in Section 7.4:

$$\text{DISPATCHER} = \text{REQ-DISPATCHER} \backslash \{start, finish\}$$

The equality holds in this case because there is no notion of time in CSP and, as a consequence, it is impossible to distinguish between the two processes. Note that without time there is no means to account for the time taken by the internal events.

7.11   Distributivity of Generalized Operators

The material in this section has been especially developed for part of our discussion in Section 7.17.6 and is outside the CSP notation.

Most CSP operators such as $\|, \sqcap$ and $\square$ have *generalized* or *indexed versions* that may be applied to any number of processes. An example is the *generalized parallel composition operator*, which may be defined as

$$\|_{i \in 1..n} P_i \overset{def}{=} P_1 \| \left(\|_{i \in 2..n} P_i \right)$$

where all the processes are given as P_i, i being an index drawn from a set of numbers $1..n$, n being the highest applicable index. If the indices are drawn from a non-numerical set S with elements $s_1, s_2, \cdots , s_n$, the same may be shown as

$$\|_{i \in S} P_i \overset{def}{=} P_{s_1} \| P_{s_2} \| \cdots \| P_{s_n}$$

The generalized versions for other CSP operators are defined analogously.

Most of the CSP operators studied so far exhibit the property of distributivity. Let us examine here how to express this property in terms of generalized operators, when necessary.

In this connection, consider two binary associative operators $\otimes$ and $\oplus$ such that $\otimes$ is distributive over $\oplus$. Let $\bigotimes$ and $\bigoplus$ be their corresponding generalized versions. Our aim here is the introduction of a concise notation, which is equivalent to

$$P \otimes (Q \oplus R) \;=\; (P \otimes Q) \oplus (P \otimes R)$$

for the generalized operators $\bigotimes$ and $\bigoplus$. When dealing with objects that are numerically indexed, the desired expression may be written as

$$
\bigotimes_{p \in 1..s} \left(\bigoplus_{q \in 1..t} a_{p,q} \right) = (a_{1,1} \oplus a_{1,2} \oplus a_{1,3} \oplus \cdots \oplus a_{1,t}) \otimes
$$

$$
(a_{2,1} \oplus a_{2,2} \oplus a_{2,3} \oplus \cdots \oplus a_{2,t}) \otimes
$$

$$
\vdots
$$

$$
(a_{s,1} \oplus a_{s,2} \oplus a_{s,3} \oplus \cdots \oplus a_{s,t})
$$

$$
= \bigoplus_{v_1,v_2,\cdots, v_s \in 1..t} (a_{1,v_1} \otimes a_{2,v_2} \otimes a_{3,v_3} \otimes \cdots \otimes a_{s,v_s}) \qquad (B)
$$

which, despite its clarity, is not convenient for algebraic manipulations. In this respect, a more convenient notation may be introduced in the following manner.

The subscripts in terms such as $a_{i,j}$ in the above are drawn from two sets of numbers. In order to be more general, let us treat these sets as arbitrary, but finite, sets S and T. Furthermore, let the elements of S be indexed with the elements of an *index set* I such that $\#S = \#I$. This allows reference to the elements of S in functional style as $s(i_1), s(i_2), \cdots, s(i_n)$, with $i_1, i_2, \cdots, i_n \in I$. In order to reduce the number of parentheses, let us instead refer to them as $\bar{s}_{i_1}, \bar{s}_{i_2}, \cdots, \bar{s}_{i_n}$ respectively. Note that each $\bar{s}_i$ here is a constant. For the sake of generality, let us also use, instead of $a_{i,j}$ appearing in the above, an arbitrary function f from $S \times T$

to some set X appropriate to the application. In our particular case, the set X will consist of CSP processes. Let us also introduce an abbreviation,

$$\underset{v_i \in T, i \in I}{\bigodot} \overset{def}{=} \underset{(v_1, v_2, \cdots, v_{\#_I}) \in T^{\#_I}}{\bigodot}$$

for any arbitrary generalized operator $\bigodot$, $(v_1, v_2, \cdots, v_n)$ being a tuple (vector) of variables $v_1, v_2, \cdots, v_n$ and T^n being the Cartesian product of T on itself n times.

Given an appropriate index set, the desired notation for expressing (B) is presented in the following observation:

Observation 7.16 Distributivity of generalized operators.

Given that S and T are finite sets, I is an index set with respect to the set S, $\otimes$ and $\oplus$ are binary associative operators, $\bigotimes$ and $\bigoplus$ are their generalized counterparts and $\otimes$ is distributive over $\oplus$:

$$\underset{p \in S}{\bigotimes} \left(\underset{q \in T}{\bigoplus} f(p, q) \right) = \underset{v_i \in T, i \in I}{\bigoplus} \left(\underset{j \in I}{\bigotimes} f(\bar{s}_j, v_j) \right)$$

provided that j is a fresh index and does not appear as a free variable in f.

7.12 Extreme Process Behaviours

The extreme behaviours discussed here apply only to processes involving the composition operators discussed earlier. These patterns of behaviour involve the following concepts:

Deadlock – Failure of two or more processes to cooperate with each other because of not being able to agree on a common event, although they are willing to participate in other events. Note that deadlock is indistinguishable from STOP; see also Section 7.6.

Divergence – An unbounded sequence of internal (hidden or unobservable) events of a process with no communication with the external world (environment).

7.13 Traces

A *trace* is a record of progress of a process in terms of events in its evolution and is represented as a finite sequence of events. Thus, each trace represents a possible pattern of observable events and communications with the outside world. Given a process P, the set of all its traces is denoted by $trace(P)$. Often, an arbitrary trace is referred to simply as tr. There are a number of operators for manipulating traces. Some of the operations are commonly associated with sequences. These are:

$x : s$	–	A non-empty sequence, the first element of which is x and the rest is s.
$head(tr)$	–	The first element in the non-empty trace tr.
$last(tr)$	–	The last element in the non-empty trace tr.
$front(tr)$	–	The front end of the non-empty trace tr without its last element.
$tail(tr)$	–	The tail end of the non-empty trace tr without its first element.
$s \frown t$	–	The concatenation of the two sequences s and t.
$tr \downarrow e$	–	The number of occurrences of the event e (or the events in e, if e is a set) in the trace tr.
$tr \lceil e$	–	The trace obtained by restricting the events in trace tr to the event e (or the events in e if e is a set).
s in tr	–	A predicate which is true if and only if s is a contiguous subtrace of the trace tr.
$\#tr$	–	The length of the trace tr.
$s \backslash t$	–	Subtraction of sequence t from sequence s. The relevant operator may be defined as

$$
\begin{aligned}
s \backslash t &= s_1 \frown s_2, && \text{if there are two sequences } s_1, s_2 \text{ such} \\
&&& \text{that } s = s_1 \frown t \frown s_2, \\
&= s, && \text{otherwise.}
\end{aligned}
$$

For example, given a finite trace tr of the form

$$tr = \langle arrive.m_1, open, next, next, delete, send.m_2, close, open, next,$$
$$delete, previous \rangle$$

the following are some observations on tr:

$$
\begin{aligned}
tr \downarrow next &= 3 \\
head(tr) &= arrive.m_1 \\
last(tr) &= previous \\
\#tr &= 11
\end{aligned}
$$

7.14   Reasoning Primitives

The following notions are useful for reasoning about the above extreme patterns of behaviour, in particular, with reference to the global properties of the system.

Sometimes they may also be treated as complementary means (along with traces) for the specification of requirements.

Refusals   –   The sets of events that a given process refuses to take part in. Any member of this set relates to a given point in one of the possible traces of the process concerned. Given a process P, the set of all its possible refusals is denoted by $refusals(P)$.

Failures   –   A mathematical concept dealing with traces and refusals. Each failure is a pair, consisting of a finite trace and a set of events that the process concerned refuses afterwards.

This discussion is continued in the next chapter.

7.15   Requirement Specification

The form of process representation considered so far is an effective means of visualizing the behaviour of processes. The representation is also highly intuitive as abstract models. However, it is often difficult, at least initially, to conceive a model that matches the customer requirements accurately. On the other hand, customer requirements are always made as statements at the outset and, therefore, formality may be introduced relatively easily by translating them first into statements in logic. In the case of CSP, such formal sentences are written with respect to traces and other primitives in the language. In order to make such requirements explicit, CSP uses a 'meta-predicate' denoted by the symbol 'sat' relating CSP processes with sentences in predicate logic that express customer requirements of the processes concerned.

This predicate is not exclusive to purposes of specification and applies equally to expressing various observations about the behaviour of formal models. Such observations are made in the process of formal reasoning, which is a crucially important part of any formal work but, as mentioned at the outset, it is outside the scope of our brief study.

Generally, customer requirements and observations about theoretical models are expressed in the form,

P sat φ

where φ is a predicate involving a trace of P.

EXAMPLE

The following examples illustrate the use of traces for stating customer requirements as applicable to our mail tool:

(a) The mail tool dispatches a message for every message the user
requests before accepting another request for sending a message.

$$\text{MAIL-TOOL sat} \quad (0 \leq tr \downarrow \{send.m \mid m \in Message\} -$$
$$tr \downarrow \{dispatch!pack(m) \mid m \in Message\} \leq 1)$$

The above relies on the fact that tr is an arbitrary trace. Alternatively, tr
may be introduced using a universal quantifier as follows:

$$\forall \; tr \in traces(\text{MAIL-TOOL}) \; \bullet \; \cdots$$

(b) The mail tool dispatches a message after every user request
and before accepting another request.

$$\text{DISPATCHER sat}$$
$$\forall m : Message; \; a, b : \Sigma \; \bullet \; \langle a, b \rangle \text{ in } tr \wedge a = send.m \Rightarrow$$
$$b = dispatch.pack(m))$$

7.16 Event Renaming

Often there are processes which have an identical pattern of behaviour at an abstract level, but differ from one another at more concrete levels, that is, by engaging
in different events. Their mathematical formalization can be facilitated by producing a process description for one of them to start with and generating others by
explicitly renaming the event labels used in the first process.

Given a process P and an injective function f from αP to a set of event labels
appropriate to a process Q, Q may be defined as

$$Q = f(P)$$

where $f \in \alpha P \rightarrowtail \alpha Q$. The events in the alphabet of Q are determined as

$$\alpha Q = \{ f(e) \mid e \in \alpha P \}$$

An example illustrating the event renaming in this manner may be found in Section 7.17.5.

Another form of event renaming is the extension of event labels implicitly with
process identifier labels. For example, given a process P it may be convenient to
produce some copies of P and label the copies before their use for unique identification. If $i : P$ is such a labelled process derived from P, its alphabet may be
defined in terms of αP as

$$\alpha(i : P) = \{ i.e \mid e \in \alpha P \}$$

EXAMPLE

As an example, suppose that a separate mail tool is required for each individual in a given set. Two such mail tools for the individuals Jane and John may be defined from MAIL-TOOL in the following manner:

> *jane* : MAIL-TOOL
> *john* : MAIL-TOOL

As a result, the process *john* : MAIL-TOOL created for John consists, for example, of the following alphabet:

> α *john* : MAIL-TOOL =
>   {*john.open*, *john.close*, *john.next*, *john.previous*,
>   *john.delete*, *john.bleep*} $\cup$ {*john.arrive.m* | *m* $\in$ *Message*} $\cup$
>   {*john.send.m* | *m* $\in$ *Message*} $\cup$
>   {*john.dispatch.pack*(*m*) | *m* $\in$ *Message*}

In this manner, the processes modelling both Jane's and John's mail bags are provided with their own 'private' events.

7.17   An Example

This section considers in CSP the interaction of a system of telephones through a network. It illustrates further the concepts in CSP introduced in this chapter. It will also serve as a running example in the next chapter. Section 5.3.3 of Chapter 5 considers the same example in timed Petri nets, but in less detail.

7.17.1   The Preliminaries

The telephone exchange may be seen as a set of telephones working in conjunction with an underlying network. In its formalization here, *Sub* denotes a non-empty finite set of telephone subscribers or telephone identifiers and *Digit* the set of digits from 0 to 9 (and any other punctuation symbols, if necessary) used in constructing the elements of *Sub*. Let us assume, without attempting their definitions, the availability of the following predicates and the function:

(a) *isTelePrefix* is a predicate of the following type:

> *isTelePrefix* : seq *Digit* $\leftrightarrow$ *Sub*

which is true only of sequences of digits which are valid prefix subsequences of telephone identifiers.

(b) *isTeleNum* is a predicate of the following type:

$$isTeleNum : \text{seq } Digit \leftrightarrow Sub$$

which is true only of sequences of digits that are telephone identifiers.

(c) *TeleNum* is a function of the following type:

$$TeleNum : \text{seq } Digit \nrightarrow Sub$$

returning the telephone identifier for a given valid sequence of digits.

Furthermore, let the Σ_T be the alphabet of any telephone when taken in isolation.

$$\Sigma_T = \{lift, hangup, seton, setoff, ring, dialtone, eng\text{-}tone, \\ rng\text{-}tone, stop\text{-}rng\text{-}tone\} \cup \{dial.i \mid i \in Digit\}$$

Obviously, *dial* is the label of a communication channel. The intended meaning of the events in Σ_T are as follows:

lift	–	The user lifting the handset to make or answer a call.
hangup	–	The user returning the handset after making or answering a call.
seton	–	Setting the bell to ring.
setoff	–	Stopping the bell ringing.
ring	–	The bell ringing.
dialtone	–	Emitting the dial tone when the handset is lifted if the telephone is neither in use nor ringing.
error	–	Detection of an error in dialling.
rng-tone	–	Emitting the ringing tone signifying that the remote telephone is ringing in response to the call being made.
stop-rng-tone	–	Stop emitting the ringing tone.
eng-tone	–	Emitting the engaged tone signifying that the called telephone is currently busy.
connect	–	A given telephone establishing a connection with some telephone.
connect.y	–	A given telephone establishing a connection with telephone y.
be-con-to.y	–	The event of a given telephone being connected to telephone y in response to a call originating from y.
dial?i, dial!i	–	The instrument accepting the dialled digit i and the caller dialling the digit i respectively.

Let us assume as a simplification that the engaged tone stops when the handset is returned to the telephone. The same applies to disconnection of an already established connection when one of the parties involved in a telephone conversation returns the handset to the instrument.

The telephones and the ancillary facilities required for delivering the service may be represented as a set of communicating or coordinating processes. These processes model the following components of the system and the environment:

USER	–	An abstraction of the user.
TELEPHONE	–	The telephone equipment consisting of a bell, a transmitter and a receiver.
HANDSET	–	The handset. In conventional telephones, the handset contains parts of the transmitter and receiver which belong to the user interface.
BELL	–	The bell.
INSTRUMENT	–	The telephone equipment excluding the handset and the bell.
SERVICE	–	An abstraction of the services provided by the network at each telephone.
NETWORK	–	An abstraction of the behaviour of the network.
EXCHANGE	–	An abstraction of the composite behaviour of the network, the telephones and the users.

The interrelationships among the above processes are indicated diagrammatically in the Figure 7.3.

7.17.2 The Environment

The environment consists of a set of telephone users, as identified by the elements of the set *Sub*. The relevant behaviour of each user may be modelled by an abstract process USER. Its alphabet is restricted to the following:

$$\alpha\text{USER} \;=\; \{lift, hangup\} \;\cup\; \{dial!i \mid i \in Digit\}$$

while its behaviour may be given by the definition

$$\text{USER} \;=\; (\text{CALLEE} \sqcap \text{CALLER}) \,\hat{}\, \text{FINISH}$$
$$\text{FINISH} \;=\; hangup \rightarrow \text{USER}$$

where

$$\text{CALLEE} \;=\; lift \rightarrow \text{STOP}$$
$$\text{CALLER} \;=\; lift \rightarrow \mu X \bullet (dial!i \rightarrow X \sqcap \text{STOP})$$

According to the above, a user may lift the handset and select a number of digits on the dialling pad and eventually return the handset to the telephone. As will

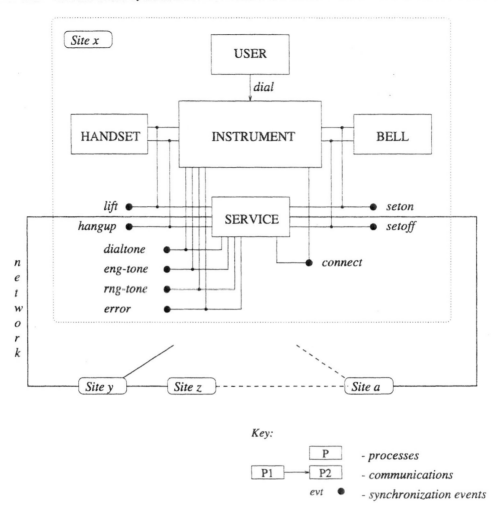

Figure 7.3 CSP example on telephone

become clear, selecting digits does not necessarily mean dialling. Obviously, this abstraction ignores the most important user activity, which is speech, because the concern here is with the mechanics of the telephone making such conversations possible among the users and not with the processes of conversations themselves.

7.17.3   Telephone

As indicated earlier, TELEPHONE represents the interactive behaviour of the processes INSTRUMENT, HANDSET and BELL. The desired behaviour can be modelled in CSP as their parallel composition:

$$\text{TELEPHONE} \ = \ \text{INSTRUMENT} \parallel \text{HANDSET} \parallel \text{BELL}$$

The alphabets of the subprocesses in TELEPHONE are restricted to the following:

$$
\begin{aligned}
\alpha\text{TELEPHONE} \ &= \ \Sigma_T \\
\alpha\text{HANDSET} \ &= \ \{lift, hangup\} \\
\alpha\text{BELL} \ &= \ \{seton, setoff, ring\} \\
\alpha\text{INSTRUMENT} \ &= \ \{seton, setoff, lift, hangup, dialtone, eng\text{-}tone, \\
& \qquad rng\text{-}tone, stop\text{-}rng\text{-}tone, connect, error\} \ \cup \\
& \qquad \{dial?i \mid i \in Digit\}
\end{aligned}
$$

The definitions of HANDSET and BELL are straightforward and are given below. The process HANDSET is used here for the sole purpose of sequencing the events *lift* and *hangup* explicitly:

$$
\begin{aligned}
\text{HANDSET} \ &= \quad lift \rightarrow hangup \rightarrow \text{HANDSET} \\
\text{BELL} \ &= \quad seton \rightarrow ((\mu X \bullet ring \rightarrow X) \,\widehat{}\, (setoff \rightarrow \text{BELL}))
\end{aligned}
$$

The definition given below for INSTRUMENT considers the behaviour of the telephone very much as an interface:

$$
\begin{aligned}
\text{INSTRUMENT} \ = \ seton \rightarrow \ &((lift \rightarrow setoff \rightarrow connect \rightarrow \text{STOP}) \,\widehat{} \\
& \qquad\qquad\qquad (hangup \rightarrow \text{INSTRUMENT}) \\
& \quad \Box \\
& (setoff \rightarrow \text{INSTRUMENT})) \\
\Box & \\
lift \rightarrow \ &((dialtone \rightarrow \text{DIAL}) \,\widehat{}\, (hangup \rightarrow \text{INSTRUMENT}))
\end{aligned}
$$

where

$$
\begin{aligned}
\text{DIAL} \ = \quad &dial?i \rightarrow \text{DIAL} \\
&\mid error \rightarrow \text{STOP} \\
&\mid rng\text{-}tone \rightarrow connect \rightarrow \text{STOP} \\
&\mid eng\text{-}tone \rightarrow \text{STOP}
\end{aligned}
$$

Let us introduce the notion of telephone site through the following:

$$
\begin{aligned}
\text{SITE} \ = \ (\text{USER} \parallel \text{TELEPHONE}) \setminus \ &(\{ring, stop\text{-}rng\text{-}tone\} \ \cup \\
&\ \{dial.i \mid i \in Digit\})
\end{aligned}
$$

where the interaction of the user with the physical components of the telephone and other purely local events are hidden.

7.17.4 Site Service

The instrument may operate in one of the two distinct modes: in IN-CALL mode for receiving incoming calls and in the calling out mode OUT-CALL. However, these operational modes are supported from outside the instrument and are a part of the service provided by the network at each telephone site. In this respect, consider a process SERVICE, the behaviour of which may be seen as the composition of the two modes using the external choice operator in CSP:

$$\text{SERVICE} \;=\; \text{IN-CALL} \;\square\; \text{OUT-CALL}$$

The use of external choice is justified by the fact that the activation of either mode is determined by the external circumstances, namely, whether or not there are incoming calls or whether the user wishes to make an outgoing call. let us restrict the alphabet of SERVICE to the following:

$$\alpha\text{SERVICE} \;=\; \{lift, hangup, seton, setoff, dialtone, eng\text{-}tone, rng\text{-}tone,$$
$$error\} \;\cup\; \{dial.i \mid i \in Digit\} \;\cup\;$$
$$\{connect.x, be\text{-}con\text{-}to.x \mid x \in Sub\}$$

As mentioned earlier, let us also assume as a simplification that the return to SERVICE of either the process IN-CALL or the process OUT-CALL implicitly disconnects any already established connection. The process IN-CALL handling incoming calls is defined as

$$\text{IN-CALL} \;=\; \prod_{y \in Sub} \text{BE-CONNECTED}_y$$
$$\text{BE-CONNECTED}_y \;=\; seton \to \; (lift \to setoff \to \; (be\text{-}con\text{-}to.y \to \text{STOP})\;\widehat{\;}$$
$$(y.hangup \to \text{STOP})\;\widehat{\;}$$
$$(hangup \to \text{SERVICE})$$
$$\square$$
$$(y.hangup \to setoff \to \text{SERVICE}))$$

Thus, in the event of more than one incoming call only one of them will succeed and the choice of the call which is to succeed is left open. The process OUT-CALL handling outgoing calls may be defined using an auxiliary process $\overline{\text{OUT-CALL}}$:

$$\overline{\text{OUT-CALL}} \;=\; lift \to ((dialtone \to \text{INDATA}_{()})\;\widehat{\;}\,(hangup \to \text{SERVICE}))$$
$$\text{INDATA}_{()} \;=\; dial.i \to \text{INDATA}_{\langle i \rangle}$$
$$\text{INDATA}_s \;=\; \text{if } isTelePrefix(s)$$
$$\text{then if } isTeleNum(s)$$
$$\text{then } \text{CONNECT}_{TeleNum(s)}$$
$$\text{else } dial.i \to \text{INDATA}_{s\;\widehat{\;}\langle i \rangle}$$
$$\text{else } error \to \text{STOP}$$

The process $\text{CONNECT}_{TeleNum(s)}$ captures the behaviour of a given telephone in making a connection with the telephone designated by the sequence of digits s. Section 7.17.5 examines in detail the desired behaviour of this process.

The definition given above for $\overline{\text{OUT-CALL}}$ is too low level in relation to the rest of our formalization and, therefore, let us define OUT-CALL from it by abstraction:

$$\text{OUT-CALL} \; = \; \overline{\text{OUT-CALL}} \setminus \{dial.i \mid i \in Digit\}$$

It is clear that $\overline{\text{OUT-CALL}}$ is a refinement of the process OUT-CALL. Because of the non-deterministic nature of the already hidden events of the form $dial.i$, an equivalent expression for the process OUT-CALL is

$$\text{OUT-CALL} \; = \; \bigsqcap_{y \in Sub} \text{OUT-CALL}_y$$

where

$$\text{OUT-CALL}_y = lift \to \quad (dialtone \to \; \text{CONNECT}_y$$
$$\square$$
$$error \to \text{STOP}) \,\widehat{}$$
$$(hangup \to \text{SERVICE})$$

7.17.5   Establishing a Telephone Connection

Let us examine closely a definition suitable for CONNECT. Obviously, it has a certain relationship with BE-CONNECTED. Consider, for example, the labelled versions of the two processes concerned in the following form:

$$x : \text{CONNECT}_y \qquad \text{and} \qquad x : \text{BE-CONNECTED}_y$$

The process $x : \text{BE-CONNECTED}_y$ describes x's behaviour in the event of y attempting the establishment of a connection with x. By contrast, $x : \text{CONNECT}_y$ describes primarily x's behaviour in the event of x attempting the establishment of a connection with y. However, the process $x : \text{CONNECT}_y$ does, in our representation, also involve events belonging to y in order to describe how y is affected in the course of this process. Note as a result that

$$x : \text{CONNECT}_y \neq y : \text{BE-CONNECTED}_x$$

However, there is a certain degree of 'symmetry' between the above two labelled processes. This should become clear from the following comparison. According to $y : \text{BE-CONNECTED}_x$, the manner in which y is affected by x attempting a connection with y is given by

$$y : \text{BE-CONNECTED}_x =$$
$$y.seton \to \; (y.lift \to y.setoff \to \; (y.be\text{-}con\text{-}to.x \to y : \text{STOP}) \,\widehat{}$$
$$(x.hangup \to y : \text{STOP}) \,\widehat{}$$
$$(y.hangup \to y : \text{SERVICE})$$
$$\square$$
$$(x.hangup \to y.setoff \to y : \text{SERVICE}))$$

The above uses the convention in process labelling and relies on $y.x.hangup$ being identical to $x.hangup$, since $x.hangup$ is one of x's private events. This is catered for shortly by the explicit renaming of events.

On the other hand, the behaviour of any telephone attempting a connection with y to be such that CONNECT$_y$ is given by

$\text{CONNECT}_y =$
$\quad y.seton \rightarrow \;\; (rng\text{-}tone \rightarrow y.lift \rightarrow y.setoff \rightarrow stop\text{-}rng\text{-}tone \rightarrow$
$\quad\quad\quad\quad\quad\quad\quad\quad\quad\quad (connect.y \rightarrow \text{STOP}))\;\widehat{}$
$\quad\quad\quad\quad\quad\quad\quad\quad\quad\quad (y.hangup \rightarrow \text{STOP})$

$\quad \square$

$\quad eng\text{-}tone \rightarrow \text{STOP}$

Note that according to the above a call ending up in an engaged tone forces termination of the call and does not permit waiting for the callee telephone to become free. The adoption of the above as a definition for CONNECT$_y$ leads to x's behaviour as given by

$x : \text{CONNECT}_y =$
$\quad x.y.seton \rightarrow \;\; (x.rng\text{-}tone \rightarrow x.y.lift \rightarrow x.y.setoff \rightarrow$
$\quad\quad\quad\quad\quad\quad\quad\quad x.stop\text{-}rng\text{-}tone \rightarrow (x.connect.y \rightarrow x : \text{STOP}))\;\widehat{}$
$\quad\quad\quad\quad\quad\quad\quad\quad\quad\quad\quad (x.y.hangup \rightarrow x : \text{STOP})$

$\quad \square$

$\quad x.eng\text{-}tone \rightarrow x : \text{STOP}$

Consideration of the synchronization of the processes $x : \text{CONNECT}_y$ and $y : \text{BE-CONNECTED}_x$:

$$f(x, y)(x : \text{CONNECT}_y) \parallel g(x, y)(y : \text{BE-CONNECTED}_x)$$

is based on two renaming functions $f(x, y)$ and $g(x, y)$ such that

$\{x.y.seton \mapsto y.seton, x.y.setoff \mapsto y.setoff,$
$x.y.lift \mapsto y.lift, x.y.hangup \mapsto y.hangup\} \quad\quad\quad\quad \subseteq \;\; f(x, y)$
$\{y.be\text{-}con\text{-}to.x \mapsto x.connect.y, \; y.x.hangup \mapsto x.hangup\} \;\; \subseteq \;\; g(x, y)$

where the functions $f(x, y)$ and $g(x, y)$ are not fully specified for the time being. The above leads to the following:

$f(x, y)(x : \text{CONNECT}_y) \parallel g(x, y)(y : \text{BE-CONNECTED}_x) =$
$\quad (y.seton \rightarrow \;\; (x.rng\text{-}tone \rightarrow y.lift \rightarrow y.setoff \rightarrow x.stop\text{-}rng\text{-}tone \rightarrow$
$\quad\quad\quad\quad\quad\quad\quad\quad\quad\quad (x.connect.y \rightarrow x : \text{STOP}))\;\widehat{}$
$\quad\quad\quad\quad\quad\quad\quad\quad\quad\quad (y.hangup \rightarrow x : \text{STOP})$

$\quad \square$

$\quad x.eng\text{-}tone \rightarrow x : \text{STOP})$
$\quad \parallel$
$\quad (y.seton \rightarrow \;\; (y.lift \rightarrow y.setoff \rightarrow \;\; (x.connect.y \rightarrow y : \text{STOP})\;\widehat{}$
$\quad\quad\quad\quad\quad\quad\quad\quad\quad\quad (x.hangup \rightarrow y : \text{STOP})\;\widehat{}$
$\quad\quad\quad\quad\quad\quad\quad\quad\quad\quad (y.hangup \rightarrow y : \text{SERVICE})$

$\quad\quad\quad\quad \square$

$\quad\quad (x.hangup \rightarrow y.setoff \rightarrow y : \text{SERVICE}))) \quad\quad\quad\quad\quad\quad (C)$

It is clear that the two processes in the above parallel composition will synchronize in the common events such as $y.seton, y.setoff, y.lift$ and $x.connect.y$ in their alphabets. The above interaction is brought about by an interaction of the form

$$f(x : \text{SERVICE}) \parallel g(y : \text{SERVICE})$$

between the processes SERVICE at x and y, leading immediately to the following outcome:

$$f(x : \text{OUT-CALL}_y) \parallel g(y : \text{BE-CONNECTED}_x)$$

Let us consider other possible outcomes of parallel composition of the processes SERVICE at x and y. Firstly, the interaction of two mutual OUT-CALL's:

$$f(x : \text{OUT-CALL}) \parallel g(y : \text{OUT-CALL})$$

Eventually, it will lead to the parallel composition of two labelled processes of CONNECT in the following manner:

$$
\begin{aligned}
f(x, y)(x : &\text{CONNECT}_y) \parallel g(x, y)(y : \text{CONNECT}_x) = \\
(y.seton \rightarrow \ &(x.rng\text{-}tone \rightarrow y.lift \rightarrow y.setoff \rightarrow x.stop\text{-}rng\text{-}tone \rightarrow \\
&\qquad\qquad (x.connect.y \rightarrow x : \text{STOP}) \,\hat{} \\
&\qquad\qquad (y.hangup \rightarrow x : \text{STOP}) \\
\square& \\
x.eng\text{-}tone &\rightarrow x : \text{STOP}) \\
\parallel& \\
(x.seton \rightarrow \ &(y.rng\text{-}tone \rightarrow x.lift \rightarrow x.setoff \rightarrow y.stop\text{-}rng\text{-}tone \rightarrow \\
&\qquad\qquad (y.connect.x \rightarrow y : \text{STOP}) \,\hat{} \\
&\qquad\qquad (x.hangup \rightarrow y : \text{STOP}) \\
\square& \\
y.eng\text{-}tone &\rightarrow y : \text{STOP})
\end{aligned}
\tag{D}
$$

The above two processes do not share any events in common in their alphabets other than $x.connect.y$ and $y.connect.x$. When considered in isolation, these two processes may interleave their private events in any arbitrary order, but according to the order in their definitions. However, there is potential deadlock because the events $x.connect.y$ and $y.connect.x$ are common to both alphabets and yet are different. However, deadlock would not take place in practice. Firstly, the two processes are subprocesses of OUT-CALL, each of which is guarded by a unique occurrence of *lift* and none can engage in this event for a second time until the control is returned to SERVICE. As each of the operand processes OUT-CALL reaches the stage of the process CONNECT, the only possible event is *eng-tone*, which leads to STOP, in turn requiring the event *hangup* to break the impasse.

Let us now consider another possible outcome of the composition of the two SERVICE's in parallel:

$$f(x : \text{IN–CALL}) \parallel g(y : \text{IN–CALL})$$

If it ever comes about, the above brings about immediately the interaction shown in (D). A set of possible first events in the above for x and y are the events $x.seton$ and $y.seton$. These two events are certainly a possibility due to telephone calls by third parties, but not on a mutual basis between a pair of telephones. This is because the process IN–CALL eventually relies on the participation of the environment. However, the model allows for this possibility. Mutually incoming calls are conceivable only if faults in the network are admissible, but no such faulty behaviour is considered here.

Returning to the more general case, a connection is established through the interaction of the processes SERVICE belonging to two separate telephones. In our model this comes about through the composition of

$$f(x : \text{SERVICE}) \parallel g(y : \text{SERVICE})$$

provided that x dials y and y dials x. The labelling functions f and g for this general case may be defined as

$$
\begin{aligned}
f = \ & \text{id } \alpha(x : \text{SERVICE}) \oplus \{x.y.seton \mapsto y.seton, \\
& x.y.setoff \mapsto y.setoff, x.y.lift \mapsto y.lift, x.y.hangup \mapsto y.hangup, \\
& x.be\text{-}con\text{-}to.y \mapsto y.connect.x, x.connect \mapsto x.connect.y \mid \\
& x, y \in Sub\} \\
g = \ & \text{id } \alpha(y : \text{SERVICE}) \oplus \{y.x.seton \mapsto x.seton, \\
& y.x.setoff \mapsto x.setoff, y.x.lift \mapsto x.lift, y.x.hangup \mapsto x.hangup, \\
& y.be\text{-}con\text{-}to.x \mapsto x.connect.y, y.connect \mapsto y.connect.x \mid \\
& x, y \in Sub\}
\end{aligned}
$$

where $\oplus$ is the relational overriding operator. The above parallel composition of the services at x and y may be manipulated algebraically in order to make more explicit the possible forms of their interaction:

$$
\begin{aligned}
& \text{CONNECTION}(x, y) \\
& = f(x : \text{SERVICE}) \parallel g(y : \text{SERVICE}) \\
& = f(x : \text{IN–CALL } \square \text{ OUT–CALL}) \parallel g(y : \text{IN–CALL } \square \text{ OUT–CALL}) \\
& = (f(x : \text{IN–CALL}) \parallel g(y : \text{IN–CALL})) \qquad \square \\
& \quad (f(x : \text{IN–CALL}) \parallel g(y : \text{OUT–CALL})) \qquad \square \\
& \quad (f(x : \text{OUT–CALL}) \parallel g(y : \text{IN–CALL})) \qquad \square \\
& \quad (f(x : \text{OUT–CALL}) \parallel g(y : \text{OUT–CALL}))
\end{aligned}
$$

If neither x dials y nor y dials x, the process CONNECTION(x, y) may never be invoked. However, the network must be prepared to provide this service, should there ever be such a request. As mentioned earlier, the following interaction:

$$(f(x : \text{IN–CALL}) \parallel g(y : \text{IN–CALL}))$$

may never take place, although it appears above in the process CONNECTION(x, y).

7.17.6   Telephone Network

In this section, let us attempt to define a formal model of the telephone network, first on the basis of our intuition and then more formally.

Telephone Network – A Preliminary Model

According to the development so far, a network of services is seen as an interaction of connections between every pair of locally available services in the network. Thus, it may be defined as the following composition:

$$\text{NETWORK} \quad = \quad \Big\|_{x,y \in Sub \ \wedge \ x \neq y} \text{CONNECTION}(x, y)$$

The interaction of the network with the individual telephones may then be defined as

$$\text{EXCHANGE} \quad = \quad \text{NETWORK} \parallel \Big(\Big\|_{x \in Sub} x : \text{SITE}\Big)$$

The parallel composition operator $\parallel$ in the above requires the correct synchronization of events both local to telephone sites and the telephone interconnection events such as $x.connect.y$ over the network.

Although the above captures the behaviour of the network and the telephones to a large extent, it has a certain limitation, namely, it is difficult to be absolutely certain about whether the model is complete with respect to possible interactions. In order to overcome this limitation, let us adopt a more formal approach. This is the subject of the rest of this section.

Telephone Network – A Rigorous Model

In developing a more rigorous model of the network, let us focus our attention on the derivation of an expression equivalent to $\text{CONNECTION}(x, y)$, introduced in Section 7.17.5. For brevity, the consideration of the interactions with the processes SITE is omitted. Also, let us treat the network as a direct interaction between the processes SERVICE without the use of any intermediate process definitions. The task is to derive an expression for such an intermediate process. As before, it is possible to achieve any desired synchronization with an appropriate renaming function $f(x)$ for each labelled process $x : \text{SERVICE}$. The derivation begins with this understanding. It also relies on Observation 7.16 given on page 131 on the distributivity of certain generalized CSP operators:

$$\text{NETWORK}$$
$$= \quad \Big\|_{x \in Sub} f(x)(x : \text{SERVICE})$$
$$= \quad \Big\|_{x \in Sub} (f(x)(x : \text{IN-CALL}) \ \Box \ f(x)(x : \text{OUT-CALL}))$$

def. of SERVICE

$$= \left\|_{x \in Sub} \left(f(x) \left(\square_{z \in \{1,2\}} (x : \text{CALL-TYPE}^z) \right) \right) \right.$$

where

$$\text{CALL-TYPE}^1 = \text{IN-CALL}$$
$$\text{CALL-TYPE}^2 = \text{OUT-CALL}$$

a notational modification

$$= \square_{z_i \in \{1,2\}, i \in I} \left(\left\|_{j \in I} f(\bar{x}_j)(\bar{x}_j : \text{CALL-TYPE}^{z_j}) \right) \right.$$

Observation 7.16

$$= \square_{z_i \in \{1,2\}, i \in I} \left(\left\|_{j \in I} \left(\square_{y \in Sub} f(\bar{x}_j, y)(\bar{x}_j : \text{CALL-TYPE}_y^{z_j}) \right) \right) \right.$$

where

$$\text{CALL-TYPE}_y^1 = \text{BE-CONNECTED}_y$$
$$\text{CALL-TYPE}_y^2 = \text{OUT-CALL}_y$$

def. of IN-CALL and OUT-CALL

$$= \square_{z_i \in \{1,2\}, i \in I} \left(\square_{y_k \in Sub, k \in I} \right.$$

$$\left. \left(\left\|_{l \in I} f(\bar{x}_j, y_l)(\bar{x}_j : \text{CALL-TYPE}_{y_l}^{z_j}) \right) \right) \right.$$

Observation 7.16

(E)

Thus, when considering the interaction of different telephones over the network, our analysis may start from the following term:

$$\left\|_{l \in I} f(\bar{x}_j, y_l)(\bar{x}_j : \text{CALL-TYPE}_{y_l}^{z_j}) \right. \tag{F}$$

$$= f(\bar{x}_j, \bar{y}_1)(\bar{x}_j : \text{BE-CONNECTED}_{\bar{y}_1}) \quad \| \quad f(\bar{x}_j, \bar{y}_2)(\bar{x}_j : \text{BE-CONNECTED}_{\bar{y}_2}) \|$$

$$\vdots \qquad\qquad\qquad\qquad \vdots$$

$$f(\bar{x}_j, \bar{y}_n)(\bar{x}_j : \text{BE-CONNECTED}_{\bar{y}_n}) \quad \| \quad f(\bar{x}_j, \bar{y}_1)(\bar{x}_j : \text{OUT-CALL}_{\bar{y}_1}) \|$$

$$\vdots \qquad\qquad\qquad\qquad \vdots$$

$$f(\bar{x}_j, \bar{y}_{n-1})(\bar{x}_j : \text{OUT-CALL}_{\bar{y}_{n-1}}) \quad \| \quad f(\bar{x}_j, \bar{y}_n)(\bar{x}_j : \text{OUT-CALL}_{\bar{y}_n})$$

with just one form of interaction. In the above, $\bar{x}_j$ is a specific element of *Sub* as identified by the index j, whereas y_l is a variable ranging over the elements in *Sub*. For example, $\bar{x}_j : \text{CALL-TYPE}_{y_l}^2$ is a process initiated by the specific site at $\bar{x}_i$ for a telephone connection potentially with any site $y_l \in Sub$. The expression (F) is therefore the most comprehensive expression and deals with all possible interactions of a range of processes when working in parallel. For example, as shown in the expanded version, it includes explicitly the potentially interleaved parallel evolution of those processes not participating in a given telephone connection. Obviously, other forms of interactions due to non-deterministic operators come into effect as we move outward from the term shown in (F) in the final expression (E) derived for the process NETWORK.

7.18 Bibliographical Notes

The theory of Communicating Sequential Processes due to Hoare [59] serves as the foundation of many important works devoted to the study of concurrent systems. Brookes [16] provides the mathematical foundations for defining CSP operators as given in this chapter. An alternative powerful framework to CSP with many similarities is used by Milner [101]. Another mathematically related reference is Hennessy [58]. The underlying mathematical frameworks of these approaches are often referred to as process algebras. A good introduction to other approaches such as LOTOS may be found in Turner [161].

In relation to the example on telephony in Section 7.17, the reader may find interesting the works by Kay and Reed [73, 74] using timed CSP and Mataga and Zave [99] using Z.

7.19 Exercises

1. State the following requirements using process traces and then give for each the definitions of processes concerned separately. Substantiate the process definitions informally.

   The requirements of a reliable transmission system include the following:

   (a) Every message input from the port *in* is eventually output from the port *out*.

   (b) The orderings of the input and output messages in (a) are the same.

   (c) No messages in (a) are duplicated.

   (d) No messages in (a) are generated internally.

   (e) Messages are input from the port *in* and are output alternately from the ports *out*1 and *out*2.

2. Revise the definitions given in Section 7.17 on telephones to account for the following additional requirements or the changes in requirements:

   (a) According to the definition of the processes IN–CALL and BELL in Section 7.17.3, once started, a telephone will continue to ring until it is answered. Make the necessary changes to all relevant processes and introduce, if required, any new processes in order to limit the ringing of the bell to M or N times depending on the current setting of a 'timer'. If the two numbers are different, for example if $M < N$, then this will provide the user with a facility to switch between a short sequence of bell rings and a longer one.

   (b) In the event of more than one incoming telephone call, the process SERVICE in Section 7.17.4 chooses just one of them for service. All other calls fail to establish a connection and are forced to terminate following an engaged tone.

Modify, if necessary, the definition of IN-CALL such that callers may wait in the engaged mode until the callee becomes free and can answer any waiting call.

(c) Provide the definitions that will enable the incorporation of a telephone answering machine as part of some telephone sites.

(d) Suggest the revisions required for providing a telephone conferencing facility.

3. An engine monitoring system monitors a number of engines at a specific regular rate. Two individual sensors in each engine monitor the temperature and the pressure at particular locations and another sensor monitors the state of a switch. If the monitored parameters are detected to be outside certain predefined limits, the monitoring system outputs a message, raises an alarm and produces the historical record of monitored variables over the last n cycles. The permitted temperatures are as follows. If the pressure is above p_1 and the switch is in the *on* position then the temperature must be below t_1 degrees and it must be below t_2 degrees otherwise; t_1 and t_2 being such that $t_2 > t_1$.

Produce a CSP model for the engine monitoring system.

4. In preparation for the discussion in the next chapter, review the deficiencies of the telephone system as modelled in Section 7.17 that can be attributed to a lack of any notion of time in CSP, except for the implicit precedence ordering of events.

Chapter 8

An Overview of Timed CSP

This chapter is a basic introduction to Timed CSP and it extends the concepts covered in the previous chapter in order to deal with time. Part of the notation used in the literature tends to vary and we have adopted that which we feel is most appropriate to our study. Such variations, however, do not apply to the basic concepts, which are well understood and can be applied to practical problems without any confusion.

To a limited extent this chapter relies on the telephone system discussed in Section 7.17 of the previous chapter, Chapter 7, as an illustrative example.

8.1 Extensions to Basic Concepts

8.1.1 Semantic Models of Timed CSP

The best way to commence our study of realtime CSP is to compare it with untimed CSP with respect to the basic concepts and fundamental ideas. A natural framework for this comparison is abstraction. Subjecting all variants of CSP, including untimed CSP, to this comparison, we observe that untimed CSP occupies the highest level of abstraction, where the events have no notion of time other than an implicit precedence relation. An important function of this relation is to define the events that are synchronized. The timed extensions of CSP become richer formalisms in this hierarchy, enabling lower levels of abstraction. This conforms with the philosophy that systems and processes have to be specified, and subsequently designed in a hierarchical manner so that the abstraction and reasoning are manageable in the simplest form in each stage of the development process.

In all timed versions of CSP, the events may be indexed (tagged) with their time of occurrence. However, the extra timing information alone is not adequate for dealing with the behaviour of typical realtime systems. As mentioned in Section 1.2.3 of Chapter 1, there are properties such as *safety* and *liveness*, which are important for qualitative characterization of realtime systems.

For dealing with such aspects, Timed CSP provides several semantic models, each with special capabilities that enable a greater understanding of a chosen aspect of the system. These models are organized in such a way that the truth about various observations is preserved as one moves from a more abstract model to a more concrete one in the hierarchy of models. Obviously, this hierarchy is defined by an ordering relation on models. For our purposes, only one of these models would suffice. In particular, our discussion is based primarily on what is called the *Timed Failures Model*, which also happens to be the most commonly used model in practice. Here it is possible to understand the potential behaviour of a system through time, as well as its precluded behaviours. It is worth noting also that the model underlying Hoare's CSP is the *Untimed Traces Model*, extended with failures in order to deal with non-determinism.

8.1.2   Timed Events

The events in CSP are 'instantaneous' events. Intuitively, each of these may correspond to the beginning or the end of a durative event. Using the terminology of Event Logic introduced in Section 3.6.4 of Chapter 3, the events in CSP may be regarded as *punctual* events. However, as we begin to consider Timed CSP, this link with Event Logic breaks down. This is because according to Timed CSP the time of occurrence of any event can be precisely located at an instant of time, whereas this is not the case in Event Logic, except in the case of a very special kind of instantaneous events – 'momentary' events.

A timed event is a pair (t, e), t being the time of occurrence (or observation, depending on the interpretation) of event e. For brevity, sometimes the same is referred to as e_t. Timed events are of the type

$$T\Sigma \stackrel{def}{=} \mathbb{R}^+ \times \Sigma$$

according to which the time values are drawn from the set of non-negative real numbers $\mathbb{R}^+$ and the event labels from a set Σ.

Although we used the term 'duration' above in relation to events, Timed CSP assumes that all events take zero time to occur. Durative events may be represented by two such instantaneous events: one for the beginning and the other for the end. On the other hand, delays and other kinds of timing information may be made explicit by other means.

Timed CSP relies on a special event ε for the purpose of reasoning. ε is a distinguished 'non-event' such that $\varepsilon \notin \Sigma$. Another special event is $\checkmark$, introduced in the previous chapter. It is a distinguished event signalling the successful termination of a process.

Another notation used in Timed CSP is δ, which is a certain fixed measure of time used for various purposes, but primarily as a default 'duration' or delay for events with unspecified durations. Although its necessity is considered fundamental in the earlier works, the more recent works have moved away from this position in favour of making such delays explicit as necessary.

8.1.3 Timed Traces

A *timed trace* is a chronologically ordered finite sequence of timed events. That is,

$$\langle (t_1, e_1), (t_2, e_2) \rangle \text{ in } tr. \Rightarrow t_1 < t_2$$

EXAMPLE

A possible timed trace of the telephone equipment is

$$\langle (1, \textit{lift}), (2, \textit{dial}.3), (4, \textit{dial}.7), (5, \textit{dial}.6), (10, \textit{eng-tone}), (11, \textit{eng-tone}),$$
$$(12, \textit{eng-tone}), (13, \textit{connect}), (20, \textit{hangup}) \rangle$$

The above corresponds to a scenario where the handset of a telephone has been lifted at time 1, three digits have been input via *dial* at times 2, 4 and 5, the engaged tone has been emitted continuously at times 10, 11 and 12, a connection with a remote telephone has been made at time 13, and, finally, at time 20, the handset has been returned to the instrument.

A more detailed discussion about traces follows in Section 8.8.3. Part of the relevant notation has already been introduced in Section 7.13 in the previous chapter.

8.2 Deterministic Processes

WAIT t is a primitive timed process, which does nothing but successfully terminate after t time units. It is a process that produces a specified delay and is a generalization of SKIP such that

WAIT $0 = $ SKIP

Event prefixing without any choice in CSP is interpreted in Timed CSP as an event prefixing with a default delay of δ time units. Thus,

$$a \to P$$

is the process which is prepared to engage in the event a first and, if a occurs, it then behaves as the process P after a delay of δ time units. This is to be interpreted as not passing the control over to P for δ units of time. The reason for adopting a default minimum 'duration' is to ensure that distinct events are separable in the trace and, more importantly, to ensure that progress takes place at a finite rate and to eliminate the occurrence of an infinite number of events in a finite interval of time.

The above process may be generalized to incur a specified delay t in the following manner:

$$a \overset{t}{\rightarrow} P \overset{def}{=} a \rightarrow \text{WAIT}(t - \delta) \; ; \; P$$

provided that $t \geq \delta$. The above denotes the process which is prepared to engage in a first and, if a occurs, then behaves as the process P after a delay of t time units. See Section 8.4.5 for the sequential composition operator ' ; '.

EXAMPLE

As an example consider, in relation to the example from telephony in the previous chapter, inputting a digit via the channel *dial*. In this respect, the following two definitions are identical if $\delta = 1$ and describes a situation where INDATA$_{()}$ (see page 140) can make any progress only three time units after the communication event *dial.i* has taken place:

$$dial.i \overset{3}{\rightarrow} \text{INDATA}_{\langle i \rangle}$$
$$= \quad dial.i \rightarrow \text{WAIT } 2; \; \text{INDATA}_{\langle i \rangle}$$

It is possible to generalize event prefixing further as

$$a \overset{t_1 .. t_2}{\rightarrow} P$$

in order to account for a non-deterministic delay of the process P lasting from t_1 to t_2 time units from the time of occurrence of the event a:

$$a \overset{t_1 .. t_2}{\rightarrow} P \overset{def}{=} a \rightarrow \text{WAIT } T \; ; \; P$$

where

$$T = \{t - \delta \mid t \in t_1 .. t_2 \wedge t \geq \delta\}$$

and the definition of WAIT T is given in Section 8.4.2.

8.3   Recursion

Recursive processes are interpreted in two different ways, namely, as,

(a) *Delayed recursion*, with an implicit delay of δ with each recursive call to X:

$$\mu X \bullet P$$

(b) *Immediate recursion*, involving no delay with recursive calls to X:

$$\mu\, X \circ P$$

This form of recursion is intended especially for use in mutual recursion between different processes. It also makes the task of keeping track of process durations easier.

EXAMPLE

As an example, consider the timing of the process BELL given in Section 7.17.3, which consists of a recursive process within it for modelling the ringing of the bell every time the event *ring* occurs. According to its timed version given below, the bell starts ringing δ time units after the event *seton* and keeps ringing every time unit until it is set off by the event *setoff*. The bell returns to its original state $(1 + \delta)$ time units after this event:

$$\text{BELL} \;=\; \textit{seton} \rightarrow ((\mu\, X \circ \textit{ring} \xrightarrow{1} X)\triangledown(\textit{setoff} \xrightarrow{1} \text{BELL}))$$

Note that the above uses the notation $\triangledown$ from Timed CSP for the CSP interrupt operator $\hat{\ }$. An interesting question here concerns the appropriateness of the instantaneous event *ring* for modelling the ringing of the telephone, since this is a durative event according to our common understanding. If it is a drawback, it can be overcome, as mentioned earlier, by having two separate events as markers for the start and the finish of each ring. Note here that the use of delayed and immediate recursion would have an effect on the time taken by the above process.

8.4 Process Composition

8.4.1 Parallel Composition

Parallel composition of the processes P and Q, denoted by $P \parallel Q$, has a number of variants in Timed CSP, each making explicit the events synchronizing the operand processes P and Q. These are as follows:

(a) Parallel composition requiring the cooperation of events in the intersection of the sets A and B only:

$$P\;_A\!\!\parallel_B Q$$

In the above, P may progress independently of Q over the events in $A - B$ and Q may do so independently of Q over the events in $B - A$, but both processes must synchronize over the events in $A \cap B$. This operator removes the restriction of the parallel composition operator $\|$ in untimed CSP on synchronization strictly over all events in $\alpha P \cap \alpha Q$.

EXAMPLE

As an example, let us modify the processes USER $\overline{\text{OUT-CALL}}$, given in Sections 7.17.2 and 7.17.4, so that the instrument behaves as a toy telephone, which allows a child to play with it continuously by pressing its buttons. Let us assume that the toy emits a message *'well done'* via the output channel *out* for every two *timely* entries of digits. Let the behaviour of both the child and the toy, including the timing aspects, be given by

$$
\begin{aligned}
\text{CHILD} \;&=\; \textit{lift} \to \mu X \bullet \textit{dial}.i \to X \\
&\quad \mid \textit{hangup} \xrightarrow{2} \text{CHILD} \\
\text{TOY} \;&=\; \textit{lift} \xrightarrow{1} \textit{dialtone} \xrightarrow{1} \text{TOY}_{\langle\rangle} \\
\text{TOY}_x \;&=\; \text{if } \#x = 2 \\
&\qquad \text{then } \textit{out!'well done'} \xrightarrow{2} \text{TOY}_{\langle\rangle} \\
&\qquad \text{else } \textit{dial}.i \xrightarrow{1} \text{TOY}_{x^\frown\langle i\rangle} \\
&\qquad \square \\
&\qquad \textit{hangup} \xrightarrow{2} \text{TOY}
\end{aligned}
$$

According to the process CHILD and assuming $\delta = 1$, the fastest speed at which the child can perform events is one event per every t time units, where $t \geq 2$. If the process TOY is placed in parallel with the process CHILD, the interaction between the two would be as follows:

$$
\text{CHILD} \parallel \text{TOY} \;=\; \textit{lift} \xrightarrow{1} \textit{dialtone} \xrightarrow{1} \text{PLAY}
$$

where

$$
\begin{aligned}
\text{PLAY} \;&=\; \textit{dial}.i \xrightarrow{1} \text{PRESS} \parallel \text{TOY}_{\langle i\rangle} \\
&\quad \mid \textit{hangup} \xrightarrow{2} \text{CHILD} \parallel \text{TOY} \\
&=\; \textit{dial}.i \xrightarrow{1} \textit{dial}.j \xrightarrow{1} \text{PRESS} \parallel \text{TOY}_{\langle i,\, j\rangle} \\
&\qquad \mid \textit{hangup} \xrightarrow{2} \text{CHILD} \parallel \text{TOY} \\
&\quad \mid \textit{hangup} \xrightarrow{2} \text{CHILD} \parallel \text{TOY} \\
&=\; \textit{dial}.i \xrightarrow{1} \textit{dial}.j \xrightarrow{1} \textit{out!'well done'} \xrightarrow{2} \text{PLAY} \\
&\qquad\qquad \mid \textit{hangup} \xrightarrow{2} \text{CHILD} \parallel \text{TOY} \\
&\qquad \mid \textit{hangup} \xrightarrow{2} \text{CHILD} \parallel \text{TOY} \\
&\quad \mid \textit{hangup} \xrightarrow{2} \text{CHILD} \parallel \text{TOY}
\end{aligned}
$$

and

$$
\begin{aligned}
\text{PRESS} \;=\; &\mu X \bullet \textit{dial}.i \to X \\
&\mid \textit{hangup} \to \text{USER}
\end{aligned}
$$

The above would not be a correct description of behaviour if $\delta \ll 1$ and the child were assumed to be able to engage in the events such as *dial!i* faster than one event per every time unit. In this case, the definition should permit the timed events from the child's alphabet, but outside the alphabet of the toy to occur freely between the synchronized events shared by the two. This is because, according to the definition of TOY, the different stages of its evolution are effectively disabled for precise lengths of time after each event, whereas the child would become free to press buttons faster with a minimum separation time δ between successive presses.

(b) Parallel composition requiring the cooperation of events in a set C is denoted by the following:

$$P \underset{C}{\parallel} Q$$

EXAMPLE

The notation is of use in situations such as

$$\text{INSTRUMENT} \underset{\{lift,hangup\}}{\parallel} \text{HANDSET}$$

$$\text{INSTRUMENT} \underset{\{seton,setoff\}}{\parallel} \text{BELL}$$

$$\text{HANDSET} \underset{\varnothing}{\parallel} \text{BELL}$$

in relation to TELEPHONE, in order to make explicit the form of the desired synchronization.

(c) *Simple parallel* composition operator $\parallel$ requiring the cooperation of all events in the alphabet. It assumes that both P and Q have identical alphabets. Therefore,

$$P \parallel Q \overset{def}{=} P \underset{\Sigma}{\parallel} Q$$

(d) The parallel composition operator has a *generalized* or an *indexed version* that may be applied to any number of processes. It is defined as

$$\underset{i \in 1..n}{\parallel} P_i \overset{def}{=} P_1 _{A_1}\parallel_{\left(\bigcup_{i \in 2..n} A_i\right)} \left(\underset{i \in 2..n}{\parallel} P_i\right)$$

where all the processes and their synchronizing events are given, respectively, as P_i and A_i, i being an index drawn from $1..n$ and n being the maximum applicable index. Analogous generalized versions exist for other composition operators discussed later.

EXAMPLE

As an illustration, consider an alternative definition of the form

$$\text{TELEPHONE} \quad = \quad \|_{i \in 1..3} \text{SUBSYS}_i$$

for the process TELEPHONE, where the subsystems SUBSYS$_i$ are

$$
\begin{aligned}
\text{SUBSYS}_1 &= \text{INSTRUMENT} \\
\text{SUBSYS}_2 &= \text{HANDSET} \\
\text{SUBSYS}_3 &= \text{BELL}
\end{aligned}
$$

The above form is useful for working out the role of the different synchronizing events of the processes concerned.

8.4.2   Composition based on Internal Choice

Timed version of *internal* or *non-deterministic choice* operator has, syntactically, the same form as that in untimed CSP:

$$P \sqcap Q$$

The above process permits two options, namely, P or Q, for the implementation of the process $P \sqcap Q$. What is distinctive in Timed CSP are the timing aspects. It is worth noting in this respect that the time taken by $P \sqcap Q$ may be either the time taken by P or the time taken by Q.

This operator also permits a non-deterministic extension to the process WAIT t. This generalized version WAIT T is defined as

$$\text{WAIT } T \stackrel{def}{=} \sqcap_{t \in T} \text{WAIT } t$$

where $\sqcap_{t \in T}$ is the generalized version of $\sqcap$. WAIT T thus incorporates a non-deterministic delay drawn from the set of time values in T. This process is used for modelling scenarios where it is impossible, or difficult, to predict which operand process might actually take place.

EXAMPLE

As an example of internal choice, consider two different types of telephone. With the telephones of one type, one can dial a telephone number of any destination, whereas the telephones of the other type are connected to a single fixed destination and, therefore, do not accept dialling. If the choice between these telephone types is to be left open, it is necessary to redefine the process $\overline{\text{OUT-CALL}}$ given in Section 7.17.4 in the following manner:

$$\overline{\text{OUT-CALL}}^1 \;=\; \textit{lift} \xrightarrow{2} ((\textit{dialtone} \to \text{INDATA}_{\langle\rangle}) \; \triangledown \; \text{TERMINATE})$$
$$\sqcap$$
$$\textit{lift} \xrightarrow{1} (\text{CONNECT}_x) \; \triangledown \; \text{TERMINATE})$$

where

$$\text{TERMINATE} = \textit{hangup} \to \text{SERVICE}$$

and $x \in Sub$ and is an unknown. The process $\overline{\text{OUT-CALL}}^1$ is always ready to engage in the event *lift*. Since this event is common to both choices, the behaviour of the service is fully predictable one unit time after it is observed for the first time. Thus, according to the above, any given telephone exhibits only one of the two possible types of behaviour in the calling out mode.

By contrast, the following version of OUT-CALL would potentially exhibit both patterns of behaviour:

$$\overline{\text{OUT-CALL}}^2 \;=\; \textit{lift} \xrightarrow{1} (\text{WAIT1} \;;\; \textit{dialtone} \to \text{INDATA}_{\langle\rangle}$$
$$\sqcap$$
$$\text{CONNECT}_x)$$
$$\triangledown$$
$$\text{TERMINATE}$$

where, as explained in Section 8.4.5, sequential composition ' ; ' incurs zero time. According to the above definition, the process $\overline{\text{OUT-CALL}}^2$ may sometimes let the user dial a telephone number and make the connection two time units after lifting the handset, and at other times connect the telephone with the telephone designated by x one time unit after lifting the handset without prompting the user to dial a number.

Thus, the internal choice operator in Timed CSP works in the same manner as in untimed CSP but, in addition, embodies the non-deterministic process delay and other implications of timed events.

8.4.3 Composition based on External Choice

The timed *external* or *deterministic* choice operator also resembles its untimed counterpart. The process

$$P \;\square\; Q$$

may behave either as P or Q, depending on the choice exercised by the environment. If the choice of the environment is exclusive to P and is a timed event of P, then the above process will behave as P. Similarly, if the choice is exclusive to Q, then the process $P \;\square\; Q$ will behave as Q. On the other hand, if the choice belongs to both P or Q, then it will behave as the non-deterministic choice $P \;\sqcap\; Q$. With respect to timing aspects, the process $P \;\square\; Q$ may last the time taken by either P or Q. Obviously, it is necessary to consider now the durations of processes, arising from choices common to both P and Q.

8.4.4   Interleaving Parallel Operator

Given two processes P and Q, the timed *parallel interleaving* operator $|||$ produces the process

$$P \,|||\, Q$$

where P and Q evolve asynchronously, neither requiring any cooperation from the other party. Any trace of $P \,|||\, Q$ is an interleaving of one trace of P and another of Q. It follows from the definitions given in Section 8.4.1 that $|||$ is a special case of the operator $\|$ such that

$$P \,|||\, Q = P \overset{\|}{\underset{\varnothing}{}} Q$$

Two events a and b in the process given below:

$$(a \longrightarrow P) \,|||\, (b \longrightarrow Q)$$

may occur simultaneously in Timed CSP, whereas in untimed CSP a and b may occur only sequentially.

8.4.5   Sequential Composition

There are two timed versions of sequential composition. These are as follows:

(a) Sequential composition without any delay:

$$P \,;\, Q$$

This process behaves as P, and if the latter successfully terminates, then it behaves as Q with the simultaneous occurrence of the last event of P, which is a $\checkmark$ taking no time at all, and the first event of Q. Note also that

$$\text{WAIT } t_1 \,;\, \text{WAIT } t_2 \overset{def}{=} \text{WAIT}(t_1 + t_2)$$

(b) Sequential composition with a delay of δ:

$$P \,\overset{\circ}{\underset{9}{}}\, Q \overset{def}{=} P \,;\, \text{WAIT } \delta \,;\, Q$$

8.5   Additional Timed Composition Operators

This section provides certain practical means for dealing with different aspects of realtime systems discussed in Section 1.1.5 of Chapter 1.

8.5.1 Timeout Operator

The *timeout operator* is denoted by $\rhd$. $P \overset{t}{\rhd} Q$ denotes a process which is willing to behave as P provided that P engages in an observable event within t time units. Otherwise, the process $P \overset{t}{\rhd} Q$ behaves as Q. Thus, P gains control first but, if unable to make any progress at all, it transfers control to Q but incurring a delay of t:

$$P \overset{t}{\rhd} Q \overset{def}{=} (P \;\square\; \text{WAIT } t \; ; \; a \rightarrow Q)\backslash a$$

Another equivalent notation is $P \rhd \{t\}\; Q$. [Let us use the latter when dealing with long variable names or expressions for t.] A non-empty trace tr of $(P \overset{t}{\rhd} Q)$ is a trace of P if the first event e_{t_1} in tr is such that $t_1 < t$; otherwise, tr is a trace of Q.

EXAMPLE

The use of this operator may be illustrated by considering a timeout after the dialling of a digit. In the revised definition given below for the process INDATA, the timeout is limited to *digit–time* time units:

$$\text{INDATA}_x \;\; = \;\; dial.i \rightarrow \text{CHECK}_{x^\frown \langle i \rangle}$$
$$\rhd \; digit{-}time$$
$$\text{TERMINATE}$$

where

$$\text{CHECK}_x \;\; = \;\; \text{if } \textit{isTelePrefix}(x)$$
$$\text{then if } \textit{isTeleNum}(x)$$
$$\text{then CONNECT}_{\textit{TeleNum}(x)}$$
$$\text{else INDATA}_x$$
$$\text{else TERMINATE}$$

According to INDATA$_x$, failure to dial a digit within *digit–time* time units leaves no option but to terminate using the instrument with the event *hangup*. On the other hand, dialling a digit within *digit–time* time units would allow the user, if dialling is yet to be completed, to dial the next digit with a newly reset timeout.

8.5.2 Timed Interrupt Operator

The timed *interrupt* operator is denoted by $\overset{t}{\underset{t}{\wr}}$. The process

$$P \overset{t}{\underset{t}{\wr}} Q$$

behaves as P for at most t time units, and if P does not terminate within t time units, then the above process behaves from then on as Q. P gains control first but transfers it to Q at t, but incurring a delay of t.

In terms of an arbitrary trace tr of $P \overset{t}{\vartriangleright} Q$, tr is a trace of P up to t, but from the time $(t + \delta)$ it is a trace of Q.

EXAMPLE

As an example, consider another revision to the process INDATA as given below:

$$\text{INDATA}_x \;=\; (dial.i \to \text{CHECK}_{x^\frown \langle i \rangle}$$
$$\vartriangleright digit\text{-}time$$
$$\text{TERMINATE)} \overset{\triangledown}{_{dial\text{-}time}} \;\; \text{TERMINATE}$$

Unlike the timeout operator, where the control is taken away when the user fails to take any action within the permitted time, the interrupt operator takes away control from the operand on its left hand side at the specified time regardless of the progress being made. Thus, in the event that the *dial-time* expires in the middle of dialling a number or its checking, the above process would force termination of the calling out process.

8.5.3   Event Interrupt Operator

The *event interrupt* operator is denoted by $P \overset{\triangledown}{_e} Q$. In the process denoted by

$$P \overset{\triangledown}{_e} Q$$

P gains control first, but transfers it to Q at the first occurrence of e and incurring a delay of δ. The trace of $P \overset{\triangledown}{_e} Q$ may again be decomposed into a trace of P up to the first occurrence of e and into a trace of Q beyond e.

The operator is useful for modelling 'cause and effect'. A particular case in point, in relation to our telephone example, are the interruptions caused by the local events *setoff* and *hangup* to the operation of the instrument.

EXAMPLE

The above is illustrated by the following revised processes for BELL and $\overline{\text{OUT-CALL}}$:

$$\text{BELL} \quad = \quad seton \to ((\mu X \bullet ring \to X) \overset{\triangledown}{_{setoff}} \text{BELL})$$
$$\overline{\text{OUT-CALL}} \;=\; lift \to ((dialtone \to \text{INDATA}_{\langle\rangle}) \overset{\triangledown}{_{hangup}} \quad \text{SERVICE})$$

Compared to the corresponding definitions in CSP, the above definitions are more explicit about the interrupting events and are clearer about the function of the process that takes over.

Table 8.1 A comparison of constructs of CSP and timed CSP

Construct in untimed CSP	Timed CSP		
	Equivalents in timed CSP	Minimum duration	Comments
STOP	STOP	∞	Timed failures models
	$\perp$	∞	do not consider these
SKIP	SKIP	0	
	WAIT t	t	The specific delay t
	WAIT T	$min\ T$	A non-deterministic delay drawn from the set T
$a \to P$	$a \to P$	$\delta + t_P$	With an implicit delay δ
	$a \xrightarrow{t} P$	$t + t_P$	With an explicit delay t
$P\ ;\ Q$	$P\ ;\ Q$	$t_P + t_Q$	With no additional delay
	$P\ \overset{\circ}{\underset{\circ}{}}\ Q$	$t_P + t_Q + \delta$	With an implicit additional delay δ
$P \sqcap Q$	$P \sqcap Q$	$min\ \{t_P, t_Q\}$	With a non-deterministic delay drawn from the possible delays of P and Q individually
$P \parallel Q$	$P \parallel Q$	$max\ \{t_P, t_Q\}$	
	$P_A \parallel_B Q$	$min\ \{t_P, t_Q\}$	
$P \mathbin{\square} Q$	$P \mathbin{\square} Q$	$min\ \{t_P, t_Q\}$	
$P \mathbin{\vert\vert\vert} Q$	$P \mathbin{\vert\vert\vert} Q$	$min\ \{t_P, t_Q\}$	
$\mu X \bullet P$	$\mu X \bullet P$		With an implicit delay δ for each recursive call
	$\mu X \circ P$		No additional delays with recursive calls
$(P \mathbin{\square} Q) \sqcap Q$	$P \overset{t}{\triangleright} Q$	$min\ \{t_P, t_Q + t\}$	
$P \char94 Q$	$P \overset{h}{\underset{t}{?}} Q$	$min\ \{t_P, t_Q + t\}$	
	$P \mathbin{\triangledown} Q$	$min\ \{t_P, t_Q + t\}$	
$P \char94 (e \to Q)$	$P \overset{\triangledown}{e} Q$	$min\ \{t_P, t_Q + \delta\}$	

8.6 Correspondence of Untimed and Timed Constructs

Table 8.1 presents a brief comparison of notations used in CSP and Timed CSP. The comparison is made mainly on a syntactic basis. The term *minimum duration* is used for the minimum time taken by the process concerned from initiation to termination. Note that t_P and t_Q in Table 8.1 denote the *minimum durations* of some (terminating) processes P and Q respectively. Also, $min\ S$ and $max\ S$ return, respectively, the minimum and maximum values of the non-empty set S of time values.

8.7   Liveness and Safety

In CSP, due to the fact that events must take place in synchronization with all the relevant processes, it is not possible to state liveness requirements with reference to any process. This is because one can always conceive of an environment where a given process deadlocks immediately. In this connection, Timed CSP relies on the notion of *refusal* in order to express liveness requirements indirectly. A refusal is basically a set of timed events that a process might refuse. Instead of requiring as a liveness requirement that a particular event e must occur at time t, it is possible to stipulate that the process concerned must not refuse to participate in the event e at time t, should its environment choose to do so. Thus refusals are an indirect means for stating liveness requirements.

Refusals are in fact a more general concept enabling the expression of not only liveness properties, but also safety properties – properties that prohibit the occurrence of certain undesirable events. The use of refusals in this sense is quite obvious from the term *refusal* itself.

In the case of events that require the participation of both the system and the environment, the events are *offered* and they *occur* with the participation of both parties. The *internal* events that belong only to one of the parties do not require the participation of the other party.

As far as the rate of progress is concerned, events common to both the system and its environment must take place as soon as both parties are willing to engage in them. The internal events, on the other hand, take place as soon as they are enabled. This understanding is often termed *maximal progress*. Implicit in this is the assumption that no events are inhibited due to lack of processors or other resources. Thus, a notion that is closely linked with maximal progress is *maximal parallelism*, introduced in Section 1.2.3 of Chapter 1.

8.8   Behaviours

8.8.1   Refusals

A *timed refusal* is a set of timed events, $\aleph$, which a given process refuses to participate in. If (t, e) is a specific timed refusal, i.e. an element of $\aleph$, it signifies that the process concerned refuses to participate in the event e at time t.

A *refusal token* is a set of timed refusals whose domain equals a finite contiguous stretch of time. That is, the events concerned are refused during that interval of time. For example, the refusal token

$$[t_1 \mathrel{..} t_2) \times \{a, b\}$$

denotes the timed refusal by a process to take part in the events a and b at or after time t_1 until time t_2 exclusively.

8.8.2   A Formal Representation of Behaviours

Liveness and safety requirements do not always relate to timed events in isolation, but to a number of events. In other words, there is always a wider context determining the occurrence of events. This contextual information is provided by pairing refusals with traces. Thus, a *behaviour* or a *timed failure* in Timed CSP is a pair

$$(tr, \aleph)$$

In effect, tr is a record of what can be observed in the behaviour of the process concerned and $\aleph$ is a record of timed events refused by the process in the same behaviour. A timed event e_t may be present in both tr and $\aleph$, meaning that no more occurrences of e_t are allowed in tr.

A process in the Timed Failures Model therefore consists of the set of all its possible behaviours. Process requirements are stated with respect to behaviours in the form

$$P \text{ sat } \varphi(tr, \aleph)$$

where φ is a formula in predicate logic involving one or both components of an arbitrary behaviour $(tr, \aleph)$. Such a statement requires all possible behaviours of the process P to satisfy φ. An example is

$$P \text{ sat } a \notin \sigma(tr)$$

where a is a specific event and $\sigma(tr)$ is the set of 'untimed' events in tr; see below for the definition.

The above form of specification concerns the behaviour of the system independently of its environment. In cases where it is necessary to consider the role of the environment specifically, the specification takes the following general form

$$P \text{ sat } (\varphi_{env}(tr, \aleph) \Rightarrow \varphi_{sys}(tr, \aleph))$$

where φ_{env} and φ_{sys} are predicates specifying, respectively, an assumed behaviour of the environment and an expected behaviour of the system. Thus, φ_{env} qualifies the environmental circumstances under which φ_{sys} has to be met. If P is supposed to meet the requirement φ_{sys} in any environment, then

$$\varphi_{env}(tr, \aleph) \Leftrightarrow \text{true}$$

leading to the original form of specification on the system on its own.

8.8.3   Traces of Processes

As explained above, each of the possible observations of a system in the Timed Failures Model is partly represented by a distinct trace. Traces in Timed CSP are finite sequences of timed events, as compared with similar sequences of untimed events in CSP. As noted earlier, a pair such as (t, e) in a trace tr denotes the occurrence of the event e at time t in the corresponding observation.

Here let us use the notation presented in Section 3.1.1 of Chapter 3 for representing contiguous stretches of time (intervals). These are: $[t_1, t_2], [t_1, t_2), (t_1, t_2]$ and (t_1, t_2), a square bracket signifying inclusion of the relevant end point in the interval, and a parenthesis signifying its exclusion from the interval.

It is often necessary to manipulate a given trace in order to produce sequences of some specific events, to consider the events over a specific stretch of time, or to extract the event label or the time of occurrence of a timed event leading (or ending) such a trace. The operations given below are intended for this purpose. Some of the operations are extensions of those given in Section 7.13 for untimed traces and some are substitute definitions.

$\sigma(tr)$ –   The set of 'untimed' events occurring in the trace tr. The events in $\sigma(tr)$ do not contain the time tag of the corresponding timed events in tr.

$tr \downarrow e$ –   The number of occurrences of the untimed event e (or the events in e, if e is a set) in the trace tr.

$tr \lfloor e$ –   The trace obtained by restricting the events in trace tr to the untimed event e (or the events in e, if e is a set).

s in tr –   A predicate stating that s is a contiguous subtrace of the trace tr.

$begin(tr)$ –   The time of the first event in the trace tr. It may be defined as

$$begin(\langle\rangle) \;=\; \infty$$
$$begin(\langle(t, a)\rangle \frown s) \;=\; t$$

$end(tr)$ –   The time of the last event in the trace tr. It may be defined as

$$end(\langle\rangle) \;=\; 0$$
$$end(s \frown \langle(t, a)\rangle) \;=\; t$$

$first(tr)$ –   The first untimed event in the trace tr. It may be defined as

$$first(\langle\rangle) \;=\; \varepsilon$$
$$first(\langle(t, a)\rangle \frown s) \;=\; a$$

$last(tr)$ –   The last untimed event in the trace tr. It may be defined as

$$last(\langle\rangle) \;=\; \varepsilon$$
$$last(s \frown \langle(t, a)\rangle) \;=\; a$$

$head(tr)$ – The first timed event in the trace tr. It may be defined as

$$head(tr) = (begin(tr), first(tr))$$

$foot(tr)$ – The last timed event in the trace tr. It may be defined as

$$foot(tr) = (end(tr), last(tr))$$

$tr{\uparrow}I$ – A subtrace obtained by restricting the times of the events in the trace tr to the times in the interval I.

$tr{\restriction}t$ – A subtrace obtained by restricting the times of the events in the trace tr to the times from 0 up to and inclusive of t.

$tr{\upharpoonright}t$ – A subtrace obtained by restricting the times of the events in the trace tr to the times beyond (and exclusive of) t.

8.8.4 Timed Refusals

Analogous notations to the above are applicable to timed refusals $\aleph$. These are outlined below:

$\sigma(\aleph)$ · – The set of untimed events occurring in the refusal set $\aleph$.

$begin(\aleph)$ – The time of the first event in the timed refusals $\aleph$. Note that if $\aleph = \varnothing$ then $begin(\aleph) = \infty$.

$end(\aleph)$ – The time of the last event in the timed refusals $\aleph$. Note that if $\aleph = \varnothing$ then $end(\aleph) = 0$.

$begin(tr, \aleph)$ – $begin(tr, \aleph) = min\{begin(tr), begin(\aleph)\}$.

$end(tr, \aleph)$ – $begin(tr, \aleph) = max\{end(tr), end(\aleph)\}$.

$\aleph{\restriction}t$ – Refusal token obtained by restricting the times of the events in $\aleph$ to the times from 0 up to t (exclusive of t).

$\aleph{\upharpoonright}t$ – Refusal token obtained by restricting the times of the events in $\aleph$ to the times beyond and inclusive of t.

8.9 High Level Constructs

There are various predicates about events and traces which recur frequently in the specification of behaviours. In this respect, it is desirable to introduce some high level constructs for convenience in specification and for improving readability of process descriptions. The following is a list of such constructs defined with respect to an arbitrary behaviour $(tr, \aleph)$. Other variables appearing there are as follows: A and B are sets of events; a is an arbitrary event; t, t_1, t_2 and t_ε are time values; and I is an arbitrary time interval. The variables which are not explicitly quantified are to be treated as universally quantified.

On events

A onlyif B $\overset{def}{\Leftrightarrow}$ $A \cap \sigma(tr) \neq \varnothing \Rightarrow B \cap \sigma(tr) \neq \varnothing$
$\Leftrightarrow$ $B \cap \sigma(tr) = \varnothing \Rightarrow A \cap \sigma(tr) = \varnothing$
Any event in A could occur only if at least one event in B occurs.

unique A $\overset{def}{\Leftrightarrow}$ $\forall a \bullet a \in A \Rightarrow \#(tr \restriction a) \leq 1$
Any given event in A could occur at most once.

· exclusive A $\overset{def}{\Leftrightarrow}$ $\#(tr \restriction A) \leq 1$
Only one event from A could occur and if it occurs then only once.

On events, times and intervals

A at I $\overset{def}{\Leftrightarrow}$ $A \cap \sigma(tr \uparrow I) \neq \varnothing$
At least one event in A occurs in the interval I.

a at t $\overset{def}{\Leftrightarrow}$ $a \in \sigma(tr \uparrow [t, t])$
The event a occurs at time t.

a not at t $\overset{def}{\Leftrightarrow}$ $\neg (a$ at $t)$
The event a does not occur at time t.

A stops$_{t_\varepsilon}$ B $\overset{def}{\Leftrightarrow}$ $\forall t \bullet A$ at $[t, t] \Rightarrow B \cap (tr \restriction t + t_\varepsilon) = \varnothing$
No events from B could occur for t_ε time units after an event from A occurs.

A causes$_{t_\varepsilon}$ B $\overset{def}{\Leftrightarrow}$ $\forall a, t \bullet a \in A \wedge a$ at $t \wedge C$ not at $(t, t + t_\varepsilon) \wedge$
unless C $\qquad end(tr, \aleph) \geq t + t_\varepsilon \Rightarrow B$ at $[t, t + t_\varepsilon]$
An event from B must occur within t_ε time units after an event from A, unless an event from C has already occurred.

A causes$_{t_\varepsilon}$ B $\overset{def}{\Leftrightarrow}$ A causes$_{t_\varepsilon}$ B unless $\varnothing$
$\Leftrightarrow$ $\forall a, t \bullet a \in A \wedge a$ at $t \wedge end(tr, \aleph) \geq t + t_\varepsilon \Rightarrow B$ at $[t, t + t_\varepsilon]$
Within t_ε time units after an event from A, an event from B must occur.

a ref t $\overset{def}{\Leftrightarrow}$ $a \in \sigma(\aleph \uparrow [t, t])$
The event a is refused at time t.

a ref I $\overset{def}{\Leftrightarrow}$ $I \times \{a\} \subseteq \aleph$
The event a is refused during the open interval I.

es ref I $\overset{def}{\Leftrightarrow}$ $I \times es \subseteq \aleph$
The events in the set es are refused during the open interval I.

a live t $\overset{def}{\Leftrightarrow}$ a at $t \vee \neg a$ ref t
The event a occurs at time t or at least it is not refused at t.

$$a \text{ live } [t_1, t_2] \overset{def}{\Leftrightarrow} \forall t \bullet t \in [t_1, t_2) \Rightarrow (\exists t' \bullet t' \in [t_1, t] \wedge a \text{ at } t') \vee \neg a \text{ ref } t$$

> The event a occurs some time during the interval $[t_1, t_2)$ or it is not refused at t.

$$es \text{ live } [t_1, t_2] \overset{def}{\Leftrightarrow} \forall a \bullet a \in es \Rightarrow a \text{ live } [t_1, t_2]$$

> All events in the set of events es are live over the interval $[t_1, t_2]$ in the above sense.

Other useful predicates may be defined in the above manner. The predicates at and ref given above are overloaded with multiple meanings. The applicable meaning of each should become clear from the context. The predicate not at is defined above only for the negation of the single event predicate at .

8.10   Extreme Process Behaviours

The Timed Failures Model allows the consideration of liveness and safety characteristics. There are other global characteristics such as *deadlock* and *divergence* relevant to the study of realtime systems, but not addressed within the Timed Failures Model. There are, however, other Timed CSP models which can deal with such issues. These global characteristics have the following temporal properties:

(a) *Deadlock*
    Deadlock may be recognized in Timed CSP after a finite amount of time.
(b) *Divergence*
    Divergence cannot be recognized after a finite amount of time. As mentioned earlier, divergence is identified by $\perp$.
(c) *Timed Stability*
    If the process P is associated with a stability value $\alpha : \mathbb{R}$, where $\alpha \geq 0$, then any internal activity of P may last at most α time units, that is, *stability* is guaranteed after α time units.

8.11   Illustrative Examples

The following examples illustrate the use of Timed CSP for the modelling and specification of realtime systems. Each example starts with an informal description prior to its formalization in Timed CSP.

8.11.1   Mouse

Informal Description:

> An object such as a text file or an executable program stored in a computer may be selected for some further manipulation

by clicking a button on the mouse (pointing device) once, while
pointing it at the displayed icon of the object concerned. At
any given time, at most only one object may be selected. Double
clicking of the button in rapid succession within some t time
units enables the object to be immediately displayed or
initiated, as applicable.

One may formalize the realtime aspects in the above problem by means of two
basic processes OBJECT and MOUSE with the obvious meanings. Furthermore, let
us consider the following events:

click	–	Clicking the appropriate button of the mouse while pointing it at a given object.
unclick	–	An event that restores the state of an already selected (that is, by a single click) object to its state prior to selection.
nilclick	–	Clicking the mouse while pointing it at no object.

Note that our formalization has no notion of a user or an environment. Had there
been one, *unclick* would not have been an event in its alphabet. Thus, *unclick* is
supposed to be an event shared only by the mouse and by the application objects.
The process alphabets are

$$\alpha\text{OBJECT} = \{click, unclick\}$$
$$\alpha\text{MOUSE} = \{nilclick\} \cup \{x.click, x.unclick \mid x \in Application\}$$

where *Application* is the set of application objects. The definition for the process
OBJECT is shown below.

$$\text{OBJECT} = click \rightarrow (click \rightarrow \text{OPEN}$$
$$\rhd (t - \delta)$$
$$\text{SELECT} \ {}_{\text{unclick}}^{\triangledown} \ \text{OBJECT})$$

where OPEN denotes the process that opens the content of the given object or
initiates it, and SELECT the process that selects the object for some other manipulation. These two processes are not defined here. The behaviour of the mouse may
be defined as

$$\text{MOUSE} = \quad x.click \rightarrow \text{MOUSE}_x$$
$$\mid nilclick \rightarrow \text{MOUSE}$$

$$\text{MOUSE}_x = \quad x.click \rightarrow \text{MOUSE}_x$$
$$\mid y.click \rightarrow x.unclick \rightarrow \text{MOUSE}_y$$
$$\mid nilclick \rightarrow x.unclick \rightarrow \text{MOUSE}$$

where $x \neq y$. The interaction of the mouse with the objects in *Application* may
be given as the parallel composition

$$\text{MOUSE} \parallel \left(\underset{x \, \in Application}{\left|\left|\right|\right.} x : \text{OBJECT} \right)$$

This situation may not be captured adequately in untimed CSP.

8.11.2 Realtime Locking System

Informal Description:

> A realtime locking system consists of two independent locks,
> which are to be operated by separate keys within a small time
> interval T_1 of each other. For security reasons, only three
> attempts may be made within any interval lasting T_2 time units,
> and consecutive attempts must be separated from each other by
> at least T_3 time units. Failure of all three attempts in
> succession disables the locking system for T_4 time units.
> Successful operation deactivates the system for T_5 time units,
> permitting access to whatever items are kept under lock. After
> this time the system automatically returns to the locked state.

Let us first attempt a process definition for the following in timed CSP, so that
it exhibits the desired timing characteristics as closely as possible. Let us then
specify the same as predicates on timed traces and timed failures.

The behaviour of the locking system may be defined using the following more
primitive processes KEY and LOCK such that:

$$\alpha\text{KEY} = \{turn\}$$
$$\alpha\text{LOCK} = \{turn, deactivate, activate\}$$

The intended meaning of these processes and events is clear from the words chosen
as identifiers. The timed versions of these processes are as follows:

$$\text{KEY} = turn \rightarrow \text{KEY}$$

$$\text{LOCK} = turn \rightarrow (\text{LOCK-AUX}$$
$$\square$$
$$(\text{WAIT } (T_3 - \delta);$$
$$(turn \rightarrow \text{LOCK-AUX}$$
$$\square$$
$$(\text{WAIT } (T_3 - \delta);$$
$$(turn \rightarrow \text{LOCK-AUX}$$
$$\square$$
$$(\text{WAIT } (T_3 - \delta) \; ; \; \text{WAIT } T_4 \; ; \; \text{LOCK})))))))$$

where

$$\text{LOCK-AUX} = deactivate \xrightarrow{T_5 - \delta} activate \rightarrow \text{LOCK}$$

In defining the complete locking system, the processes KEY and LOCK may be
composed in the following manner:

$$\text{LOCK-SYS} = f_1(l : \text{LOCK}) \parallel f_2(r : \text{LOCK}) \parallel (l : \text{KEY}) \parallel\mid r : \text{KEY})$$

where

$$
\begin{aligned}
f_1 &= \{l.turn \mapsto l.turn, \; l.deactivate \mapsto deact, \; l.activate \mapsto act\} \\
f_2 &= \{r.turn \mapsto r.turn, \; r.deactivate \mapsto deact, \; r.activate \mapsto act\}
\end{aligned}
$$

Note that the above does not capture all the timing requirements and, in particular, the requirements that the two locks have to be operated within T_1 time units and that the number of attempts in any interval of length T_2 time units is limited to three attempts.

An alternative to a process definition intended as a specification such as the above is to state the requirements as sentences in predicate logic. These are written with respect to the set of traces and the set of refusals.

One may state some of the requirements as follows as behavioural specifications. The temporal variables such as the t and t_is appearing there are universally quantified. Given that $tr \in traces(\text{LOCK})$:

(a) The consecutive key turnings must be T_3 time units apart:

$$turn \text{ at } t \Rightarrow turn \text{ ref } (t, t + T_3)$$

(b) Three consecutive turns within any interval of length T_2 disable the locking system for T_4 time units:

$$\langle(t_1, turn), (t_2, turn), (t_3, turn)\rangle \text{ in } tr \wedge (t_3 - t_1) \le T_2 \Rightarrow$$
$$turn \text{ ref } (t_3, t_3 + T_4)$$

(c) The lock is activated $T_5 - \delta$ time units after the deactivation:

$$deactivate \text{ at } t \Rightarrow activate \notin \sigma(tr{\uparrow}(t, t + T_5 - \delta)) \wedge$$
$$activate \in \sigma(tr{\mid}t + T_5 - \delta)$$

A similar statement may be made with respect to the operability of the lock by key.

Similarly, given that $tr \in traces(\text{LOCK-SYS})$, one may state that

(d) If the locks are operated by keys within T_1 time units of each other, then the locking system will be deactivated some time afterwards:

$$(\langle(t_1, l.turn), (t_2, r.turn)\rangle \text{ in } tr \vee \langle(t_1, r.turn), (t_2, l.turn)\rangle \text{ in } tr)$$
$$\wedge (t_2 - t_1) \le T_1 \Rightarrow deact \notin \sigma(\aleph{\mid}t_2)$$

8.11.3   Railway Level Crossing

The physical features of the system being considered are based on level crossings[1]
found commonly in many urban areas. The timing requirements considered are
purely hypothetical.

Informal Description:

> The system being considered is a level crossing, operated
> automatically using information provided by sensors monitoring
> incoming trains. The crossing consists of a barrier preventing
> access to the railway tracks while they are in use by the rail
> transport. It also consists of a set of lights indicating, as
> appropriate, the current, or the impending, state of the tracks
> for the benefit of the road users (i.e. pedestrians and
> motorists).
>
> The times of approach and passing of trains (as monitored by
> sensors) can be arbitrary from the point of view of the system.
> Twin red warning lights are to be activated within T_1 time
> units from the time of approach, and each must continue to
> flash by being on and off for T_2 time units alternately. The
> green lights for the road users come into effect within T_3 time
> units after raising the barrier. Raising and lowering the
> barrier take up to a maximum of T_4 time units altogether. The
> lowering of the barrier takes T_5 time units after detecting
> an approaching train but completes before the train begins to
> cross the junction. The barrier is raised T_6 time units after
> the train has passed the crossing.

Specification in Untimed CSP

The first task is to represent the problem in untimed CSP. In this respect, consider
the following processes:

RED	–	The behaviour of a red light.
GREEN	–	The behaviour of a green light.
ALT-RED	–	Alternately flashing red lights.
LIGHTS	–	A system coordinating one green light and a pair of alternately flashing red lights.
RAIL-TRAFFIC	–	The behaviour of rail traffic as detected by the sensors.
BARRIER	–	The behaviour of the barrier across the road at the level crossing.

---

[1] A level crossing is an intersection of a railway and a road at ground level.

The alphabets of the above processes are as follows:

$$
\begin{aligned}
\alpha\text{RED} &= \{red\text{-}on,\ red\text{-}off\} \\
\alpha\text{GREEN} &= \{turn\text{-}green\} \\
\alpha\text{ALT-RED} &= \{left,\ right\} \\
\alpha\text{LIGHTS} &= \{approach,\ left,\ right,\ raise,\ turn\text{-}green\} \\
\alpha\text{RAIL-TRAFFIC} &= \{approach,\ gone\} \\
\alpha\text{BARRIER} &= \{approach,\ gone,\ raise,\ lower\}
\end{aligned}
$$

The event *approach* signifies a train approaching the crossing and the event *gone* signifies a train clearing the junction after crossing it. Both events are as detected by the sensors. Note that sensors have no means of identifying trains and, therefore, the events are not associated with specific trains. In other words, these events correspond to arrival of sensor signals. The identifiers *left* and *right* denote the events of turning on the red warning lights on the left and right hand sides respectively (and not the end points of time intervals referred to in Sections 3.1.1 and 3.2). The labels of other events are sufficiently intuitive to infer their intended meaning. The behaviour of the system of lights may be formalized as follows:

$$
\begin{aligned}
\text{RED} &= \mu X \bullet (red\text{-}on \rightarrow red\text{-}off \rightarrow X) \\
\text{ALT-RED} &= f_1(l : \text{RED}) \parallel f_2(r : (red\text{-}off \rightarrow \text{RED})) \\
\text{GREEN} &= turn\text{-}green \rightarrow \text{STOP} \\
\text{LIGHTS} &= \text{GREEN} \,\widehat{}\ (approach \rightarrow \text{ALT-RED}) \,\widehat{}\ (raise \rightarrow \text{LIGHTS})
\end{aligned}
$$

f_1 and f_2 are functions for renaming the events of labelled processes l and r, and designed to achieve the desired synchronization of flashing red lights.

$$
\begin{aligned}
f_1 &= \{l.red\text{-}on \mapsto left,\ l.red\text{-}off \mapsto right\} \\
f_2 &= \{r.red\text{-}on \mapsto right,\ r.red\text{-}off \mapsto left\}
\end{aligned}
$$

The rest of the level crossing may be defined as

$$
\begin{aligned}
\text{RAIL-TRAFFIC} &= approach \rightarrow gone \rightarrow \text{RAIL-TRAFFIC} \\
\text{BARRIER} &= approach \rightarrow lower \rightarrow gone \rightarrow raise \rightarrow \text{BARRIER}
\end{aligned}
$$

Finally, let us define the behaviour of the process LEVEL-CROSSING by composing the above two processes and the process LIGHTS in parallel:

$$
\text{LEVEL-CROSSING} = \text{LIGHTS} \parallel \text{BARRIER} \parallel \text{RAIL-TRAFFIC}
$$

The above abstraction models only the synchronization of events and ignores the states brought about by their occurrence.

Specification in Timed CSP

The timing of events concerned may now be dealt with by enriching the above CSP model in the following manner:

$$\text{RED} \;=\; \mu X \circ (\textit{red-on} \xrightarrow{T_2} \textit{red-off} \xrightarrow{T_2} X)$$

$$\text{ALT--RED} \;=\; f_1(l : \text{RED}) \parallel f_2(r : (\textit{red-off} \xrightarrow{T_2} \text{RED}))$$

$$\text{GREEN} \;=\; \textit{turn-green} \rightarrow \text{STOP}$$

$$\text{LIGHTS} \;=\; \text{GREEN} \underset{\textit{approach}}{\overset{\triangledown}{}} \text{WAIT } 0 \,.\,.\, T_1; \; \text{ALT--RED} \underset{\textit{raise}}{\overset{\triangledown}{}}$$

$$\text{WAIT } 0 \,.\,.\, T_3; \; \text{LIGHTS}$$

Other timing aspects are as shown below:

$$\text{RAIL--TRAFFIC} \;=\; (\textit{approach} \rightarrow \text{STOP}) \underset{\textit{gone}}{\overset{\triangledown}{}} \text{RAIL--TRAFFIC}$$

$$\text{BARRIER} \;=\; (\textit{approach} \xrightarrow{T_5} \textit{lower} \xrightarrow{0..T_4} \text{STOP}) \underset{\textit{gone}}{\overset{\triangledown}{}}$$

$$(\text{WAIT } T_6; \; (\textit{raise} \xrightarrow{0..T_4} \text{BARRIER}))$$

with the expression for LEVEL--CROSSING remaining unchanged. Note that the events *lower* and *raise* in the timed version of the process BARRIER correspond respectively to the events of starting to lower the barrier and starting to raise it.

Enhancements

The above includes a number of simplifications. For example, it assumes that the crossing consists of a single track and that it may be used only by one train in a given cycle of operation. This may not be acceptable and, on the contrary, the crossing may be required to accommodate any number of trains within a single cycle of operation. This applies especially to crossings that consist of multiple tracks.

In order to allow for this, let us revise one of the CSP definitions given earlier as follows:

$$\text{BARRIER} \;=\; (\textit{approach} \rightarrow \mu X \bullet (\textit{lower} \rightarrow \text{SKIP}$$

$$\mid \textit{approach} \rightarrow (X \; ; \; \widetilde{Z}))) \; ;$$

$$(\textit{gone} \rightarrow \text{SKIP}) \; ; \; \widetilde{V} \; ;$$

$$(\textit{raise} \rightarrow \text{BARRIER})$$

where

$$\widetilde{Z} \;=\; \mu Z \bullet (\textit{gone} \rightarrow \text{SKIP}$$

$$\mid \textit{approach} \rightarrow (\widetilde{Y} \; ; \; Z))$$

$$\widetilde{V} \;=\; \mu V \bullet ((U \; ; \; V) \;\square\; \text{SKIP})$$

$$\widetilde{Y} \;=\; \mu Y \bullet (\textit{gone} \rightarrow \text{SKIP}$$

$$\mid \textit{approach} \rightarrow (Y \; ; \; Y))$$

$$U \;=\; (\textit{approach} \rightarrow \widetilde{Y})$$

Note that the new definition of BARRIER allows for multiple crossings of rail traffic in a single cycle of barrier operation. Further, the recursive process $\widetilde{V}$ allows more trains to enter the crossing subsequent to clearing of any previous batches of trains.

The above definition has a complex structure. The specific scenario shown in Table 8.2 illustrates how it works. Note that this illustration has imposed a temporal order using 'timed events', although the above definition does not incorporate time.

Table 8.2 Unfolding of the process BARRIER illustrating the barrier operation

Timed event	Number of trains crossing	Outstanding (recursive) calls
		Note: W is an abbreviation.
		$W = (gone \rightarrow \text{SKIP})$;
		$\tilde{V}$; $(raise \rightarrow \text{BARRIER})$
$(0, approach)$	1	$\mu X \circ (\cdots)$; W
$(1, approach)$	2	X ; $\tilde{Z}$; W
$(2, approach)$	3	X ; $\tilde{Z}$; $\tilde{Z}$; W
$(3, approach)$	4	X ; $\tilde{Z}$; $\tilde{Z}$; $\tilde{Z}$; W
$(4, lower)$	4	SKIP ; $\tilde{Z}$; $\tilde{Z}$; $\tilde{Z}$; W
$(5, approach)$	5	$\tilde{Y}$; Z ; $\tilde{Z}$; $\tilde{Z}$; W
$(6, approach)$	6	Y ; Y ; Z ; $\tilde{Z}$; $\tilde{Z}$; W
$(7, gone)$	5	Y ; Z ; $\tilde{Z}$; $\tilde{Z}$; W
$(8, approach)$	6	Y ; Y ; Z ; $\tilde{Z}$; $\tilde{Z}$; W
$(9, approach)$	7	Y ; Y ; Y ; Z ; $\tilde{Z}$; $\tilde{Z}$; W
$(10, gone)$	6	Y ; Y ; Z ; $\tilde{Z}$; $\tilde{Z}$; W
$(11, gone)$	5	Y ; Z ; $\tilde{Z}$; $\tilde{Z}$; W
$(12, gone)$	4	Z ; $\tilde{Z}$; $\tilde{Z}$; W
$(13, gone)$	3	$\tilde{Z}$; $\tilde{Z}$; W
$(14, approach)$	4	$\tilde{Y}$; Z ; $\tilde{Z}$; W
$(15, gone)$	3	Z; $\tilde{Z}$; W
$(16, gone)$	2	$\tilde{Z}$; W
$(17, approach)$	3	$\tilde{Y}$; Z ; W
$(18, gone)$	2	Z ; W
$(19, gone)$	1	$(gone \rightarrow \text{SKIP})$; $\tilde{V}$; $\cdots$
$(20, gone)$	0	$\tilde{V}$; $(raise \rightarrow \text{BARRIER})$; $\cdots$
$(21, approach)$	1	$\tilde{Y}$; V ; $(raise \rightarrow \text{BARRIER})$; $\cdots$
$(22, gone)$	0	V ; $(raise \rightarrow \text{BARRIER})$; $\cdots$
$(23, \checkmark)$	0	SKIP ; $(raise \rightarrow \text{BARRIER})$; $\cdots$
$(24, raise)$	0	BARRIER ; $\cdots$

The new definition for the crossing is

$$\text{LEVEL-CROSSING} \ = \ \text{BARRIER} \ \| \ \text{LIGHTS} \ \| \ \left(\Big\|\Big\|_{i \in S} \ \text{RAIL-TRAFFIC}_i \right)$$

where S is an appropriate (unspecified) set of indices, for example, identifying tracks. Let us use the subscript i in RAIL-TRAFFIC$_i$ in order to avoid labelling it i, which affects the event labels. It is clear from the illustration given in Table 8.2 that the timing of the events may not be easily shown on, or inferred from, the structural process definition given above. It would be more convenient in this case to describe the timing requirements by referring to possible traces of BARRIER, that is, by giving a behavioural specification.

Consideration of multiple train crossings is likely to require more stringent timing requirements. These may be given as below for an arbitrary trace tr, $tr \in traces(\text{BARRIER})$.

The following is a predicate used in formalizing the relevant requirements and concerns subtraces, each of which corresponds to a separate cycle of the barrier operation:

$$cycle(s) \ \stackrel{def}{\Leftrightarrow} \ \exists \, t, tr \bullet s \, \frown \langle (t, raise) \rangle \ \text{in} \ tr \wedge first(s) = raise \, \wedge$$
$$raise \notin \sigma(tail(s))$$

Below are some generally applicable requirements (a)–(c), among them non-temporal requirements.

(a) No trains may use the crossing without approaching it:

$$tr \downarrow approach \geq tr \downarrow gone$$

(b) The barrier is open initially; raising and lowering it are alternate events:

$$tr \downarrow raise = tr \downarrow lower \ \vee \ tr \downarrow raise = tr \downarrow lower + 1$$

(c) The barrier may not open for road users whilst the crossing is in use by rail traffic:

$$s \ \text{in} \ tr \ \wedge \ first(s) = raise \ \wedge \ last(s) = lower \ \wedge$$
$$lower \notin \sigma(front(s)) \Rightarrow s \downarrow gone = 0$$

(d) Trains may not pass the crossing unless the red warning lights are in operation:

$$cycle(s) \ \wedge \ t_1 = begin(s) \ \wedge \ t_2 = begin(s \lceil \{left, \ right\}) \Rightarrow$$
$$gone \ \text{ref} \ [t_1, \ t_2]$$

(e) Rail crossings must be duly accompanied by barrier lowering and the operation of red warning lights:

$$s \text{ in } tr \ \wedge \ t = begin(s\lfloor\{approach\}) \ \Rightarrow$$
$$\exists\, t_1, \ t_2 \ \bullet \ t_2 > t_1 > t \ \wedge \ \{lower, left\} \text{ live } [t_1, \ t_2]$$

(f) Similarly, road users must be allowed through the barrier sometimes:

$$s \text{ in } tr \ \wedge \ t = begin(s\lfloor\{gone\}) \ \Rightarrow$$
$$\exists\, t_1, \ t_2 \ \bullet \ t_2 > t_1 > t \ \wedge \ \{raise, \ turn\text{-}green\} \text{ live } [t_1, \ t_2]$$

The requirements stated informally under (e) and (f) are not explicit about the desired order of the events concerned. A more accurate formalization may be made following a clarification of these requirements. Some more specialized requirements are:

(g) The red lights are sensitive only to the first *approach* event, and no more than two trains may be allowed to approach the crossing until the red lights begin to function:

$$cycle(s) \wedge t_1 = begin(s\lfloor\{approach\}) \wedge t_2 = begin(s\lfloor\{left, \ right\}) \Rightarrow$$
$$t_1 \ < \ t_2 \le t_1 \ + \ T_1 \ \wedge \ \#((s\uparrow[t_1, \ t_2])\lfloor\{approach\}) \le 2$$

(h) No more than two trains are allowed to be on the crossing for any time interval shorter than T_7 time units:

$$s \text{ in } tr \ \wedge \ end(s) - begin(s) \le \ T_7 \ \Rightarrow$$
$$(s \downarrow gone) \le (s \downarrow approach) \le (s_1 \downarrow gone \ + \ 2)$$

(i) Trains should approach the crossing at least T_8 time units apart:

$$s \text{ in } (tr \ \lfloor approach) \ \Rightarrow \ begin(tail(s)) - begin(s) \ge T_8$$

(j) The barrier should open T_9 time units after the last train passing, but for not less than T_{10} time units:

$$cycle(s) \ \wedge \ gone \text{ at } t \ \Rightarrow \ end(s) - t \ge T_9$$

$$s \text{ in } (tr \ \lfloor\{lower, \ raise\}) \ \wedge \ first(s) = raise \ \Rightarrow$$
$$begin(tail(s)) - begin(s) \ge T_{10}$$

(k) If the time between consecutive train approaches is greater than T_{11} time units, then the barrier should open within that time for the benefit of road users. Otherwise, the barrier should remain closed:

$$s \text{ in } (tr \ \lfloor approach) \ \wedge \ t_1 = begin(s) \ \wedge$$
$$t_2 = begin(tail(s)) \ \wedge \ t_2 - t_1 \ge \ T_{11} \ \Rightarrow$$
$$\{raise, \ lower\} \subseteq \sigma(tr\uparrow[t_1, \ t_2])$$

8.12   Safety and Liveness Requirements

As mentioned in Section 1.2.3 of Chapter 1, *safety* and *liveness* are two important properties encountered in the specification, analysis and development of safety critical systems. The last example discussed above is a typical scenario where such issues are paramount. Since there are other functional requirements, the two properties do not provide for an exhaustive classification of system requirements. The criteria distinguishing safety and liveness also lack precise definitions, and are based on the notions of the *desirability* or *undesirability* of certain specific behaviour patterns of the system in order to provide a required level of service and safety.

EXAMPLE

(1) Referring to the example on realtime lock in Section 8.11.2, the requirements (a) and (b) may be identified as *safety* requirements. This is because these requirements forbid the occurrence of the event *turn* following certain sequences of events. On the other hand, the requirements (c) and (d) are *liveness* requirements; (c) requires the occurrence of the event *activate* following *deactivate* in a certain temporally ordered sequence of events, whereas (d) stipulates that *deactivate* may not be refused under certain circumstances.

(2) Some desirable features of the example on railway level crossing, discussed in Section 8.11.3, are stated in the requirements (e), (f) and (k), and are intended to make sure that all users of the system have access to it. By contrast, the requirements (g)–(j) state the rules of engagement of different events; when they should or should not occur and under what circumstances. Thus, desirability characterizes the *liveness* required of the system and undesirability – its *safety* aspects. In this respect, as mentioned earlier, the concept of refusal in Timed CSP may be used directly to state what is not required, and indirectly through the converse to state what is desired. Note that the traces also provide for an alternative means for stating timing requirements, although in a different sense.

8.13   Bibliographical Notes

For a more comprehensive and definitive coverage of this material the reader should consult sources such as Davies [34], Davies and Schneider [35, 36], Reed [131], Reed and Roscoe [132] and Schneider [142]. It is worth noting that there have been other attempts such as those by Hooman [61] and Liu and Shyamasundar [95] to extend the theory of Communicating Sequential Processes to include time. There are also other formal frameworks for dealing with realtime issues at specification and design stages, namely, Jahanian and Mok [66] based on predicate logic and many works such as [9, 54, 114] on temporal logic. A general discussion on applications of formal approaches may be found in van Tilborg and Knob [163].

A behavioural specification of a telephone system in Timed CSP may be found in Kay and Reed [73, 74]. With reference to the example in Section 8.11.3, the reader might find the work by Davies and Schneider [36] in timed CSP interesting. Another relevant work is the specification by Simpson [150] of an automatic train protection system in CSP. Both these works may be useful when attempting the extended exercise in Section A.4 of Appendix A.

8.14　Exercises

1. Provide a full timing specification for the illustrative example on telephones presented in Section 7.17 of the previous chapter. Because of the familiarity of telephony from ordinary life, no timing requirements are provided and the reader is expected to commence this exercise with the production of an informal timing specification first. This may be based on an appropriate set of timing parameters and not absolute time values.
2-6. Attempt the exercises given in Section 5.8 of Chapter 5 on timed Petri nets in Timed CSP.

Chapter 9

Software Partitioning

Software partitioning is the definition of the general structure of a software system with a view to ensuring the optimality of its major implementation parameters. It is an engineering activity undertaken during the early design phases, and may be conducted with limited knowledge about the system. Since partitioning aims at establishing a clear link between the initial conceptual design of software and the form of its final implementation, it can significantly aid the process of subsequent validation and verification of software.

Some of the concepts discussed here are not unique to partitioning and are common to task allocation – the subject of the next chapter, which expands on these concepts in greater detail. The discussion here differs in one important respect, namely, in that it pays little attention to hardware capabilities and places emphasis almost exclusively on global software structure, which facilitates the objectives of task allocation. Note also that some of the notation and concepts introduced in this chapter are reproduced or elaborated further in the next chapter with reference to task allocation.

The approach discussed here has a close link with the data flow paradigm of computing; Section 9.11 provides some bibliographical references on the subject and a relevant application.

9.1 Software Tasks

Software partitioning is the activity associated with the identification and definition of tasks early in the development process. Its aim is to translate the conceptual (logical) modules reflecting the user's point of view of software to a set of tasks which at the implementation level is able to deliver the functionality expected by the user. The software tasks thus identified can form the basis for the subsequent design process.

The notion of *task* is central to the detailed design of any computer system and permeates through most stages of the development process. It is an indispensable term when dealing with task allocation, scheduling and implementation issues. Proper identification of tasks and their possible execution sequences therefore has a crucial bearing on the design and the attainment of a desired level of performance. An inescapable question in this respect is how specific tasks come about in relation to a given application.

A *task* is a software entity or a program intended to process some specific input or to respond in a specific manner to events conveyed to it in the form of signals or messages. In realtime applications specific timing requirements are likely to be associated with tasks both in isolation and in relation to one another.

Any software task may be traced back in some form, albeit a rudimentary form, to the early design activities during or immediately following high level functional design. Therefore, partitioning may begin with functional designs, usually depicted diagrammatically. How and when tasks are identified at this stage is to a large extent a matter of professional experience. Systematic design does not leave partitioning to *ad-hoc* processes, but requires a formal treatment with a longer term view on how tasks are to be refined and eventually implemented. Once the system is implemented, partitioning will serve as a continuous thread linking software requirements and the means employed for achieving them, facilitating greatly the post-implementation activities such as system verification. On the other hand, partitioning permits the setting up of design parameters and design targets for different components early, so that they can guide the design process and help to monitor and evaluate its progress.

A number of partitioning criteria may be envisaged. Among them are the minimization of response time, the reduction of cumulative execution time, effective resource utilization, low intertask communications and off-loading the bottleneck processors. These are too diverse to be addressed at the partitioning stage individually and, therefore, partitioning strives to achieve them by focussing attention on a unified criterion. These issues receive greater attention later at the task allocation stage.

9.2   Overhead Costs in Processing

Partitioning brings about both benefits and costs. Achievement of partitioning criteria is therefore a complex task because of the inevitable trade-offs to be made between the two.

The direct costs associated with tasks concern the processing involved, namely, retrieval of data, their interpretation, obeying commands or performing a required action, communicating with other tasks as necessary and storage of output for the tasks that follow. In addition, there are other indirect costs or overheads associated with tasks. These are typically the costs incurred through the operating system in relation to, for example, scheduling, task dispatching and synchronization. Any reduction in the two kinds of cost has to be sought in rather different ways: in the case of direct costs by concentrating on the internal characteristics of the tasks, and in the case of indirect costs on their external organization.

Let us examine two aspects that may be affected by partitioning; firstly, load balancing. This aims at an 'even' distribution of load on individual processors in order to avoid what is known as 'non-linear' response degradation, that is, greater degradation of performance with workload than that predicted by a simple rule based on proportionality. As an example, consider the allocation of two tasks τ_1 and τ_2 with computation times c_1 and c_2, such that $c_1 \ll c_2$, to two identical processors A and B. Assume that τ_1 is allocated to A and τ_2 to B. It is obvious that this could severely overload B, unless some processing of τ_2 is off-loaded to A.

Secondly, there may also be a need for timely servicing of interrupts, required for providing access to remotely located files, or processing of higher priority tasks. In the context of the above example, if τ_1 requires remote access to a data file used by τ_2 at B, τ_1 may be forced to wait c_2 time units. In this connection, it is prudent to decompose τ_2 further into smaller tasks in order to limit the execution time of tasks to be processed on B, or to provide τ_2 with realtime interrupts. The latter may be acceptable if the interrupts are not excessive in terms of overheads.

Different partitioning schemes may result in significantly different overhead costs in terms of intertask communication, task dispatches and temporary storage required. The example shown in Figure 9.1 illustrates partitioning of the modules m_1, m_2, m_3, and m_4 into two tasks τ_1 and τ_2 under two different partitioning schemes. Table 9.1 illustrates the effects of these two different schemes on overheads.

Table 9.1 Example: overheads due to different partitioning schemes

Partitioning scheme	Intertask communications (transmission+receipt)	Task dispatches	Temporary storage
I	m_1 of τ_1 with m_2 of τ_2	τ_1 at m_1	τ_1 after m_3
	m_2 of τ_2 with m_4 of τ_1	τ_2	
		τ_1 at m_4	
II	m_2 of τ_1 with m_4 of τ_2	τ_1	none
	m_3 of τ_1 with m_4 of τ_2	τ_2	

Greater overhead costs may be anticipated with partitioning scheme I. The above example illustrates two key objectives in partitioning, namely, load balancing and limiting interrupt service times or waiting times. Both these can be achieved by keeping tasks to reasonable sizes.

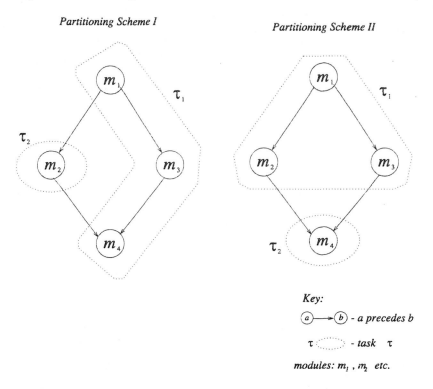

Figure 9.1 An example illustrating two partitioning schemes

9.3   Software Partitioning Parameters

In generalizing our discussion so far, let us limit the size of all software tasks by using two global parameters: processing cost (time) limit E_{max} on tasks and storage (memory) limit D_{max} on tasks. Alternatively, these may be interpreted as a crude model of hardware features: E_{max} denoting a uniform processor cost and D_{max} a uniform storage cost. In this case these attributes assume a homogeneous system of processors. Furthermore, let us use the following sets of values:

$\mathbb{E}$ – The set $\mathbb{E}$ is an arbitrary type, the elements of which denote an appropriate measure of direct and indirect (overhead) execution costs. If the execution cost is measured in terms of computation time, the set of lengths $\mathcal{T}$ of time in $\mathbb{T}$ (see Chapter 2) may be used for $\mathbb{E}$.

$\mathbb{S}$ – $\mathbb{S}$ is another arbitrary set, the elements of which denote storage or memory capacities of processor nodes in a suitable unit of measurement.

The aspects of any application relevant to software partitioning may be seen as a quadruple

$$\mathcal{A} = (\mathcal{M}, \prec_m, \mathcal{E}, \mathcal{D})$$

the elements of which are all application dependent partitioning parameters. These are:

$\mathcal{M}$ –   A non-empty finite set of conceptual (logical) modules.

$\prec_m$ –   The immediate predecessor relation on $\mathcal{M}$:

$$\prec_m: \mathcal{M} \leftrightarrow \mathcal{M}$$

reflecting the logical execution sequence of modules. Interpretation of $\prec_m$ is such that, given any two modules m_1 and m_2, the predicate $m_1 \prec_m m_2$ is true if and only if 'the execution of m_1 precedes immediately before that of m_2'. Section 9.4 below considers further other aspects of this relation.

$\mathcal{E}$ – $\mathcal{E}$ represents the maximum execution costs of conceptual modules. It is a function from $\mathcal{M}$ to set $\mathbb{E}$.

$\mathcal{D}$ – $\mathcal{D}$ denotes the demand for storage (memory) by modules. It is a function from $\mathcal{M}$ to $\mathbb{S}$.

In relation to the above, the following must hold:

$$
\begin{aligned}
\mathcal{M} &= \operatorname{dom} \mathcal{E} \\
&= \operatorname{dom} \mathcal{D} \\
&= (\operatorname{dom} \prec_m) \cup (\operatorname{ran} \prec_m)
\end{aligned}
$$

9.4   Precedence Relation on Modules

A precedence relation on modules specifies the order of execution of modules. As mentioned in Section 11.4.2 of Chapter 11 on scheduling, an analogous relation may exist on tasks. Although the precedence relations on modules and tasks are necessarily different, the effectiveness of partitioning, measured with respect to criteria mentioned earlier, would greatly depend on the maintenance of a 'proper' correspondence between the two precedence relations. This can be seen clearly in the example given in Section 9.2.

The relation $\prec_m$ is irreflexive and not necessarily symmetrical or anti-symmetrical; see Figure 9.2. This is because there can be symmetrical pairs in $\prec_m$ accounting for specific concurrent modules. Some further relations that may be founded on the immediate predecessor relation are

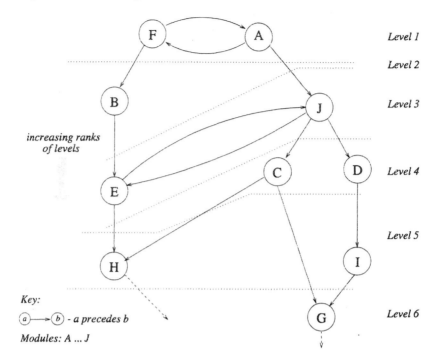

Figure 9.2 A module precedence relation

$\preceq_m$ – $m_1 \preceq_m m_2$ if and only if the execution of m_1 either precedes immediately before, or is concurrent with, that of m_2. Obviously,

$$\mathrm{id}\,\mathcal{M} \subseteq \preceq_m$$

$\succ_m$ –   The complementary predicate to $\prec_m$ is $\succ_m$, symbolizing the immediate successor relation on $\mathcal{M}$, and equals the inverse of the immediate predecessor relation. Thus,

$$\succ_m = \prec_m{}^{-1}$$

$\nprec_m$ –   The negation of the immediate predecessor relation

$$m_1 \nprec_m m_2 \overset{def}{\Leftrightarrow} \neg\,(m_1 \prec_m m_2)$$

$\prec_m^*$ –   The predecessor relation on $\mathcal{M}$, defined as the reflexive transitive closure of $\prec_m$.

$\prec_m^{sym}$ –   The symmetric closure of $\prec_m$.

$\prec'_m$ — The 'acyclic' subgraph of $\prec_m$ defined as

$$\prec'_m = \prec^{sym}_m - \prec_m{}^{-1}$$

and thus representing the pairs of the precedence relation $\prec_m$ corresponding to non-concurrent modules only; see below for the definition. In order to ensure that $\prec'_m$ is acyclic, let us require the following:

$$\text{id}\,\mathcal{M} \cap \prec'^{+}_m = \varnothing$$

$\prec''_m$ — The subgraph of $\prec_m$ containing cyclic parts and is defined as

$$\prec''_m = \prec^{sym}_m - \prec'_m$$

The pairs in this relation represent the concurrent modules.

$\prec_{ms}$ — The predecessor relation on the power set of $\mathcal{M}$:

$$\prec_{ms}: \mathbb{P}\mathcal{M} \leftrightarrow \mathbb{P}\mathcal{M}$$

$$\forall\, s,\, t: \mathbb{P}\mathcal{M} \bullet$$

$$s \prec_{ms} t \overset{def}{\Leftrightarrow} \forall\, m_1,\, m_2: \mathcal{M} \bullet$$
$$m_1 \in s \,\wedge\, m_2 \in t \;\Rightarrow\; m_1 \prec^+_m m_2$$

According to the above, given any two sets of modules s and t, $s \prec_{ms} t$ if and only if every module in s precedes every module in t. As a consequence of this, s and t must also be disjoint.

Two distinct modules m_1 and m_2 are said to be *concurrent modules* if and only if

$$m_1 \prec_m m_2 \wedge m_2 \prec_m m_1$$

That is, neither m_1 nor m_2 may complete, for example, because of the need for exchanging data during execution. In other words, they must be executed *concurrently*. On the other hand, two modules m_1 and m_2 are said to be *independent modules*, or that they may be executed independently of each other if and only if

$$m_1 \not\prec_m m_2 \wedge m_2 \not\prec_m m_1$$

9.5 Module Execution Levels

On the basis of the module precedence relation introduced above, it is possible to rank the modules into *levels* such that the module levels correspond to the execution order of modules in time; see Figure 9.2. According to these levels, for example, modules which precede no other module will be in the first level and concurrent modules will be in one and the same level. The module levels may be determined according to the following rules:

(i) Modules with no preceding modules in $\prec'_m$ and modules in $\prec''_m$ but not reachable by pairs in $\prec'_m$ are in *Level* 1.

(ii) A module with just a single immediately preceding module in *Level* i is in *Level* $(i+k)$ for some minimal k, k being either 1, or as determined by (iv) below.

(iii) A module with more than one immediately preceding module has a level one greater than the highest level among its immediately preceding modules.

(iv) Mutually communicating modules are in the same level.

The above rules defining the execution levels may be expressed mathematically as follows. Note that $\mathcal{L}$ denotes the set of all possible levels for the set of modules under consideration and forms a contiguous segment of natural numbers $\mathbb{N}$ starting from 1. The module belonging to a given level as defined by a given precedence relation is a function *Level* of the type:[1]

$$Level : (\mathcal{M} \leftrightarrow \mathcal{M}) \rightarrow \mathcal{L} \rightarrow \mathbb{P}\mathcal{M}$$

It is convenient to define another function $Level_{\prec_m}$ applicable to a given context as

$$Level_{\prec_m} \quad \overset{def}{=} \quad Level \ \prec_m$$
$$Level_{\prec_m} \ 1 \ = \ (\text{dom} \ \prec'_m - \text{ran} \ \prec'_m) \ \cup$$
$$\text{fld} \ \{(a,b) \mid (a,b) \in \prec''_m \wedge \{a,b\} \cap \text{ran} \ \prec'_m = \emptyset\}$$

For any $n > 1$, the $Level_{\prec_m} \ n$ may be defined as a closure:

$$(\prec'_m \ (\!| \ Level_{\prec_m}(n-1) \ |\!) \ ) \cup \{m_1 \mid \exists \ m_2 \bullet \ m_2 \in Level_{\prec_m} \ n \wedge m_1 \prec''_m m_2\} - \bigcup_{i \in n+1..} Level_{\prec_m} \ i) \subseteq Level_{\prec_m} \ n$$

In other words, $Level_{\prec_m} \ n$

(i) comprises the modules reachable from the preceding level; and

(ii) comprises all mutually concurrent modules at that level; but

(iii) excludes those modules which may be executed at a higher level.

9.6   Definition of Tasks

Software partitioning forms tasks by grouping modules into non-empty pairwise disjoint sets of modules. However, it is important that the task definitions retain the dependencies between modules in any given task. Therefore, it is natural to

---

[1] See page 416 in Appendix C (under *curried functions*) for an explanation of function abstraction used in *Level*.

represent each task as a pair that consists of a set of modules and a relation on the latter. Let the following set:

$$Task \stackrel{def}{=} \{(ms, g) \bullet ms : \mathbb{P}\mathcal{M}; \ g : \mathcal{M} \leftrightarrow \mathcal{M} \mid ms \neq \varnothing \wedge g \subseteq \prec_m \wedge \\ (\forall \ m_1, m_2 : \mathcal{M} \bullet (m_1, m_2) \in g \Rightarrow m_1 \in ms \vee m_2 \in ms)\}$$

contain all possible tasks at the level of abstraction appropriate to our discussion in this chapter. Given a task (ms, g), let us refer to ms as the module set of the task concerned and g as its module graph. The conjunct on the second line in the above definition ensures that the modules appearing in the module graph but not in the module set of any given task are those just outside the boundary of the given task, possibly belonging to some other task. The set of lowest level modules of a task $\tau \in Task$ may be defined as

$$lowest(\tau) \stackrel{def}{=} \{m \bullet m : \mathcal{M} \mid \exists\, ms : \mathbb{P}\mathcal{M}; \ g : \mathcal{M} \leftrightarrow \mathcal{M} \bullet \tau = (ms, g) \wedge \\ m \in ms \wedge (\forall m_1 : \mathcal{M} \bullet m_1 \in ms \Rightarrow \\ Level_{\prec_m} m \leq Level_{\prec_m} m_1)\}$$

The terminology '*non-trivial task*' refers to a task which contains more than one module in its module set.

9.7   Software Partitioning Concepts

9.7.1   Task Activation and Executability

Let us first introduce two important definitions. A module is said to be *completely executable* if and only if it has no predecessor modules or all its predecessor modules have already been completely executed. Underlying this is a model of data flow driven computation. Implicit in the definition of executability is a certain notion of state in which some modules have already been executed and some are yet to be executed. The notion of executability may be extended to tasks. A task is said to be *completely executable* if and only if all its modules are *completely executable*.

A task is said to be *properly activated* if at the time of its activation it has access to all external data required by its modules of the lowest level. An immediate consequence of this definition is the following:

> Observation 9.1 A task may be properly activated if and only if none of its modules of the lowest level may both precede and succeed a module outside the task module set.

Consider a task τ such that $\tau = (ms, g)$. Let $act(\tau)$ be a predicate meaning that the task τ may be properly activated in the above sense. Then the above observation may be restated as

$$act(\tau) \iff (\forall\, m_1, m_2 : \mathcal{M} \bullet m_1 \in lowest(\tau) \Rightarrow$$
$$m_2 \in ms \lor m_1 \prec_m m_2 \lor m_2 \prec_m m_1)$$

The plan of the rest of this section is to study the executability of tasks on the basis of the following characterization of tasks:

(a) Tasks that always release the results produced by their modules as the modules terminate.

(b) Tasks that release none of the results produced by their modules prior to the termination of each task as a whole.

The above classification is intended as the basis for partitioning modules into tasks under two distinct sets of circumstances. With this in mind, the two cases (a) and (b) above are considered separately in Sections 9.7.2 and 9.7.3.

9.7.2   Release of Results by Tasks before Termination

This section considers the executability of tasks under the assumption that tasks release their results as their modules terminate. In this connection, the following must hold:

> **Observation 9.2** In order to guarantee that a properly activated task τ is completely executable, the modules in τ must satisfy:
>
> (i) the immediate predecessors of every module in τ, other than those of the modules of its lowest level, are in its module set, or
>
> (ii) each of the immediate predecessors of every module in τ that does not belong to its module set also precedes the modules of the lowest level in τ.

The word 'guarantee' is used to signify the complete executability of the task concerned irrespective of the size of the modules concerned. Given a task $\tau \in Task$ such that $\tau = (ms, g)$, let $exec(\tau)$ be a predicate meaning that the task τ is executable in the above sense. Then, the above requirement may be stated as

$$exec(\tau) \iff act(\tau) \land \forall\, m_1, m_2 : \mathcal{M} \bullet m_2 \in ms \land m_1 \prec_m m_2 \Rightarrow$$
$$m_1 \in ms \lor \{m_1\} \prec_{ms} lowest(\tau)$$

It follows from the definitions given so far that there can be tasks that may be properly activated at a certain time, but not completely executable because of unavailability of data or information required by modules at higher levels. Here is another related observation:

> **Observation 9.3** A non-trivial task is completely executable if and only if none of its modules may precede and succeed another module which does not belong to the task module set.

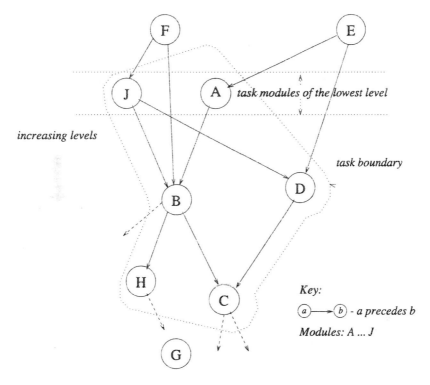

Figure 9.3 Executability with release of results prior to task termination

The above concerns in particular those tasks which may be executed to completion independently of other tasks. Observation 9.2 taken in conjunction with Observation 9.3 forms the basis of one of the partitioning schemes. Certain circumstances covered by the above observation are illustrated in Figure 9.3.

9.7.3 Release of Results by Tasks only after Termination

Let us now consider a scenario where no task releases its results prior to its termination.

Observation 9.3 in the previous section remains applicable here. However, software partitioning based on Observations 9.2 and 9.3 could be too liberal. This is because a predecessor task τ_j of a task τ_i can make some of its results available to τ_i before τ_j's completion. In applications where such a requirement may be not admissible, it may be constrained by replacing it with the following:

> Observation 9.4 In order to guarantee that a properly activated task τ_i is completely executable, the modules in the task τ_i must satisfy:
>
> (i) the immediate predecessors of every module of τ_i, other than those

of the modules of its lowest level, are in the module set of τ_i, or

(ii) each and every immediate predecessor of every module in τ_i that does not belong to τ_i's module set belongs to the module set of another task τ_j, which contains a module that precedes at least one of the lowest level modules of τ_i.

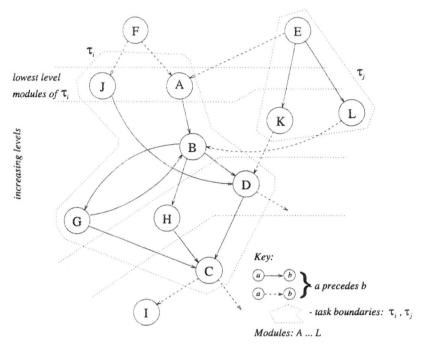

Figure 9.4 Executability with release of results only after task termination

Note that (ii) above makes sure that τ_i cannot be activated until τ_j terminates, since τ_j does not release any of the data produced by its modules, which the lowest level modules in τ_i require for τ_i to start. The predicate *exec* introduced in the previous section may be redefined for a task τ_i in the above sense as follows:

$$exec(\tau_i) \;\Leftrightarrow\; act(\tau_i) \wedge (\forall\, m_1, m_2 : \mathcal{M} \;\bullet\; m_1 \in ms \wedge m_2 \prec_m m_1 \Rightarrow$$
$$m_2 \in ms \vee (\exists\, \tau_j : Task;\; ms_j : \mathbb{P}\,\mathcal{M};\; g_j : \mathcal{M} \leftrightarrow \mathcal{M};$$
$$m_3 : \mathcal{M} \;\bullet\; \tau_j = (ms_j, g_j) \wedge \{m_2, m_3\} \subseteq ms_j \wedge$$
$$\{m_3\} \prec_{ms} lowest(\tau_i)))$$

The above, together with Observation 9.3, leads to the second partitioning scheme, where no task can rely on another task for its execution until the latter has terminated. This is illustrated in Figure 9.4.

9.8 Partitioning Considerations and Schemes

9.8.1 Resource Constraints

The task attributes are obviously dependent on how the modules are partitioned and, therefore, have to be determined with respect to each partition separately. Task attributes are partial functions from *Task* to the relevant domain of values and the ones relevant to partitioning are

$E(\tau)$ –   The direct cost of the task τ. Obviously, given that $\tau = (ms, g)$ for some ms and g,

$$E(\tau) = \sum_{m \in ms} \mathcal{E}(m)$$

$I(\tau)$ –   The indirect cost of the task τ. This is measured in the same units as $E(\tau)$. $I(\tau)$ needs to be computed by adding the costs associated with the task dispatches, temporary storage and other overheads resulting from the given partitioning.

$D(\tau)$ –   Memory requirements of τ measured in units consistent with D_{max}. Obviously, given that $\tau = (ms, g)$ for some ms and g,

$$D(\tau) = \sum_{m \in ms} \mathcal{D}(m)$$

Together, $E(\tau)$ and $I(\tau)$ constitute the total processing cost of τ. The resource or implementation constraints on tasks in any partition may be written as

$$E(\tau) + I(\tau) \leq T_{max}$$
$$D(\tau) \leq D_{max}$$

9.8.2 Logical Constraints

Let $\wp$ denote the set of tasks to be established by software partitioning. Note that $\wp \in \mathbb{P}$ *Task*. The determination of $\wp$ is subject to the following logical constraints:

$$\forall (ms_1, g_1), (ms_2, g_2) \in Task \bullet \{(ms_1, g_1), (ms_2, g_2)\} \subseteq \wp \wedge$$
$$ms_1 \cap ms_2 \neq \varnothing \Rightarrow ms_1 = ms_2 \wedge g_1 = g_2 \tag{i}$$

$$\left(\bigcup_{\tau \in \wp \wedge \tau = (ms,g)} ms \right) = \bigcup (\text{fld} \prec_m) \tag{ii}$$

$$\prec_m = \bigcup \{g \bullet g : \mathcal{M} \leftrightarrow \mathcal{M} \mid \exists ms : \mathbb{P}\mathcal{M} \bullet (ms, g) \in \wp\} \tag{iii}$$

Clause (i) above requires that no two tasks share any module in their module sets. According to (ii), all modules in the task module sets must appear in the module precedence relation. Condition (iii) requires that the individual module graph of each task in $\wp$ is within the immediate precedence relation $\prec_m$ on modules and no part of $\prec_m$ may be omitted in defining the tasks. However, the task module graphs are not required to be pairwise disjoint, since some arcs in module graphs, namely, those on task boundaries related to inter-task communications, may appear in more than one task.

9.8.3   Partitioning Schemes

The partitioning of the modules into tasks may be carried out under the two different schemes discussed in Sections 9.7.3 and 9.7.2. The two schemes are referred to as Scheme I and Scheme II respectively. The considerations behind these two schemes are summarized below.

(a) Both schemes require that every task in $\wp$ is executable in the sense of Observation 9.3 given in Section 9.7.2.

(b) Scheme I requires that every task in $\wp$ is completely executable in the sense of Observation 9.2 given in Section 9.7.2; see Figure 9.3.

(c) Scheme II requires that every task in $\wp$ is completely executable in the sense of Observation 9.4 given in Section 9.7.3; see Figure 9.4.

The distinction between Schemes I and II is that the former establishes task executability only by referring to the already executed modules irrespective of whether the relevant tasks have terminated, whereas the latter establishes the same strictly within the rule that no task relies on other tasks for their results prior to their termination.

A software partition that serves the partitioning objectives well may be established by optimizing the following objective function within a chosen partitioning scheme:

$$\frac{\displaystyle\sum_{\tau\in\wp} D(\tau)}{\displaystyle\sum_{\tau\in\wp} D(\tau)+I(\tau)}$$

The optimization of the above corresponds to the minimization of the overheads resulting from the partitioning and, thus, to maximizing the partitioning efficiency. The partition $\wp$ resulting from the optimization is the required solution.

9.9   An Example

Figures 9.5 and 9.6 illustrate two partitions that obey the rules of both partitioning Schemes I and II, the diagrams of Figure 9.6 showing a more complex partition. Table 9.2 gives further details of task analysis in the latter case.

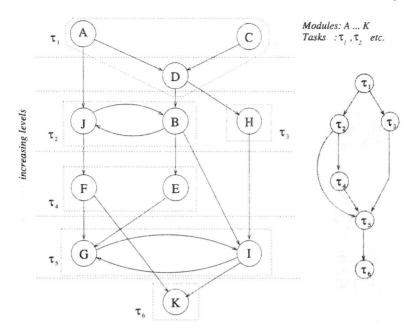

Figure 9.5 Example: a partition obeying Schemes I and II

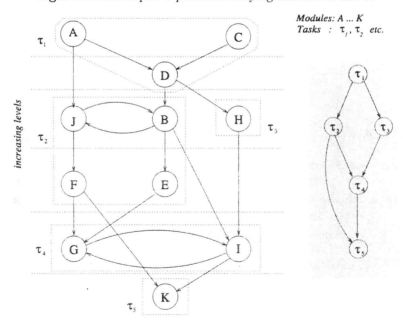

Figure 9.6 Example: a partition obeying Schemes I and II

Table 9.2 A partition obeying Schemes I and II

Task	The truth value of $exec(\tau)$	
τ	*Scheme I*	*Scheme II*
τ_1	**true** (The task has no predecessors.)	as in Scheme I
τ_2	**true** (All predecessor modules are either in its module set or precede its two lowest level modules, which are B and J.)	as in Scheme I
τ_3	**true** (The task has only one module and only one predecessor module, which is outside its module set.)	as in Scheme I
τ_4	**true** (The task consists of only two modules of the same level and has four predecessor modules, namely, F, E, B and H, which are of lower levels.)	**true** (The predecessors F, E and B of the task modules G and I are in the task τ_2. Since they precede each other, G and I happen to be its only lowest level modules. The other predecessor module H of τ_4 is in τ_2 and τ_2's only lowest module.)
τ_5	(The task has only two predecessor modules F and I, which are at lower levels than τ_5's only module K.)	as in Scheme I

The partition shown in Figure 9.7, on the other hand, does not conform to either of the schemes. Table 9.3 shows how the different tasks in this case meet or violate the requirements of the two schemes.

9.10   Applicability of the Approach

It should be noted that the approach offers only a framework for guiding the partitioning, and does not offer a method for doing it, namely, an algorithm. General solutions to this problem are not available. However, as illustrated in Chapter 10, more promising in this respect are the heuristic algorithms.

It is evident that partitioning Scheme I offers a greater choice in partitioning, but at the expense of greater vulnerability to delays at run time in the event of lack of data. Although motivated by similar considerations such as short response time, better load balance, etc., as in task allocation, partitioning does not target its effort at specific criteria, but aims at meeting a single high level criterion such as efficient use of resources.

The approach is intended especially for high level software design, but there is no reason to preclude it from other design stages, provided that greater account is taken of the hardware features in appropriate detail. Alternatively, the detailed design may take into account other finer details in the task allocation stage later and improve such performance characteristics as response time then.

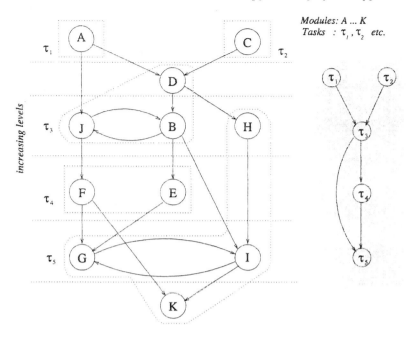

Figure 9.7 Example: a partition not obeying Schemes I and II

Table 9.3 Violation of rules on Schemes I and II

Task	The truth value of $exec(\tau)$	
τ	*Scheme I*	*Scheme II*
τ_1	true (The task has no predecessors.)	as in Scheme I
τ_2	true (The task has no predecessors.)	as in Scheme I
τ_3	true (All predecessor modules are either in the task module set or precede its lowest level modules.)	as in Scheme I
τ_4	true (All predecessor modules precede its lowest level modules.)	as in Scheme I
τ_5	false (The module F, which precedes both G and K of τ_5 does not precede H, which is the only one lowest level module of τ_5.)	false (One of the predecessor tasks of τ_5, namely τ_4, does not contain any module which precedes H, which is the only one lowest level module of τ_5. However, note that τ_3, the other predecessor task of τ_5, does contain D which precede H, but this is not sufficient.)

9.11   Bibliographical Notes

This chapter is based on the work due to Huang [64]. Experimental findings in the cited reference indicate that partitioning Scheme I results in lower response times than Scheme II. According to the same results, higher partitioning efficiency is shown to lead to better performance with respect to response time.

Further information on the data flow paradigm of computing, referred to in Section 9.7.1 in relation to complete executabilty of modules and tasks, may be found in Ackerman [2], Dennis [37], Lee and Messerschmitt [90] and Watson and Gurd [167].

9.12   Exercises

1. Investigate other possible partitioning schemes of the set of modules considered in the example in Section 9.9.
2. Assuming the execution costs and the overheads given in the table below and a uniform task dispatch cost of three units for each dispatch, assess the partitioning efficiency of the solutions in the answer to (1) above and those given as illustrative partitions for the example in Section 9.9. Assume that the communication costs are incurred only across task boundaries. All costs are given in a single consistent cost unit.

Execution costs		*Overheads*			
Module	*Cost*	*Modules*		*Comm. cost*	*Temp. storage*
		m_1	m_2	*from m_1 to m_2*	*between m_1 and m_2*
A	3	A	D	5	3
B	7	C	D	1	2
C	5	A	J	6	3
D	4	D	B	2	1
E	4	J	F	2	3
F	3	B	E	5	4
G	1	F	G	3	3
H	2	F	K	2	3
I	5	E	G	1	2
J	5	B	I	3	2
		I	K	3	1
		J	B	4	3
		B	J	3	5
		G	I	2	4
		I	G	2	3

Chapter 10

Task Allocation

This chapter continues the theme started in the previous chapter – Chapter 9. It brings to the forefront the notion of resources, which is of prime importance as we begin to address the implementation issues of realtime systems. There can be different kinds of resource such as processors, storage media, peripherals, etc., but it is sufficient for our purpose to consider just the first two. The major concern of this chapter is how best to utilize a given set of resources in order to achieve the performance parameters set at a higher level by the application requirements.

Task allocation is often viewed as part of static scheduling in distributed systems, where task allocation determines the assignment of processors to tasks, which are then scheduled statically on the assigned processors (see Section 11.8.2 of Chapter 11 and Chapters 12 and 13).

Note that we continue to use the term 'module' when dealing with 'tasks' in task allocation. This is an anomaly in the terminology, resulting from the highly context dependent usage of the term 'module' in computing.

10.1   The Aims

Task allocation is the problem of determining an optimal allocation of tasks in an application to a number of distributed processors. Thus, its concern is the spatial ordering of tasks. It arises due to the fact that the final number of software tasks usually exceeds the number of available processors at the implementation level. Its primary objective is to achieve, in relation to the given application, a desired level of system performance in terms of throughput, response time or cost. These cannot be achieved merely by increasing resources, because, apart from the cost involved, there is a limit to productive and efficient use of increased resources. This trend of diminishing returns, or sometimes even a drop in performance, at high resource levels is often referred to as the *saturation effect*. This is because increased resources bring about extra resource management overheads and extra *interprocessor communications*. A common problem encountered in multi-processor architectures is the potential load imbalances among the processors, often leading to queueing delays – the delays caused by the assignment of more than one module to any given processor. Further complications arise if we are to consider at the time of task allocation the dynamics of the system configuration or the fluctuations of its current workload. The optimality of task allocation may therefore be judged according to such criteria as:

- minimization of the total execution cost of the application;
- minimization of the interprocessor communication, measured, for example, in terms of the amount of data to be communicated between processors, message propagation delays and queueing delays;
- a 'fair' distribution of load or *load balancing* among processors (in order to achieve a high throughput or a fast response time);
- minimization of the maximum processor loading (in order to avoid processing bottlenecks);
- maximization of the minimum processor loading and minimization of the number of resource units (in order to achieve greater resource utilization, ideally at the least cost).

Some of these criteria have already been mentioned in Chapter 9.

10.2   The Allocation Problem

From the viewpoint of task allocation, let us treat the system abstractly as a triple

$$Sys = (\mathcal{H}, \mathcal{S}, \chi)$$

where

(a) $\mathcal{H}$ is an n-tuple (see Section 10.3.1) representing an abstract model of the hardware or the architecture of the distributed system. It incorporates, among others, a set of processors $\mathcal{P}$ and a connectivity graph CON on $\mathcal{P}$, the latter reflecting the network topology and other features of the network. $\mathcal{H}$ may have other components with features for representing channel bandwidth and any heterogeneity of the processors with respect to capabilities, speed and storage capacity.

(b) $\mathcal{S}$ is an n-tuple (see Section 10.4.1) representing an application at the software level. Typically, $\mathcal{S}$ reflects the communication and processing requirements of the application. It incorporates, among others, a communication graph (or a data flow graph) COM. It is a weighted directed graph, nodes representing computational modules (tasks) and the arcs and their weighting representing the communication demands. The definition of COM depends to a large extent on the chosen problem decomposition.

(c) χ is a mapping from suitably partitioned subgraphs of COM to the processor nodes $\mathcal{P}$.

When addressing the task allocation of any specific application, $\mathcal{S}$ and $\mathcal{H}$ are usually considered as being fixed by prior design. The aim of task allocation is to establish χ such that certain chosen optimality criteria are met. The problem of task allocation then consists of three subproblems:

- partitioning of COM;
- determination of χ such that the selected criteria are met in a certain optimal sense; and
- performance analysis of different architectures for testing their appropriateness to the application concerned.

The three subproblems are closely interwoven and the outcome of each may have important repercussions on the effectiveness of the subsequent ones.

Partitioning is done under two conflicting demands. On the one hand, one has to aim at minimizing the interprocessor communications among the modules belonging to different subgraphs and, therefore, residing on different processors. This cannot be done indefinitely since, in the limit, the whole application must be allocated to a single processor, possibly resulting in the worst response time. On the other hand, partitioning must aim, as far as possible, at nearly an even distribution of tasks among the processors for achieving greater throughput or better response time. However, this, too, cannot be done with no limit, except in the case of simple data processing applications exhibiting limited or no data inter-dependence. Thus, load balancing in an even manner cannot be a goal in itself, since this would limit the kind of applications to be dealt with. Generally, load balancing relies heavily on a high degree of parallelism in the implementation. This requires the exploitation of both inherent concurrency in the problem and the capability of the architecture to support parallel execution of computations. The notion of tasks at the allocation level must already incorporate the outcome of such endeavours.

The following are some general types of values used here:

$\mathbb{E}$ –   The set $\mathbb{E}$ is an arbitrary type, the elements of which denote an appropriate measure of execution costs. If the execution cost is measured in terms of computation time, the set of lengths $\mathcal{T}$ of time in $\mathbb{T}$ (see Chapter 2) may be used for $\mathbb{E}$.

$\mathbb{C}$ – $\mathbb{C}$ is an arbitrary set, the elements of which denote an appropriate measure of the *intermodule communication cost* (IMC). The set $\mathbb{N}$ may often fulfil this role.

$\mathbb{S}$ – $\mathbb{S}$ is another arbitrary set, the elements of which denote storage or memory capacities of processor nodes in a suitable unit of measurement.

10.3 Allocation Parameters of the System

10.3.1 A Model of the System

The system supporting the application may be seen generally as an n-tuple, its elements representing various features and capabilities of the system. Let us adopt for our purpose a tuple with seven elements:

$$\mathcal{H} = (\mathcal{P}, \mathcal{F}, \text{CON}, \sigma, \rho, \eta, \varphi)$$

where

$\mathcal{P}$ –   A non-empty finite set of processors.

$\mathcal{F}$ –   A non-empty set of files.

CON   –   A connectivity graph representing, as mentioned in Section 10.2, the network topology. Obviously, CON is a relation and CON $\in \mathbb{P}(\mathcal{P} \times \mathcal{P})$. Given two processors p_i and p_j, CON(p_i, p_j) means that processor p_i can communicate with processor p_j (or has access to processor p_j).

σ – σ denotes processor storage capacities. It is a function from $\mathcal{P}$ to $\mathbb{S}$.

ρ – ρ denotes a measure of the processing capabilities of processors, given as a rate of processing power (e.g. processor time per unit real time). It is a function from $\mathcal{P}$ to $\mathbb{E}$.

η – η is a record of the permitted maximum utilization factors for the processors. It is a function from $\mathcal{P}$ to $\mathbb{R}$. Given a processor p, $\eta(p)$ denotes the utilization factor of p as a fraction of its processing capability. Obviously, $0 < \eta(p) \leq 1$.

φ – φ represents the allocation of files to processors for storage. It is a relation (or a predicate) from $\mathcal{F}$ to $\mathcal{P}$. Note that although each file may have a unique processor for permanent storage, its replicas may reside at other processors temporarily. When interpreted as a predicate, $\varphi(f, p)$ is to be taken as true if and only if the file f or one of its copies is located at the processor p.

The components of $\mathcal{H}$ must satisfy the following:

$$\mathcal{P} = \text{dom } \sigma = \text{dom } \rho = \text{dom } \eta$$
$$= \text{dom CON} \cup \text{ran CON}$$

Furthermore, CON is a connected graph in the sense that there are no totally disjointed subgraphs. It may not necessarily be fully interconnected, that is, there may be pairs of nodes with no arcs between them.

For obvious reasons, CON must be reflexive. It may be defined in different ways depending on the communication capabilities of the network. For example, it may be defined:

(a) Purely in terms of adjacent pairs of processors, thus restricting the model to direct connections between immediately accessible processors in the specified directions only.

(b) As the symmetric closure of a relation, but otherwise formed according to (a), in order to provide bi-directional communication capabilities between those adjacent pairs of processors with any link between them.

(c) As the transitive closure of a relation formed according to (a), if the processors are capable of forwarding messages to other processors in the direction of the arcs.

(d) As an equivalence relation, endowing the network with all three capabilities listed above.

As a simplification, we may sometimes assume full interconnectivity of CON, whereby all processors are assumed to be able to communicate with one another. In this case, CON may be simply omitted from the definition of $\mathcal{H}$. In many cases, it may be possible to reduce $\mathcal{H}$ further to the set of processors $\mathcal{P}$.

10.3.2 Interprocessor Communication Scaling Factors

Let us make explicit the implications of the connectivity graph in terms of certain scaling factors for (logically) possible communications between pairs of processors. In general, these scaling factors may be chosen to reflect such requirements as communication overheads and physically impossible communications. The scaling factors adopted below conform with the commonly accepted factors in task allocation problems.

(a) Communications within any processor incur no cost. As indicated above, a small non-zero value may sometimes be appropriate in order to account for any processor overhead with respect to internal communication.

(b) Communication costs between pairs of processors unreachable by CON are infinitely costly.

(c) The scaling factor for communication costs between pairs of all other processors reachable by CON is unity. This may be scaled down (up) in order to encourage (discourage) communication traffic over certain links in a desired manner.

These requirements may be taken care of by the following network scaling function:

$$
\begin{aligned}
\text{SCL} \quad &: \quad (\mathcal{P} \times \mathcal{P}) \to \mathbb{R}^+ \cup \{\infty\} \\
\text{SCL} \quad &= \quad \{(pair, 0) \quad \bullet \quad pair : \mathcal{P} \times \mathcal{P} \mid pair \in \text{id } \mathcal{P}\} \cup \\
&\qquad \{(pair, 1) \quad \bullet \quad pair : \mathcal{P} \times \mathcal{P} \mid pair \in \text{CON} - \text{id } \mathcal{P}\} \cup \\
&\qquad \{(pair, \infty) \quad \bullet \quad pair : \mathcal{P} \times \mathcal{P} \mid pair \notin \text{CON} \wedge pair \notin \text{id } \mathcal{P}\}
\end{aligned}
$$

The set $\mathbb{R}^+$ in above denotes the set of non-negative real numbers and is obviously intended to make sure that all scaling factors are non-negative. It is worth noting that the function SCL already incorporates fully the information given in CON and, therefore, is an alternative mathematical entity to CON.

Multi-processor architectures may be represented accurately using fixed scaling functions. Because of the unpredictabilities and uncertainties characteristic to distributed systems, fixed scaling functions are not applicable to them generally, except when dealing with statistically meaningful scenarios such as the average or the worst case. A static approach for dealing with the general case of distributed systems is to adopt a variable scaling function based on predicted estimates of communication costs. Obviously, these costs must account for their fluctuation in time sufficiently accurately and make an allowance for possible network delays.

10.4   Allocation Parameters of the Application

10.4.1   A Model of the Application

From the point of task allocation, an application may be viewed as an n-tuple. This study adopts a tuple with seven elements,

$$S = (\mathcal{M}, \, \mathcal{E}, \, \text{COM}, \, \gamma, \, \text{OPT}, \, \text{FXD}, \, \mathcal{D})$$

the elements of which are all application dependent allocation parameters. These are:

$\mathcal{M}$ –   A non-empty finite set of modules (tasks). As mentioned at the very outset, this chapter uses the terms 'module' and 'task' interchangeably. By contrast, Chapter 9 uses a different notion of 'module', which is an abstract user oriented notion.

$\mathcal{E}$ – $\mathcal{E}$ represents the execution costs of modules. It is a function from $\mathcal{M} \times \mathcal{P}$ to set $\mathbb{E}$.

COM   –   A communication graph, representing the communication links between the modules. It is a relation on $\mathcal{M}$ and, therefore, COM $\in$ $\mathbb{P}(\mathcal{M} \times \mathcal{M})$. This graph is reflexive since every module must be able to communicate with itself. Sometimes other properties such as symmetry and transitivity may also be appropriate. Taking reflexivity for granted, enumeration of reflexive terms in COM may be omitted for convenience.

γ – γ represents the intermodule communication cost (IMC) or a measure of communication traffic and acts as a weighting on COM. It is a function from $\mathcal{M} \times \mathcal{M}$ to $\mathbb{C}$.

OPT   –   OPT is a relation from $\mathcal{M}$ to $\mathcal{P}$, specifying a certain processor option (a choice of processors) for a subset of modules. It is discussed further in Section 10.4.8.

FXD   —   FXD is a partial function from $\mathcal{M}$ to $\mathcal{P}$, specifying a certain subset of module allocations fixed beforehand. It is also discussed further in Section 10.4.8.

$\mathcal{D}$ — $\mathcal{D}$ denotes the demand for storage (memory) by modules. It is a function from $\mathcal{M}$ to $\mathbb{S}$.

Another obvious component that may be incorporated in $\mathcal{S}$ is a precedence relation on modules, which is not considered in this study. In relation to the components mentioned in $\mathcal{S}$ above, it is necessary that the following:

$$
\begin{aligned}
\text{COM} \ &= \ \text{dom } \gamma \\
\mathcal{M} \ &= \ \{m \mid \exists p \in \mathcal{P} \bullet (m, p) \in \text{dom } \mathcal{E}\} \\
&= \ \text{dom COM} \cup \text{ran COM}
\end{aligned}
$$

are satisfied. The subsections below discuss the execution costs, communication costs and the notions of modules and the module allocation function χ in greater detail.

10.4.2   Execution Costs

Given a module m and a processor p, $\mathcal{E}(m, p)$ denotes the cumulative execution cost of m on the processor p. As mentioned in Section 10.4.1, execution costs may be measured in terms of computation time, which may be established by approximate estimations or empirically. Obviously, the measure of the execution cost on whatever the chosen unit depends on the particular execution or run of the program. An indirect measure of the computation time is the number of machine language instructions to be executed in an appropriate run of the program. If the application concerns a program that terminates, the cumulative cost may represent the execution cost from the start to the termination. In the case of a non-terminating program, this should apply to a given period of time.

An approximation to the cumulative execution cost of a module m on a processor p over a given interval (t_1, t_2) may be computed, for example, knowing the mean (average) execution cost of m per execution and the number of executions of m over (t_1, t_2). Other alternatives to the use of the mean execution cost exist. Their choice would depend on the particular design issue being addressed. The maximum execution cost would suit when one were addressing the worst case, namely, peak demands on processor time. The median cost, on the other hand, would better suit investigations into the most likely demand for processor time in situations, where a skew due to a small number of abnormally high or low values in a sample of execution costs (measured or estimated) may drastically distort the average execution cost.

Note that $\mathcal{E}(m, p)$ is strictly positive. If $\mathcal{E}(m, p) = \infty$, then the execution of m on p is prohibitively costly. However, a 'zero execution cost' may be adopted for modules which have fixed processor assignments because of their possible dependence on facilities available only within their assigned processors. These are instances where the actual costs are replaced by fictitious values so that the algorithm which determines the module allocation ensures a desired processor assignment indirectly. An alternative to such indirect ways of achieving a fixed prior assignment is discussed in Section 10.4.8.

The function $\mathcal{E}$, and hence the allocation problem, may be simplified without much loss of generality by assuming identical capabilities for all processors.

10.4.3 Intermodule Communication Costs

Intermodule communication costs (IMC) are estimated on the assumption that each and every communicating module invariably incurs an interprocessor communication cost (IPC), and are therefore specified with no reference to a particular architecture. Thus, the module allocation function χ_m (introduced in Section 10.4.5) plays no role in the determination of IMC, which consists of two contributions: the cost incurred through control messages between modules and the cost of accessing data or files located at remote processors. Control messages may account for overheads such as synchronization, task scheduling, resource management and maintaining consistency of any shared information. Direct communication costs associated with accessing data or files (shared information) may consist of two kinds of cost, one dealing with the extent of data, which is problem dependent, and the other the message propagation time, which is hardware dependent. When dealing with the amount of data to be communicated between two modules, it may be measured in bits, words, packets or some other unit.

In situations involving file updates, any pair of communicating modules may keep replicas of any shared files at both processors or, in the more general case, at a third processor. Any update made to such a replica at a given processor as its current computation progresses (state changes) requires the same update to be made at the original kept at the remote processor as well as in its replicas used by other processors. The cost at the sender consists of the cost involved in message composition and message dispatch while the cost at each recipient consists of that involved in unpacking and reading the message.

Given two modules m_i and m_j, $\gamma(m_i, m_j)$ denotes the IMC from the module m_i to the module m_j. Extreme values of IMC, whether they are actual or fictitious, correspond to two plausible situations:

$\gamma(m_i, m_j) = 0$ In this case, the module m_i incurs a zero communication cost when communicating with m_j. If the same applies to communication from m_j to m_i, the two modules may be allocated to different processors.

$\gamma(m_i, m_j) = \infty$ In this case, the communication cost from module m_i to module m_j is prohibitively high. Obviously, any viable allocation algorithm must allocate the two modules concerned to the same processor.

10.4.4 Modules and Module Clusters

At the task allocation level, *module (task)* constitutes the smallest computationally indivisible software entity. The aim of partitioning is to merge modules into *module clusters* in order to achieve a low IPC with an appropriate processor assignment. This results in a set of clusters of modules where the communications between modules belonging to different clusters may be seen as inter-cluster communications.

The quadruple

$$(\mathcal{M}, \text{COM}, \mathcal{E}, \gamma)$$

may be seen as a *module graph,* where the nodes $\mathcal{M}$ and the arcs COM are both weighted by the weighting functions $\mathcal{E}$ and and γ respectively. This section considers smaller clusters of modules in a module graph and how to partition a module graph into a set of clusters.

As a simplifiction, let us view module graphs, as well as clusters and partitions based on module graphs, through their nodes and arcs only. The nodal and arc weighting of these graphs are implicit and are the same as $\mathcal{E}$ and γ.

Being a subgraph of the module graph, each *cluster* consists of a set of nodes and a set of arcs. Let the set of all possible clusters that may be formed from the module graph be the set CLU:

$$\text{CLU} \stackrel{def}{=} \{(c, g) \mid c \in \mathbb{P}\,\mathcal{M} \wedge g \in \mathbb{P}(\mathcal{M} \times \mathcal{M}) \wedge \ c \neq \varnothing \wedge g = c \triangleleft \text{COM} \triangleright c\}$$

which is clearly a subset of $\mathbb{P}\,\mathcal{M} \times \mathbb{P}(\mathcal{M} \times \mathcal{M})$. It follows from the above that each subgraph of the module graph which is a cluster confines its arcs to be strictly on the modules within its cluster. The above definition permits module clusters to consist of single modules, in which case their internal communication graphs consist of a singleton, which is a reflexive pair. There can also be larger clusters consisting only of reflexive terms, effectively with no intermodule communication graphs. Obviously, the module graph itself is a cluster, that is, $(\mathcal{M}, \text{COM}) \in \text{CLU}$. Intuitively, clusters enable us to ignore the pairing of modules within clusters and view each module cluster simply as a collection of modules.

Clustering of the module graph as a whole results in a partition of the module graph. Since a unique set of arcs is associated with each cluster, a given partition may be seen as a function from $\mathbb{P}\,\mathcal{M}$ to $\mathbb{P}(\mathcal{M} \times \mathcal{M})$. Let us define the set of these functions as a set $\overline{\text{PARTN}}$:

$$\overline{\text{PARTN}} \stackrel{def}{=} \{ f : \mathbb{P}\mathcal{M} \rightarrow \mathbb{P}(\mathcal{M} \times \mathcal{M}) \mid$$
$$\forall \, clu \bullet \; clu \in f \Rightarrow clu \in \text{CLU} \; \wedge \qquad\qquad\qquad\text{(i)}$$
$$\forall \, c_1, c_2 : \mathbb{P}\mathcal{M}; \; g_1, g_2 : \mathbb{P}(\mathcal{M} \times \mathcal{M}) \bullet$$
$$\{(c_1, g_1), (c_2, g_2)\} \subseteq f \wedge (c_1 \cap c_2 \neq \emptyset \vee$$
$$g_1 \cap g_2 \neq \emptyset) \Rightarrow c_1 = c_2 \wedge g_1 = g_2\} \qquad\text{(ii)}$$

Predicate (i) requires that each cluster of modules in any given partition is an element of CLU, whereas predicate (ii) requires that each module and each arc are unique to a specific cluster. The above set $\overline{\text{PARTN}}$ is a useful interim definition. The final definition of *partition* is given by

$$\text{PARTN} \stackrel{def}{=} \{ f \in \overline{\text{PARTN}} \mid \bigcup (\text{dom } f) = \mathcal{M} \}$$

which requires that, given any partition, the modules in all its clusters when taken together constitute exactly the modules of the module graph. A partition of a module graph into clusters is shown in Figure 10.1.

10.4.5   Module and Module Cluster Allocation Functions

It follows from the grouping of modules into (non-empty) larger clusters that our intention is to allocate each module cluster to only one processor. This explains why χ is considered to be a mapping.

In order to distinguish between module cluster allocation and module allocation, let us introduce two separate functions for the two purposes: χ_c for cluster based module allocation, and χ_m for the allocation of modules where the affiliation of modules with clusters is hidden. The intended usage of these functions may be clearer from their type definitions:[1]

$$\chi_c \quad : \overline{\text{PARTN}} \rightarrow \text{CLU} \twoheadrightarrow \mathcal{P}$$
$$\chi_m \quad : \overline{\text{PARTN}} \rightarrow \mathcal{M} \twoheadrightarrow \mathcal{P}$$

The above uses $\overline{\text{PARTN}}$ in order to retain the flexibility of using these functions in relation to partially defined partitions. In the case of module clusters, each module cluster is being allocated to a single processor. However, since a given partition may not contain every possible module cluster, $\chi_c(ptn)$ is a partial function for any given $ptn \in \overline{\text{PARTN}}$. On the other hand, $\mathcal{M}$ being a set consisting of nothing more than the modules of interest to a given application, each and every module must be allocated to a processor. However, since $\overline{\text{PARTN}}$ may not contain some module clusters and, therefore, some modules of $\mathcal{M}$, $\chi_m(ptn)$ is also a partial function. It is obvious that, knowing χ_c, one can establish χ_m as

---

[1] See page 416 in Appendix C (under *curried functions*) for an explanation of function abstraction used in χ_m and χ_c.

$$\forall\, ptn \in \overline{\text{PARTN}}\ \bullet$$
$$\chi_m(ptn) = \{(m,p)\ \bullet\ m:\mathcal{M};\ p:\mathcal{P}\ |\ \exists\, c:\mathbb{P}\mathcal{M};\ g:\mathbb{P}(\mathcal{M}\times\mathcal{M})\ \bullet$$
$$(c,g)\in\text{CLU}\wedge(c,g)\in\text{dom}(\chi_c(ptn))\wedge$$
$$\chi_c(ptn,(c,g))=p\wedge m\in c\}$$

For the purpose of simplifying the notation, let us omit writing ptn in $\chi_m(ptn)$ and $\chi_c(ptn)$ and instead write χ_m and χ_c respectively.

10.4.6　Cluster Graphs

Given a module graph, it is possible to develop an equivalent *cluster graph*, that is, a graph where the nodes are clusters of modules.

Each function $f\in\text{PARTN}$ represents a partition of the module graph into a set of module clusters. It accounts for the arcs in COM which are solely within each of its clusters. In developing the notion of *cluster graph*, the elements of a partition f are treated as the nodes of the cluster graph. The arcs of the cluster graph due to f are the arcs of the module graph that are not accounted for in f. These arcs represent the communications between modules belonging to different clusters. Analogous to module graphs, the nodes and the arcs of cluster graph are also weighted. The weight of nodes represents the total execution costs of the modules in each cluster. The weight of an arc between a pair of nodes represents the total communication cost between different modules belonging to the two corresponding clusters. The two weighting functions of the cluster graph are: $\mathcal{E}_g$ and γ_g, $\mathcal{E}_g$ determining the total execution cost of clusters and γ_g determining inter-cluster communication costs. These functions[2] are

$$\mathcal{E}_g\quad:\quad\overline{\text{PARTN}}\rightarrow(\text{CLU}\times\mathcal{P})\nrightarrow\mathbb{E}$$
$$\gamma_g\quad:\quad\overline{\text{PARTN}}\rightarrow\text{CLU}^2\nrightarrow\mathbb{C}$$

$$\forall\, ptn\in\overline{\text{PARTN}}\ \bullet$$
$$\mathcal{E}_g(ptn)\ =\ \{((cl,p,),a)\ \bullet\ cl\in ptn;\ p:\mathcal{P};\ a\in\mathbb{E}\ |\ \chi_c(cl)=p\wedge$$
$$(\exists\, c,g\ \bullet\ cl=(c,g)\wedge a=\sum_{m\in c}\mathcal{E}(m,p))\}$$
$$\gamma_g(ptn)\ =\ \{((cl_1,cl_2),a)\ \bullet\ cl_1,cl_2\in ptn;\ a\in\mathbb{C}\ |\ (\exists\, c_1,c_2,g_1,g_2\ \bullet$$
$$cl_1=(c_1,g_1)\wedge cl_2=(c_2,g_2)\wedge\chi_c(cl_1)\neq\chi_c(cl_2)\wedge$$
$$a=\sum_{\substack{m_1\in c_1\ \wedge\\ m_2\in c_2}}\gamma(m_1,m_2))\}$$

where χ_c is a module allocation function defined above in Section 10.4.5.
EXAMPLE

Consider the application shown in Figure 10.1. For the module clusters indicated

---

[2]See page 416 in Appendix C (under *curried functions*) for an explanation of the function type used in $\mathcal{E}_g$ and γ_g.

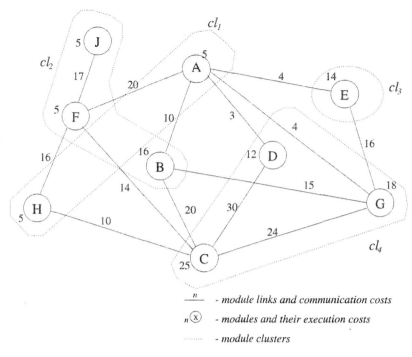

Figure 10.1 Partitioning a communication graph into clusters

there, the details of the corresponding module graph are given in the table below
and are shown in the Figure 10.2.

Constituents of cluster graph, ptn			Exec. cost	Comm. cost		
Clusters	Modules, c	Arcs, g	$\mathcal{E}_g(ptn, cl)$	cl_i	cl_j	$\gamma_g(ptn, (cl_i, cl_j))$
cl_1	H, A	$(H,H), (A,A)$	10	cl_1	cl_2	46
cl_2	J, F, B	$(F,J), (J,F)$, etc.	26	cl_1	cl_3	4
cl_3	E	(E,E)	14	cl_1	cl_4	17
cl_4	C, D, G	$(C,D), (C,H),$	55	cl_2	cl_3	0
		$(D,C), (H,C)$, etc.		cl_2	cl_4	49
				cl_3	cl_4	16

10.4.7   Interprocessor Communication Costs

The intermodule cost between any pair of modules becomes a real cost only if they
are allocated to different processors. Let λ denote the interprocessor communication costs incurred by the modules. This is a function dependent on both γ,
which defines the IMC, and the allocation function χ_m. Note that λ depends also
on the partition of the module graph into clusters and this dependence is implicit
in χ_m and χ_c. The dependence of λ on χ_m may be separated from that on γ by

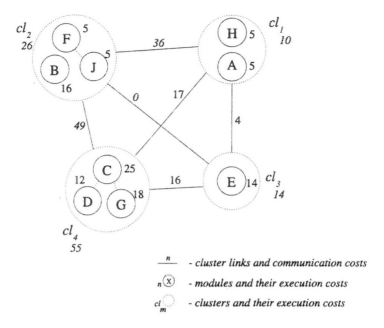

$\dfrac{n}{}$ - *cluster links and communication costs*

$n\!\!\bigcirc\!\!\times$ - *modules and their execution costs*

$cl_m\ \raisebox{0pt}{$\vdots$}$ - *clusters and their execution costs*

Figure 10.2 Clusters and their execution and communication costs

considering an intermediate function $\lambda(\chi_m)$,[3] which has the same type as γ. That is, $\lambda(\chi_m)$ is a function from $\mathcal{M} \times \mathcal{M}$ to $\mathbb{C}$.

In the event of the allocation of two modules m_i and m_j to the same processor, their communication does not incur interprocessor communications and, therefore, the relevant IPC, $\lambda(\chi_m, m_i, m_j)$, becomes equal to zero. In other cases, when they reside on different processors, m_i and m_j do incur an IPC. Following our discussion in Section 10.3.2, the IPCs have to be determined by using both the IMCs and the interprocessor scaling factors. Thus, the interprocessor module communication cost function λ may be defined as

$$\lambda(\chi_m) \;=\; \{((m, n), x) \;\bullet\; m, n : \mathcal{M};\; x : \mathbb{C} \mid (m, n) \in \mathrm{dom}\ \gamma \wedge$$
$$x = \gamma(m, n) \times \mathrm{SCL}(\chi_m(m), \chi_m(n))\}$$

where the scaling function SCL is as given in Section 10.3.2. As a result:

(a) The IPC incurred by pairs of co-resident modules is zero.
(b) The IPCs between pairs of modules that have been assigned to processors unreachable by CON are ∞ – a large cost resulting from an inappropriate choice of χ_m.
(c) The IPC between pairs of modules allocated to processors reachable by (CON – id $\mathcal{P}$) is identical to the IMC specified by γ.

---

[3]See page 416 in Appendix C (under *curried functions*) for an explanation of function abstraction used in $\lambda(\chi_m)$.

It is obvious that because of the associated 'infinite costs' the presence of unconnected processors significantly complicates the choice of χ_m. In this respect, the assumption of full interconnectivity eliminates this difficulty since it results in a simpler form of the function λ, namely,

$$\lambda(\chi_m) = \gamma \; \oplus \; \{((m,n),0) \bullet \; m, n : \mathcal{M} \mid \chi_m(m) = \chi_m(n)\}$$

where $\lambda(\chi_m)$ is obtained in the following manner:

(a) by overwriting communication costs defined in γ between pairs of co-resident modules with zero; and
(b) retaining the communication costs in γ for all other pairs.

With knowledge of λ, it is possible to compute as follows the interprocessor communication costs λ_g incurred by clusters from the inter-cluster communication cost γ_g (introduced in Section 10.4.6) due to a given partition *ptn*:

$$\lambda_g \qquad : \quad \overline{\text{PARTN}} \to \text{CLU}^2 \nrightarrow \mathbb{C}$$

$$\forall \, ptn : \overline{\text{PARTN}} \bullet$$
$$\lambda_g(ptn) \;\; = \;\; \{((cl_1, cl_2), a) \bullet \; cl_1, cl_2 \in ptn; \; a : \mathbb{C} \mid$$
$$a = \gamma_g(cl_1, cl_2) \times \text{SCL}(\chi_c(cl_1), \chi_c(cl_2))\}$$

10.4.8 Placement Constraints

Task allocation may be further constrained by various application dependent requirements. Some of these are:

(a) allocation preference relations, specifying preferred processors for the execution of particular modules;
(b) module exclusion relations, excluding the execution of particular modules on the same processor;
(c) module redundancy relations, replicating the execution of selected modules on a number of processors in order to provide a required level of fault tolerance.

Some of them have already been mentioned in Sections 10.4.2, 10.4.3 and 10.4.7, which made use of various fictitious cost values to model such requirements indirectly. A better way of dealing with such constraints is to state them explicitly using, for example, relations and functions.

The requirements (b) and (c) are not considered any further. The requirement (a), on the other hand, has been made stronger by insisting that the assignment of certain modules is fixed *a priori* by two relations:

FXD : $\mathcal{M} \twoheadrightarrow \mathcal{P}$
OPT : $\mathcal{M} \leftrightarrow \mathcal{P}$

The interpretation of FXD is such that given a module m and a processor $p \in \mathcal{P}$, $(m, p) \in$ FXD is true if and only if **module m must be executed on the processor p**. The interpretation of OPT is such that, given a module m and a set of processors $s : \mathbb{P}\mathcal{P}$ such that $s \neq \varnothing$, the formula

$$\{(m, p) \bullet p : \mathcal{P} \mid p \in s\} = \{m\} \lhd \text{OPT}$$

is true if and only if **module m must be executed on one of the processors in the set** s. Such requirements may be motivated by the desire to exploit features or capabilities specific to one or more selected processors. These may include, for example, processing capabilities, local database facilities and the availability of specific peripheral devices. Allocation of modules to certain fixed processors by FXD and OPT requires that

$$\text{FXD} = (\text{dom FXD}) \lhd \text{OPT}$$

according to which the modules with fixed allocations have exactly one processor option.

In practical terms, different values of OPT also signify different computational models. These are,

- Shared memory model

  In the case of a shared memory model involving a homogeneous set of processors, the shared global memory extends the homogeneity beyond the individual processors. Therefore, modules may be executed on any processor. In this case,

  $$\text{OPT} = \mathcal{M} \times \mathcal{P}$$

- Local memory model

  The local memory model generally introduces heterogeneity with respect to resident nodes of code as well as memory capacities. As a result, the execution of specific modules may be restricted to specific processors. In this case,

  $$\varnothing \subset \text{OPT} \subset \mathcal{M} \times \mathcal{P}$$

10.5 Allocation as Optimization

The primary aim of treating task allocation as an optimization problem is to benefit from the general framework of optimization. Certain problems of task allocation have been solved as optimization problems. Optimization is a separate subject in its own right with a considerable body of advanced knowledge and is beyond the scope of this text. Therefore, we have chosen to confine ourselves to just the terminology of optimization and not to the techniques.

10.5.1   Objective Functions

Clearly, it may be impossible to meet all evaluatory criteria fully in any design task. Trade-offs must be made and compromises must be reached in the event of conflicting demands. The goal here is the achievement of a certain optimality in the allocation, which may be approximated by the optimization of an *objective function* under the physical constraints of available resources and the realtime requirements of the application. An *objective function* produces a certain 'aggregated' or a 'weighted' cost (benefit) measured in a single unit from a set of costs (benefits) which are different in nature and are generally measured in a number of disparate units. Each of these disparate costs may in turn be a function of system parameters. The optimization constraints of the objective function may also be geared towards achieving other performance criteria such as load balancing among processors.

10.5.2   Total Processing Costs

The total workload $\mathcal{L}(\chi_m, p)$ of a processor p under the allocation χ_m is

$$
\mathcal{L}(\chi_m, p) = r_e \left(\sum_{\substack{m \in \mathcal{M} \,\wedge \\ \chi_m(m)=p}} \mathcal{E}(m, p) \right) +
$$

$$
r_c \sum_{\substack{m \in \mathcal{M} \,\wedge \\ \chi_m(m)=p}} \left(\sum_{\substack{n \in \mathcal{M} \,\wedge \\ \chi_m(n)\neq p \,\wedge \\ (m,n)\in\text{dom } \gamma}} \lambda(\chi_m, m, n) + \sum_{\substack{n \in \mathcal{M} \,\wedge \\ \chi_m(n)\neq p \,\wedge \\ (n,m)\in\text{dom } \gamma}} \lambda(\chi_m, n, m) \right)
$$

The summation of $\mathcal{E}(m, p)$ over modules m accounts for the total execution cost incurred by the modules allocated to p by χ_m. The term $\lambda(\chi_m, m, n)$ in the second summation over modules m and n accounts for the total communication cost due to outgoing messages from all modules allocated to p, while the second term $\lambda(\chi_m, n, m)$ there accounts for the total communication cost due to incoming messages to all modules allocated to p. Note that r_e and r_c are conversion factors for converting execution costs and communication costs, respectively, to a common cost unit suitable for defining an objective function for the system as a whole. The cost due to outgoing control and file update messages at p may be computed as

$$
\sum_{\substack{m \in \mathcal{M} \,\wedge \\ \chi_m(m)=p}} \sum_{\substack{n \in \mathcal{M} \,\wedge \\ \chi_m(n)\neq p \,\wedge \\ (m,n)\in\text{dom } \gamma}} \lambda(\chi_m, m, n) = V_c(\chi_m, m, n) + \sum_{\substack{f \in \mathcal{F} \,\wedge \\ \varphi(f, \chi_m(n))}} V_f(\chi_m, m, f)
$$

where

$\mathcal{F}, \varphi$ – $\mathcal{F}$ is a set of files and φ is a predicate. Both have been introduced in Section 10.3.1.

$V_c(\chi_m, m, n)$ –   is a measure of the control data (for example, in bytes) being transferred from the module m to the module n under the allocation scheme χ_m.

$V_f(\chi_m, m, f)$ –   is a measure of the data being transferred from the module m to update file f under the allocation scheme χ_m.

One may define the cost $\lambda(\chi_m, n, m)$ analogously for incoming messages to m.

The total processing cost, that is, the sum of both execution and communication costs, in a given implementation of application S within the given configuration $\mathcal{H}$ thus becomes

$$Cost(Sys) = \sum_{p \in \mathcal{P}} \mathcal{L}(\chi_m, p)$$

In other words, the aggregated cost is the sum of the processing costs and the communication costs incurred by the modules allocated to different processors.

10.5.3   Bottleneck Processors

A processor is said to be a *bottleneck* processor if it is one of the excessively loaded processors. It is clear that an even distribution of work load among the processors is likely to result in a better response time performance than a distribution where one or a few processors are heavily loaded almost to their full capacity while others are lightly loaded. A factor contributing to this fall in performance is the rapid growth of queueing delay at processors with high processor utilization levels.

The load on the most heavily loaded processor, which may possibly be a bottleneck, is

$$maxL = max\ \{\mathcal{L}(\chi_m, p) \mid p \in \mathcal{P}\}$$

where *max* returns the maximum value in its operand set appearing on its right hand side. Obviously, the determination of bottleneck processors depends also on processor capabilities.

Minimization of the above expression for $maxL$ is shown to lead to balanced processor loads in peak load regimes, although there can be greater variations in low load regimes.

10.6   Optimization Constraints

10.6.1   Resource Constraints

Optimization of a given objective function is often subject to various system constraints such as limited storage (memory) capacity at processor nodes and the limited processing capability of processors.

The demand for storage at processor p and its storage capacity is subject to the following constraint:

$$\sum_{\substack{m \in M \,\wedge \\ \chi_m(m)=p}} \mathcal{D}(m) \leq \sigma(p)$$

where, as mentioned in Section 10.4.1, $\mathcal{D}(m)$ denotes the demand for storage by the module m. Variations of constraints of the above form may be formulated for other different kinds of resource.

10.6.2   Utilization Constraints

Assuming that the expression derived for the workload $\mathcal{L}(\chi_m, p)$ on processor p derived in Section 10.5.2 is over a time interval (t_1, t_2) and the processing capability of processor p is given by $\rho(p)$, one can write a constraint on the demand and supply of the processing power at p as

$$\frac{1}{t_2 - t_1} \mathcal{L}(\chi_m, p) \leq \eta(p) \times \rho(p)$$

where, as mentioned in Section 10.3.1, $\eta(p)$ denotes the maximum utilization factor for processor p. The actual value of $\eta(p)$ may be motivated, for example, by the need to guarantee schedule feasibility (see Section 12.6.4 of Chapter 12 for the uniprocessor case) or on the grounds of experimental observations on performance as a function of processor utilization.

Utilization constraints may also be applied on a system-wide scale. In this case, a constraint of the form

$$\frac{1}{t_2 - t_1} \sum_{p \in P} \mathcal{L}(\chi_m, p) \leq \eta_s \sum_{p \in P} \rho(p)$$

may be formulated using a single utilization factor η_s for the system as a whole.

10.6.3   Timing Constraints

It is sometimes necessary to introduce realtime constraints for specifying that the total demand for processor time by the modules allocated to a particular processor does not exceed a certain prescribed fixed length of time. Such constraints may be written in an analogous manner to utilization constraints developed in the previous subsection.

10.7 Approaches to Task Allocation

An *optimal* solution to allocation will either minimize or maximize the chosen objective function, depending on whether the objective function represents a cost or a benefit, subject to other constraints mentioned earlier.

Different objective functions tend to result in different performance measures. For example, optimization of the total processing cost over all processors and involving both execution costs and interprocessor communications costs may achieve a high throughput. This may suit environments which involve a number of non-realtime applications sharing the resources of a distributed system. However, this might not be the case in highly specialized realtime applications, where each application relies on its own exclusive computer system.

Since, as it was discussed earlier, minimization of the interprocessor communication cost tends to concentrate modules on as few processors as possible, such an approach could result in a relatively poor response time. This could be a real possibility in systems where the total processing cost is dominated by the IPC.

Module partitioning is accomplished alongside the allocation of modules to processors. Task allocation is a complex task because of the potentially large number of processor assignments. The scale of this may be seen from the number of possible different allocation schemes. Given that $\#\mathcal{P}$ and $\#\mathcal{M}$ denote, respectively, the number of processors and the number of modules in the application, an exhaustive search for an optimal solution would involve the search of a tree of depth $\#\mathcal{M}$ with $\#\mathcal{P}$ branches at every node, resulting in a total of $(\#\mathcal{P})^{\#\mathcal{M}}$ leaves. Clearly, such an exhaustive search is not a practically viable approach for the allocation problem.

Practical approaches to task allocation fall into three different categories:

- heuristic algorithms (discussed in Section 10.8);
- graph theoretic (discussed in Section 10.9); and
- linear (integer) programming.

Our study is limited to the first two approaches only and, as mentioned earlier in Section 10.5, excludes the third. This omission is also due to the fact that the approaches based only on optimization appear to suffer from certain drawbacks when considering precedence constraints and the effects of current system states on realtime constraints.

10.8   Heuristic Algorithm: Clustering and Reassignment

This section discusses a particular heuristic algorithm which consists of two distinct subalgorithms: algorithm MCA (Module Clustering Algorithm) to be introduced in Section 10.8.3 and algorithm MRA (Module Reassignment Algorithm) to be introduced in Section 10.8.4. The algorithm as a whole works iteratively. In each cycle, MCA first produces an initial clustering of modules and allocates the resulting clusters to processors. Subsequently, MRA transfers modules from the heavily loaded processors to other processors in order to achieve a better distribution of processor loads. The emphasis placed on reducing the IPC and that on load balancing thus alternate during the course of the algorithm, trading off the IPC for better load balance each time.

Thus, the algorithm as presented assumes a simple notion of processor utilization, with a degree of decoupling between the module execution costs and the IPC in favour of load balancing. This could be inadequate in certain circumstances, since optimization with a bias towards one or the other may not necessarily result in the minimization of total running costs. However, this limitation may be overcome with a more realistic notion of processor utilization based on both execution and communication costs.

The system consists of a fully interconnected set of processors. It is also homogeneous with respect to processor capabilities and, in particular, with respect to execution costs. Furthermore, both the communication capabilities between processors and the communication needs of modules are symmetric, thus making it unnecessary to consider directed graphs for CON and COM. However, no assumptions are made as to how the communication costs are apportioned between communicating processors. The algorithm does not consider a precedence relation on modules.

10.8.1   A Processor Loading Classification

The algorithm discussed in this section aims at load balancing according to queue length, which is taken as the sum of the execution costs of modules allocated to a processor. The notion of 'queue' here does not consider the frequency of task requests and, therefore, does not represent a queueing model. The queue length of processor p under a partitioning scheme ptn is defined here by $\mathrm{QUE}(ptn, p)$

$$\mathrm{QUE}(ptn, p) \;=\; \sum_{\substack{cl \in ptn\ \wedge \\ \chi_c(cl)=p}} \mathcal{E}_g(ptn, (cl, p)), \qquad \text{if } ptn \in \overline{\mathrm{PARTN}}$$

$$=\; \sum_{\substack{m \in \mathcal{M}\ \wedge \\ \chi_m(m)=p}} \mathcal{E}(m, p), \qquad \text{if } ptn \in \mathrm{PARTN}$$

The first is a more general expression than the second and applies also to partial module allocations. The utilization level of each processor p as a fraction of the average utilization level of all processors may then be computed as

$$\text{QUE}'(ptn, p) \;=\; \frac{\text{QUE}(ptn,p)}{\frac{1}{\#(\text{ran } \chi_m)} \sum_{cl \in ptn} \mathcal{E}_g(ptn,(cl,p))}, \qquad \text{if } ptn \in \overline{\text{PARTN}}$$

$$\;=\; \frac{\text{QUE}(ptn,p)}{\frac{1}{\#\mathcal{P}} \sum_{m \in \mathcal{M}} \mathcal{E}(m,p)}, \qquad \text{if } ptn \in \text{PARTN} \wedge \text{ran } \chi_m = \mathcal{P}$$

Again, the first expression is more general and applies also to situations where a sufficiently high processor utilization level is desired but without necessarily using all the processors. The second expression concerns completed module allocation with the utilization of all processors at one's disposal. The above also assumes that there are no initial processor loads. Given a permitted deviation δ ($\delta \geq 0$) from the ideal utilization level of unity, the overloaded, the underloaded and the acceptably loaded processors in the context of a given partition ptn may be identified as

$$\begin{aligned}
ov\text{--}loaded(ptn, p) &\Leftrightarrow \text{QUE}'(ptn, p) > 1 + \delta \\
ud\text{--}loaded(ptn, p) &\Leftrightarrow \text{QUE}'(ptn, p) < 1 - \delta \\
ok\text{--}loaded(ptn, p) &\Leftrightarrow 1 - \delta \leq \text{QUE}'(ptn, p) \leq 1 + \delta
\end{aligned}$$

where $ov\text{--}loaded$, $ud\text{--}loaded$ and $ok\text{--}loaded$ are predicates with the indicated meanings.

10.8.2 An IPC Classification

In assessing possible module allocations, it is necessary to compare intermodule and interprocessor communication costs between alternative allocations. For generality, let us base such comparisons on the interprocessor communication costs, since this would enable us to take into account not only the actual network topology, but also certain fictitious penalty factors introduced later (see Step 7 of the algorithm MRA presented in Section 10.8.4) for shifting modules from heavily loaded to lightly loaded processors. With this in mind, let us introduce two predicates $hi\text{--}ipc(m, n)$ and $lo\text{--}ipc(m, n)$:

$$\begin{aligned}
hi\text{--}ipc(m, n) &\Leftrightarrow \forall\, p, q : \mathcal{P} \;\bullet\; p \neq q \wedge (p, q) \in \text{CON} \Rightarrow \\
&\qquad\qquad \gamma(m, n) \times Scale(p, q) > H \\
lo\text{--}ipc(m, n) &\Leftrightarrow \exists\, p, q : \mathcal{P} \;\bullet\; p \neq q \wedge (p, q) \in \text{CON} \wedge \\
&\qquad\qquad \gamma(m, n) \times Scale(p, q) < L
\end{aligned}$$

where H and L are threshold IPCs such that $0 < L < H$ adopted for the purpose of defining, respectively, high and low IPCs, and $Scale$ is a function which is defined as a variable in the algorithm. Initially, $Scale$ is identical to SCL, but generally contains analogous information adjusted during the course of the algorithm for the purpose of penalizing communications that result in excessive load imbalances. The predicate $hi\text{-}ipc(m, n)$ is true if and only if 'the modules m and n result in a high IPC when allocated to every pair of distinct but connected processors'. On the other hand, the predicate $lo\text{-}ipc(m, n)$ is true if and only if 'the modules m and n result in a low IPC when allocated to certain pairs of distinct but connected processors'. The values of H and L may be revised in different calls for the algorithms concerned. Note that Sections 10.8.3 and 10.8.4 rely on the above understanding of high and low IPC.

10.8.3   Module Clustering Algorithm (MCA)

The purpose of this algorithm is to partition the module graph subject to certain allocation constraints. It is guided only by possible interprocessor communication costs between modules under different allocation schemes. The steps of this algorithm are as follows:

Preamble Algorithm *MCA*

$$MCA(Mods, Coms, Opts, Scale, \chi_m, \chi_c)$$

where the arguments are:

Mods is an input set of modules and $Mods \subseteq \mathcal{M}$.

Coms is an input relation on modules and $Coms \subseteq \text{COM}$.

Opts is an input relation from modules to processors. Its intended usage may be clear from the fact that $Opts = \text{OPT}$ when the algorithm is first called.

Scale is an input function from processors to $\mathbb{R}^+$. Its intended usage has been mentioned in Section 10.8.2.

χ_m, χ_c are two variables both serving as inputs and as outputs. These are module allocation functions to be established by the algorithm.

Let *Modules* and *Arcs* be two local variables for keeping track of modules yet to be allocated and the arcs of COM associated with these modules. These are the elements of the following sets:

$$Modules \ \in \ \mathbb{P}\mathcal{M}$$
$$Arcs \quad \ \in \ \mathbb{P}(\mathcal{M} \times \mathcal{M})$$

Step 1. Initialize these variables as follows:

$$Modules := Mods; \ Arcs := Coms$$

Step 2. Find a function $f : \mathcal{M} \twoheadrightarrow \mathcal{P}$ such that

$$f \subseteq Opts \wedge \mathrm{dom}\ f = \mathrm{dom}\ Opts$$

If there are any pairs of modules m_i and m_j such that $Opts$ permits their allocation to the same processor p, that is,

$$\{(m_i, p), (m_j, p)\} \subseteq Opts$$

and they also result in high IPC, that is, $hi\text{-}ipc(m_i, m_j)$ is true (see Section 10.8.2), then choose f such that

$$\{(m_i, p), (m_j, p)\} \subseteq f$$

Step 3. Update χ_c using f in the following manner:

$$\begin{aligned} \chi_c := \ & \chi_c \oplus \{((ms, as), p) \ \bullet \ ms : \mathbb{P}\mathcal{M}; \ as : \mathbb{P}(\mathcal{M} \times \mathcal{M}); \ p : \mathcal{P} \ | \\ & ms \neq \varnothing \wedge ms = \mathrm{dom}(f \rhd \{p\}) \wedge \\ & as = ms \lhd \mathrm{COM} \rhd ms\} \end{aligned}$$

and compute χ_m accordingly. Remove the modules so allocated to processors by f from *Modules* and any associated arcs from *Arcs*:

$$\begin{aligned} Modules \ &:= Modules - \mathrm{dom}\ f; \\ Arcs \ &:= Arcs - \{(m_i, m_j) \ \bullet \ m_i, m_j : \mathcal{M} \ | \ \{m_i, m_j\} \subseteq \mathrm{dom}\ f \wedge \\ & \qquad (m_i, m_j) \in \mathrm{COM}\} \end{aligned}$$

Step 4. Establish those modules in the domain of χ_m and those yet in *Modules* sharing between them a high interprocessor communication cost. In other words, given two modules m_i and m_j, if $m_i \in \mathrm{dom}\ \chi_m$ and $m_j \in Modules$ and $hi\text{-}ipc(m_i, m_j)$ is true, then make the following updates:

$$\begin{aligned} \chi_c \ &:= \chi_c \oplus \{((ms \cup \{m_j\}, as \cup \{(m_i, m_j)\}), p) \ | \\ & \qquad ((ms, as), p) \in \chi_c \wedge m_i \in ms \wedge m_j \in Modules \wedge \\ & \qquad hi\text{-}ipc(m_i, m_j)\}; \\ Modules \ &:= Modules - \{m_j\}; \\ Arcs \ &:= Arcs - \{(m_i, m_j)\} \end{aligned}$$

Step 5. Repeat Step 4 until the IPC between modules which have already been allocated by χ_c and those in *Modules* are no longer high.

Step 6. Compare the IPC between pairs of modules remaining in *Modules* according to the criteria set out in Section 10.8.2.

- If a pair with a high IPC is found, then allocate them to a single processor.

- If a pair with a zero or with a low non-zero IPC is found, then allocate them to different processors, if necessary.

As in Step 4, record the allocated modules and processors by updating the allocation function χ_c. Repeat this process until all modules have been clustered. Although the above algorithm is not described formally, its correctness would require the following to be true:

$$Modules = \varnothing \wedge (\text{dom } \chi_c) \in \text{PARTN}$$

at the completion of the allocation process. According to the above, all modules must have been allocated and the resulting clustering constitute a partitioning as understood by the definition of PARTN. Note that χ_c in the above relies on the simplification of the notation adopted in Section 10.4.5.

End of algorithm *MCA*

The determination of pairs of modules with high IPCs in Steps 3, 4 and 6 may be facilitated by ordering λ (based on SCL, or *Scale* to be introduced in Section 10.8.4) first in the descending order of IPC between module pairs. Furthermore, in order to avoid excessive reassignment of modules between module clusters later, it may be prudent to maintain a tally of current processor utilization levels of all processors as the allocation progresses. This would allow:

- firstly, a more informed choice of processors in Steps 3, 4 and 6 so that processor loads are maintained at an appropriate level; and
- secondly, as an additional benefit, a way to account for any initial processor loads just prior to execution of the application.

10.8.4   Module Reassignment Algorithm: MRA

This algorithm aims at achieving a specific level in processor loadings in each iteration by reassigning module allocations established initially by MCA. MRA achieves this by first modifying interprocessor communication scaling factors depending on the processor loads under the current allocation and then relying on the sensitivity of MCA to such changes to result in a different outcome in the subsequent call. The steps of this algorithm are as follows:

Preamble Algorithm *MRA*

$$MRA(\chi_m, \chi_c)$$

where the arguments χ_m, χ_c are two input/output variables giving the module allocation established by the algorithm.

Let *ptn, Modules, Arcs, Opts* and *Scale* below be some local variables:

$$
\begin{aligned}
ptn &\in \mathbb{P}\,\overline{\text{PARTN}} \\
Modules &\in \mathbb{P}\,\mathcal{M} \\
Arcs &\in \mathbb{P}(\mathcal{M} \times \mathcal{M}) \\
Opts &\in \mathcal{M} \leftrightarrow \mathcal{P} \\
Scale &\in (\mathcal{P} \times \mathcal{P}) \to \mathbb{R}^+
\end{aligned}
$$

intended for keeping track of the current state of clusters as module reassignments progress: *ptn* for the cluster configuration, *Modules* for the current set of modules in *ptn*, *Arcs* for the current set of communication links in *ptn* and *Scale* for factors used for scaling up interprocessor communication costs between disparately loaded module clusters.

Step 1. Initialize the variables in the algorithm as follows:

$$
\begin{aligned}
Modules &:= \mathcal{M}; \\
Arcs &:= \text{COM}; \\
Opts &:= \text{OPT}; \\
Scale &:= \text{SCL}; \\
\chi_c &:= \emptyset; \\
\chi_m &:= \emptyset
\end{aligned}
$$

Step 2. Call $MCA(Modules, Arcs, Opts, Scale, \chi_m, \chi_c)$ with the current values of the arguments.

Step 3. Compute the initial value of *ptn* using the allocation function χ_c:

$$ptn := \text{dom } \chi_c$$

Step 4. Following Section 10.8.1, compute the queue lengths. Based on the average queue length and the permissible deviation δ, determine:

(i) the overloaded processors;

(ii) the underloaded processors;

(iii) the acceptably loaded processors.

Step 5. Remove from *ptn* the module clusters allocated to processors which are acceptably loaded and adjust *Modules* and *Arcs* accordingly:

$$
\begin{aligned}
ptn &:= ptn - \text{dom}(\chi_c \triangleright \{p : \mathcal{P} \mid ok\text{-}loaded(p)\}); \\
Modules &:= \bigcup (\text{dom } ptn); \\
Arcs &:= Modules \triangleleft \text{COM} \triangleright Modules; \\
Opts &:= Modules \triangleleft Opts
\end{aligned}
$$

Step 6. Treat the modules allocated to underloaded processors as supplementing the fixed module allocations and processor options given by OPT. That is,

$$Opts := Opts \oplus (\chi_m \triangleright \{p : \mathcal{P} \mid ud\text{-}loaded(p)\})$$

This would prevent the shift of modules from the underloaded processors during the subsequent process of module reassignments.

Step 7. Identify the pairs of processors such that in each pair (p_i, p_j):

(i) One of the processors of p_i and p_j is overloaded and the other is underloaded.

(ii) $(p_i, p_j) \in$ CON.

(iii) There are some modules m_k and m_l such that $\chi_m(m_k) = p_i$ and $\chi_m(m_l) = p_j$.

Thus, there must be some communicating modules resident on both processors in each pair according to the current value of *ptn*.

Increase network scaling factors as given below:

$$
\begin{aligned}
Scale \; := \; & Scale \oplus \{((p_i, p_j), x) \mid ((ud\text{-}loaded(p_i) \wedge ov\text{-}loaded(p_j)) \vee \\
& (ov\text{-}loaded(p_i) \wedge ud\text{-}loaded(p_j))) \wedge \\
& x = Scale(p_i, p_j) + \tfrac{r_c}{r_e} \times abs(\text{QUE}'(p_i) - \text{QUE}'(p_j))\}
\end{aligned}
$$

where r_e and r_c are the conversion factors mentioned in Section 10.5.2. The above treats $abs(\text{QUE}'(p_i) - \text{QUE}'(p_j))$ as a penalty factor attributable to the differential load between the two processors. The modifications to *Opts* in Step 6 and to *Scale* here in effect force the tasks to gravitate towards underloaded processors from the overloaded.

Step 8. Call *MCA(Modules, Arcs, Opts, χ_m, χ_c)* with the current values of the first three arguments.

Step 9. Repeat Steps 3–8 until one of the following states has been reached:

- All modules in $\mathcal{M}$ have been allocated and all processors are acceptably loaded, in which case the task of module allocation has been successfully accomplished.

- MCA results in the same value of *ptn* as in the previous call to MCA. In this case, it is impossible to achieve a balanced loading of processors within the criteria adopted at the outset. If appropriate, adjust the thresholds H, L and δ in any combination as necessary in order to obtain a less optimal solution and repeat the algorithm from Step 1.

End of algorithm *MRA*

EXAMPLE

Consider a task allocation problem involving the set of modules and processors given below:

$$
\begin{aligned}
\mathcal{M} \; &= \; \{A, B, C, D, E, F, G, H, J\} \\
\mathcal{P} \; &= \; \{P_1, P_2, P_3\}
\end{aligned}
$$

Other details are as shown in the Figure 10.3. Note among them that

$$
\text{FXD} = \text{OPT} = \{(H, P_1), (C, P_2), (G, P_3)\}
$$

Table 10.1 An example in task allocation: initial module clustering

Step	*Processors*								
in MCA		P_1			P_2			P_3	
or MRA	$m^{\ddagger}$	$\mathcal{E}(m)$	*Load*	m	$\mathcal{E}(m)$	*Load*	m	$\mathcal{E}(m)$	*Load*
MCA: Step 2	H†	5		C†	25		G†	18	
	F	5		B	16		E	14	
	A	5		D	12				
MRA: Step 2	J	5							
MRA: Step 4									
$QUE(p)^{\ddagger}$			20			53			32
$QUE'(p)$			0.571			1.514			0.914
utiliz. level	$ud\text{-}loaded(ptn, P_1)$			$ov\text{-}loaded(ptn, P_2)$			$ok\text{-}loaded(ptn, P_3)$		

‡ m being a module and p a processor

† modules with fixed assignments

Simplifications and Assumptions:

- Let us assume that the cost types $\mathbb{E}$ and $\mathbb{C}$ are identical and are given in some processing time unit.
- Processors P_1, P_2 and P_3 are fully interconnected and identical in terms of capabilities.
- Let the various cost thresholds be: $H = 15, L = 5$ and $\delta = 0.15$.

Steps 1–6 Initial Clustering of Modules by MCA

See Table 10.8.4 for more details about the module clustering process. Various cost parameters of the application after the initial clustering of modules are as follows:

The total interprocessor communication cost
$$= 10 + 14 + 10 + 3 + 24 + 15 + 4 + 4$$
$$= 84$$
The execution cost of modules on P_1
$$= 20$$
The execution cost of modules on P_2
$$= 53$$
The execution cost of modules on P_3
$$= 32$$
The total processing cost
$$= 20 + 53 + 32 + 84$$
$$= 189 \text{ units.}$$

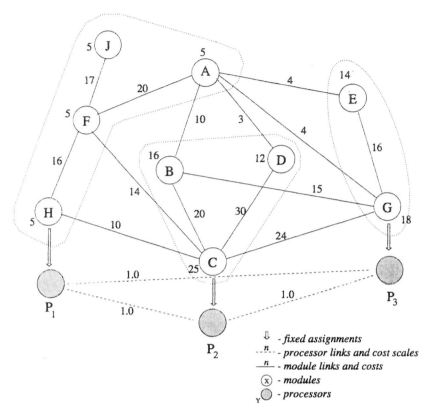

Figure 10.3 An example in task allocation: initial module clustering

The worst case execution time
$$= max(20 + 10 + 14 + 10 + 3 + 4 + 4,$$
$$53 + 10 + 14 + 10 + 3 + 24 + 15,$$
$$32 + 24 + 15 + 4 + 4)$$
$$= max(65, 129, 79)$$
$$= 129$$

The worst case execution time given above assumes that the costs are measured in processor time and that the total IPC between any pair of processors is attributable to the processor carrying the greater load. The latter assumption may not be quite reasonable since the communication costs are likely to be shared between processors. Also, our use of the terminology 'worst case execution time' has a limited meaning here and covers only the most unfavourable apportioning of communicating costs between processors.

Steps 7–8 Module Reassignment by MRA and MCA

The adjusted scale factor for interprocessor communications between processors P_1 and $P_2 = 1.0 + 0.943 = 1.943$. See Table 10.8.4 for more details

Table 10.2 An example in task allocation: module reassignment

Step	Processors						
in MCA	P_1			P_2			P_3
or MRA	$m^\ddagger$	$\mathcal{E}(m)$	Load	m	$\mathcal{E}(m)$	Load	
MRA: Step 7	F†	5		C†	25		(eliminated)
MCA: End	A†	5		D	12		
	H†	$\cdot$ 5					
	J†	5					
	B	16					
MRA: Step 4							
(2nd round)							
$QUE(p)^\ddagger$			36			37	
$QUE'(p)$			0.99			1.01	
utiliz. level	ok-$loaded(ptn, P_1)$			ok-$loaded(ptn, P_2)$			

$\ddagger$ m being a module and p a processor

$\dagger$ modules with fixed assignments

about the module reassignment process. Various cost parameters after the module reassignment are as follows:

The total interprocessor communication cost
$$= 10 + 14 + 20 + 3 + 24 + 15 + 4 + 4$$
$$= 94$$
The execution cost of modules on P_1
$$= 36$$
The execution cost of modules on P_2
$$= 37$$
The execution cost of modules on P_3 (unchanged from the previous value)
$$= 32$$
The total processing cost
$$= 36 + 37 + 32 + 94$$
$$= 199 \text{ units.}$$
The worst case execution time of the application as a whole
$$= max(36 + 10 + 14 + 20 + 3 + 15 + 4 + 4,$$
$$37 + 10 + 14 + 20 + 3 + 24,$$
$$32 + 24 + 15 + 4 + 4)$$
$$= max(106, 108, 79)$$
$$= 108$$

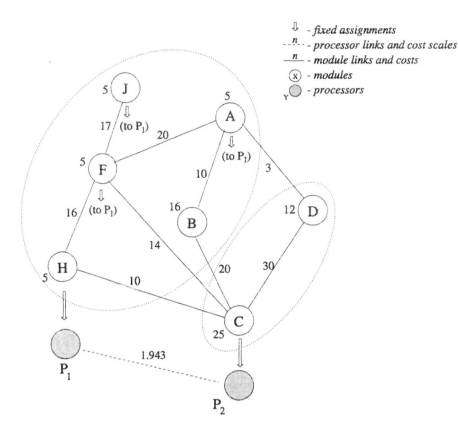

Figure 10.4 An example in task allocation: module reassignment

10.9   A Graph Theoretic Approach

This section introduces a solution to the task allocation problem based on what is known as *maximum network flow* problems.

10.9.1   Network Flow Graphs (NFG)

Below is a basic introduction to the main terminology used in network flow algorithms. Network flow graphs are based on the concept of *commodity networks*. A commodity network consists of three distinct types of nodes: *source*, *sink* and *interior* nodes and a set of weighted arcs. Source nodes are capable of producing an infinite amount of a commodity and sink nodes are capable of consuming an infinite amount of the commodity. The arcs in the graph represent transport links and are doubly weighted. One of the weights of the arcs indicates the capacity of each link and the other indicates the actual flow along it.

A *feasible commodity flow* is one that originates at the source nodes and terminates at the sink nodes subject to the constraints:

(a) The net outgoing flow from a source node is non-negative.
(b) The net incoming flow to a sink node is non-negative.
(c) The net flow at other nodes is zero.
(d) The flow in any link connecting an adjacent pair of nodes does not exceed the capacity.

Since a flow must have an origin and a destination, the direction of a flow along an arc is shown by an arrow. The *value* of a commodity flow is the sum of flows emanating from the source nodes. A *maximum flow* is a feasible flow that maximizes the value among all feasible flows.

A *cutset* is a set of arcs the removal of which from the graph disconnects the source nodes from the sink nodes. However, no proper subset of a cutset can be a cutset. In this sense, a cutset is the minimal (smallest) set. The *weight of a cutset* is the sum of capacities of the arcs in the cutset. The value of a maximum flow and the weight of cutset has an interesting relationship which is expressed in Observation 10.1:

> **Observation 10.1** The value of a maximum flow in a commodity network and the weight of the minimum weight cutset of that network are equal.

The above is known as the *max-flow min-cut theorem* due to Ford and Fulkerson. A proof of this is not essential for our study, but the example in the Figure 10.5 does illustrate this point. It also illustrates the important property of cutsets, namely, that no proper subset of a cutset is a cutset.

10.9.2   Task Allocation Problem as a Network Flow Problem

In this framework, let us view the general problem of task allocation as a tuple:

$$Sys = (\mathcal{P}, \mathcal{M}, \mathcal{E}, \text{COM}, \gamma)$$

every element of which is as given in Sections 10.3.1 and 10.4.1. Also, unless otherwise stated, let $n = \#\mathcal{P}$. It is an underlying assumption that the communication needs of modules are symmetric. Therefore, COM too is symmetric and the arcs in COM are undirected.

Now consider an extended network flow graph Sys_{nfg} defined as a triple:

$$Sys_{nfg} = (V, A, W)$$

obtained from Sys as follows:

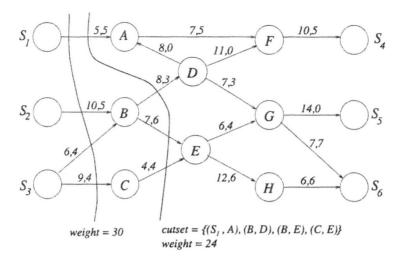

weight = 30   cutset = {(S₁ , A), (B, D), (B, E), (C, E)}
                   weight = 24

Figure 10.5 A commodity flow network

(a) V is a set of nodes and $V = \mathcal{P} \cup \mathcal{M}$.

Nodes of the type P are referred to as *distinguished* or *terminal* nodes. In the case of allocation problems involving only two processors, the literature on the subject continues to use the terminology *source* and *sink*, distinguishing one processor as the source and the other as the sink.

(b) A is a set of arcs such that $A \subseteq V \times V$ and

$$A = \text{CON} \cup \{(m, p) \mid m \in \mathcal{M} \wedge p \in \mathcal{P}\}$$

(c) W is a function from $V \times V$ to a unified type of cost values such as time (based on $\mathbb{C}$, $\mathbb{E}$ or some other measure) giving the arc weights. W is defined as

$$W = \gamma \cup \overline{\gamma}$$

where, for any module m and a processor k,

$$\overline{\gamma}(m, k) = \frac{E_{\Sigma}^{m}}{n-1} - E_{k}^{m}$$

and

$$E_{\Sigma}^{m} = \sum_{i \in \mathcal{P}} E_{i}^{m}$$

E_{k}^{m} is an abbreviation for $\mathcal{E}(m, k)$ and denotes the execution cost of the module m on the processor k. Thus, $\overline{\gamma}$ incorporates the execution costs of modules in an extended communication weighting function W. Note, for example, for some intermediate k between 1 and n that

$$\overline{\gamma}(m,k) = \tfrac{1}{n-1}(E_1^m + E_2^m + E_3^m + \cdots + E_{k-1}^m + E_{k+1}^m +$$

$$\cdots + E_n^m - (n-2)E_k^m)$$

Essentially, $\overline{\gamma}(m,k)$ in the above gives the cost of <u>not executing</u> the module m on the processor k, which obviously may not be attributed uniquely to a given processor in the case of multi-processor systems, except in the case of two-processor systems. What is important here is that the cost of executing m on k (or of assigning m to k) is identical to the cost of not executing m on all other processors. The weights of the newly added arcs for each module m are therefore chosen in such a manner that the total weight of these arcs intersected by a 'cut' equals the execution costs of the module m. Figure 10.6 illustrates this by examining the arcs from the module m to some processors $p_1, p_2, \cdots, p_n$ in a cutset that assigns m to the processor p_k. The assignment of m to p_k thus contributes to the weight of the cutset by

$$(n-1)\tfrac{E_\Sigma^m}{n-1} - \left(\sum_{i\in\mathcal{P}} E_i^m\right) + E_k^m = E_k^m$$

As a result, the total weight of all arcs intersected by a 'cut' equals the total processing cost of the application, which includes all communication costs and the execution costs of all the modules.

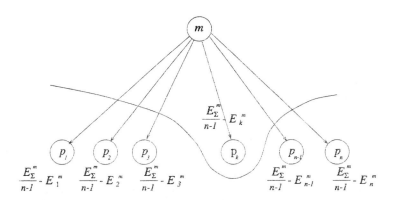

Figure 10.6 Cost to other processors of allocating m to P_k

The modified notion of network flow graphs requires a new definition for cutsets. A *cutset* of a network flow graph Sys_{nfg}, which is equivalent to a task allocation problem Sys, is a subset of arcs in A, the removal of which partitions the NFG into n disjoint subgraphs, each of which contains a unique terminal node. Note also that as in conventional NFGs, no proper subset of a cutset is a cutset.

NFGs derived from COM have extra nodes for processors as well as related additional arcs and, therefore, cutsets in NFGs may not be directly related to partitions

Table 10.3 An example: task allocation as a network flow problem

Module Execution costs			Arc weights				
			Communication costs		$\gamma(m_1, m_2)$	'Inverse' exec. costs	
Module	Processors		Modules			$\overline{\gamma}(m, p_1)$	$\gamma(m, p_2)$
m	$E^m_{P_1}$	$E^m_{P_2}$	m_1	m_2			
A	5	10	A	B	10	10	5
B	16	10	A	D	3	10	16
C	25	30	A	F	20	30	25
D	∞	12	A	G	4	12	∞
E	30	∞	B	C	20	∞	30
F	15	20	B	G	15	20	15
G	18	30	C	D	30	30	18
			C	E	10		
			C	F	14		
			E	F	16		

of the module graph discussed in Section 10.4.4. However, if one views a partition of an NFG by a cutset as a 'network partition' *nptn*, which is an element of:

$$\mathbb{P}\,V \twoheadrightarrow \mathbb{P}(V \times V)$$

the partition implicit in *nptn* may be given as the cutset *cutset(nptn)*

$$cutset(nptn) = A - \mathsf{U}\ (ran\ nptn)$$

Note that module assignment algorithms based on NFGs are of the order $O(n^3)$, n being the number of nodes in the NFG here.

EXAMPLE

Two-Processor Task Allocation

The approach is best illustrated using a task allocation problem with just two processors. In this connection, consider the set of tasks $\{A, B, C, D, E, F, G\}$ with the execution costs and the communication costs given in the Table 10.9.2. Its equivalent NFG is shown in Figure 10.7.

The additional arcs between modules and processors represent the execution costs of modules on different processors. As mentioned earlier, the number shown on any arc between a module and a processor corresponds to the cost of not executing that module on the given processor, which is termed the 'inverse costs' in the table above and in Figure 10.7.

The shaded area in Figure 10.7 shows the 'cut' resulting in the cutset giving the minimum total processing cost. Figure 10.8 and the data below perhaps give a fuller and a clearer picture of the result.

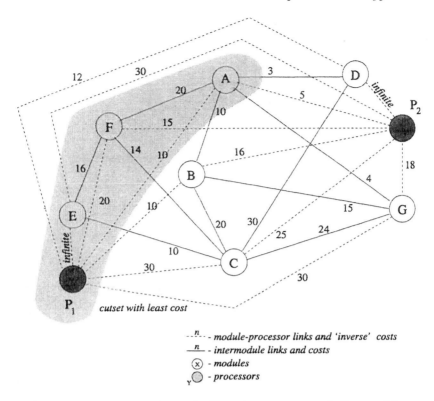

Figure 10.7 An example: task allocation as a network flow problem

The total processing cost
$$= 12 + 30 + 3 + 5 + 4 + 10 + 15 + 14 + 10 + 10 + 30 + 30$$
$$= 173$$
The total interprocessor communication cost
$$= 10 + 14 + 10 + 4 + 3$$
$$= 41$$
The execution cost of modules on P_1
$$= 30 + 15 + 5$$
$$= 50$$
The execution cost of modules on P_2
$$= 10 + 30 + 12 + 30$$
$$= 82$$
The worst case execution time
$$= 82 + 41$$
$$= 123$$

As mentioned on page 224, the worst case execution time given above assumes that the costs are measured in processor time and that the total IPC is attributable to the processor with the greater load, that is, P_2. Again, this may not be a reasonable assumption.

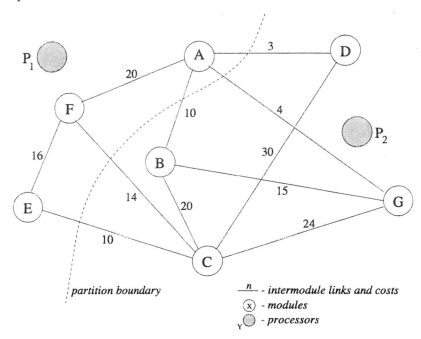

Figure 10.8 An example: the partitioning due to network flow approach

Despite the mathematical elegance, the applicability of this approach is limited to relatively small NFGs with two to three processors since no min-cut algorithms are available for greater number of processors except for special cases of COM. The general solution requires n-dimensional min-cut algorithms which are computationally intractable. Other drawbacks include the inability of the approach to consider resource, precedence and realtime constraints.

10.10   Bibliographical Notes

A good introduction to task allocation may be found in Chu, Holloway, Lan and Efe [24]. The algorithm discussed in Section 10.8 may be found in Efe [42]. Related algorithms may be found in Houstis [63] and Ma, Lee and Tsuchiya [97]. Houstis [63] considers additional eligibility criteria for merging modules, among them the amount of information access required by modules, and the interconnection network utilization level. Ma, Lee and Tsuchiya [97] describe a *branch-and-bound* method, which is based on the search of the task allocation tree guided by rules for selecting search steps and a sequence of ordered checks for checking the satisfiability of allocation constraints. Bannister and Trivedi [10] provide a best fit algorithm for the allocation of tasks, with possible replications of tasks as applicable to fault tolerant multi-processor systems. In relation to task allocation in predominantly pipelined architectures, Bokhari [15] considers some specialized forms of communication graphs and connectivity graphs, namely chains and trees.

More details on the approach based on network flow graphs discussed in Section 10.9 may be found in Stone [159] with more recent developments reported in Rao, Stone and Hu [127] and Indurkhya, Stone and Xi-Cheng [65]. Chu and Lan [25] propose an algorithm for optimal allocation of tasks that considers the execution costs, intermodule communication costs and, more importantly, a precedence relation on modules. Palis, Liou and Wei [116] consider, in the context of parallel distributed architectures, optimal task clustering with task duplication.

10.11 Exercises

1. Using an appropriate algorithm for each case allocate the sets of modules given below to the specified number of processors. All intermodule communication costs cover communications in both directions of the modules concerned. Note that this exercise continues to use the abbreviation $E_k^m = \mathcal{E}(m, k)$.

   If appropriate, compute for each case the following:

   (i) the load (the total execution cost of modules) on each processor;

   (ii) the total interprocessor communication cost;

   (iii) the worst case execution time of the application as a whole;

   (iv) the total processing cost of the application as a whole.

(a) The number of processors $= 2$, processor identification: P_1 and P_2

Module Execution and Communication Costs

Execution costs			Communication costs		
Module	*Processors*		*Modules*		$\gamma(m_1, m_2)$
m	$E_{P_1}^m$	$E_{P_2}^m$	m_1	m_2	
A	6	∞	A	B	7
B	7	7	A	C	2
C	5	5	A	D	6
D	4	4	A	E	1
E	∞	4	B	F	4
F	3	3	C	E	5
			D	E	3
			D	F	2
			E	F	8

(b) The number of processors = 3, processor identification: P_1, P_2 and P_3

Module Execution and Communication Costs

Module	Execution costs Processors			Communication costs Modules		$\gamma(m_1, m_2)$
m	$E_{P_1}^m$	$E_{P_2}^m$	$E_{P_3}^m$	m_1	m_2	
A	∞	∞	10	A	B	15
B	25	25	25	A	E	10
C	15	15	15	A	F	15
D	30	∞	∞	A	I	50
E	∞	20	∞	B	C	30
F	20	20	20	B	E	30
G	15	15	15	C	D	20
H	25	25	25	D	E	15
I	35	35	35	D	G	40
J	25	25	25	F	H	10
				G	H	20
				H	I	20
				I	J	25

(c) The number of processors = 2, processor identification: P_1 and P_2

Module Execution and Communication Costs

Module	Execution costs Processors		Communication costs Modules		$\gamma(m_1, m_2)$
m	$E_{P_1}^m$	$E_{P_2}^m$	m_1	m_2	
A	5	10	A	B	6
B	2	∞	A	C	4
C	4	4	A	F	12
D	6	3	B	C	8
E	5	2	B	D	12
F	∞	4	B	E	3
			D	E	5

Chapter 11

Scheduling

Scheduling in realtime systems concerns the determination of a temporal ordering of tasks allocated to a set of processors within the constraints of some specified timing, precedence and resource requirements. The consideration of a set of processors, rather than a single processor, may be justified in two ways. It is possible that scheduling has not been preceded by task allocation as discussed in the previous chapter. On the other hand, it is also possible that allocation of tasks has taken place not on the basis of actual individual processors, but on the basis of 'processor clusters', where each cluster is assumed to consist of a set of processors. The resources may comprise just the processors, but in typical realtime applications, they may include other equipments, materials and operators.

The objective of this chapter is a familiarization with the general concepts in scheduling and with the problem of scheduling in the multi-processor context.

11.1 Classification of Scheduling

11.1.1 Problem Dependent Classification

Depending on the nature of the problem being addressed, scheduling may be classified into different kinds: static scheduling, dynamic scheduling and mixed scheduling. This may also be seen to conform with an operational viewpoint as well.

Static scheduling assumes prior knowledge of the relevant characteristics of all tasks, which may be taken into account in scheduling. It offers the prospects of off-line scheduling, both for establishing specific schedules and for schedulability analysis. Static scheduling is applicable to problems with well-understood scheduling requirements such as frequency of processing requests and computation times, etc. Such requirements are typical in industrial process control. Schedules produced by static scheduling algorithms or, alternatively, the priorities assigned by them to tasks, are fixed for the duration of the application. However, any change in the information provided to the scheduler, especially with respect to any new tasks, requires complete rescheduling of the tasks and, as a result, static scheduling algorithms cannot cope with unpredictable circumstances. Despite this inflexibility, static scheduling has a number of attractions, namely, its low cost, due partly to the possibility of off-line scheduling and partly to low runtime costs, and greater predictability, which is a characteristic especially relevant in safety critical applications. Specific schedules produced off-line by a static scheduling algorithm may be implemented efficiently in the form of lookup tables.

On the other hand, dynamic scheduling algorithms are designed to work with unpredictable arrival times of tasks and possible uncertainties in their execution times. By definition, dynamic scheduling is required to be responsive to changing environmental demands and, therefore, there is no option but to conduct it online. It follows therefore that dynamic scheduling has the opposite properties of static scheduling algorithms. By virtue of the required functionality, dynamic scheduling is flexible, but it is expensive because of potentially extensive runtime rescheduling costs with changes in the environment.

Mixed scheduling tends to combine the two, scheduling those tasks with *a priori* known characteristics statically and accommodating others as they arrive.

11.1.2   System Dependent Classification

The nature of scheduling also varies with the system configuration of the processors and is classified as uni-processor scheduling, centralized multi-processor scheduling and distributed scheduling. Uni-processor scheduling is the simplest in terms of the issues involved, but it is unrealistic and is increasingly out of step with modern information processing, which involves large and complex applications.

Centralized multi-processor systems meet the needs of many applications. They are cheap in terms of communication costs, and allow scheduling to be carried out centrally. However, a characteristic of such systems is the resource sharing (memory, peripherals, etc.), dictating additional inter-task constraints, which introduces another dimension of complexity to scheduling.

Distributed scheduling is by far the most complex since it requires scheduling with limited, and often uncertain, global knowledge about processor workload because of the autonomous operation of the processors involved. A common strategy adopted in this respect is to schedule the tasks in an integrated manner, combining centralized scheduling within smaller 'clusters' of processors with limited global scheduling. Distributed scheduling, too, brings in additional sources of complexity, particularly in terms of interprocess communications and the need for possible task migration between processors. Let us return to this topic again in Section 11.8.2.

11.1.3   A Classification based on Task Preemptablity

Scheduling may also be classified into *preemptive* and *non-preemptive* scheduling on the basis of opportunities available for task preemption should it be necessary for scheduling the tasks in a given set.

A task is said to be *preemptable* by other tasks if it can be interrupted and resumed later without jeopardizing the achievement of its overall goal but observing any associated timing constraints. Preemptability of tasks usually depends on the application. In many industrial realtime systems, such as those found in manufacturing, tasks may not be preemptable if such systems involve non-interruptible industrial processes. On the other hand, this might not be the case in systems involving computational processes, as well as in suitably equipped industrial systems. Obviously, task preemption permits greater room for manoeuvre in scheduling. However, preemptive schedules carry greater runtime overheads because of the need for context switching – storage and retrieval of partially computed results. Non-preemptive algorithms do not incur such overheads. Other advantages of non-preemptive algorithms include their better understandability, greater predictability, ease of testing and their inherent capability for guaranteeing exclusive access to any shared resource or data.

11.2   Priority Ordering of Tasks

Priority ordering reflects considerations such as the criticality of tasks with respect to realtime constraints such as deadlines and the importance of individual tasks with respect to the mission of the system. Priority ordering is meaningful only when there are tasks which may be preemptable by other tasks.

A task τ_1 is said to have a *higher priority* over another task τ_2 when τ_2 has to be interrupted in order to execute a new request for τ_1. Obviously, if more than one higher priority task is requested simultaneously, then it is the highest priority task that will be executed. Any tie among a number of competing tasks is broken arbitrarily.

If the above holds for τ_1 and τ_2 whenever τ_1 is requested, then their priority assignment is said to be *fixed*. Scheduling where the priority ordering is fixed in advance for all the tasks concerned is known as *fixed priority scheduling*, and is found typically in static scheduling. In addition to its low runtime costs, fixed priority driven scheduling has another major attraction, that is, the possibility of implementing prioritized interrupt handling services in hardware.

By contrast, in dynamic scheduling algorithms the actual priorities assigned to tasks may vary over time from request to request, although the principle according to which priorities are assigned remains the same. Thus, given two tasks τ_1 and τ_2, τ_1 may have a higher priority over τ_2 at a certain time, while τ_2 may enjoy the same over τ_1 at another time. Therefore, priorities of tasks have to be determined at the time of execution or dynamically.

11.3   Optimality

11.3.1   Performance Optimality

There are various metrics for evaluating the performance of particular scheduling algorithms. In hard realtime systems, where no realtime constraints may be missed, performance is sometimes mistakenly equated to meeting such constraints. Although realtime constraints may often express expected performance levels, they may not be directly relevant for evaluating and comparing designs. In this respect, there are various efficiency measures. Some of the common ones are:

- the total schedule length (the time taken to execute the set of tasks being scheduled);
- the number of processors required;
- processor utilization levels;
- processor idling levels (related to above);
- throughput (the number of tasks processed per unit time).

Obviously, as was seen in the previous two chapters, such metrics are not always fully compatible with one another and there are no algorithms which will allow the achievement of the highest performance level in every metric. Most promising in this respect is optimization of a combined benefit (cost) function subject to various resource constraints; see Section 10.5 of Chapter 10. The notion of *optimality* here reflects the 'best' design, as expressed in terms of an agreed set of system parameters, which results in a high value of such a unified criterion.

The above performance metrics concern the actual service delivered by the system. Another related measure is the *guarantee ratio*, which is a predictability metric. It expresses the extent to which an algorithm is able to guarantee the execution of any newly arriving tasks within their timing constraints, while fulfilling its current obligations. The execution of tasks may be guaranteed only on the basis of certain assumptions regarding the worst case execution times and the likelihood of possible unforeseen failures. In addition, the usual demands on meeting timing constraints remain applicable. This is a measure which is extremely useful in guiding task migrations in distributed multi-processor architectures.

11.3.2   Algorithmic Optimality

Algorithmic optimality concerns the competitive advantage of one algorithm over others in a given class of algorithms. The classes of such algorithms relevant to our study consist of the class of all fixed priority scheduling algorithms and the class of all multi-processor dynamic scheduling algorithms. A scheduling algorithm is said to be *optimal* if it can schedule any given set of tasks that can be scheduled by another algorithm of the same class. Algorithmic optimality enables maximizing the guarantee ratio mentioned in the previous subsection.

11.4   Tasks and their Interrelationships

11.4.1   Scheduling Characteristics of Tasks

Task Parameters

From the scheduling point of view any task may be specified by the following parameters, namely,

- task arrival time (or task invocation time), a;
- ready time (the permitted earliest start time), r;
- computation time (or processing time), c;
- deadline for task completion, d;
- regularity of task arrival.

  Depending on the regularity, the tasks may be classified into:

  (a) Periodic tasks, with T denoting the period.

  Note that periodic tasks typically occur in realtime monitoring.

  (b) Sporadic tasks with arbitrary arrival times, computation times and deadlines.

  These are typical in realtime control, where they are more frequent, and in system initialization and error state recovery, where they may occur infrequently.

Derived Characteristics

The following are characteristics that may be determined from the schedule or estimated by considering the implementation aspects of the scheduler.

- Start time, s.

  Start time is often determined by scheduling or inter-task constraints and is the time when all resources required by the task become available.

- Waiting time.

  Waiting time is the time a task has to wait for service because of other (possibly higher priority) tasks, or because of being blocked for accessing a resource. It depends on the implementation of the scheduler.

- Turnaround time.

  Turnaround time is the total elapsed time taken by a task since becoming ready until completion. If the overheads are ignored, it is the sum of the required computation time and the waiting time.

11.4.2   Inter-Task Dependencies

Inter-task dependencies arise for a number of reasons. Among them are the following.

Precedence Relations

These constraints may be induced by:

.   • application dependent process ordering;
   • the need for inter-task exchange of data;
   • inter-task communication.

Tasks without any precedence constraints on them are said to be *independent*.

Resource Dependencies

   • use of active resources (i.e. those with processing capabilities), usually in exclusive mode;
   • use of passive resources (eg. files); both in shared and exclusive mode.

The above are usually translated as mutual exclusion (or overlapping) constraints.

Policy directed constraints

These are policy directed because they make flexibilities tolerable by the application explicit so that the scheduler can take advantage of them. These concern mainly the preemptabilty of tasks by other tasks and are dependent on the nature of applications involved.

   • Preemptable tasks may be interrupted at any time by another task in the latter's favour.
   • Once started, non-preemptable tasks may not be stopped before completion.
   • Certain tasks may be selectively preemptable depending on the applications involved.

Policy induced constraints

These may be purely artificial and may be introduced from extra-application considerations. They may include, for example, preferred placement of tasks on particular processors on the grounds of security, physical characteristics and fault tolerance, etc. On similar grounds, such constraints may include preferred times for executing certain tasks.

11.5   A Definition of Tasks

As mentioned in Section 9.6 in Chapter 9, a *task* is a software entity or a program specialized to perform a specific action. From the scheduling point of view, a task is also the smallest entity that may be dispatched by an operating system.

Section 9.6 also introduced a mathematical notion for tasks that is relevant to software partitioning. This section adopts an alternative definition applicable to task scheduling.

Let us introduce a set of task identifiers TID for uniquely distinguishing between tasks. Let $\mathcal{T}$ denote the set of lengths of clock times $\mathbb{T}$ and let '0' represent a zero time length. Henceforth the following set is used as a mathematical abstraction of all possible sporadic (or aperiodic) tasks:

$$\text{TASK} \overset{def}{=} \{(tid, a, c, d) \bullet tid : \text{TID}; \; c : \mathcal{T}; \; a, d : \mathbb{T} \mid c \geq 0 \wedge a + c \leq d\}$$

where as a simplification other possible task parameters such as ready time are ignored. Thus, each task is represented as a quadruple, the elements of which form a subset of the task parameters introduced in Section 11.4.1, but satisfying certain mathematical relations.

The following are alternative notations for referring to task parameters. For a sporadic task $\tau_i : \text{TASK}$:

$$\tau_i \overset{def}{=} (tid_i, a_i, c_i, d_i)$$

and

$$
\begin{aligned}
\tau_i.tid &= tid_i \\
\tau_i.a &= a_i \\
\tau_i.c &= c_i \\
\tau_i.d &= d_i
\end{aligned}
$$

When using such notation, we rely implicitly on the constraints on task parameters stated in the set definition given above.

Analogously, periodic tasks may be seen as a set PTASK:

$$\text{PTASK} \overset{def}{=} \{(tid, a, c, d, \mathrm{T}) \bullet tid : \text{TID}; \; c, \mathrm{T} : \mathcal{T}; \; a, d : \mathbb{T} \mid 0 \leq c \leq \mathrm{T} \wedge \\ \exists k : \mathrm{N}_1 \bullet a + k \times \mathrm{T} + c \leq d \wedge a + (k+1) \times \mathrm{T} > d\}$$

Note that it has been assumed that all periodic tasks must come to an end. This may be too restrictive as some periodic tasks may be required to take place literally for ever, in which case, one may easily produce an alternative definition. What is essential is that there must be sufficient time in the last occurrence of a periodic task for that instance to complete.

For any natural number k, the $(k+1)$th instance of a periodic task $\tau : \text{PTASK}$ may be seen as a (once-only) sporadic task $\tau_{k+1} : \text{TASK}$ such that

$$\tau_{k+1}.a = (\tau.a) + k \times (\tau.T)$$
$$\tau_{k+1}.c = \tau.c$$
$$\tau_{k+1}.d = (\tau.a) + (k+1) \times (\tau.T)$$

For the $(k+1)$th instance of periodic task τ_i : PTASK:

$$\tau_i^{k+1} \overset{def}{=} (tid_i, a_i + k \times T_i, c_i, a_i + (k+1) \times T_i)$$

11.6   Mathematical Scheduling Relations on Tasks

It is convenient to use the following mathematical relations for dealing with inter-task dependencies introduced in Sections 11.2 and 11.4.2.

11.6.1   Precedence Relation

The set of all tasks to be scheduled may be partially ordered by a relation $\prec$ which is to be interpreted as a precedence relation on TASK, that is,

$\prec$: TASK $\leftrightarrow$ TASK

such that $\prec$ is irreflexive, antisymmetric and transitive. For any two tasks τ_1 and τ_2, the predicate $\tau_1 \prec \tau_2$ means that 'the execution of τ_1 must be completed before the execution of τ_2 is begun'.

11.6.2   Priority Ordering

Given a non-empty set TASK denoting the set of tasks to be scheduled, TASK may be priority ordered (see Section 11.2) by a relation $\overset{p}{>}$ on TASK, that is,

$\overset{p}{>}$: TASK $\leftrightarrow$ TASK

such that $\overset{p}{>}$ is irreflexive, antisymmetric and transitive. Given two tasks τ_i and τ_j, the predicate $\tau_i \overset{p}{>} \tau_j$ means that 'τ_i has higher priority than τ_j'.

Preemptive priority driven scheduling algorithms require the immediate interruption of the current task in favour of any newly arrived higher priority task, but with provisions for resumption of the former later. In other words, the processor always executes the task with the highest priority. As discussed earlier, how these priorities are assigned is distinctly different with static and dynamic scheduling strategies.

In fixed priority scheduling, the relation $\overset{p}{>}$ is a constant with respect to time, whereas in scheduling with dynamic priorities, $\overset{p}{>}$ is a function of time.

11.6.3   Resource Dependencies

The relationships introduced in Section 3.4 of Chapter 3 are particularly useful for specifying inter-task constraints arising from any dependency, particularly from resource dependencies. Some of the temporal relations relevant to task scheduling are

$$before, \ equal, \ meets, \ overlaps, \ during, starts, finishes \ : \Gamma \leftrightarrow \Gamma$$

Chapter 3 discusses in detail how the above may be related to temporal relations in clock time. It may be shown that the above temporal relations may be represented in terms of two primitive constraints:

$e_1 \ precedes \ e_2 \ by\_at\_most \ k_1$
$e_1 \ precedes \ e_2 \ by\_at\_least \ k_2$

involving a pair of instantaneous events e_1 and e_2 and two constants k_1 and k_2. For example, the first is to be interpreted as 'e_1 precedes e_2 by at most k_1 time units'. This is discussed in Nissanke and Loader [110]. The two instantaneous events, in our case, signify the start and end points of any given durative event.

11.7   Multi-Processor Scheduling – The Problem

This section presents a general description of the problem of scheduling in the multi-processor context.

11.7.1   An Abstract Representation of Processors

Let PID be a set of processor identifiers. Let us denote the set of all possible processors at the given level of abstraction by PROC, each element of which is a triple:

$(pid, \ \text{T–SET}, \ \text{SCH})$

where

pid	–	$pid \in$ PID and is intended for unique identification of the given processor.
T–SET	–	T–SET is the set of tasks allocated to the processor *pid* or to be scheduled on it. Obviously, T–SET : $\mathbb{P}$ TASK.
SCH	–	SCH is a partial function from TASK to $\mathbb{O}_f$. $\mathbb{O}_f$ was introduced in Section 3.2 of Chapter 3 and is a set, each element of which in turn is a finite set of disjoint (finite) right-open intervalss in real time. Thus,

$$\text{SCH} : \text{TASK} \nrightarrow \mathbb{O}_f$$

Figure 11.1 illustrates a diagrammatic representation of SCH for a schedule involving two tasks τ_i and τ_j on a single processor.

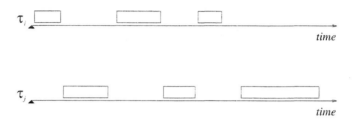

Figure 11.1 A processor schedule involving two tasks

The information in Figure 11.1 is presented in Figure 11.2 in an alternative form known as a processor *Gantt chart*. A Gantt chart may be defined as a function related to SCH as given below:

$$\text{G--CHT} : \Gamma \nrightarrow \text{TASK}$$
$$\text{G--CHT} = \{(x, \tau) \bullet x : \Gamma;\ \tau : \text{TASK} \mid \exists \theta : \mathbb{O}_f \bullet (\tau, \theta) \in \text{SCH} \wedge x \in \theta\}$$

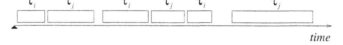

Figure 11.2 A processor Gantt chart

The triples of the form $(pid,\ \text{T--SET},\ \text{SCH})$ assumes PROC to be

$$\text{PROC} \subseteq \text{PID} \times (\mathbb{P}\,\text{TASK}) \times (\text{TASK} \times \mathbb{O}_f)$$

Each triple in PROC is an abstract representation of the processor identified by *pid*. However, its various components are subject to further constraints, which are discussed in the next section. The components of any processor will be identified using the dot notation. Thus, for example, given a processor p : PROC, $p.\text{T--SET}$ denotes the task set to be scheduled on p.

11.7.2   Schedules of Individual Processors

SCH is an abstract representation of possible schedules, giving a schedule for each task in T--SET as it is to be executed on the processor *pid*. The executions of tasks on a single processor or on a set of processors often have to be interleaved with each other for various reasons, notably because of preemption of certain tasks in favour of others or because of temporal or resource constraints. This results in fragmentation of task execution times, but over mutually non-overlapping intervals of time. The information held in SCH must account for this. Therefore, to start with,

$$\text{dom SCH} = \text{T-SET}$$

Furthermore, in relation to the task characteristics the following must hold:

$$\forall \tau : \text{TASK} \bullet \quad \begin{aligned} \mathit{left}(\mathit{first}(\text{SCH}(\tau))) &\geq \tau.a \\ \mathit{right}(\mathit{last}(\text{SCH}(\tau))) &\leq \tau.d \\ \mathit{total}(\text{SCH}(\tau)) &\leq \tau.c \end{aligned}$$

where *left* and *right* are as on page 38 in Section 3.2, while others are as given below. Given that $\theta : \mathbb{O}_f$,

$$\mathit{first}(\theta) = x, \quad \text{such that} \quad \forall y : \Gamma \bullet y \in \theta \Rightarrow x \text{ before } y \vee x = y$$

$$\mathit{last}(\theta) = x, \quad \text{such that} \quad \forall y : \Gamma \bullet y \in \theta \Rightarrow y \text{ before } x \vee x = y$$

$$\mathit{total}(\theta) = \sum_{x \in \theta} \mathit{length}(x)$$

where $\mathit{length}(x)$ is as defined on page 38 in Section 3.2. Furthermore, SCH as a whole must be such that at no time does the processor execute more than one task. Therefore,

$$(\bigcup (\text{ran SCH})) \in \mathbb{O}_f$$

which in terms of the corresponding Gantt chart becomes

$$\text{dom G-CHT} \in \mathbb{O}$$

In other words, the intervals over which the tasks in T-SET are scheduled as a whole on the given processor must themselves constitute a set of disjoint finite right-open intervalss.

11.7.3 A System of Processors with Independent Tasks

The system may be characterized by the set of processors used in the application and a system-wide schedule. Let us confine ourselves initially to fully independent tasks, that is, when $\prec = \varnothing$. Then the system may be viewed as a pair

$$\text{SYS} \stackrel{\mathit{def}}{=} (\text{SITE}, \text{SYS-SCH})$$

where

SITE   –   SITE is a finite set of processors, that is, SITE : $\mathbb{F}$ PROC.

SYS–SCH   –   SYS–SCH contains the same information as in SCH for each processor and, therefore, is a system-wide schedule for all tasks under consideration over the processors in SITE.

In view of the multiplicity of processors and the convenience in having individual processor schedules in the form of Gantt charts, let us consider SYS–SCH as a function[1] of the form,

$$\text{SYS–SCH} : \text{PROC} \rightarrow \Gamma \rightarrow \text{TASK}$$

The components of SYS must also satisfy further integrity requirements. These are as follows. Firstly, the system-wide schedule SYS–SCH must consist of the individual processor schedules expressed as Gantt charts, that is,

$$\text{SYS–SCH} \;=\; \{ p \mapsto p.\text{G–CHT} \mid p \in \text{PROC} \} \,,$$

The above continues to use the dot notation $p.\text{G–CHT}$ to refer to the Gantt chart of the processor p. This, however, does not preclude the simultaneous execution of a given task over overlapping or identical stretches of real time on more than one processor. Therefore, it may be appropriate to require that

$$\forall\, p_1, p_2 : \text{PROC}; \; \tau : \text{TASK} \; \bullet \; \{ p_1, p_2 \} \subseteq \text{SITE} \land$$
$$(\exists\, x, y : \Gamma \; \bullet \; x \in p_1.\text{SCH}(\tau) \land y \in p_2.\text{SCH}(\tau) \land x \cap y \neq \varnothing) \Rightarrow p_1 = p_2$$

Furthermore, the system may be required not to execute any task longer than necessary. Assuming that the computation times of tasks are exact computation times, this requirement may be stated as

$$total \, \{ x \bullet x : \Gamma; \; p : \text{PROC} \mid \text{SYS–SCH}(p, x) = \tau \} = \tau.c$$

for every τ : TASK. If the computation times c represent the worst case computation times then the second equality sign in the above requirement must be replaced with $\leq$.

The above model may be easily extended to include dependencies among tasks as

$$\text{SYS} \stackrel{def}{=} (\text{SITE}, \; \text{SYS–SCH}, \; \prec)$$

where $\prec$ is a precedence relation on TASK such that $\prec \neq \varnothing$. The precedence relation introduces further constraints on possible execution times of tasks. These constraints are expressed in

---

[1] See page 416 in Appendix C (under *curried functions*) for an explanation of the function type used in SYS–SCH.

$$\forall\, \tau_1, \tau_2 : \text{TASK} \ \bullet \ \{\tau_1, \tau_2\} \subseteq \left(\bigcup_{p \in \text{SITE}} (\text{ran SYS-SCH}(p)) \right) \land \tau_1 \prec \tau_2 \Rightarrow$$

$$(\forall\, p_1, p_2 : \text{PROC};\ x_1, x_2 : \Gamma \ \bullet \ \{(p_1, x_1, \tau_1), (p_2, x_2, \tau_2)\} \subseteq \text{SYS-SCH} \Rightarrow$$
$$x_1 \ before \ x_2)$$

whereby if $\tau_1 \prec \tau_2$ all executions of task τ_1 are required to precede all executions of τ_2, irrespective of the processors where the two tasks are being scheduled at the times concerned.

In conclusion, the task of scheduling is the establishment of schedules in SCH for each and every task, and thereby the system-wide schedule SYS-SCH, in such a way that all aforementioned constraints are satisfied. Following that, the schedules may be expressed in clock times using the results established in Chapter 3.

11.8 Overview of Solutions

11.8.1 A Note on Efficiency of Scheduling Algorithms

Scheduling is a search problem, similar to that outlined in Section 10.7 of Chapter 10 in relation to task allocation. Search problems are typically represented as a search tree, where any intermediate node represents a partial schedule and any leaf a complete schedule. Because of the various application dependent scheduling constraints, not every complete schedule is feasible. Furthermore, because of the multitude of options available at each intermediate node, an exhaustive search of such a tree is computationally intractable.

Using well-known mathematical techniques in algorithm analysis, one can be more specific about the degree of difficulty in obtaining a solution to a particular scheduling problem. An important concept in this respect is *time complexity* or *efficiency* of the algorithm, expressed as a function of the problem size, which in the case of scheduling is typically the number of tasks to be scheduled. Another related concept is *space complexity* – the storage or memory costs of the algorithm.

In our brief discussion, let us confine ourselves to just time complexity. Let us regard as efficient scheduling algorithms those algorithms, where the time complexity is bounded by a polynomial expression of the problem size. It follows from this that the inefficient scheduling algorithms are those, where the time complexity is above this bound. A more specific estimate of the time complexity of inefficient scheduling algorithms is that it grows exponentially with the problem size.

Most general scheduling problems are equally hard or computationally intractable. A mathematical terminology used in this connection is the notion of *NP-hard problems*. A problem is said to be NP-hard if it is possible to find an efficient algorithm for solving it; then it is also possible to solve likewise a large family of computationally intractable problems. In relation to scheduling, it follows from this that solving the general scheduling problem is at least as hard as solving the hardest problem in the family of NP-hard problems.

11.8.2 Comments on Scheduling Algorithms

As has already been stated, no solutions exist for the general problem of scheduling. However, scheduling is also a problem which has been widely studied. As a result, there are solutions to a significant number of restricted subproblems with varying computational complexity. Below is an overview of the available solutions.

- Static scheduling of independent tasks

  As indicated in Section 11.1.3, preemption offers greater prospects for scheduling. The known solutions based on preemption involve reasonable computational costs, that is, they are of polynomial time complexity. The more difficult problem of multi-processor scheduling may be solved by its decomposition initially into a task allocation problem (see Chapter 10) and subsequent uni-processor scheduling of tasks on individual processors.

  Scheduling of independent tasks without preemption is generally harder than the corresponding preemptive problem and many non-preemptive scheduling problems are known to be NP-hard.

  A static scheduling algorithm enabling a fixed priority assignment to periodic tasks is discussed in Section 12.3 of Chapter 12.

- Static scheduling of dependent tasks

  Scheduling of a set of tasks with an arbitrary precedence relation is known to be NP-hard. As with all NP-hard problems, more promising in this respect are the heuristic algorithms and those based on restricting the precedence relation to a simple form such as a tree. The latter is the subject of Chapter 13, which discusses a static scheduling algorithm intended for computing schedules explicitly.

- Dynamic Scheduling

  Dynamic scheduling algorithms such as Earliest Deadline First and Least Laxity First are optimal in the uni-processor case, but this ceases to be the case in the general multi-processor case. It is known in particular that there is no optimal scheduling algorithms without *a priori* knowledge of task characteristics.

  More about these observations may be found in Chapter 14. A dynamic scheduling algorithm for uni-processor case is presented in Section 12.8 of Chapter 12.

- Distributed Scheduling

  Distributed scheduling was discussed briefly in Section 11.1.2. Generally, it has all the characteristics of a dynamic scheduling problem, where the arrival times as well as the computation times of tasks could be unpredictable and uncertain. In situations where it has the characteristics of a static problem, scheduling in distributed systems is often seen as a combined problem of task allocation (see Chapter 10) and local static scheduling (see Chapters 12 and 13).

In addition to unpredictabilities and uncertainties associated with tasks at the application level, dynamic distributed scheduling involves uncertainties in relation to the information held at each node about the states of other nodes in the system. This is because the information about any remote node is inherently out of date, and sometimes can be even totally obsolete, since it has to be acquired at runtime over a network, incurring unpredictable delays. As in static scheduling outlined above, a natural decomposition of the problem leads to a well-known solution, involving two subproblems:

(a) A *distributed scheduler*, which on the one hand determines a site where any newly task arrived could be processed, and on the other enables the migration of any task that cannot be scheduled on the assigned node to another node with spare capacity.

(b) A *local scheduler*, which first determines the schedulability of any newly allocated task locally and then, depending on the outcome, either accommodates it locally using a dynamic scheduling algorithm or coordinates with the distributed scheduler for its migration to another node.

Distributed scheduling is not covered further in this book (see the next section for bibliographic references).

11.9 Bibliographical Notes

General discussions on scheduling may be found in [20, 23, 50, 158, 156]. Formal descriptions of the general scheduling problem may be found from various sources, including Xu and Parnas [172, 173] and Xu [171]. A survey of algorithms and a more detailed discussion about their computational efficiency may be found in Cheng and Stankovic [23]. Viaravan and DeMillo [162] also address the computational complexity of scheduling problems.

An important contribution to distributed scheduling is the work carried out as part of the Spring Kernel; see Niehaus *et al.* [107] and Stankovic and Ramamritham [154, 155].

Chapter 12

Uni-processor Scheduling

Despite the increasing use of multi-processor and distributed systems, uni-processor systems will continue to play an important role, particularly in process control environments and in non-critical embedded systems requiring no redundancies. The uni-processor systems considered here have strict realtime constraints on their tasks and, in this respect, differ from uni-processor systems that support the common multi-programming environments.

12.1 The Preliminaries

12.1.1 Assumptions about the Environment

The assumptions made here conform closely with conditions prevalent in process control environments, requiring periodic monitoring of the environment and regulating its characteristics. With such applications in mind, all tasks are assumed to be periodic. In reality, any non-periodic task has to be treated as a special task, effectively taking over the processor completely.

By definition, periodic tasks may not have concurrent multiple instances of the same task. Although the scheduler may anticipate future occurrences of a task, the notion of queueing is not practised. In other words, new entries may be made only after the completion of the current one. No other constraints are assumed to affect the task deadlines and, as a consequence, the deadline of any given instance of a task coincides with the arrival time of its next instance. That is, if at time a a task arrives for the first time, or it is requested again, then the deadline for that instance of the task is at time $a + T$, T being the request period.

The tasks are considered independent in terms of initiation and completion of other tasks. This entails the absence of any precedence relation on the tasks, with the exception of that which is implicit in the periodicity between different instances of the same task.

As a simplification, the computation time of tasks is considered independent of the time of the execution. This may be acceptable if the computation times specified are based on the maximum processing time required by the task, otherwise some allowance may have to be made in order to compensate for the drop in processor performance under heavy workload.

12.1.2   Terminology and Definitions

Let us use some of the notation introduced in Chapter 11. In particular, *Task* denotes the set of all possible tasks. Terminology and notations specific to this chapter are as follows:

Request Period	– The interval between two successive requests for a given periodic task. It is denoted by T, with subscripts as necessary.
Request Rate	– Reciprocal of the request period, that is, $\frac{1}{T}$.
Overflow	– Non-fulfillment of a task deadline at its due time.
Response Time	– The time interval from the receipt of a request to the end of response upon task completion.
Critical Instant	– Critical instant of a task is the request time of an instance of that task having the longest response time, but without incurring an overflow. This may occur when multiple instances of other tasks are requested before the completion of the task in question.
Critical Response Time	– The response time associated with the critical instant of a task.
Critical Time Zone	– The time interval between the critical instant of a task and its completion time.
S	– The set of tasks involved. S is non-empty and is finite. Thus, $S \in \mathbb{F}\,Task$.
m	– The size of the set S above, that is, $m = \#S$.

12.2   Schedule Overflow and Schedule Feasibility

Let us attempt a more precise definition for '*schedule overflow*' than that given above. The notion of schedule overflow is closely tied with the notion of demand for processor time during a particular time interval, which is an important concept in scheduling in general and deserves a separate treatment. As will become clear, both notions depend on the underlying scheduling discipline.

12.2.1   Demand for Processor Time

The notion of the processor may be considered implicitly through a function $P_D(S, (t_1, t_2))$, denoting the processor time spent on, or required for, executing the set of tasks S over an interval of time (t_1, t_2) following some given scheduling strategy D. [It is immaterial here whether the interval from t_1 to t_2 is open or closed.] The function P_D does not account for processor time required in future on current commitments, but exactly that required over the given period. An alternative simpler notation being used is $P_D(S, t)$, applicable to an interval $(0, t)$ starting from zero. When $P_D(S, t) > t$, $P_D(S, t)$ denotes the minimum total demand on processor time at time t, which obviously cannot be met on a single processor. When $P_D(S, t) \leq t$, since the demand may be met by a single processor, it denotes the net total (actual) processor time. Note that $P_D(S, t)$ includes the time spent on partially computed tasks at t and, therefore,

$$P_D(S, t) \geq P_0(S, t)$$

where $P_0(S, t)$ denotes the processor time required for executing the tasks in S that must have been fully completed by time t. Since our concern here is periodic tasks, these tasks must have been executed an integral number of times. Therefore,

$$P_0(S, t) = \sum_{\tau \in S \wedge \tau.d \leq t} \tau.c = \sum_{\tau_i \in S} \lfloor t/T_i \rfloor \times c_i$$

See Appendix C for the notations $\lfloor x \rfloor$ and $\lceil x \rceil$. These are to be read as '*floor of x*' and '*ceiling of x*' respectively. Following the notations introduced in Chapter 11, $\tau.d$ (the dot notation) denotes the deadline d of the task τ.

Note that $P_0(S, t)$ itself is independent of the scheduling discipline, since it concerns the tasks that should have been already completed by time t. By contrast, $P_D(S, t)$ does depend on the manner tasks with pending deadlines are being executed. Because of the complications in accounting for time spent on partially computed tasks, which are also potentially preemptable, no attempt is made to define $P_D(S, t)$ formally. It is worth noting, however, that $P_D(S, t)$ is a non-decreasing function of time, and for any periods $(0, t_1)$ and $(0, t_2)$,

$$t_2 \geq t_1 \Rightarrow P_D(S, t_2) \geq P_D(S, t_1) .$$

12.2.2   Schedule Overflow

The notion of schedule overflow varies with the scheduling strategy. A very straightforward notion corresponds with the situation where the primary concern is that a task has missed its deadline at the specified time. Thus, in this case, no attention is paid to the circumstances that caused the failure to meet the given deadline.

Given a scheduling discipline D, let us define a predicate $overflow_D(S, t)$ meaning that 'the overflow of a task in the set S at time t is justifiable according to the scheduling discipline D'.

For example, bearing in mind the scheduling strategy Rate Monotonic Priority Assignment (RMPA), which is to be introduced in Sections 12.3 and 12.4 and whereby higher priorities are assigned to tasks with higher request rates, the predicate $overflow_{\text{RMPA}}(S, t)$ may be defined as

$$overflow_{\text{RMPA}}(S, t) \stackrel{def}{\Leftrightarrow} (\exists \ \tau : Task \bullet \tau \in S \wedge \tau.d = t) \wedge$$
$$P_{\text{RMPA}}(S, (0, t)) > t$$

Thus, according to RMPA, a schedule overflow signifies that the demand for processor time exceeds the available processor time at time t.

Another notion of schedule overflow is related to the Deadline Driven Scheduling algorithm discussed in Section 12.8. It considers the circumstances surrounding failure in greater detail. For example, this notion of overflow addresses whether there has been a period of unwarranted processor idling just prior to failure or whether the processor has been busy in processing non-urgent tasks prior to failure.

Let us first define a subsidiary predicate $idle_D(S, t)$ meaning that 'The processor idles immediately prior to t in executing S according to the scheduling discipline D'.

$$idle_D(S, t) \stackrel{def}{\Leftrightarrow} \exists \ t' : \mathbb{T} \bullet t' < t \wedge P_D(S, (t', t)) = 0$$

No scheduling discipline could justify processor idling immediately prior to an overflow. In the context of deadline driven scheduling, the processor should not be devoting any time to computing the tasks with deadlines beyond t. These requirements justifying a schedule overflow in the context of deadline driven scheduling may be summarized as follows:

$$overflow_{\text{DDS}}(S, t) \stackrel{def}{\Leftrightarrow} (\exists \ \tau : Task \bullet \tau \in S \wedge \tau.d = t) \wedge \qquad \text{(i)}$$
$$\neg \ idle_{\text{DDS}}(S, t) \wedge \qquad \text{(ii)}$$
$$(S' = \varnothing \Rightarrow P_0(S, t) > t) \wedge \qquad \text{(iii)}$$
$$(S' \neq \varnothing \Rightarrow (\exists \ t' : \mathbb{T} \bullet t' < t \wedge$$
$$P_{\text{DDS}}(S - S', (t', t)) = P_{\text{DDS}}(S, (t', t)) \wedge \quad \text{(iv)}$$
$$P_0(S, (t', t)) > t - t')) \qquad \text{(v)}$$

where S' is the subset of partially computed tasks in S, that is, the tasks whose deadlines are beyond t:

$$S' = \{\tau \mid \tau \in S \wedge \tau.d > t\} \ .$$

In the definition of $overflow_{\text{DDS}}(S, t)$ given above:

- The conjunct (i) requires that a deadline has been missed at time t.

- The conjunct (ii) requires that there has not been processor idling just prior to the overflow.
- The conjunct (iii) requires that, in the absence of tasks with deadlines beyond the overflow, the demand for processor time up to time t has exceeded the available time, which in the case of a uni-processor system is t time units.
- The conjunct (iv) requires that, in the presence of tasks with deadlines beyond the overflow, the processor has not been busy executing these tasks immediately prior to the overflow.
- The conjunct (v) requires that, in the presence of tasks with deadlines beyond the overflow, the demand for processor time just before t has exceeded the available time.

It would have been more appropriate to use $P_{\text{DDS}}(S, t)$ instead of $P_0(S, t)$ in the definition of $overflow_{\text{DDS}}(S, t)$ above, but $P_0(S, t)$ has been adopted for convenience in reasoning about certain observations.

12.2.3   Processor Utilization and Schedule Feasibility

Processor utilization factor U is defined as the fraction of processor time spent on executing tasks, and equals the total average rate of processor utilization by all tasks individually. That is,

$$U = \sum_{\tau_i \in S} (c_i / T_i) \, .$$

The processor utilization has to be optimized under conflicting requirements. From the point of view of resource use, U must be minimized, while from the point of view of productive completion of tasks, U must be maximized. However, U may not be increased arbitrarily since it must also satisfy the task deadlines. Let us return to this topic in Section 12.6.1.

Schedule feasibility signifies a guarantee that schedule overflow does not occur under certain circumstances. Obviously, the two concepts are linked and are meaningful only in the context of a specific scheduling strategy.

Observation 12.1 Schedule Feasibility

The feasibility of scheduling a set of tasks S with respect to a scheduling discipline D requires that

$$feasible_D(S) \Leftrightarrow (\forall t : \mathbb{T} \bullet 0 < t \leq T_1 \times T_2 \times \cdots \times T_m \Rightarrow$$
$$\neg \, overflow_D(S, t))$$

where $T_1, T_2, \cdots, T_m$ are the periods of the given set S of m tasks.

Obviously, it is sufficient to consider in the above an interval of length equal to the least common multiple of the periods, instead of the length $T_1 \times T_2 \times \cdots \times T_m$. Informally, the predicate $feasible_D(S)$ is true if and only if 'the set of tasks S may be scheduled by the scheduling discipline D without an overflow'. Note that the predicate $overflow_D(S,t)$ has to be interpreted according to the scheduling strategy.

Processor utilization is extremely important in addressing schedule feasibility. The following, which follows from the observation given above and the definitions given in Section 12.2.2, expresses an important but obvious relationship between the two concepts:

> **Observation 12.2** An implication of the feasibility of scheduling a set of tasks S by the scheduling discipline D.
>
> $$feasible_D(S) \Rightarrow U \leq 1$$

12.3 Uni-processor Static Scheduling

This section makes a case for the static scheduling algorithm known as *rate monotonic scheduling* (RMPA), which is a fixed priority algorithm; see Section 11.2 of Chapter 11.

12.3.1 Priority Ordering and Critical Response Time

Consider two periodic tasks τ_1 and τ_2 (see Figure 12.1) such that

(i) τ_1 has higher priority than τ_2, i.e.,

$$\tau_1 \overset{p}{>} \tau_2$$

(ii) τ_1 arrives within $(k+1)$th instance of τ_2, i.e.,

$$a_2 + kT_2 \leq a_1 < a_2 + (k+1)T_2$$

(iii) τ_1 has a higher request rate than τ_2, i.e.,

$$T_1 < T_2 .$$

Let us examine how the arrival time of τ_1 affects the completion time of τ_2.

Best Case: τ_1 arrives within $(k+1)$th instance of τ_2, but after its completion, that is,

$$a_2 + kT_2 + c_2 \leq a_1 < a_2 + (k+1)T_2$$

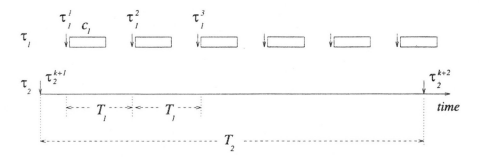

Figure 12.1 Priority ordering based on request rate

and therefore, there is no adverse effect.

Worst Case: τ_1 and the $(k+1)$th instance of τ_2 arrive simultaneously, that is,

$$a_1 = a_2 + kT_2 .$$

This is the worst case, as otherwise τ_1 may be advanced forward until the above holds. The worst of all is that, as soon as τ_2 arrives, all its higher priority tasks also arrive.

The following observations follow from the above:

> **Observation 12.3** A critical instant of a given task occurs whenever the request is accompanied simultaneously with requests for all its higher priority tasks.

> **Observation 12.4** If a set of tasks is schedulable at the critical instant of its every task, then the same set of tasks is schedulable with arbitrary arrival times of the tasks concerned.

12.3.2   Priority Ordering in Scheduling

The above observations are suggestive of an important approach to establishing the schedule feasibility, namely by checking the feasibility of scheduling every task at its critical instant.

EXAMPLE

Consider two tasks,

Task	a	c	T
τ_1	t_0	1	2
τ_2	t_0	1	5

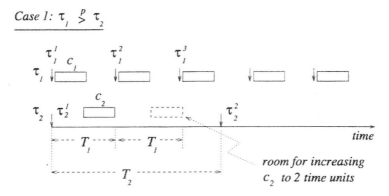

Figure 12.2 With higher priority for more frequent requests

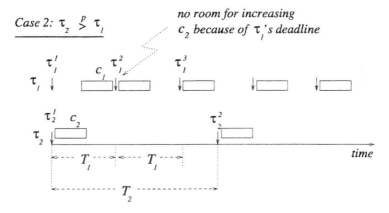

Figure 12.3 With higher priority for less. frequent requests

under two separate priority assignments, namely, $\tau_1 \overset{p}{>} \tau_2$ and $\tau_2 \overset{p}{>} \tau_1$.

As illustrated in Figures 12.2 and 12.3, this example leads to an important conclusion, namely, that, it makes sense to assign higher priority to τ_1 than τ_2.

Let us examine the conclusion of the above example by generalizing it. Following our convention, let

$$\tau_i \overset{def}{=} (tid_i, a_i, c_i, d_i, \mathrm{T}_i)$$
$$\tau_j \overset{def}{=} (tid_j, a_j, c_j, d_j, \mathrm{T}_j)$$

and assume that $\mathrm{T}_i < \mathrm{T}_j$. Since the intention is to convince ourselves about the validity of the conclusion drawn from the above example, let us consider the possible forms of priority assignment.

Case 1: $\tau_i \overset{p}{>} \tau_j$

The schedule feasibility in this case dictates that:

(i) All instances of τ_i within T_j must be completed.
(ii) In addition, the instance of τ_j due within T_j must also be completed.

The above two requirements may be stated mathematically as

$$\lfloor T_j/T_i \rfloor \times c_i + c_j \le T_j \tag{1}$$

Case 2: $\tau_j \overset{p}{>} \tau_i$

In this case, we must insist that

(i) τ_i completes within T_i.
(ii) T_i must be long enough to accommodate an instance of τ_j, if τ_j is ever requested within T_i.

That is,

$$c_i + c_j \le T_i \tag{2}$$

Now let us consider the relationship between the two cases and, in particular, whether it is better to assign higher priority to τ_i or τ_j, or whether it is immaterial. This judgement is to be made by examining whether any given condition out of the conditions (1) or (2) above logically implies the other, namely,

$$(c_i + c_j \le T_i) \Rightarrow (\lfloor T_j/T_i \rfloor \times c_i + c_j \le T_j) \tag{a}$$
$$(\lfloor T_j/T_i \rfloor \times c_i + c_j \le T_j) \Rightarrow (c_i + c_j \le T_i) \tag{b}$$

It may be shown that (a) is identically true, whereas (b) is not.

Proof of the Implication in (a):

1.	$c_i + c_j \le T_i$	assumption
2.	$\lfloor T_j/T_i \rfloor \times c_i + \lfloor T_j/T_i \rfloor \times c_j \le \lfloor T_j/T_i \rfloor T_i$	from (1); i.e. from line 1
3.	$\lfloor T_j/T_i \rfloor T_i \le T_j$	def. of $\lfloor \; \rfloor$
4.	$\lfloor T_j/T_i \rfloor \times c_i + \lfloor T_j/T_i \rfloor \times c_j \le T_j$	from (2) and (3)
5.	$c_j \le \lfloor T_j/T_i \rfloor \times c_j$	Since $T_j > T_i$
6.	$\lfloor T_j/T_i \rfloor \times c_i + c_j \le T_j$	from (4) and (5)
7.	$(c_i + c_j \le T_i) \Rightarrow (\lfloor T_j/T_i \rfloor \times c_i + c_j \le T_j)$	Discharging assumption (1) with the introduction of implication

Hence, the required proof.

Demonstration of the Invalidity of the Implication in (b):

The invalidity of (b) may be shown by providing a counter example which demonstrates that (b) does not necessarily hold. Consider the case with

$$c_i = 0.5, \ T_i = 2; \ c_j = 2, \ T_j = 5$$

for which

$$
\begin{aligned}
\lfloor T_j/T_i \rfloor \times c_i + c_j \leq T_j \quad &\Leftrightarrow \quad \lfloor 5/2 \rfloor \times 0.5 + 2 \leq 5.0 \\
&\Leftrightarrow \quad \text{True} \\
c_i + c_j \leq T_i \quad\quad\quad\quad\; &\Leftrightarrow \quad 0.5 + 2.0 \leq 2.0 \\
&\Leftrightarrow \quad \text{False}
\end{aligned}
$$

Hence, the implication in (b) is not a logical implication.

In conclusion, it may be observed that if the scheduling of two tasks τ_i and τ_j with

(i) $T_i < T_j$, and
(ii) $\tau_j \overset{p}{>} \tau_i$.

is feasible, then the scheduling of the same is also feasible with swapped priorities. However, the converse is not necessarily true. Thus, tasks with lower request rates may be given lower priority.

12.4   Some Observations about RMPA

Let us first summarize the main conclusion of the previous section through the following observation, which generalizes the result established there for two tasks to any number of tasks.

Observation 12.5 Principle of Rate Monotonic Priority Assignment.

According to this principle, increasing priorities are assigned to tasks in the ascending order of their request rates, or, in other words, in the decreasing order of their request periods.

The above forms the basis of the scheduling strategy known as *Rate Monotonic Priority Assignment*, or RMPA for short. Below is another observation about RMPA:

Observation 12.6 Rate monotonic priority assignment can schedule any set of tasks if it can be scheduled by some other fixed priority assignment.

RMPA is considered optimal in the above sense; see Section 11.3.2 of Chapter 11. This notion of optimality may be shown by pairwise consideration of the tasks involved. For example, if two tasks τ_i and τ_j may be scheduled with $\tau_i \overset{p}{>} \tau_j$ but $T_i > T_j$, then it may be seen that they can also be scheduled with $\tau_j \overset{p}{>} \tau_i$ by swapping the order of execution.

Let us also restate Observation 12.2 made in Section 12.2.3 for RMPA:

Observation 12.7 Schedule Feasibility with RMPA.

Given a set of tasks S,

$$feasible_{\text{RMPA}}(S) \Rightarrow U \leq 1$$

It is instructive to compare the above observation with Observation 12.16 made in the Section 12.8. The reader may verify the invalidity of the reverse implication of Observation 12.7 by considering the counter example given by the following set of tasks:

Task	Period	Computation time
τ_1	2	1
τ_2	3	$\frac{1}{2}$
τ_3	4	$\frac{2}{3}$
τ_4	5	$\frac{1}{2}$

12.5   Fixed Priority Schedulability Constraints

This section examines the constraints determining schedulability by RMPA of a set of tasks $\tau_1, \tau_2, \cdots, \tau_n$ respectively with periods $T_1, T_2, \cdots, T_n$ such that $T_n > T_{n-1} > \cdots > T_2 > T_1$ and computation times $c_1, c_2, \cdots, c_n$.

Let $D_2, D_3, \cdots, D_n$ be the *implicit deadlines* at the critical instant of the tasks $\tau_2, \tau_3, \cdots, \tau_m$ implicit from the above task periods. In the case of an arbitrary task τ_i, D_i is an implicit deadline for the following two reasons:

- During the interval starting from D_i and ending at T_i at the critical instant of τ_i, only the higher priority tasks τ_k of τ_i (that is, tasks with $T_k < T_i$) may be executed.

- The task τ_i may be executed up to the implicit deadline D_i, as otherwise the deadline must in effect be before D_i.

As a consequence, if the implicit deadline of the task τ_i does not coincide with the next request for τ_i, then it must coincide with the request time of the first higher priority task τ_k (within the critical instant) beyond which τ_i cannot be executed because of the need to execute τ_k, and possibly other subsequent higher priority tasks.

Let us focus our attention on the implicit deadline of τ_n, the task with the longest period. It follows from the above that, firstly, the implicit deadline D_n of a task τ_n must be an element of the following set of time values:

$$\{t \mid 0 < t \le T_n \wedge \exists \tau_k : Task; \ i : \mathbb{N}_1 \ \bullet \ t = i \times T_k\}$$

The time values in the above set are known as *scheduling points* of the task τ_n, which are the deadlines of the tasks $\tau_1, \tau_2, \cdots, \tau_n$ calculated for the critical instant of τ_n. As shown below, however, it is sufficient to consider just a subset of the scheduling points. Secondly, D_n must satisfy the following criteria:

$$D_n + \sum_{j=1}^{n-1} (\lceil T_n/T_j \rceil - \lceil D_n/T_j \rceil) c_j \ \ge \ T_n \tag{i}$$

$$\sum_{j=1}^{n} \lceil D_n/T_j \rceil c_j \ \le \ D_n \tag{ii}$$

The inequality (i) specifies the circumstances under which D_n is the implicit deadline of τ_n, namely, either when D_n happens to coincide with T_n or when the interval between D_n and T_n has to be devoted fully to the execution of higher priority tasks. The inequality (ii) stipulates that D_n must be long enough to accommodate τ_n and all requests for its higher priority tasks. Furthermore, D_n must be the earliest deadline if (i) and (ii) happen to hold for more than one request of higher priority tasks. As a result, D_n may be found as

$$D_n = min\{t \mid 0 < t \le T_n \wedge \exists \tau_k : Task; \ i : \mathbb{N}_1 \ \bullet \ t = i \times T_k \wedge$$
$$t + \sum_{j=1}^{n-1} (\lceil T_n/T_j \rceil - \lceil t/T_j \rceil) c_j \ge T_n\}$$

which is the smallest element of the indicated subset of the scheduling points.

As an example, let us first consider a set of two tasks τ_1 and τ_2. In this case, the inequalities (i) and (ii) amount to the following:

$$D_2 + (\lceil T_2/T_1 \rceil - \lceil D_2/T_1 \rceil) c_1 \ \ge \ T_2 \tag{i(a)}$$
$$\lceil D_2/T_1 \rceil c_1 + \lceil D_2/T_2 \rceil c_2 \ \le \ D_2 \tag{ii(a)}$$

Analogous inequalities may be derived for a set of three tasks τ_1, τ_2 and τ_3 as:

$$D_3 + (\lceil T_3/T_1 \rceil - \lceil D_3/T_1 \rceil) c_1 + (\lceil T_3/T_2 \rceil - \lceil D_3/T_2 \rceil) c_2 \ \ge \ T_3 \tag{i(b)}$$
$$\lceil D_3/T_1 \rceil c_1 + \lceil D_3/T_2 \rceil c_2 + \lceil D_3/T_3 \rceil c_3 \ \le \ D_3 \tag{ii(b)}$$

This discussion is continued in the next two sections, which derive certain relations useful in schedulability analysis.

12.6   Processor Utilization Bounds

12.6.1   The Relevance

Processor utilization bounds are of interest for two reasons. Firstly, as the term implies, the utilization concerns rational use of resources and, therefore, an awareness of the proximity of actual utilization to any known theoretical utilization bounds may help in design decisions. Secondly, utilization bounds may serve as a measure indicative of schedule feasibility. Our concern here is this second aspect, namely, the use of the processor utilization bound as a tool in schedulability analysis.

The rational use of any resource requires the accomplishment of some given set of tasks, while making the most effective use of the resource. This might often mean modifying the tasks, wherever possible, in order to achieve this rational use of the resource. Although it is desirable to use a resource to 100% of its availability and capability, this is not always possible. The objective must therefore be to maximize the throughput while minimizing the use of the resource.

In the context of scheduling according to a given fixed priority assignment, a set of tasks is said to *fully utilize* the processor if any increase in their computation times makes the priority assignment infeasible. It is important to realize that 'full processor utilization' as understood here is not an absolute notion but a relative one, which is tied to a particular principle of priority assignment.

The *least upper bound* of the processor utilization factor is the minimum of the processor utilization factors of all possible sets of tasks that fully utilize the processor. Since the least upper bound implies full processor utilization and, hence, the schedule feasibility according to a given priority assignment, utilization factors below this bound signify schedule feasibility automatically. It is this fact which makes the least upper bound of processor utilization factors a useful practical tool. However, it must be emphasized that utilization factors above this bound do not necessarily signify the infeasibility of the priority assignment. Feasibility would depend on the actual task periods involved. The notation $lub(U)$ is used later to denote the least upper bound of the processor utilization factor.

12.6.2   Processor Utilization with Two Tasks

This section examines the schedulability of two tasks τ_1 and τ_2, respectively, with computation times c_1 and c_2 and periods T_1 and T_2 such that $T_2 > T_1$. Let

$$\frac{T_2}{T_1} = h + f$$

where $h = \left\lfloor \frac{T_2}{T_1} \right\rfloor$. Obviously, $0 \leq f < 1$. The considerations (i(b)) and (ii(b)) given in Section 12.5 may be written in a slightly different form for τ_1 and τ_2:

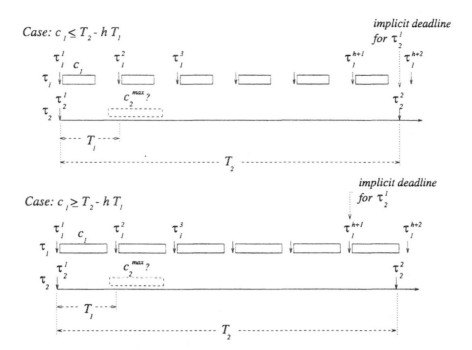

Figure 12.4 Maximizing processor utilization with two tasks

$$c_2^{max} = \begin{cases} T_2 - (h+1)c_1 & \text{if } c_1 \le T_2 - h\ T_1 \\ h(T_1 - c_1) & \text{if } c_1 \ge T_2 - h\ T_1 \end{cases}$$

$$= \begin{cases} h(T_1 - c_1) + fT_1 - c_1 & \text{if } fT_1 - c_1 \ge 0 \\ h(T_1 - c_1) & \text{if } fT_1 - c_1 \le 0 \end{cases}$$

The reasoning behind the above is also illustrated in Figure 12.4. It follows from the above that the processor utilization factor U becomes

$$U = \begin{cases} 1 + \frac{c_1}{T_2}(f-1) & \text{if } fT_1 - c_1 \ge 0 \\ \frac{h}{h+f} + \frac{c_1}{T_2}f & \text{if } fT_1 - c_1 \le 0 \end{cases}$$

As a result, U is a minimum with respect to c_1 when $c_1 = fT_1$ and is given by U':

$$U' = \frac{h+f^2}{h+f}$$

On the other hand, U' is a maximum with respect to h when $h = 1$, since $T_2 > T_1 > 0$, and it is a maximum with respect to f when

$$f = 2^{\frac{1}{2}} - 1 \approx 0.414$$

This results in a least upperbound of U

$$lub(U) = 2(\sqrt{2} - 1) \approx 0.828$$

The above holds for $h = 1$. A more general expression may be obtained without minimizing with respect to h. This corresponds to

$$f = (h^2 + 1)^{\frac{1}{2}} - h$$

and results in the least upperbounds of U given by

h	1	2	3	..	∞
$lub(U)$	0.83	0.90	0.93	..	1

12.6.3   A Property of Tasks Minimizing Processor Utilization

Let us establish here an important property of tasks that minimizes the processor utilization. This property is restricted to tasks with periods differing from each other by a factor of less than 2.

> **Observation 12.8** Given that the tasks $\tau_1, \tau_2, \cdots, \tau_m$ fully utilize the processor and minimizes the processor utilization factor, the following holds:
>
> $$\begin{aligned} C_1 &= T_2 - T_1 \\ C_2 &= T_3 - T_2 \\ &\vdots \\ C_i &= T_{i+1} - T_i \\ &\vdots \\ C_{m-1} &= T_m - T_{m-1} \end{aligned}$$
>
> where $C_1, C_2, \cdots, C_m$ are the respective computation times and $T_1, T_2, \cdots, T_m$ are the periods such that $T_1 < T_2 < \cdots < T_m$ and
>
> $$T_j/T_i < 2 ,$$
>
> for all i and j such that $i < j$.

The above may be proved as follows. Let us show for an arbitrary $i \in 1..(m-1)$ that

$$C_i = T_{i+1} - T_i$$

by providing a proof by contradiction, where we first assume that

$$C_i = T_{i+1} - T_i + \delta$$

and $\delta \neq 0$. Note that δ can be arbitrary, but in any case it must be sufficiently small or be of a magnitude such that $C_{i+1} + 2\delta > 0$. Let us consider the cases where $\delta > 0$ and $\delta < 0$ separately.

Case 1: $\delta > 0$

Since $\tau_1, \tau_2, \cdots, \tau_m$ fully utilize the processor by definition, the set of tasks $\tau_1', \tau_2', \cdots, \tau_m'$ with the following computation times:

$$
\begin{aligned}
C_1' &= C_1 \\
C_2' &= C_2 \\
&\vdots \\
C_{i-1}' &= C_{i-1} \\
C_i' &= T_{i+1} - T_i \\
C_{i+1}' &= C_{i+1} + \delta \\
C_{i+2}' &= C_{i+2} \\
&\vdots \\
C_m' &= C_m
\end{aligned}
$$

must also be feasible under the same priority assignment; see Figure 12.5. The change in the processor utilization factor resulting from the above reallocation of computation time is

$$U - U' = \frac{\delta}{T_i} - \frac{\delta}{T_{i+1}} = \frac{\delta}{T_i}\left(1 - \frac{T_i}{T_{i+1}}\right) > 0$$

since, by definition, $T_{i+1} > T_i$. It thus follows from the above that $U > U'$.

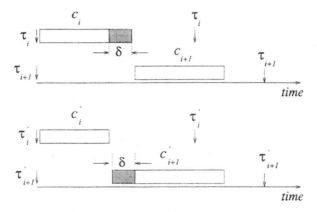

Figure 12.5 Task modification in Case 1

Case 2: $\delta < 0$

Now consider a slightly different reallocation of computation times, where the new set of tasks $\tau_1'', \tau_2'', \cdots, \tau_m''$ will have the following computation times:

$$
\begin{aligned}
C_1'' &= C_1 \\
C_2'' &= C_2 \\
&\vdots \\
C_{i-1}'' &= C_{i-1} \\
C_i'' &= T_{i+1} - T_i \\
C_{i+1}'' &= C_{i+1} + 2\delta \\
C_{i+2}'' &= C_{i+2} \\
&\vdots \\
C_m'' &= C_m
\end{aligned}
$$

Again, the above constitutes a feasible set of tasks under the same priority assignment; see Figure 12.6. The change in the processor utilization factor resulting from the above is

$$
U - U'' = \frac{\delta}{T_i} - \frac{2\delta}{T_{i+1}} = \frac{\delta}{T_i}\left(1 - 2\frac{T_i}{T_{i+1}}\right) > 0
$$

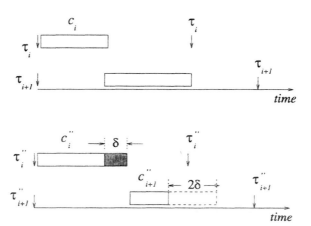

Figure 12.6 Task modification in Case 2

The above case analysis shows that the assumption of $C_i \neq T_{i+1} - T_i$ leads to a conclusion which contradicts our original premise that the tasks $\tau_1, \tau_2, \cdots, \tau_m$ minimize the processor utilization factor. Therefore, it must be the case that $C_i = T_{i+1} - T_i$. Since our choice of i is arbitrary, the result holds for all $i \in 1 .. (m-1)$.

12.6.4   Processor Utilization with Two or More Tasks

The result established in the previous section is an important step in establishing the least upper bound of the processor utilization factor for any set of tasks:

Observation 12.9 The least upper bound of the processor utilization factor for a set of m tasks scheduled with a fixed priority assignment is:

$$lub(U) = m(2^{\frac{1}{m}} - 1) .$$

The above is quite a general statement and applies, as mentioned, to any set of tasks. Let us reason about this claim in two stages:

Stage 1 Let us first show that the processor utilization factor of any arbitrary set of tasks is bounded from below by the least upper bound of the processor utilization factor that applies to a set of tasks whose periods do not differ from each other by more than a factor of 2.

Stage 2 Let us then show that the least upper bound of the processor utilization factor that applies to a set of tasks whose periods do not differ from each other by more than a factor of 2 is given by

$$lub(U) = m(2^{\frac{1}{m}} - 1)$$

which is identical to the formula given under Observation 12.9.

Stage 1

Let the arbitrary set of tasks be, as before, $\tau_1, \tau_2, \cdots, \tau_m$, with $C_1, C_2, \cdots, C_m$ being the computation times and $T_1, T_2, \cdots, T_m$ the periods. Let us also introduce the notations:

$$\begin{aligned} g_i &= \frac{T_m}{T_i} = h_i + f_i \\ h_i &= \lfloor g_i \rfloor \end{aligned}$$

where $i \in 1..m$. Obviously, $0 \le f_i < 1$. Without loss of generality, we also assume that $h_i > 1$. Note that this restriction may be removed easily. In relation to the above set of tasks, consider another set of tasks $\tau_1', \tau_2', \cdots, \tau_m'$ derived from the former by letting

$$\begin{aligned} C_1' &= C_1 \\ C_2' &= C_2 \\ &\vdots \\ C_{m-1}' &= C_{m-1} \\ C_m' &= C_m + \sum_{i=1}^{m-1} (h_i - 1) C_i \end{aligned}$$

and

$$T_1' = h_1 T_1$$
$$T_2' = h_2 T_2$$
$$\vdots$$
$$T_{m-1}' = h_{m-1} T_{m-1}$$
$$T_m' = T_m$$

In effect, the above modification is suggesting that the periods of every task, other than that of τ_m, are raised to the highest integral multiple of its original period within T_m, while maintaining its computation time unchanged. However, in order to maintain the processor utilization at the full utilization level, the computation time of the task τ_m must be correspondingly increased. Given a task τ_i such that $i \neq m$, the corresponding increase called for in C_m' is at most $(h_i - 1)C_i$. This is illustrated in Figure 12.7.

Original tasks

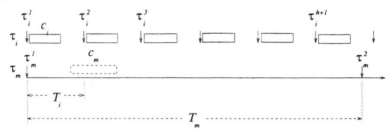

Modified tasks

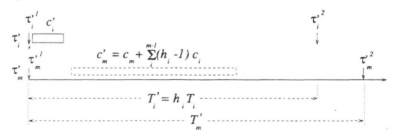

Figure 12.7 Task modification in Stage 1

It follows from the above that

$$\frac{T_m'}{T_i'} = \frac{T_m}{h_i T_i} = 1 + \frac{f_i}{h_i} < 2$$

The new set of tasks results in a processor utilization factor U':

$$U' \leq U + \sum_{i=1}^{m-1} \left(\frac{(h_i-1)C_i}{T_m} + \frac{C_i}{T_i'} - \frac{C_i}{T_i} \right)$$
$$\leq U - \sum_{i=1}^{m-1} \frac{(h_i-1)f_i C_i}{T_m h_i}$$

Since the sum in the last line is non-negative, our new set of tasks has a lower processor utilization, but maintains practically the same level of processing capability. Furthermore, the ratio of periods for any pair of tasks in the modified set of tasks is less than 2, thus justifying the next stage of the analysis.

Stage 2

Let us continue our analysis using Observation 12.8 established in Section 12.6.3. Note that this result concerns only tasks that fully utilize the processor and at the same time have periods the ratios of which lie within 0 and 2.

First, it may be noted from Observation 12.8 that

$$C_m \leq 2T_1 - T_m .$$

The processor utilization factor U resulting from a set of tasks that fully utilize the processor and at the same time have the required periods is

$$
\begin{aligned}
U &= \sum_{i=1}^{m} \frac{C_i}{T_i} \\
&= \frac{2T_1 - T_m}{T_m} + \sum_{i=1}^{m-1} \frac{T_{i+1} - T_i}{T_i} \\
&= \frac{2T_1}{T_m} - 1 + \sum_{i=1}^{m-1} \left(\frac{T_{i+1}}{T_i} - 1 \right) \\
&= \frac{2}{g_1} - 1 - (m-1) + \sum_{i=1}^{m-1} \frac{g_i}{g_{i+1}} \\
&= -m + \sum_{i=0}^{m-1} \frac{g_i}{g_{i+1}} \\
&= -m + \frac{g_0}{g_1} + \frac{g_1}{g_2} + \cdots + \frac{g_{i-1}}{g_i} + \frac{g_i}{g_{i+1}} + \cdots + \frac{g_{m-1}}{g_m} .
\end{aligned}
$$

where we have let $g_0 = 2$.

The least upper bound of U may be established by minimizing U with respect to all unknown g_is. That is,

$$\frac{\partial U}{\partial g_i} = -\frac{g_{i-1}}{g_i^2} + \frac{1}{g_{i+1}} = 0, \qquad \text{for } i = 1, \cdots, m-1$$

The above is a system of equations of the form

$$
\begin{aligned}
g_2 &= \frac{g_1^2}{g_0} \\
g_3 &= \frac{g_2^2}{g_1} \\
&\vdots \\
g_m &= \frac{g_{m-1}^2}{g_{m-2}}
\end{aligned}
$$

for the unknowns $g_1, g_2, \cdots, g_{m-1}$. It may also be viewed as a recurrence relation

$$g_i = \frac{g_{i-1}^2}{g_{i-2}}$$

for $i \in 2 ..\ m$ and with $g_0 = 2$. It is obvious that $g_m = 1$. It may also be easily seen that

$$g_i = 2^{(m-i)/m}$$

is the solution of the above recurrence relation and may be verified, if required, by mathematical induction. Substitution of the above solution in the expression for U leads to

$$
\begin{aligned}
U &= -m + \sum_{i=0}^{m-1} \frac{g_i}{g_{i+1}} \\
&= -m + \sum_{i=0}^{m-1} 2^{\frac{1}{m}} \\
&= m(2^{\frac{1}{m}} - 1)
\end{aligned}
$$

which is the desired result. This completes the proof of Observation 12.9. The practical significance of the above result lies in the following observation:

> **Observation 12.10** A set of n independent tasks with arbitrary periods can be scheduled by RMPA if its processor utilization factor U satisfies the following:
>
> $$U \le n(2^{\frac{1}{n}} - 1)$$

The above may thus be used as a criterion in schedulability tests. However, the set of tasks may still be schedulable when

$$n(2^{\frac{1}{n}} - 1) < U \le 1,$$

provided that the periods and the computation times are such that any intervening processor idling can be eliminated.

12.7   General Schedulability Criteria

12.7.1   Exact Schedulability Criterion

Although Observation 12.10 expresses a sufficient condition for schedulability, its use is limited since it does not address a necessary condition. However, the discussion in Section 12.5 enables the formulation of a more general criterion, which is stated below:

Observation 12.11 A Necessary and Sufficient Schedulability Criterion

A set of n tasks $S = \{\tau_1, \tau_2, \cdots, \tau_n\}$, respectively, with periods $T_1, T_2, \cdots, T_n$ such that $T_n > T_{n-1} > \cdots > T_2 > T_1$ and computation times $c_1, c_2, \cdots, c_n$, is schedulable by RMPA if and only if the following conditions hold for the <u>earliest</u> implicit deadline D_i of each and every task τ_i:

$$D_i + \sum_{j=1}^{i-1}(\lceil T_i/T_j \rceil - \lceil D_i/T_j \rceil)c_j \geq T_i \qquad (i)$$

$$\sum_{j=1}^{i} \lceil D_i/T_j \rceil c_j \leq D_i \qquad (ii)$$

The above may be proved informally as follows. Let us consider first the necessity of the given criterion. Assume that the set of tasks is schedulable. That means that every task τ_i in S is also schedulable. If τ_i is schedulable then it meets its deadline, which lies at T_i at its critical instant. Its completion time is at T_i or some time earlier and, in any case, before the arrival time of one or more higher priority tasks beyond which that instance of τ_i cannot be executed. If τ_i is the last task to complete before T_i, then T_i is the implicit deadline and (i) is automatically satisfied. The truth of (ii) in this case follows from

$$\neg\, overflow_{\text{RMPA}}(S_i, T_i))$$ since τ_i is schedulable
$$\Rightarrow P_{\text{RMPA}}(S_i, (0, T_i)) \leq T_i$$ def. of $overflow_{\text{RMPA}}$
$$\Leftrightarrow \sum_{j=1}^{i} \lceil T_i/T_j \rceil c_j \leq T_i$$ def. of P_{RMPA} (see below)

where $S_i = \{\tau_1, \tau_2, \cdots, \tau_i\}$. Note that in the above

$$P_{\text{RMPA}}(S_i, (0, T_i)) = \sum_{j=1}^{i} \lceil T_i/T_j \rceil c_j$$

holds because, since τ_i is the last task to complete, one request of τ_i and all requests of other higher priority tasks must therefore have been executed by time T_i.

On the other hand, if τ_i is required to complete before T_i in order to comply with its deadline, then there must exist a time value D_i by which time τ_i is to complete execution. The value of D_i is determined by the arrival of a higher priority task, beyond which that instance of τ_i cannot be executed. Consequently, the value of D_i must equal the arrival time of the earliest task among them. In that case, by definition, D_i is the implicit deadline and also satisfies (i). Since τ_i is schedulable before D_i, it can be shown through an analogous argument to the above that the condition (ii) must also be true for the implicit deadline D_i. Thus, the necessity of the above criterion can be justified.

Let us now turn our attention to sufficiency of the criterion. Let us assume that D_i is the earliest implicit deadline and (ii) is true. Condition (i) follows from the definition of D_i itself. There are two cases to consider, namely, $D_i = T_i$ and $D_i < T_i$. If $D_i = T_i$, then

$$\sum_{j=1}^{i} \lceil T_i/T_j \rceil c_j \leq T_i \qquad \qquad \text{condition } (ii) \text{ for } D_i = T_i$$

$$\Leftrightarrow \quad P_{\text{RMPA}}(S_i, (0, T_i)) \leq T_i \qquad \qquad \text{def. of } P_{\text{RMPA}}$$

$$\Rightarrow \quad \neg \; overflow_{\text{RMPA}}(S_i, T_i)) \qquad \qquad \text{def. of } overflow_{\text{RMPA}}$$

Thus, since there cannot be an overflow at T_i, the set of tasks must be schedulable. For the case $D_i < T_i$, an identical argument holds for D_i in place of T_i. Thus, there cannot be an overflow at D_i either and, therefore, the set of tasks is again schedulable. Thus, the sufficiency of the above criterion holds for $D_i \leq T_i$, and hence, with its necessity already proved, Observation 12.11 can be justified.

EXAMPLE

As an illustration of the use of the above criterion, consider three tasks with the following parameters:

Task	c	T
τ_1	30	100
τ_2	50	150
τ_3	100	350

The processor utilization factor is

$$U = \frac{30}{100} + \frac{50}{150} + \frac{100}{350}$$
$$= 0.92$$
$$> 0.78$$
$$= 3(2^{\frac{1}{3}} - 1)$$
$$= n(2^{\frac{1}{n}} - 1), \qquad \text{for } n = 3$$

and hence, the criterion given in Observation 12.10 does not help us in establishing schedule feasibility. Let us examine the schedulability of the tasks according to the the criterion given in Observation 12.11 when τ_3 is under consideration. As given in Section 12.5, the three tasks must satisfy the following inequalities:

$$D_3 + (\lceil T_3/T_1 \rceil - \lceil D_3/T_1 \rceil)c_1 + (\lceil T_3/T_2 \rceil - \lceil D_3/T_2 \rceil)c_2 \geq T_3 \qquad \text{(i(b))}$$
$$\lceil D_3/T_1 \rceil c_1 + \lceil D_3/T_2 \rceil c_2 + \lceil D_3/T_3 \rceil c_3 \leq D_3 \qquad \text{(ii(b))}$$

The scheduling points of τ_3 (the candidate values of D_3) are as follows:

$100, 150, 200, 300, 350$ time units.

The simple check given below establishes that only the scheduling points at 300 and 350 time units satisfy condition (i(b)).

Scheduling point : 100 and 150 time units

    Condition (i(b))
    $\vdots$
$\Leftrightarrow$ False

Scheduling point : 200 time units

    Condition (i(b))
$\Leftrightarrow$ $200 + (\lceil 350/100 \rceil - \lceil 200/100 \rceil)30 + (\lceil 350/150 \rceil - \lceil 200/150 \rceil)50 \geq 350$
$\Leftrightarrow$ $200 + (4 - 2)30 + (3 - 2)50 \geq 350$
$\Leftrightarrow$ $310 \geq 350$
$\Leftrightarrow$ False

Scheduling point : 300 time units

    Condition (i(b))
$\Leftrightarrow$ $300 + (\lceil 350/100 \rceil - \lceil 300/100 \rceil)30 + (\lceil 350/150 \rceil - \lceil 300/150 \rceil)50 \geq 350$
$\Leftrightarrow$ $300 + (4 - 3)30 + (3 - 2)50 \geq 350$
$\Leftrightarrow$ $380 \geq 350$
$\Leftrightarrow$ True

Scheduling point : 350 time units

    Condition (i(b))
    $\vdots$
$\Leftrightarrow$ True

The implicit deadline of τ_3 is

    $D_3 = min\{300, 350\} = 300$ time units.

Condition (ii(b)) at the implicit deadline may be stated as

    Condition (ii(b))
$\Leftrightarrow$ $\lceil 300/100 \rceil \, 30 + \lceil 300/150 \rceil \, 50 + \lceil 300/350 \rceil \, 100 \leq 300$
$\Leftrightarrow$ $3 \times 30 + 2 \times 50 + 1 \times 100 \leq 300$
$\Leftrightarrow$ $90 + 100 + 100 \leq 300$
$\Leftrightarrow$ $290 \leq 300$
$\Leftrightarrow$ True

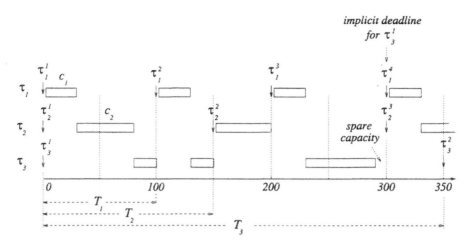

Figure 12.8 RMPA schedule for the three tasks with $c_1 = 30$ time units

Since both conditions (i(b)) and (ii(b)) are satisfied, the schedulability of the three tasks is assured when τ_3 is under consideration. The schedule at the critical instant is shown in Figure 12.8.

Let us increase the computation time of c_1 to 35 time units, while maintaining all other task parameters unchanged. This raises the processor utilization factor to

$$U = \frac{35}{100} + \frac{50}{150} + \frac{100}{350}$$
$$= 0.97$$

but still keeps it below unity. Let us again examine the schedulability of the three tasks according to Observation 12.11 when τ_3 is under consideration. The scheduling points of τ_3 remain unchanged. Verification of condition (i(b)) at 200 and 300 units of time is as follows:

Scheduling point : 200 time units

        Condition (i(b))
   ⇔ $200 + (\lceil 350/100 \rceil - \lceil 200/100 \rceil)35 + (\lceil 350/150 \rceil - \lceil 200/150 \rceil)50 \geq 350$
   ⇔ $200 + (4 - 2)35 + (3 - 2)50 \geq 350$
   ⇔ $320 \geq 350$
   ⇔ False

Scheduling point : 300 time units

Condition (i(b))

$\Leftrightarrow$ $300 + (\lceil 350/100 \rceil - \lceil 300/100 \rceil)35 + (\lceil 350/150 \rceil - \lceil 300/150 \rceil)50 \geq 350$

$\Leftrightarrow$ $300 + (4-3)35 + (3-2)50 \geq 350$

$\Leftrightarrow$ $385 \geq 350$

$\Leftrightarrow$ True

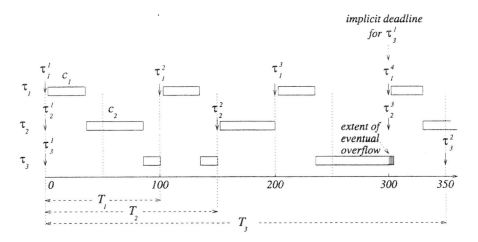

Figure 12.9 Partial RMPA schedule with c_1 increased to 35 time units

The implicit deadline D_3 is 300 time units.
Condition (ii(b)) at the implicit deadline may be stated as

Condition (ii(b))

$\Leftrightarrow$ $\lceil 300/100 \rceil\, 35 + \lceil 300/150 \rceil\, 50 + \lceil 300/350 \rceil\, 100 \leq 300$

$\Leftrightarrow$ $3 \times 35 + 2 \times 50 + 1 \times 100 \leq 300$

$\Leftrightarrow$ $105 + 100 + 100 \leq 300$

$\Leftrightarrow$ $305 \leq 300$

$\Leftrightarrow$ False

Thus, condition (ii(b)) is not satisfied at the implicit deadline $D_3 = 300$ and, therefore, the tasks are not schedulable when c_1 is increased to 35 time units. This failure is evident from the partial schedule shown in Figure 12.9

An alternative exact schedulability criterion, which is widely known in the literature, is the following:

Observation 12.12 A Necessary and Sufficient Schedulability Criterion

A set of tasks $\tau_1, \tau_2, \cdots, \tau_n$, respectively, with periods $T_1, T_2, \cdots, T_n$ such that $T_n > T_{n-1} > \cdots > T_2 > T_1$ and computation times

$c_1, c_2, \cdots, c_n$, is schedulable by RMPA if and only if for each and every task τ_i:

$$\left(min \left\{ \frac{1}{l\ T_k} \sum_{j=1}^{i} c_j \left\lceil \frac{l\ T_k}{T_j} \right\rceil \mid (k,l) \in R_i \right\} \right) \leq 1$$

where

$$R_i = \{(k,l) \mid k \in 1 .. i \wedge l \in 1 .. \lfloor T_i / T_k \rfloor \}$$

12.7.2   Scheduling under Priority Inversion

An assumption made in this study at the outset (in Section 12.1.1) is that all tasks are mutually independent. This is not a realistic assumption in certain situations. There can be all kinds of inter-dependence between tasks, among which are the dependencies introduced by critical resources such as files and shared data structures. In order to maintain their consistency, access to such resources must be controlled, typically by serialization. This, however, introduces an anomaly to priority based access scheduling. Occasionally, a higher priority task may be forced to wait or, in other words, be *blocked*, for the completion of a lower priority task if the former arrives after the latter has gained access to the resource. Furthermore, a higher priority task may be unnecessarily blocked by a lower priority task using a resource even if the higher priority task does not require access to the resource itself. The result is an effective *inversion* of the priorities of the tasks concerned. As a consequence, not only will the principles underlying the scheduling strategies be violated but also the computation times of blocked tasks will effectively be lengthened, affecting both schedulability and the level of processor utilization.

Another problem is that the duration of blocking of a higher priority task by a lower priority task is unpredictable because of the possible preemption of the lower priority task by other tasks of intermediate priorities. This leads to what is called *unbounded priority inversion*. This is addressed by a *priority ceiling protocol*, which prevents the blocking of any higher priority task at any time by more than one lower priority task. Further details about this protocol may be found in the references cited under bibliographical notes in Section 12.10.

In order to account for the possible blocking of higher priority tasks by lower priority ones, the results given under Observations 12.10 and 12.12 need to be modified. The following is thus a generalization of Observation 12.10:

Observation 12.13 A·set of n periodic tasks with arbitrary periods can be scheduled by RMPA (using priority ceiling protocol) provided that

$$\frac{c_1}{T_1} + \frac{c_2}{T_2} + \cdots + \frac{c_n}{T_n} + max \left\{ \frac{B_1}{T_1}, \frac{B_2}{T_2}, \cdots, \frac{B_{n-1}}{T_{n-1}} \right\} \leq n(2^{\frac{1}{n}} - 1)$$

where B_i is the duration of the longest blocking experienced by the task τ_i.

The above is established effectively by raising the computation times of each task by its worst possible blocking delay and relying on the priority ceiling protocol. Note that $B_n = 0$ since τ_n is the lowest priority task and, by definition, cannot be blocked by a lower priority task. Similarly, Observation 12.12 is generalized as:

Observation 12.14 A Necessary and Sufficient Schedulability Criterion

A set of tasks $\tau_1, \tau_2, \cdots, \tau_n$ is schedulable by RMPA if and only if for each and every task τ_i:

$$\left(min \left\{ \frac{1}{l\ T_k} \left(\sum_{j=1}^{i-1} c_j \left\lceil \frac{l\ T_k}{T_j} \right\rceil + c_i + B_i \right) \mid (k, l) \in R_i \right\} \right) \le 1$$

where the periods, the computation times and the expression for R_i are as given in Observation 12.12, while B_i is the worst case blocking time of the task τ_i.

12.8 Uni-processor Dynamic Scheduling

The best-known dynamic scheduling algorithm is based on *deadline driven scheduling*, referred to below simply as DDS.

Observation 12.15 Deadline Driven Scheduling

According to deadline driven scheduling, increasing priorities are assigned to tasks in the descending order of their deadlines. In other words,

(i) The task with the nearest deadline at any moment is given the highest priority.

(ii) Priorities of other tasks decrease with increasing time to their deadlines.

The following serves as a criterion for establishing schedule feasibility by DDS.

Observation 12.16 Deadline driven scheduling of a set of tasks is feasible if and only if $U \le 1$. That is,

$$feasible_{\text{DDS}}(S) \Leftrightarrow U \le 1\ ,$$

Note that, following the discussion in Section 12.2.3, $feasible_{\text{DDS}}(S)$ is true if and only if S may be scheduled by DDS. The practical significance of this observation lies in the fact that a calculation of the processor utilization factor U would immediately establish the feasibility of scheduling a given set of tasks by the Deadline Driven Scheduling Algorithm. Section B.3 of Appendix B substantiates the above observation with a proof.

12.9   Mixed Scheduling

It is possible to adopt, where necessary, a Mixed Scheduling strategy by using Rate-Monotonic Priority assigned static scheduling for the first k tasks with highest request rates, and using deadline driven scheduling for the remaining $(m-k)$ tasks with lower request rates, but when the processor is not attending to the first set. Mixed scheduling may be justified on the grounds of better compatibility with interrupt mechanisms with a fixed priority scheduler and the marginal scheduling cost when long period tasks are handled dynamically.

12.10   Bibliographical Notes

This chapter is based largely on work by Liu and Layland [94], widely used as a general framework for scheduling; see, for example, Klein *et al.* [76, 77]. The reader may also benefit from van Tilborg and Knob [164]. The place of the rate monotonic scheduling in the general theory of scheduling is discussed in Stankovic *et al.* [156]. More details on the general scheduling criterion in Observation 12.12 and other criteria introduced in Section 12.7.2 may be found in Lehoczky *et al.* [91] and Sha *et al.* [145, 146, 147].

12.11   Exercises

1. Referring to the set of periodic tasks given at the very end of Section 12.4, that is,

Task	Period	Computation time
τ_1	2	1
τ_2	3	$\frac{1}{2}$
τ_3	4	$\frac{2}{3}$
τ_4	5	$\frac{1}{2}$

   construct, if possible, a dynamic schedule.
2. Establish the applicability of the notions of overflow discussed in Section 12.2.2 in relation to the following set of two tasks:

Task	c	T
τ_1	1	2
τ_2	2.1	5

if they are to be scheduled in accordance with the rate monotonic priority assignment discussed in Sections 12.3 and 12.4 and the deadline driven algorithm discussed in Section 12.8.

3. Investigate the schedulability of the set of tasks considered in the Example on page 272 in accordance with the schedulability criterion given under Observation 12.12. Investigate also the scope for raising the processor utilization without changing the periods of the tasks concerned.

Chapter 13

Multi-processor Static Scheduling

This chapter presents an approach to multi-processor static scheduling of tasks. The temporal order of the tasks is represented by a precedence relation, which implicitly defines the deadlines on task completions. The approach is applicable to precedence relations resulting in acyclic graphs and contains a special solution to those corresponding to rooted computation trees.

13.1 Problem Statement

The problem addressed here is a computation which consists of a set of tasks with an associated precedence relation $\prec$ defined on it. The precedence relation corresponds to an acyclic graph, which is irreflexive and strictly non-symmetric. It is also to be interpreted as immediate precedence. That is, a pair of tasks (τ_1, τ_2) is in this relation if and only if τ_1 is to be executed immediately before τ_2 is begun. An alternative terminology used here for referring to a precedence relation given as part of a scheduling problem is a *computation graph*.

EXAMPLE

Let the set of tasks be

$$Task = \{\tau_1, \tau_2, \tau_3, \tau_4, \tau_5\}$$

A possible precedence relation on *Task* may be (see Figure 13.1)

$$\prec = \{(\tau_1, \tau_3), (\tau_2, \tau_3), (\tau_2, \tau_5), (\tau_4, \tau_5)\}$$

meaning that τ_1 is to be executed before τ_3, τ_4 before τ_5, and τ_2 before both τ_3 and τ_5.

The computation is to be performed on a non-empty set of identical processors, each capable of executing at most one task at any given time. The only optimization criterion is the schedule length.

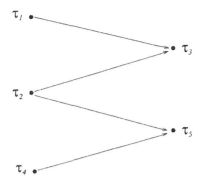

Figure 13.1 A precedence relation on a set of tasks

13.2 Scheduling Disciplines

The scheduling disciplines may be classified as:

(i) Basic (or non-preemptive) scheduling, BS.

Once started each task is executed to its completion.

(ii) Preemptive scheduling, PS.

Tasks may be interrupted in order to execute other tasks. Note that task preemption here is not necessarily priority based.

(iii) General scheduling, GS.

This is a theoretical notion. In essence, general scheduling amounts to potential 'processor sharing' by more than one task at any moment and, thus, contravenes the assumption set out at the beginning that each processor executes at most one task at a time. It is based on the premise that processors can devote, if necessary, a certain fraction α of their full computing capability to any task at a given time, with $0 \leq \alpha \leq 1$. A consequence of this assumption is that the elapsed computation time of any task executed at reduced rates increases in inverse proportion to α. In other words, a task taking c time units on a dedicated processor would take $\frac{c}{\alpha}$ time units in real time if computed at a constant rate of α with processor sharing.

Note that given k identical processors, it is always the case that $\sum \alpha \leq k$. Note also that no task may be executed simultaneously in parallel on more than one processor. Let us assume that task definitions already account for inter-process communications and resource dependencies.

In relation to the above scheduling disciplines:

Definition: $C_D(G, k)$

The notation $C_D(G, k)$ denotes the *minimum computation time* required for the computation given by a graph G by employing the scheduling discipline D on a system with k identical processors.

An important observation on the minimum computation time defined above is expressed in the following observation:

Observation 13.1 Preemptive and general scheduling are equivalent with respect to minimum computation time. That is, for any graph G with k processors

$$C_{GS}(G, k) = C_{PS}(G, k)$$

The utility of this relationship lies in the fact that general scheduling may be used as a stepping stone in constructing a preemptive schedule with the same schedule length as the corresponding general schedule.

Proof of Observation 13.1: The proof consists of two separate proofs for the following subgoals:

$$C_{GS}(G, k) \leq C_{PS}(G, k) \tag{a}$$
$$C_{GS}(G, k) \geq C_{PS}(G, k) \tag{b}$$

The proof of (a) follows immediately from the fact that PS is also a GS for the special case of $\alpha = 1$ and, therefore, that a PS cannot improve upon the minimum computation time of the corresponding GS .

The proof of (b) is not so obvious. It amounts to the claim that for any GS schedule S, it is possible to construct a PS schedule which is no longer than S.

The proof, which is a 'proof by construction', is as follows. Let

$$t_s = \{ t_i \mid i \in 1 \mathbin{..} m \}$$

be the set of completion times of m nodes in the graph G ordered in the ascending order of time by the indices i; see Figure 13.2.

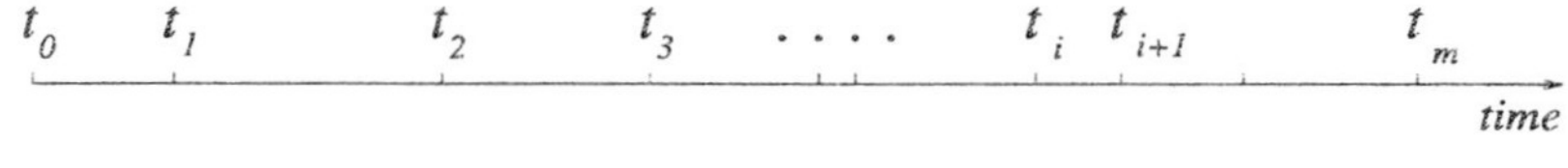

Figure 13.2 Task completion times

The intervals marked off by consecutive t_is have an interesting property, namely, that any tasks executed in any given interval are independent. If this were not the case then there could be two tasks τ_i and τ_j in some interval such that $\tau_i \prec \tau_j$, requiring τ_i to complete before τ_j and, thus, an additional completion time in the interval concerned. Obviously, this contradicts the definition of t_s, namely, that the time values in t_s are the only completion times.

Let the completion times in t_s correspond to a GS schedule S. Then, as proof of (b) one may convert S to a PS schedule S' such that

$$\text{length of } S' \leq \text{length of } S$$

The construction of S' is based on the arguments:

1. S already satisfies the precedence relation associated with the set of tasks.

2. Processor sharing within any interval may therefore be altered without violating the precedence relation since all tasks executed within the interval are independent.

   Therefore, S is convertible to another equivalent GS schedule, including a PS schedule, provided that the sum total of effective (not elapsed) computation time devoted to each task within each interval is not affected.

3. On the basis of the above, one may compute the total effective computation time spent on each and every task individually, and reallocate the tasks one per processor and for durations equal to the respective effective computation times. That is, the tasks are redistributed with α equal to unity.

The above may be illustrated as follows. Let the pth task τ_p be computed over non-overlapping time stretches $l_1, l_2, \cdots, l_m$ within the interval $\langle t_i, t_{i+1} \rangle$ at the rates of $\alpha_1, \alpha_2, \cdots, \alpha_m$ respectively (see Figure 13.3).

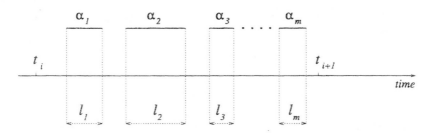

Figure 13.3 Task computation under general scheduling

Then the total computing power spent on the task τ_p over $\langle t_i, t_{i+1} \rangle$ is

$$\delta c_p = \sum_{j \in 1..m} \alpha_j l_j \leq t_{i+1} - t_i \tag{1}$$

Also, the total computing power spent on all tasks executed over $\langle t_i, t_{i+1} \rangle$ is

$$\sum_{\tau_p \in Task} \delta c_p \le k \times (t_{i+1} - t_i) \tag{2}$$

Thus, according to (1) above, we never need more than one processor per task within $\langle t_i, t_{i+1} \rangle$ and, according to (2), there is sufficient computing power for all tasks executed within $\langle t_i, t_{i+1} \rangle$. This argument remains applicable to any interval in the GS schedule S.

Having computed the δc_ps according to (1) for all tasks and all intervals, it is now possible to redistribute them without processor sharing. For example, dealing with a given time interval and starting off with any processor, one may allocate δc_p time units of that processor to τ_p (with $\alpha = 1$). If there remains enough computing time on the same processor then full δc_q time units on it may be allocated to some τ_q, otherwise as much time as possible on it may be allocated to τ_q making up for the shortfall on a second processor. This process is carried out for all tasks executed in that interval, employing a new processor as the computing time on the current processor runs out.

The resulting schedule S' is a PS schedule and, by virtue of (1) and (2), never needs more time than the original GS schedule. Thus, the method of construction outlined and observations (1) and (2) prove (b) and, thus, conclude the proof of Observation 13.1. Following this procedure, knowing a GS schedule it is always possible to construct an equivalent PS schedule of the same length; see Figure 13.4.

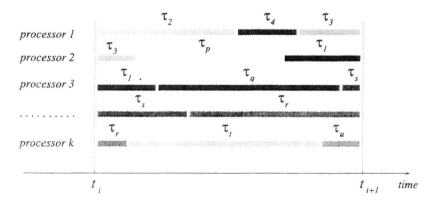

Figure 13.4 Task computation under preemptive scheduling

13.3   Acyclic Computation Graphs

As a direct illustration of the above construction, consider the computation presented by the graph in Figure 13.5, which is to be performed using at most two identical

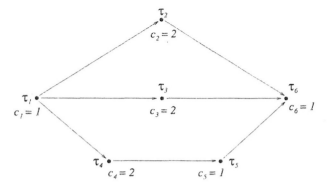

Figure 13.5 An acyclic computation graph

processors within the shortest time possible. The computation times of tasks shown on the graph are in units of 'processor time' (e.g. τ_2 requires a single dedicated processor for two time units). Figure 13.6 shows the changes in demand for processor time by the given set of tasks, as well as the possible maximum aggregate consumption levels of the available processing power.

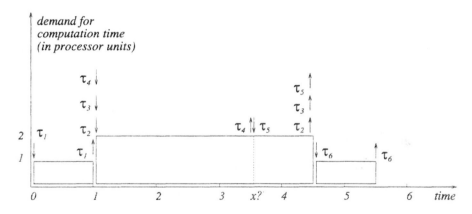

Figure 13.6 Demand for processor time

The GS schedule for the above is constructed as follows. The tasks τ_1 and τ_6 have to be executed on their own and each may be allocated a single processor, one time unit for τ_1 at the very beginning and one time unit for τ_6 at the end. The tasks τ_2, τ_3 and τ_4 are to be executed as soon as τ_1 is completed. Since τ_5 may not begin until τ_4 is completed, the two tasks together may be combined into a single task and computed at a single rate. Let us refer to this combined task as $\tilde{\tau}_4$. As a consequence, τ_2, τ_3 and $\tilde{\tau}_4$ can be treated as arriving at the same time. These three tasks together require seven processor time units and, therefore, may be completed in $3\frac{1}{2}$ time units using the two processors at our disposal. Assuming uniform computing rates for them over this interval, it is possible to arrive at the α rates shown below:

	T_1	T_2	T_3	T_4	T_5	T_6
α_i	1	$\frac{4}{7}$	$\frac{4}{7}$	$\frac{6}{7}$	$\frac{6}{7}$	1
l_i	1	$3\frac{1}{2}$	$3\frac{1}{2}$	$2\frac{1}{3}$	$1\frac{1}{6}$	1

Using above, one may establish the task completion times given below:

Time, t_i	Tasks completed	Tasks begun
$t_0 = 0$	None	T_1
$t_1 = 1$	T_1	T_2, T_3, T_4
$t_2 = 3\frac{1}{3}$	T_4	T_5
$t_3 = 4\frac{1}{2}$	T_2, T_3, T_5	T_6
$t_4 = 5\frac{1}{2}$	T_6	None

This allows the construction of a System Gantt Chart based on General Scheduling; see Figure 13.7.

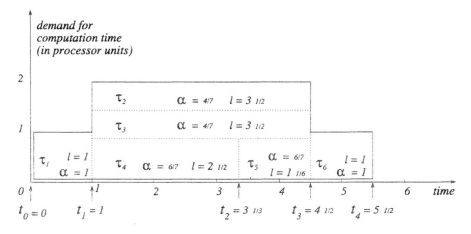

Figure 13.7 System Gantt chart

The above may now be converted to a preemptive schedule in the following manner. Consider the tasks scheduled for execution over an interval between a pair of adjacent completion times. For example, according to the GS schedule shown in Figure 13.7, three tasks, namely, T_2, T_3 and T_4, are to be executed over the interval $\langle 1, 3\frac{1}{3} \rangle$. Knowing their α rates and the length of the interval, it is a simple calculation to establish the cumulative processing power required by each one of them over this interval. The next step is to reallocate processor time at the rate of $\alpha = 1$ to the three tasks concerned, but meeting their cumulative processing requirements. Since it is necessary to avoid executing any task simultaneously on two processors, consider one task at a time and make sure that its computing requirements are first met fully using one or, if necessary, two processors before moving on to the next task. Since $\alpha < 1$, no task need be executed on more than two processors over this interval. The results of these calculations and the processor allocation schemes are shown in the following table and in Figure 13.8 as Processor Gantt Charts.

Processor 1		Processor 2	
Time interval	*Task executed*	*Time interval*	*Task executed*
$\langle 0, 1 \rangle$	τ_1	$\langle 0, 1 \rangle$	Idling
$\langle 1, 2\frac{1}{3} \rangle$	τ_2	$\langle 1, 1\frac{1}{3} \rangle$	τ_3
$\langle 2\frac{1}{3}, 3\frac{1}{3} \rangle$	τ_3	$\langle 1\frac{1}{3}, 3\frac{1}{3} \rangle$	τ_4
$\langle 3\frac{1}{3}, 4 \rangle$	τ_2	$\langle 3\frac{1}{3}, 3\frac{1}{2} \rangle$	τ_3
$\langle 4, 4\frac{1}{2} \rangle$	τ_3	$\langle 3\frac{1}{2}, 4\frac{1}{2} \rangle$	τ_5
$\langle 4\frac{1}{2}, 5\frac{1}{2} \rangle$	τ_6	$\langle 4\frac{1}{2}, 5\frac{1}{2} \rangle$	Idling

Processor 1

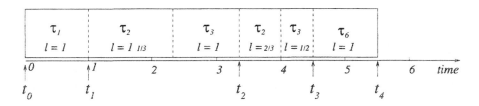

Processor 2

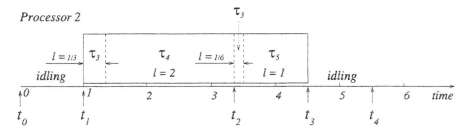

Figure 13.8 Processor Gantt charts

13.4   Rooted Computation Trees

This section considers a special case of the precedence relation, which takes the form of a tree structure. It is called a *rooted computation tree*. The root of the tree corresponds to the terminating task, the leaves to tasks which do not rely on the results produced by other tasks and the remaining nodes to various intermediate tasks with interdependencies.

13.4.1   Preliminaries

Some Mathematical Terminology:

Mathematically, a rooted computation tree is an acyclic graph defined by a precedence relation $\prec$ of the form discussed earlier but with two additional properties:

(i) Every task in the domain of the precedence relation may have at most one successor, that is, the precedence relation is a function.
(ii) There is a unique task in the precedence relation having predecessors but not successors, that is, there is a single terminating task.

$$\exists_1 \tau : Task \bullet \tau \in (\mathrm{ran} \prec) \wedge \tau \notin (\mathrm{dom} \prec)$$

Below is given part of the graph theoretic terminology being used. For any tasks τ_i and τ_j such that $\tau_i \prec^+ \tau_j$ ($\prec^+$ being the transitive closure of $\prec$),

Distance between	–	Inclusive sum of computation times of some tasks τ_i,
τ_i *and* τ_j		$\tau_k, \tau_l, \cdots, \tau_m, \tau_j$ such that $\tau_i \prec \tau_k$, $\tau_k \prec \tau_l$, $\cdots$, $\tau_m \prec \tau_j$
Height of τ_i	–	Distance between τ_i and the root of the tree, τ.

An Assumption:

Let us assume as a simplification that task computation times are mutually commensurable, that is, they are integer multiples of some standard computation time.

13.4.2   Computation Process

The computational model underlying the construction of a GS schedule is as follows. At any one time, only the tasks represented by the leaves are executed, as the execution of tasks with nodes anywhere else in the tree would otherwise violate the precedence relation. With the progress of the computational process in time, the height of those tasks being executed monotonically decreases. It is part of the strategy not to execute these tasks at different rates, but at the same rate. As a result, all the tasks at the highest level are executed at the same rate in such a way that the height of the tree reduces uniformly everywhere within the tree. However, any idling processors, resulting from the fact that there are more processors than the number of leaf nodes at the tree height, may be utilized, if necessary, to compute any lower level leaves. Reaching a joint in the tree signifies the completion of one or more leaf nodes and reaching a fresh leaf signifies the need to execute a new independent task. On both occasions, processing power has to be distributed equitably among the outstanding leaves lying at the current tree height. This could mean a change in the rate of reduction of tree height. The computation terminates after the completion of the terminal task corresponding to the root.

The principles underlying the above may be expressed in terms of the following rules:

(i) Always execute only independent tasks, but observing precedence requirements, if any.

A consequence of this is that only a non-empty subset of leaves of the tree remaining may be computed at any moment.

(ii) Allow processor sharing if the number of tasks to be executed exceeds the number of available processors.

In this respect, the other principles discussed in previous sections on processor sharing remain applicable. Note in particular that $\alpha \leq 1$. Thus, if there are more processors than the number of tasks to be computed, then assign at most one processor per task.

(iii) Assign processing power in such a way that the tasks further away (in terms of *distance*) complete, at current rate, no later than those which are close by.

A consequence of this principle is that the subset of tasks mentioned in (i) is best chosen as the set of leaves equidistant from the root as, otherwise, the computation of the leaves nearer the root would violate (iii). However, as mentioned earlier, this is not an absolutely necessary requirement.

On similar grounds, the processing power has to be evenly distributed among the competing tasks.

(iv) As a consequence of the above, processing power can be reassigned whenever:

(a) A task is completed.

(b) The height of the tree remaining to be computed is reduced to such a level, where there is at least one new task which is yet to be computed.

The following example illustrates the application of the above principles in constructing a GS schedule.

EXAMPLE

Construct a GS schedule for a set of tasks $\tau_1, \cdots, \tau_9$ with computation times as shown in Table 13.1 for computing them under the precedence relation,

$$\prec = \{(\tau_1, \tau_4), (\tau_2, \tau_4), (\tau_3, \tau_4), (\tau_4, \tau_6), (\tau_5, \tau_6), (\tau_6, \tau_9), (\tau_7, \tau_9), (\tau_8, \tau_9)\}$$

Table 13.1 Task computation times

Task	τ_1	τ_2	τ_3	τ_4	τ_5	τ_6	τ_7	τ_8	τ_9
Computation Time	$7\frac{1}{2}$	$7\frac{1}{2}$	$7\frac{1}{2}$	1	5	$1\frac{1}{2}$	2	2	$\frac{1}{2}$

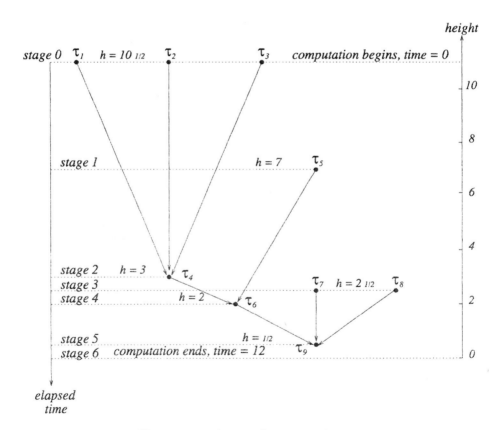

Figure 13.9 A rooted computation tree

Table 13.2 Computation of a static GS schedule

Stage	τ_1	τ_2	τ_3	τ_4	τ_5	τ_6	τ_7	τ_8	τ_9	Tasks being computed	α	Height reduction	Time taken	Elapsed time
0	$7\frac{1}{2}$	$7\frac{1}{2}$	$7\frac{1}{2}$	1	5	$1\frac{1}{2}$	2	2	$\frac{1}{2}$			0	–	0
										τ_1,τ_2,τ_3	1			
1	4	4	4	1	5	$1\frac{1}{2}$	2	2	$\frac{1}{2}$			$3\frac{1}{2}$	$3\frac{1}{2}$	$3\frac{1}{2}$
										$\tau_1,\tau_2,\tau_3,\tau_5$	$\frac{3}{4}$			
2	0	0	0	1	1	$1\frac{1}{2}$	2	2	$\frac{1}{2}$			4	$5\frac{1}{3}$	$8\frac{5}{6}$
										τ_4,τ_5	1			
3	0	0	0	$\frac{1}{2}$	$\frac{1}{2}$	$1\frac{1}{2}$	2	2	$\frac{1}{2}$			$\frac{1}{2}$	$\frac{1}{2}$	$9\frac{1}{3}$
										$\tau_4,\tau_5,\tau_7,\tau_8$	$\frac{3}{4}$			
4	0	0	0	0	0	$1\frac{1}{2}$	$1\frac{1}{2}$	$1\frac{1}{2}$	$\frac{1}{2}$			$\frac{1}{2}$	$\frac{2}{3}$	10
										τ_6,τ_7,τ_8	1			
5	0	0	0	0	0	0	0	0	$\frac{1}{2}$			$1\frac{1}{2}$	$1\frac{1}{2}$	$11\frac{1}{2}$
										τ_9	1			
6	0	0	0	0	0	0	0	0	0			$\frac{1}{2}$	$\frac{1}{2}$	12

The heights of the vertices are given in the graph shown in Figure 13.9. Table 13.2 presents a summary of the computations in the relevant GS schedule.

Once a general schedule is constructed as outlined above, a preemptive schedule of an identical length may be derived following the procedure described in Section 13.3.

13.5 Bibliographical Notes

This chapter is based on work due to Muntz and Coffman [104]. The reader may also benefit from van Tilborg and Knob [164].

13.6 Exercises

1. Construct a general schedule first and then transform it to a preemptive schedule for processing each of the following sets of tasks with the associated computation graph using two identical processors:

(a) Task set:

Task	τ_1	τ_2	τ_3	τ_4	τ_5	τ_6
Computation time	1	2	2	2	1	1

Computation graph:

$$\{(\tau_1,\ \tau_2),\ (\tau_1,\ \tau_3),\ (\tau_1,\ \tau_4),\ (\tau_4,\ \tau_5),\ (\tau_3,\ \tau_5),\ (\tau_2,\ \tau_6),\ (\tau_3,\ \tau_6),$$
$$(\tau_5,\ \tau_6)\}$$

(b) Task set:

Task	τ_1	τ_2	τ_3	τ_4	τ_5	τ_6	τ_7
Computation time	1	2	3	2	2	2	2

Computation graph:

$$\{(\tau_1,\ \tau_2),\ (\tau_1,\ \tau_3),\ (\tau_2,\ \tau_4),\ (\tau_2,\ \tau_5),\ (\tau_4,\ \tau_6),\ (\tau_5,\ \tau_6),\ (\tau_3,\ \tau_7),$$
$$(\tau_5,\ \tau_7)\}$$

(c) Task set:

Task	τ_1	τ_2	τ_3	τ_4	τ_5	τ_6	τ_7	τ_8
Computation time	3	1	2	3	5	4	5	2

Computation graph:

$$\{(\tau_5,\ \tau_3),\ (\tau_8,\ \tau_4),\ (\tau_1,\ \tau_2),\ (\tau_3,\ \tau_2),\ (\tau_4,\ \tau_2),\ (\tau_7,\ \tau_3),\ (\tau_6,\ \tau_4)\}$$

Chapter 14

Multi-processor Dynamic Scheduling

Dynamic scheduling algorithms derive their effectiveness from focussing on simple criteria, typically on a single task parameter such as the deadline or the urgency of tasks. The aim is to avoid computationally expensive optimization of schedules, so that the system can respond rapidly to changes in the environment. This may be facilitated greatly by having a clear snapshot view of the environment, scope for strategic planning and a full appreciation of any inherent limitations. These are certain aspects that characterize well the material presented in this chapter.

14.1   Laxity

Consider a task τ:

$$\tau = (tid, a, c(t), d)$$

where $c(t)$ denotes the outstanding computation time at time t. Obviously, $c(t) \geq 0$. *Laxity* $l(t)$ of τ at time t is then defined as

$$\begin{aligned} l(t) &= d - c(t) - t \\ &= \tilde{d} - c(t) \end{aligned}$$

where $\tilde{d}$ is the length of time from the current time or the time of arrival, whichever is the latest, to the deadline. The notion of laxity indicates how urgent the execution of a task is, as well as whether there is any leeway in its execution. Therefore, an alternative term for laxity is *urgency*. The significance of $l(t)$ in relation to task execution is as follows:

$l(t) > 0$ –   There is enough time for the task to be executed and completed by the deadline, provided that there is no undue competition for the resources required by it.

$l(t) = 0$ —   The task is being executed, or is to be executed immediately, to completion and without interruption.

$l(t) < 0$ —   The deadline of the task is bound to be missed.

14.2   A Scheduling Game

14.2.1   Representation of Scheduling Task

Let us assume as a simplification a unit clock granularity, that is, $\Delta = 1$. The overall situation of the tasks to be scheduled may be visualized in the form of a graphical display (see Figure 14.1), where the status of each task is characterized by a point (token, in the terminology used henceforth, with the tasks shown by small circles) in a continuously changing two-dimensional plane with an orthogonal system of coordinates $c(t)$ versus $l(t)$. This system of coordinates is later referred to as l–c space, with c pointing upwards and l pointing rightward in our graphs.

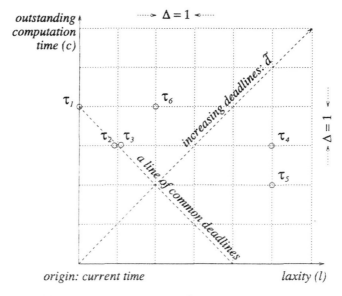

Figure 14.1 Task representation in l–c space

The passage of time is considered in this visualization by having a separate display for each time value t. With the progression of time these displays are played in the right order of their time values and at the right speed. As time progresses, the state of the tasks is represented by the continuous movement of tokens in the negative direction of one of the axes. The significance of token movements in the interpretation is as follows:

Task *Execution*	– The task execution corresponds to token movements downwards. This follows from

$$
\begin{aligned}
c(t+1) &= c(t) - 1 \\
l(t+1) &= d - c(t+1) - (t+1) \\
&= d - (c(t) - 1) - (t+1) \\
&= d - c(t) - t \\
&= l(t)
\end{aligned}
$$

Task *Non-execution*	– The non-execution of tasks corresponds to token movements leftward. This may be seen from

$$
\begin{aligned}
c(t+1) &= c(t) \\
l(t+1) &= d - c(t+1) - (t+1) \\
&= d - c(t) - t - 1 \\
&= l(t) - 1
\end{aligned}
$$

Tasks *with Common* *Deadlines*	– Since

$$
\tilde{d} = d - t = l + c
$$

tasks with common deadlines lie on lines with

$$
l + c = constant
$$

Tasks *Definitely* *Expected in* *Future*	– Tasks with known parameters (deadline, laxity, etc.) but yet to arrive are denoted by squares labelled with the arrival time and are referred to as 'restricted tokens'. These are held stationary until their arrival times. This is because, although already known, the parameters of these tasks must remain constant until their arrival.

14.2.2   Simulation of a Multi-processor System

The scheduler's task in a system consisting of m identical processors may be described as follows. Starting from some initial configuration of tokens, the scheduler moves at most m tokens one division downwards at each clock tick. In accomplishing this, the scheduler's task is to decide which ones to move, but bearing the following in mind:

- A token reaching the l-axis signifies the successful completion of the corresponding task and, therefore, the elimination of the token.
- A token reaching the c-axis signifies the failure of the corresponding task to meet its deadline.
- New tasks may arrive at any time, and are shown by the appearance of new tokens in the l–c space.
- The environment may consist of, as mentioned earlier, tasks with known characteristics but not yet arrived. The tokens corresponding to these tasks may become active at any time, as with other newly arriving tasks.

14.3   Surplus Computing Power

Surplus computing power of a multi-processor system may be defined by partitioning the l–c space, introduced in Section 14.2.1, as shown in Figure 14.2. It is meaningful only with respect to a given period of time. Here, the surplus computing power of a multi-processor system with m processors is defined with reference to the next x time units. It is a function of both x and t and is denoted by $F(x, t)$:

$$F(x, t) = m \times x - \sum_{\tau \in R_1} c_\tau(t) - \sum_{\tau \in R_2} (x - l_\tau(t))$$

where

$c_\tau(t)$	–	denotes the outstanding computation time of task τ at time t. Note that $c_\tau(t) \stackrel{def}{=} \tau.c(t)$.
$l_\tau(t)$	–	denotes the laxity of task τ at time t. Note that $l_\tau(t) \stackrel{def}{=} \tau.l(t)$.
R_1	–	denotes the region in l–c space with deadlines within the next x time units.
R_2	–	denotes the region in l–c space with laxities not exceeding x time units, and deadlines beyond x time units.
R_3	–	denotes the region in l–c space with laxities beyond x time units.

The first summation in the above denotes the exact total demand for processing power by the tasks in region R_1. Each of the tasks in the second summation, that is, those in region R_2, requires exactly $c_\tau(t) = d_\tau(t) - l_\tau(t)$ time units of processing power for their completion. However, our concern is the lowest demand within the next x time units and, therefore, the demand for processing power by each of those tasks within the next x time units is $x - l_\tau(t)$ processor time units.

14.4   Scheduling Algorithms and their Optimality

14.4.1   Scheduling Algorithms

The representation introduced in Section 14.2 is amenable to scheduling tasks with two known algorithms, namely,

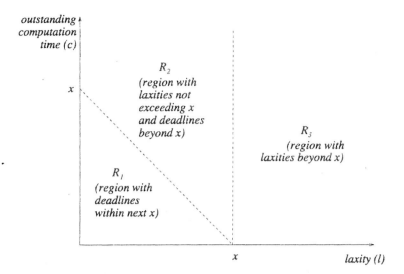

Figure 14.2 Partition of l–c space

(i) *Earliest Deadline First*, EDF

This algorithm is based on the execution of the task with the closest deadline, always, making a non-deterministic choice in the case of a tie. [Note: The same algorithm has been referred to earlier in Chapter 12 as *Deadline Driven Scheduling*, DDS; the alternative terminology is used for consistency with the source of this material.]

(i) *Least Laxity First*, LLF

This algorithm is based on the execution of the task (among those which have already arrived) with least laxity, always, making, as in the above, a non-deterministic choice in the case of a tie.

14.4.2   Optimality in Uni-Processor Scheduling

This section is a brief supplement to our coverage of uni-processor scheduling in Chapter 12. As mentioned in Section 11.3.2 of Chapter 11, a scheduling algorithm is said to be *optimal* if it can schedule any set of tasks which can be scheduled by any other algorithm of the same class.

Observation 14.1 Optimality of EDF (DDS) and LLF

Both Earliest Deadline and Least Laxity algorithms are optimal in the uni-processor case.

The above may be proved as a theorem, and the proof follows from the fact that a schedule produced by any third algorithm can always be transformed to either EDF or LLF by an appropriate pairwise swapping of tasks. This may require the breakup of task execution times, if task decomposition is permitted.

14.4.3   Optimality in Multi-processor Scheduling

The Earliest Deadline and Least Laxity algorithms are not optimal in multi-processor case. This may be demonstrated by providing a simple counter example against optimality.

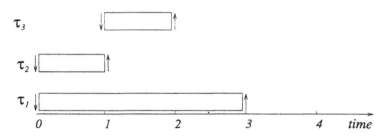

Figure 14.3 Example demonstrating schedule infeasibility in EDF

Case of EDF: Consider the scheduling of the three tasks

$$\tau_1 = (tid_1, 0, 3, 3)$$
$$\tau_2 = (tid_2, 0, 1, 1)$$
$$\tau_3 = (tid_3, 1, 1, 2)$$

also shown in Figure 14.3. EDF fails to schedule the above; the Gantt chart in Figure 14.4 demonstrates the schedule feasibility.

14.4.4   Optimality and Prior Task Knowledge in Multi-processor Scheduling

A question posed in respect of optimality is the extent of prior knowledge required by an optimal algorithm. Alternatively, one may ask whether there is any optimal algorithm which can schedule a set of tasks with partial knowledge about them.

   The answer to this question is that there is no such optimal algorithm, and this may be substantiated by an exhaustive examination of the three different cases of partial knowledge about task characteristics. The first two cases deal with immediate failure modes of the scheduler (at the next scheduling moment), whereas the third one deals with a possible future failure mode (some time after the next scheduling moment).

processor 1

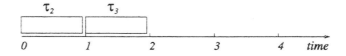

processor 2

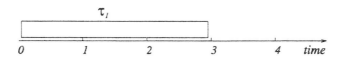

Figure 14.4 Feasibility of scheduling tasks in the example

However, this does not apply to deadline driven scheduling of a set of tasks, the computation times of which are all equal. The optimality of deadline driven scheduling in this case follows from the fact that a deadline driven schedule may always be obtained from another produced by a competing algorithm by simply swapping the tasks around independently of the number of processors and without executing the same task on more than one processor simultaneously.

Case 1: Lack of Knowledge about Computation Time

This case demonstrates the following observation:

> **Observation 14.2** There is no optimal algorithm if computation times are not known a priori.

As a particular instance, consider the case with two processors and a set of tasks with a common deadline. From the scheduler's perspective, for each task,

$$c(t), \; l(t) \quad - \quad \text{are unknowns, and}$$
$$d, \; a \quad\quad - \quad \text{are knowns}$$

although we assume them to be known in our own reasoning here. Let one of them, say a certain τ_1, have zero laxity. Figure 14.5 shows a possible scenario (our view) with a set of tasks with a common deadline and the scheduler's restricted viewpoint. It is obvious that the scheduler has no guaranteed means of avoiding failure; success would depend on the execution of τ_1 first.

Case 2: Lack of Knowledge about Deadlines

This case demonstrates the following observation:

> **Observation 14.3** There is no optimal algorithm if task deadlines are not known a priori.

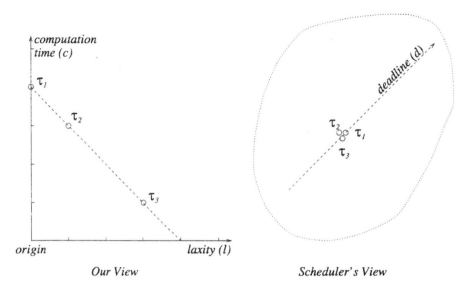

Our View   Scheduler's View

Figure 14.5 Non-optimality and lack of knowledge about computation time

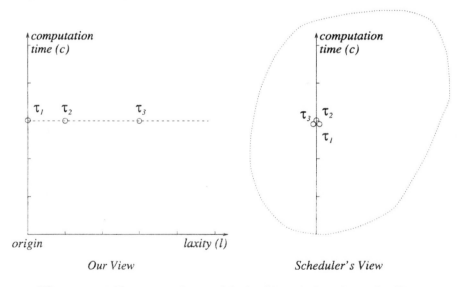

Our View   Scheduler's View

Figure 14.6 Non-optimality and lack of knowledge about deadlines

As in the above case, let us consider the case with two processors and a set of tasks with a common computation time. In this case, from the scheduler's perspective, for each task,

$$d,\ l(t) \qquad - \qquad \text{are unknowns, and}$$
$$c,\ a \qquad - \qquad \text{are knowns.}$$

Let one of the tasks, say τ_1, have zero laxity. Figure 14.6 shows our and the scheduler's view of a possible scenario. Here again, the scheduler has no guaranteed means of avoiding failure; the success would depend on the execution of τ_1 first.

Case 3: Lack of Knowledge about Arrival Times

This case demonstrates the following observation:

> **Observation 14.4** There is no optimal algorithm if task arrival times are not known a priori.

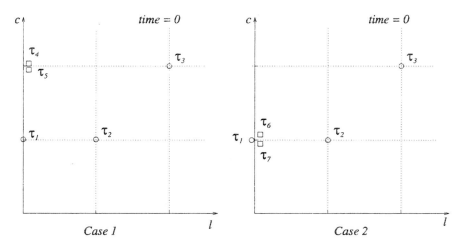

Figure 14.7 Our view of two sets of tasks (Cases 1 and 2)

In this case, since the computation times and the deadlines of all tasks are assumed to be known to the scheduler, token positions of the tasks in the l-c plane are fully specified, although their arrival times are unknown to the scheduler.

Let us examine a specific scenario with tasks τ_i with $i \in 1..6$ with characteristics as presented in the table below:

Task	Laxity (l_{τ_i})	Computation time (c_{τ_i})	Arrival time (a_{τ_i})
τ_1	0	1	0
τ_2	1	1	0
τ_3	2	2	0
τ_4, τ_5	0	2	2
τ_6, τ_7	0	1	1

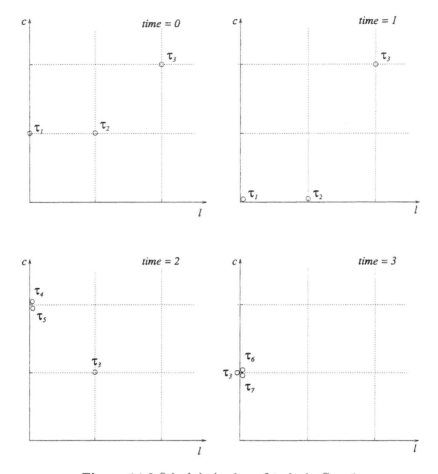

Figure 14.8 Scheduler's view of tasks in Case 1

and consider two cases of scheduling, each involving two separate subsets of tasks. In scheduling each set of tasks, the scheduler has only two choices at $t = 0$. For both cases, the scheduler is shown to fail.

The two sets of tasks are as shown in Figure 14.7. The three tasks τ_1, τ_2 and τ_3 are common to both sets and are assumed to have already arrived and, therefore, the information about these three tasks is assumed to be already known to the scheduler. The tasks τ_4 and τ_5 belong to only one of the task sets and τ_6 and τ_7 belong to the other. All four tasks τ_i with $i \in 4 \ldots 6$ are yet to arrive at the scheduling moment under consideration and thus are unknown to the scheduler. Therefore, the information given in the table is meant for our own reasoning only.

Dealing with the scenario involving the first task set, a perfectly possible sequence of moves by the scheduler, is shown in Figure 14.8. Because of the lack of

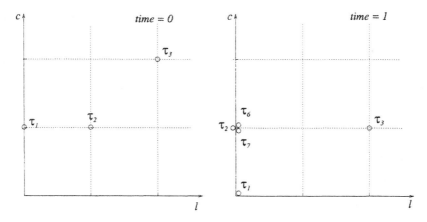

Figure 14.9 Scheduler's view of tasks in Case 2

knowledge about tasks τ_4 and τ_5, the scheduler may find itself unprepared for the situation at time $t = 2$ and fails at $t = 3$.

In the scenario involving the second task set, a similar possible sequence of moves by the scheduler is shown in Figure 14.9 and, this time, the scheduler may fail at $t = 1$ on the grounds of lack of knowledge about tasks τ_6 and τ_7 .

In both choices, the task sets may be scheduled separately and, therefore, the optimality of the dynamic scheduling algorithms is not generally assured without full information on the scheduling characteristics of the tasks. However, the optimality prevails in restricted cases, for instance, in the case of EDF with tasks of identical computation times. This applies to the multi-processor case without any restriction on the number of processors.

Given that all scheduling characteristics are available to the scheduler, it may be designed to take advantage of them intelligently in avoiding such unwarranted failures as those shown above.

14.5 Schedule Feasibility

14.5.1 Necessary Condition for Scheduling

Observation 14.5 A necessary condition for schedule feasibility of a set of tasks with identical arrival times (without restricted tokens) is

$$F(x, t) \geq 0$$

for all $x > 0$.

Using the notation introduced in Section 14.3, the above observation may be justified as follows:

Available computing power within the next x time units. $= m \times x$

Demand for computing power by tasks with deadlines within the next x time units. $= \sum_{\tau \in R_1} c_\tau(t)$

Demand for computing power by tasks in R_2 within the next x time units. $= \sum_{\tau \in R_2} (x - l_\tau(t))$

[Note that each task τ may be left unattended for at most $l_\tau(t)$ time units, but its completion requires execution during the remainder of the next x time units.]

Thus, the total demand can only be met if

$$F(x, t) = m \times x - \sum_{\tau \in R_1} c_\tau(t) - \sum_{\tau \in R_2} (x - l_\tau(t)) \geq 0$$

Since x was chosen arbitrarily, the above must hold for all x, leading to Observation 14.5.

14.5.2   Sufficient Condition for Runtime Scheduling

Observation 14.6 If it is feasible to schedule a set of tasks when their arrival times are identical, then it is also feasible to schedule them by a runtime algorithm even with differing arrival times. That is, the arrival times are immaterial.

One may reason about the above statement in two stages:

Stage 1 Show that there is never an 'immediate failure mode' (that is, at the next scheduling moment).

Stage 2 Show that there is never a 'future failure mode' (that is, some time after the next scheduling moment), if LLF is used.

Stage 1

If there is a schedule for the case with identical arrival times, then

$$F(x, t) \geq 0$$

for all x. However, since our interest is in the next scheduling moment, that is, at $x = 1$:

$$\begin{aligned}
F(1, t) &= m - \sum_{\tau \in R_1} c_\tau(t) - \sum_{\tau \in R_2} (1 - l_\tau(t)) \\
&= m - \sum_{\tau \in R_1} 1 - \sum_{\substack{\tau \in R_2 \wedge \\ l_\tau = 1}} (1 - 1) - \sum_{\substack{\tau \in R_2 \wedge \\ l_\tau = 0}} 1 \\
&= m - \sum_{\tau \in R_1} 1 - \sum_{\substack{\tau \in R_2 \wedge \\ l_\tau = 0}} 1
\end{aligned}$$

Note that the two summations on the last line of the above represent the number of tokens on the c-axis. Since $F(1, t) \geq 0$, the number of processors m is therefore greater than or equal to the number of tokens on the c-axis at time t. Thus, there cannot be an immediate failure if LLF is used.

Stage 2

Here it is necessary to show that,

$$F(x, t) \geq 0$$

for all x and for all t. This may be shown by induction with

(i) $\forall x \bullet F(x, 0) \geq 0$ — the base case
(ii) $(\forall x \bullet F(x, t) \geq 0) \Rightarrow (\forall x \bullet F(x, t+1) \geq 0)$ — the inductive step

Base Case:

This follows immediately from Observation 14.5 for arrival time $t = 0$.

Inductive Step:

The induction step (ii) relies on

$$\forall x \bullet F(x, t) \geq 0$$

as the induction hypothesis. It then requires a proof for

$$\forall x \bullet F(x, t+1) \geq 0$$

Let us show the latter indirectly by showing first that, given any t, for all x there exists an x' such that

$$F(x, t+1) \geq F(x', t)$$

and then relying on $F(x', t) \geq 0$ for all x' due to Observation 14.5. Let

$$\delta F = F(x, t+1) - F(x', t)$$

and consider x' with

$$x' = x + 1$$

Our reasoning below relies on Figure 14.10 showing the partitioning of the l-c plane by x and x' diagonals and verticals into regions R_1, R_2 and R_3. Note that R_1^t, R_2^t and R_3^t denote the regions as partitioned by x, and R_1^{t+1}, R_2^{t+1} and R_3^{t+1} denote the regions as partitioned by x'.

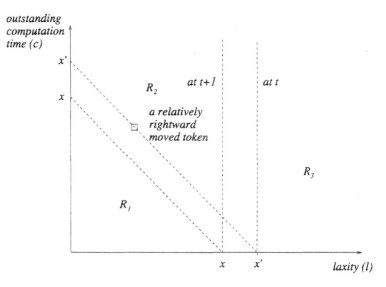

Figure 14.10 Change of demand for processor time with time

At time t, LLF may execute at most m tasks left of the laxity vertical x'. The contribution of each of these tasks to δF defined above may be assessed as follows. Consider, for example, the downward movement of a specific token in R_2. Its contribution to δF appears through the summation term $\sum_{\tau \in R_2} (x - l_\tau(t))$ in both $F(x, t+1)$ and $F(x', t)$ and may be worked out as

$$
\begin{aligned}
F(x, t+1) &= \cdots &&-(x - l(t+1)) \\
F(x', t) &= \cdots &&-(x' - l(t)) \\
\delta F &= \cdots &&+(x' - l(t)) - (x - l(t+1)) \\
&= \cdots &&+(x+1 - l(t)) - (x - l(t+1)) \\
&= \cdots &&+1
\end{aligned}
$$

Note that $l(t) = l(t+1)$ in the above. Other contributions to δF, resulting from the movement of different tokens depending on their locations in the three regions R_1, R_2 and R_3, follow analogously. Table 14.1 presents a summary of such reasoning.

Since, according to the above $\delta F \geq 0$, it follows that

$$
F(x, t+1) \geq F(x', t)
$$

but

$$
F(x', t) \geq 0
$$

on the strength of the induction hypothesis. With this follows the induction step and, hence, the proof of Observation 14.6.

Table 14.1 Demonstration of $\delta F \geq 0$

Token movement	Contribution to δF by each token
1. Downward moved tokens in R_2	$-(x - l(t+1)) + ((x+1) - l(t)) = 1$
2. Downward moved tokens from line $l + c = x'$ to line $l + c = x$ (and, hence, in R_2)	$-c(t+1) + c(t) = 1$
3. Other downward moved tokens in R_1	$-c(t+1) + c(t) = 1$
4. Leftward moved tokens in R_2	$-(x - l(t+1)) + ((x+1) - l(t)) = 0$
5. Leftward moved tokens from R_3 to R_1	$-x + l(t+1) = 0$
6. Leftward moved tokens in R_1	$-c(t+1) + c(t) = 0$
7. Stationary tokens that remained in R_1	$-c(t+1) + c(t) = 0$
8. 'Relatively rightward moved' stationary tokens from R_1^{t+1} to R_2^t (note that these tokens come under different terms in F)	$\begin{aligned} & -(x - l(t+1)) + c(t) \\ = & -(x - l(t+1)) + (x+1) - l(t) \\ = & 1 \\ & \text{since } c(t) + l(t) = (x+1). \end{aligned}$
Therefore, the net contribution by all token movements	$\delta F \geq 0$

14.6 Bibliographical Notes

This chapter is based on work due to Dertouzos and Mok [38]. In the light of computational limitations of dynamic scheduling algorithms, such as the restriction of algorithmic optimality to uni-processor scheduling using DDS and LLF and the non-existence of optimal algorithms for the general multi-processor case, considerable effort has been directed towards the development of heuristic approaches. A noteworthy effort in this connection is the Spring kernel (see Niehaus *et al.* [107] and Stankovic and Ramamritham [154, 155]), mentioned also in Chapter 11 in relation to distributed scheduling.

14.7   Exercises

1. Given are the two sets of tasks $\tau_1, \tau_2, \cdots, \tau_{11}$ with the following characteristics:

Set of Tasks: A

Task	Arrival time (clock time)	Time to deadline since arrival (length of time)	Computation time (length of time)
τ_1	0	4	3
τ_2	0	4	2
τ_3	0	3	1
τ_4	0	6	4
τ_5	0	8	5
τ_6	0	6	3
τ_7	0	8	3
τ_8	0	7	2
τ_9	0	6	1
τ_{10}	0	8	2
τ_{11}	0	10	3

Set of Tasks: B

Task	Arrival time (clock time)	Time to deadline since arrival (length of time)	Computation time (length of time)
τ_1	0	3	1
τ_2	0	4	2
τ_3	unknown	6	2
τ_4	unknown	6	4
τ_5	0	8	4
τ_6	0	10	2
τ_7	0	10	7
τ_8	0	10	5
τ_9	unknown	10	4
τ_{10}	0	12	5
τ_{11}	0	16	7

(i) Determine the smallest number of processors required to guarantee sufficient computing power to prevent any failure within the first ten units of time in the runtime scheduling of the tasks.

(ii) How would the prior knowledge of arrival times of tasks τ_3, τ_4 and τ_9 affect the answer to (i) above?

(iii) Assuming that all tasks arrive at the same time, investigate whether the use of the Least Laxity First (LLF) algorithm at runtime can produce a schedule that uses fewer processes.

(iv) Investigate whether the tasks can be scheduled at runtime by Deadline Driven Scheduling (Earliest Deadline First algorithm) with the same number of processors as that in the answer to (i).

Chapter 15

Fault Tolerance

Fault tolerance is a topic that is closely linked with safety critical systems and dependable systems, particularly with those which are required to meet stringent real-time requirements. Fault tolerance is a collection of measures undertaken alongside conventional forms of good design practice, but in recognition of runtime failures caused by all kinds of faults, including those due to design faults. This chapter is an overview of issues addressed by fault tolerance, approaches to fault tolerance and their implications, and the relevant techniques. The reader should consult the cited references for further details.

15.1 Safety, Reliability and Fault Tolerance

For the reasons given above, it is appropriate to begin this discussion with an understanding of concepts closely related to fault tolerance.

15.1.1 Safety and Reliability

The design of critical systems involves two independent sets of requirements: functional requirements and safety requirements. The two are different notions addressing different issues. The functional requirements address the expected service, which usually allows some leeway in terms of the extent of its provision over time. This flexibility is quantified through system *reliability* – a notion covered also under system dependability. *Safety requirements* concern the system behaviour patterns forbidden on the grounds of danger to human life, property or the system itself. Although they can be in conflict, safety and reliability measures frequently coincide and are assured to a great extent by fault tolerance.

15.1.2   Safety Requirements

Safety critical systems are so called for a number of reasons, among them, the high consequential costs in the event of failure, tight constraints on the use of resources and their hazardous operational environments. As a consequence of such factors these systems have to operate within narrow margins of error. Furthermore, the time available for taking corrective actions in the event of failure with realtime systems may be extremely limited, especially in the critical stages. This is exemplified by such routine, yet vulnerable, operations as the take-off and landing of aircraft.

The design of safety critical systems begins with the acknowledgement that safety is a supreme design objective considered at the system level, which may not be traded-off in favour of other technical design objectives and cost savings. It also begins with an explicit statement of what 'safety' is. This involves:

(a) Identification of the hazards involved.
(b) What safety means in terms of undesirable system behaviours; these must be identified explicitly in the requirement specification and are referred to as *safety requirements*.
(c) How tightly the safety requirements must be observed. These requirements are expressed through normative probabilistic criteria partially reflecting the different risk levels.
(d) What safety means in terms of the extent of losses in the event of failures.

Requirements (c) and (d) together constitute what is usually termed 'risk'. Thus, high risk provisions reflect both high costs incurred from failure and a high anticipated probability of failure.

The objective of fault tolerance measures, in the context of safety critical systems, is to localize the effects of faults in such way that the overall system performance is not affected unduly by minor component failures and that the system fails safely in the event of a major component failure. Such multi-level failure mechanisms, effected in proportion to the degree of 'criticalness' of failures, form the key to the cost-effectiveness of any design philosophy.

15.1.3   Dependability Requirements

The dependability requirements cover in general one or more of the following major aspects:

(a) Reliability considerations admitting no failures at all,
(b) System availability considerations tolerating failures to some limited extent,
(c) Security aspects of the system.

Assuring a high degree of dependability as understood in (a), (b) and (c) is the function of fault tolerance.

Note that (a) above may be an expression of safety. Providing the required reliability as understood in (a) and (b) happens to be the most costly item in many embedded computer systems, since the measures associated may have significant performance penalties. Our discussion of dependability is confined to (a) and (b), and is continued further in Sections 15.4 and 15.5.

15.1.4   Fault Avoidance versus Fault Tolerance

Our attitude to fault tolerance may be confusing and sometimes conflicting. As rigorous mathematical techniques begin to address the development of correct computer systems, there is a danger in underestimating the need for fault tolerance. Fault tolerance is not unique to computing technology; it appears under the guise of 'factors of safety', 'reserve strength', and 'ductility', etc., in other branches of engineering founded on well-established science. Such properties are imparted to engineering structures through the use of stronger materials, or through a combination of materials. What is distinctive about the branch of engineering dealing with computer systems is that its artefacts are judged by precise criteria. Being systems that operate characteristically in discrete domains, computer systems either work, or they do not. 'Factors of safety' have to be introduced here not through 'extra and stronger materials', but by employing 'redundant units' of critical components – the major weapon against failures in computer systems.

Therefore, fault tolerance should not be regarded as a design philosophy on its own, but as a supplementary means of securing the desired level of confidence in combatting failures along with all other means of assuring correct behaviour and reliability. In other words, fault tolerance and fault avoidance (or fault intolerance) constitute two independent sets of activities, aiming at identical goals but from different standpoints.

Fault avoidance measures consist of the more conventional means for ensuring the correct behaviour of any given system purely by preventing the introduction of faults during the development process. In the analysis and design of any particular subsystem, fault avoidance fully relies on the correct behaviour of the rest of the system. On the other hand, fault tolerance drops this assumption, and makes allowances for failures outside the subsystem under consideration, despite all other measures undertaken to assure the correct behaviour of the rest of the system. Thus, fault tolerance places partial reliance on the behaviour of the integrated system and shifts the emphasis from the prevention of faults to coping with them and to preventing faults causing runtime failures. An essential objective of such measures is to ensure continuity of service above a predefined level of acceptability in the presence of faults.

The diagram in Figure 15.1 presents a taxonomy of the concepts dealing with fault tolerance. Note that each arrow there links a concept with a more specific form of its manifestation. Our discussion of the topic is based roughly on this taxonomy.

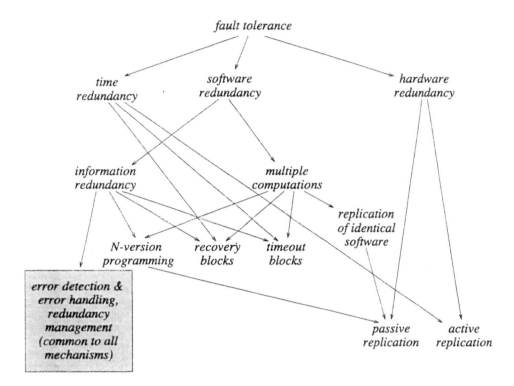

Figure 15.1 Fault tolerance techniques

15.2   Failures, Errors and Faults

The terminology introduced here is intended not merely for clarifying concepts often used in fault tolerance literature, but also as a classification that would alert the designer to the possible sources of failure. The terms 'fault', 'error' and 'failure' are often used quite interchangeably, resulting in the context dependence of the intended meaning. Such ambiguities may be resolved by adopting the following usage, according to which the three notions in the given order form a chain of actual or potential 'cause–effect' relations. These are dealt with below in reverse order.

15.2.1   Failures

A failure is a non-conformity of the external behaviour of a component with its specification, expressed in terms of anticipated product history. Failures may have operational and design origins. Operational failures arise primarily due to component failures, whether due to the physical conditions of the component or unexpected environmental conditions (including power failures), and may sometimes be transient in nature. Design failures, on the other hand, are permanent and are brought about by logical and timing errors unrelated to any operational failure.

Any formal discussion of failures necessarily involves a trace of the component's operational history as, for example, was done in CSP discussed in Chapter 7. A failure may be identified with a *finite prefix* of the component's local history which specifically violates the specification. A *failure event* may be defined as the first event of local history which identifies the latter with a failure. Given the notion of a historical trace of component behaviour, the 'time related failures' may be classified as follows.

(i) *Omission Failure*

A failure is regarded as an omission failure if the local history satisfies the specification upon the insertion of an output event to it.

One may generalize omission failures to include inputs as well. The *generalized omission failures* include the input events, the removal of which from the local history satisfies the specification. In other words, the output behaviour is not affected by the occurrence of such input events.

(ii) *Timing Failure*

A failure is regarded as a timing failure if the local history satisfies the specification upon the alteration of the time of occurrence of one or more output events in it. One may further distinguish between early timing failures and late timing failures, depending, respectively, on early and late outputs.

(iii) *Clock Failure*

A failure is regarded as a clock failure if the local history satisfies the specification upon a change in the temporal order of two or more output events in it.

The failure of a process is classed as a clock failure on the implicit assumption that it is the clock which caused the failure, either by failing to respond to a clock reading request or by issuing an incorrect clock value in response to such a request.

(iv) *Crash*

A crash is a failure characterized by the omission of all outputs required by the specification after some point in time in the local history.

Failures such as omission and timing failures are indicative of more serious problems in the operation of a system and, therefore, appropriate safety measures must be invoked unless the system is designed to tolerate their occasional occurrence. Other 'higher-order' failures such as duration failures may be defined in terms of the above.

The above failures concern only the timing aspects of outputs. There are also, however, the failures related to the magnitudes or the values of the outputs produced but with no time related failures.

(v) *Output Failure*

An output failure is the production of a logically invalid output and may be detected by checking against a given range of permitted values.

(vi) *Drift Failure*

These are related to excessive deviations between successive outputs, usually on the same communication channel and may be detected by checking against the permitted rate of change of the relevant output. A drift failure may not constitute a proper failure by itself and may be regarded as a precursor to an output failure.

(vii) *Byzantine Failure*

These are related to the production of conflicting outputs in communications. Byzantine failures are confined to distributed systems with autonomously operating processors required to work in consensus even in the presence of inconsistent data. In fault tolerant systems, a reason for the distribution of processors is the replication of hardware components operating largely independently, and the conflicting information is often created by the malfunctioning communication links between the processors. See Section 16.9 of Chapter 16 for specific examples.

15.2.2 Errors

Errors are incorrect information held in the system and, therefore, the correct usage of the term 'error' should refer to the system state not conforming with the its specification. Any system failure results from, and may be attributed to, an earlier error in this sense.

A well designed system should prevent the realization of such states and provide for error notification procedures. Error handling procedures provided as part of fault tolerance, on the other hand, may deal with error detection, error diagnosis, error recovery and the provision of immediate means for ensuring the continued service. It is prudent to provide, in addition, the means for assessing the consequences of the error and the extent of damage caused, as well as more permanent means for ensuring the continued service. The latter may include error rectifying measures, namely, repair or reconfiguration of the system.

In terms of consequences, the errors may be classified as:

(i) *Internal Errors*

An internal error is local to the process in which it is detected and is handled locally such that its consequences are not propagated to other processes.

(ii) *External Errors*

An external error may not be adequately handled by the process where it is detected.

(iii) *Pervasive Errors*

These are external errors with respect to the given process but leading also to errors in other processes.

In terms of frequency of occurrence and duration, errors may be classified as:

(iv) *Intermittent Errors*

These are errors whose frequency falls below a predefined (or permissible) threshold and is irregular over long periods of observation.

(v) *Persistent Errors*

These are errors whose frequency exceeds a predefined (or permissible) threshold.

(vi) *Transient Errors*

These errors are associated with an 'unstable' operational environment and lead to different results depending on the time of execution of the process concerned. These may include, for example, hardware malfunctioning, electromagnetic interference and transaction aborts.

The detection of transient errors requires multiple execution of the process, which is often infeasible in the case of hard realtime systems with tight timing constraints. Also, care must be taken to ensure unnecessary system reconfiguration caused by transient errors and performance degradation caused by their persistence.

(vii) *Permanent Errors*

Permanent errors are those which continue to exist right through the system history.

15.2.3   Faults

A fault is an identified or potential cause for the occurrence of an error and, thereby, for the failure of the system. Faults may be classified as physical or design faults. Physical faults are those which may be rectified by repair or replacement of one or more physical components.

Design faults are those responsible for design failures, namely, logical and timing failures, and may be traced back to a decision or an oversight in an earlier phase of the product life cycle, namely, specification, design or implementation. Prevention of such faults forms the major responsibility of fault avoidance measures.

15.3   Deterministic and Probabilistic Models

The characteristics of operational environments of fault tolerant realtime systems, as well as the physical properties of their component materials, necessarily involve a degree of randomness. Therefore, the extreme behaviour affecting the reliability of a system may be described realistically only by means of probabilistic concepts. Let us consider briefly how such probabilistic aspects may be taken into account in analysis.

A fault tolerant computer system may be studied using two different kinds of model: deterministic models and probabilistic models. These models of fault tolerance form the basis of two fundamentally different analytical approaches. Deterministic models attempt to answer the question as to whether a design meets its requirements in absolute and definitive terms. When addressing fault tolerance within a deterministic framework, the requirements may be stated, for example, in terms of a certain minimum number m component failures to be tolerated without a system failure. In other words, component failure in excess of m is interpreted as a system failure.

By contrast, probabilistic models attempt to answer the same question using notions such as randomness of failures, variability of component quality and confidence in empirical observations (data). Such models make use of relative values such as the expected rate of component failure, which itself may vary as a function of time or remains as a constant. The advantage of probabilistic models is that the analysis can differentiate between failure rates of different components rather than treating the failures of different components in absolute terms and in a uniform manner. Thus, probabilistic models can give a more realistic approximation to any problem in hand.

In summary, the two approaches provide qualitatively different answers to the same question and are based on qualitatively different kinds of argument: a deductive argument based on certainty in deterministic models and an argument based on the logic of plausible reasoning in probabilistic models. The two kinds of analysis are not alternatives. A fault tolerant system may be studied both deterministically and probabilistically. The two approaches are, however, distinct from each other, especially with respect to underlying assumptions, outcomes and intellectual tools.

15.4   Reliability Requirements

The following are some system validation requirements dictating the degree of fault tolerance to be achieved in realtime systems.

15.4.1   Relevance of Reliability Models

It must be emphasized that the reliability criteria such as those discussed below are meaningful only if there are practical viable means for the validation of their fulfillment. This turns out to be an extremely difficult, if not an impossible, task.

Furthermore, the reliability models used in fault tolerant systems have their origins predominantly in reliability theories of hardware. Although the distinction between hardware and software tends to be blurred at certain conceptual levels, there are fundamental differences at the physical level between failures in hardware and software. The differences are so significant that substitution of software for hardware carries some unquantifiable additional risks. The faults in hardware (with the exception of those due to poor design) develop with the 'extent of usage' over time, and their reliability metrics can be satisfactorily computed knowing the empirical data on material behaviour and, therefore, the component behaviour. However, the faults in software exist from the very beginning and are only exposed with usage. They are brought about not by its intrinsic 'material' features, but result purely from the technological processes employed in bringing the software into existence. As a result, reliability metrics on software are related to the pattern of exposure of faults and, therefore, to the 'pattern of usage'. As a consequence of the shift of reliance from well-understood physical laws of materials to more complex abstract structures and machines, software tends to be relatively more vulnerable to design errors and, therefore, the failure patterns and frequencies are theoretically unpredictable.

This poses a valid question about the applicability of such models to software systems. However, there are practical arguments in favour of a unified approach for dealing with both hardware and software. Moreover, hardware and software coexist in any system and it is quite difficult to apportion any system unreliability between hardware and software in a rigorous manner which takes into account the distinctions outlined above. The absence of a better model for software results in the use of a hardware model instead.

15.4.2   Definitions of Reliability

Mathematically, *reliability*[1] is a metric quantifying the time span over which a system continually provides the service expected of it. Another way to view reliability is as a survivability metric. Reliability is only applicable to failure-critical systems – systems which do not tolerate failures at all. This could be due to inadmissibility of even temporary disruptions to service on the grounds of, for example, safety considerations, the high cost of repair or the impossibility of conducting repairs at all while the system is in operation.

---

[1] Outline definitions of the relevant terminology and notations are given on pages 417 and 418 in Appendix C

The reliability may be defined in a number of ways with respect to a class of strategically chosen faults F and an appropriate time span t – a unit time such as a year, mission time or the time taken by a number of trials or operational missions. The metrics commonly applicable to reliable systems are given below.

(a) The *system reliability* $R_F(t)$ is defined as the probability that no fault of the class F occurs during time t. In other words,

$$R_F(t) = Pr[t_{init} \leq t < t_f \land f \in F],$$

where t_{init} and t_f are, respectively, the time of initialization (or the time of introduction of the system to service) and the time of occurrence of the first failure f drawn from F.

A complementary notion to $R_F(t)$ is the notion of *failure probability* $Q_F(t)$ such that

$$R_F(t) + Q_F(t) = 1$$

By definition, both $R_F(t)$ and $Q_F(t)$ lie in the range between zero and unity. As a simplification, the subscript F in $R_F(t)$ and $Q_F(t)$ will be omitted later.

(b) The *mean time to (first) failure (MTTF)* is defined as the expected value of t_f:

$$MTTF = E[t_f] = \int_0^\infty R_F(t)\, dt .$$

The *MTTF* of a system (or a component) is the *expected time* of the first failure in a sample of identical initially perfect systems (components).

(c) The *mean time to repair* $(MTTR)$, which is defined as the expected time for repair.

(d) The *mean time between failures* $(MTBF)$.

MTBF may be approximated by the following expression:

$$MTBF = MTTF + MTTR$$

Note that $R(t)$ and $MTTF$ are applicable to ultra-reliable systems that permit no failures at all, whereas $MTBF$ and $MTTR$ are applicable to systems that can be repaired. The latter are considered in Section 15.5.

In dealing with fault tolerant redundant systems, probabilistic models need to consider the following:

- system structure;
- redundant units;
- possibility of repair following failures.

15.4.3   Systems with Internal Structure and Redundancies

Serially Connected Components

For a better appreciation of the above concepts, let us first consider a system consisting of n components with no redundancies. In other words, all the components are essential components. The components may in general be totally heterogeneous and may represent different hardware units or even software units. At the given level of abstraction, the possibility of the components themselves having internal redundancies is ignored. Let the reliability of a single component k be given by

$$R_k(t) = e^{-\lambda_k t}$$

where λ_k is a constant failure rate. The above assumes what is called an exponential distribution of failures. Let us assume that the failure rates of components are statistically independent.

Consider the reliability of a system expressed below as the product of the reliabilities of its components:

$$R_1(t) \times R_2(t) \times \cdots \times R_n(t)$$

The above conforms with the most common expectation that the reliability of a complex system is no greater than the reliability of its weakest (least reliable) link or component and that the reliability of each component contributes to the overall reliability. In fact, the above is the reliability of a system constructed by connecting a set of components serially (sequentially) as shown in Figure 15.2. This is denoted by $R_{seq}(t)$:

$$R_{seq}(t) = \prod_{i=1}^{n} R_i(t)$$

where $\prod$ is the multiplication (product) operator.

Figure 15.2 Serial (sequential) composition of n units

Since the above system does not employ any redundancy, and hence relies on the proper functioning of each and every component, each $R_i(t)$ may be replaced by the corresponding $e^{-\lambda_k t}$. Therefore,

$$R_{seq}(t) = e^{-\left(\sum_{i=1}^{n} \lambda_i\right) t}$$

Comparison of the above with that of R_k shows that the failure rate of a system with no redundancies is the sum of the failure rates of the individual components. That is,

$$\lambda_{seq} = \sum_{i=1}^{n} \lambda_i$$

Then, $MTTF$ for such a system becomes

$$MTTF_{seq} = \int_0^\infty R_s(t)\ dt = \int_0^\infty e^{-\left(\sum\limits_{i=1}^{n} \lambda_i\right)t}\ dt = \left(\sum_{i=1}^{n} \lambda_i\right)^{-1} = \frac{1}{\lambda_{seq}}$$

Again, the above is analogous in form to the $MTTF$ of individual components, as seen, for example, from the $MTTF$ for the component k given by

$$MTTF_k = \frac{1}{\lambda_k}$$

The above expression for the system as a whole may be used to compute the $MTBF$ and $MTTR$. In analogy with λ_k here, the $MTTR$ may be taken as the reciprocal of a constant repair rate.

Components Connected in Parallel

Let us now consider the parallel composition of a collection of units as shown in Figure 15.3. In this case, the different units can again be totally heterogeneous, but in fault tolerant architectures they are typically redundant units and could well be identical. A system consisting of a set of units connected in parallel fails as a whole only if all individual units fail. This is reflected in the following expression of reliability of a system constructed by the parallel composition of a set of components:

$$Q_{par}(t) = \prod_{i=1}^{n} Q_i(t)$$

in which the different Q values may be replaced by $(1 - R)$ to obtain the corresponding expression for reliability.

Systems of More Complex Internal Forms

The expressions given above for $R_{seq}(t)$ and $Q_{par}(t)$ may thus be used to compute the reliability of any configuration, subsystems of which fall into either of the two categories of composition considered above. Redundant components may be modelled by components connected in parallel, while essential components are modelled by serially connected components.

Our discussion so far has helped us to understand the reliability of a complex system in terms of the reliability of its components. Some of the components may

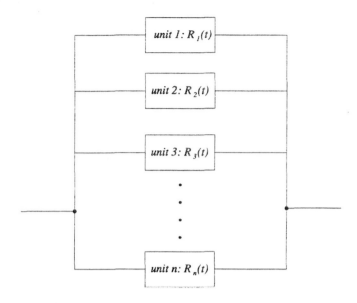

Figure 15.3 Parallel composition of n units

model redundancies. However, it is inadequate for the study of fault tolerant systems, any failed component of which may be repaired and returned to service. This can be dealt with by incorporating in the model possible patterns of component failures and subsequent repairs. In this connection, there are two analytical options when dealing with failures of redundant units, namely,

(a) *Failure to exhaustion*

   Failure to exhaustion assumes that any failed unit is irreparable and remains failed. The expressions derived for R_{seq} and R_{par} above are based on this assumption.

(b) *Failure with repair.*

   Failure with repair assumes that any failed unit can be repaired and brought into operation with some time delay.

The former is generally regarded as too pessimistic compared to the latter, but the applicability of either depends on the circumstances applicable. Failure to exhaustion could well be the only option in circumstances where there is no possibility of repairing a failed unit. However, such detailed probabilistic models are beyond the scope of this text and, therefore, the interested reader may refer to Siewiorek and Swarz [149] for further details.

15.4.4 Classification of Systems based on Reliability

The reliability requirements of ultra-reliable systems may be specified only by means of the desired probabilities of failure. These range typically from 10^{-4}/hour to 10^{-6}/hour in the case of failures in mission critical applications with relatively low cost penalties (e.g. suspension of mission or task), through 10^{-6}/hour to 10^{-7}/hour in the case of failures in technology critical applications with high cost penalties but with satisfactory life saving means (e.g. high technology defence equipment manned by highly trained crew), to 10^{-10}/hour in the case of failures in life critical applications with risks to civilian life. Figures known for specific applications include 10^{-4} for the primary protection system of the Sizewell B Nuclear Power Station, UK, and 10^{-9} per flight hour in the case of the flight control system A320 Airbus. Thus, one has to be quite clear about the reliability criteria applicable to safety critical applications, as these depend, in general, on the actual technology employed, likely failure rates and the risk to the human life.

15.5 Other Dependability Requirements

15.5.1 Availability Requirements

In contrast to reliability, *availability* is a metric quantifying the time spans unaffected by temporary disruptions to the service expected and is obviously meaningful only if such disruptions do not constitute failure in the sense of the discussion in the previous section. It is a metric that is useful for determining the extent to which the operation of a system may be halted for short periods of time. According to Littlewood [93], there are two notions of availability:

- *Pointwise availability A(t)*, which is the probability of the system being operational at time t.
  $A(t)$ differs from the reliability metric $R(t)$ in that $A(t)$ permits a specified, or an unspecified, number of failures prior to time t, whereas $R(t)$ permits no failures at all prior to t.
- *Interval availability*, which is the statistically expected fraction of time when the system is operational over a given interval (t_1, t_2).

If it exists, as t tends to infinity, the limit of $A(t)$ becomes the expected fraction of time that the system is operational. Therefore, in the case of large t and large intervals, the two notions of availability converge to the same, thus justifying the adoption of a single term '*availability*'. A simple measure of availability may be given as

$$A(t) = \frac{\mu}{\lambda + \mu}$$

where μ is a constant repair rate and λ is a constant failure rate. In this case, $A(t)$ is also constant and denotes the steady state availability.

Again, certain distinctions apply to hardware and software with respect to the cost of non-availability. The '*down-time*' in hardware, and the resulting repair costs are fairly well understood and the hardware may be returned to service at the state prior to failure. The failures of software, on the other hand, are less well understood. The direct remedial cost may be minimal and may concern just '*reloading*', but in many cases it is practically impossible to return software to the state of service at the state immediately prior to failure.

It is important to realize, however, that in the cases of both hardware and software consideration of the direct costs alone is often misleading. For instance, the down-times may not reflect the true cost of disruptions. This is because the permissible down-time (or the permissible reloading time) may be specified in a number of ways, namely, in terms of:

(a) *bounded down-time*, restricting the down-time due to a single failure;
(b) *cumulative down-time*, restricting the total down-time due to a number of failures;
(c) *frequency of down-times*, restricting the total number of failures, with no reference to durations of disruptions to the service.

Also, excessive down-times may affect the tasks being executed just prior to disruptions in different ways. This is because some tasks may require repetition of processing, others a simple resumption, and yet a third category the resumption of disrupted tasks, but with penalties in terms of processing time. As a consequence, if the actual down-time is less than whatever the permissible down-times, then the cost of disruption may be considered as equal to that due to the loss of time during the actual down-time, plus the reloading cost. Otherwise, the cost may include in addition the re-processing time and other indirect costs.

15.5.2   Validation of Dependability Requirements

Apart from system requirements, there are also requirements on fault tolerant methodologies themselves. Among them is the means for static validation because of the physical impossibility of dynamic testing of systems with relatively long life spans for extremely low failure rates. Furthermore, the design of such systems may involve crisis scenarios which may not be staged for testing purposes. Such systems may be tested only in specially controlled simulated environments.

15.6   Error Recovery Mechanisms

Prevention of runtime failures involves satisfactory recovery from error states or errors within the processes of their origin. There are two major recovery mechanisms: (1) pursuing alternative computations chosen from a *recovery block* of ordered computations and (2) *roll-back* to a previous error free state and repeating the computation (or the processing). Note that recovery blocks may be employed also in roll-back recovery. The next three sections deal with these techniques separately.

15.7   Recovery Blocks

15.7.1   Recovery Block Structure

A *recovery block* is implemented in software as a program fragment consisting of an *acceptance test*, a cascaded block of commands whose order corresponds to some preference relation, and an *error handling facility*. The first in the cascade of commands is called the *primary module* and others the *alternates* or *backup modules*. Although the modules may be ordered according to some preference criterion such as better performance (or diminishing returns) they are all supposed to satisfy the same specification. Any alternate module is attempted only when those modules ahead of it have already failed the acceptance test. The error handling facility is invoked only upon the failure of the acceptance test by all modules. In common with roll-back recovery, the invocation of an alternate module must be preceded by restoration of the state and data altered by the execution of the failed module.

In pseudo-code a recovery block is of the form

$$
\begin{array}{rl}
\text{ensure} & accpt \\
\text{by} & module_1 \\
\text{else--by} & module_2 \\
\text{else--by} & module_3 \\
\cdots & \cdots \\
\text{else--by} & module_n \\
\text{else} & error
\end{array}
$$

where *accpt* is a predicate defining an acceptance condition, and the indices indicating the desired order of module execution in the case of the failure of those with lower indices. The same structure is employed in many hardware configurations aimed at fault tolerance and is illustrated in Figure 15.4.

15.7.2   Acceptance Tests

Acceptance tests are aimed at detecting errors at runtime both under development and production systems. Since the correctness in realtime applications also covers the timing correctness, the acceptance test may incorporate a *watchdog timer* for monitoring the expiry of any deadline or other timing constraints. Since the acceptance test may be performed potentially for every alternate module executed,

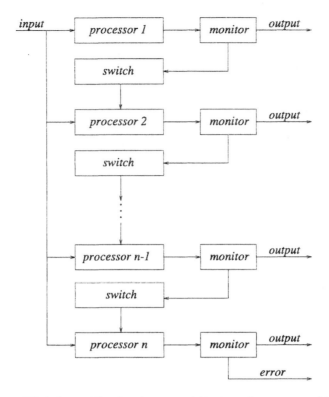

Figure 15.4 An outline hardware architecture for recovery blocks

the execution cost of the acceptance test may be quite significant. This justifies subjecting the acceptance test itself to the same design considerations as the
alternate modules.

Because of the potentially high execution cost, the acceptance test may not
be expected to verify the correctness in absolute terms, but in some 'relaxed'
form. Alternatively, the acceptance test may be viewed as an interim test at an
intermediate stage of any computation aimed at trapping highly plausible errors
early. Primarily with the execution costs in mind, the design of acceptance tests
may focus on the verification of the following (see Hecht [56]).

(a) The logical requirements of the system

Let P be a program expressed mathematically in the form of

$$\{pre\}\ P\ \{post\}$$

in terms of some predicates *pre* and *post* describing, respectively, its pre and
post conditions. In addition to being a specification, *pre* and *post* may also be
utilized in the derivation of programs and reasoning about them. Once a program has been coded in an executable language, the two predicates become

mere program annotations and are never checked at runtime, partly due to their intended role as design aids and partly because their evaluation can be too complex and expensive as runtime checks. For the latter reason, *post* is in general unsuitable as the condition of the acceptance test *accpt*. However, *accpt* may be designed to cover certain logical and/or timing requirements considered appropriate for runtime checks. It is important, therefore, to realize the difference between the roles of *accpt* and *post*: the former tests the consistency of the actual state at runtime against the state asserted by *post*, whereas *post*, in conjunction with *pre*, forms the basis for static verification of the correctness of the program with respect to its specification.

When it addresses the requirement issues, the predicate *accpt* is made weaker than *post* by design; thus resulting in the following logical implication:

$$post \Rightarrow accpt$$

The acceptance tests which specialize on logical requirements may be further classified as:

(i) Those checking the logical correctness of the values of non-cumulative program (state) variables.

For example, the acceptance test of a sorting algorithm may check just two aspects: (1) the output array of elements is sorted by the given ordering relation and (2) the length of the input and output arrays are the same during the computation. The acceptance test may thus omit an important aspect of the requirement specification, namely, that the two arrays are permutations of each other, that is, the two arrays are identical in terms of the number of occurrences of different elements in each array.

(ii) Those checking the logical correctness of the values of the cumulative program (state) variables.

These checks are especially applicable to transaction oriented applications, where it is possible to keep track of the cumulative effects of multiple passes of the program at different times on certain program variables. Some illustrative examples are: (1) bank accounts where it is possible to conduct 'accounting checks' by keeping track of the total amounts of credits and debits and making sure that their difference always equals the balance, and (2) a continuous process performing some input–output operation which may be monitored simply by ensuring that the counts of inputs and outputs are in some relation to each other, without verifying the actual input–output relation.

(b) Domain specific acceptance tests.

It may be possible in certain cases to devise acceptance tests such that *accpt* and *post* are logically independent. In this case, *accpt* is formulated in terms of domain specific secondary requirements which are outside the scope of the requirement specification. Such acceptance tests may embody 'rules of thumb' or past experience. For example, the acceptance test for a program processing analog quantities such as the outputs (e.g. speed, temperature) from a sensor may check that the value of the program input is not 'excessive', or is within a 'meaningful' range, with respect to itself (absolute value) or relative to the previous ones (increments or higher derivatives).

(c) Deficiencies in implementation

Deviations from systematic software development may result in loopholes in the implementation. Although it is bad practice to shield them by other means, failures due to such loopholes may be trapped by relying on runtime support provided by the 'underlying' machine, namely, programming language and the operating system. Some typical examples are division by zero, violation of array boundaries and violation of other memory access rights.

15.7.3   Timeout Blocks

Timeout blocks due to Harrison [55] have certain similarities to recovery blocks. Timeout blocks use an interrupt operator $P_1 \overset{t}{\triangledown} P_2$ involving two processes P_1 and P_2, denoting the process P_1 if the process $P_1 \overset{t}{\triangledown} P_2$ terminates within time t and P_2 otherwise; see Section 8.5.2 of Chapter 8 for the same operator in the context of Timed CSP. The general form of timeout blocks may be given as below:

$\text{get}\Omega(\overline{t})$;

$(s := f_1(x_0) \overset{t}{\triangledown}_{t_1} skip)$;

   $(s := f_2(x_0) \overset{t}{\triangledown}_{t_2} skip)$;

      $\cdots$

         $(s := f_{n-1}(x_0) \overset{t}{\triangledown}_{t_{n-1}} skip)$;

            $(s := f_n(x_0) \overset{t}{\triangledown}_{t_n} skip)$;

wait-until$(\overline{t} + t_1 + t_2 + \cdots + t_{n-1} + t_n)$

In the above, x_0 is the initial value of the state variable vector just prior to invocation of the timeout block, s the variable altered by the timeout block (referred to as the 'timeout block variable'), and $f_1, f_2, \cdots, f_{n-1}, f_n$ are functions computing the new value of s with better accuracy with increasing indices. Thus, the alternates are ordered according to increasing returns. The procedure $\text{get}\Omega(\overline{t})$ is for setting the variable $\overline{t}$ (which is distinct from s) to the clock reading at the time of procedure invocation, and wait-until($\bar{t}$) is a process which waits until time $\bar{t}$ and successfully terminates. Note that the commands get$\Omega(\bar{t})$ and wait-until($\bar{t}$) may be made optional.

The timeout block variable s is updated with every completed evaluation of the functions of the form f_i. If the time set against the function being executed expires, control is passed to the next statement in the timeout block. The timeout block terminates successfully with the evaluation of the last function f_n or at the expiry of time set against it. Thus, provided that f_1 is successfully evaluated within its deadline, s has the most accurate result computed at the termination of the timeout block, otherwise, the timeout block variable is unchanged. An important feature of the expression assigned to the block variable in each approximation is the function application carried out in the paradigm of functional programming in order to ensure that no updates are made to the state during its evaluation. Consequently, any aborted evaluation of function application by an interrupt does not require backtracking. Alternatively, each assignment of the form $s := f_i(x_0)$ may be viewed as an 'atomic action' – an action that takes place completely or not at all.

It is useful to draw a comparison between timeout blocks and recovery blocks. Alternates in timeout blocks are not merely alternative routines, but each makes a better approximation to the block variable afresh. Note that these approximations are not successive approximations since no use is made of the latest computed value of the block variable. The reason for this is that some alternates may potentially be skipped because of interrupts caused, for example, because of runtime environmental factors. The role of the acceptance test in recovery blocks is played by an interrupt against each approximation. Another important feature is that the timeout blocks always successfully terminate whereas recovery blocks raise exception handling if no alternate succeeds.

15.8 Roll-back Recovery

The aim of roll-back recovery is the restoration of a system to a consistent global state, which consists of the recovery points of individual processes allocated to different nodes. This approach is intended only for overcoming transient errors in single *channel* architectures (see Section 15.11.1 for the terminology '*channel*') and is inappropriate for dealing with permanent errors. Recovery of a process subsequent to a failure or error detection, does not involve the complete restart of the process, but restoration to a *recovery point* or *checkpoint*, which is the full state information of the process at some point in the past, and allows the repetition of the computation between the recovery and the failure point. However, restoration of recovery points is a complex exercise, because of the interprocess communications and interactions with the environment. In the case of interprocess communications, it is essential to select the recovery points of the processes concerned so that no communication has taken place following any of the chosen recovery points of individual processes. Since recovery points are established by different processes at different times, processes may have to *roll-back* to a past common recovery point so that the interprocess communications since the last recovery have been fully taken care of by the state corresponding to the chosen recovery point. When more than two processes are involved, this may quickly become very expensive in overheads, and complex.

However, the mere restoration of the internal state at the chosen recovery point is not sufficient for the recovery and it is essential that any interaction of the system with its environment between the recovery and failure points is also reproduced. This kind of interaction is quite typical and, by definition, is outside the control of the system. The faulty input behaviour on the environmental interface may be addressed somehow, either by retaining an input history for use in the event of failures, regeneration of inputs, or discarding the past inputs in favour of more up to date new inputs. In the case of outputs, however, there are no corrective means for undoing any consequences of the outputs generated by the system. The only means are preventative means, namely, thorough internal checks, generating the outputs only after passing all points of possible recovery invocation and deferring the outputs as late as possible.

15.8.1 Synchronization Graphs

Synchronization graphs proposed by Anderson and Knight [7] show the structure of a computational process, the synchronization times of its subprocesses and the start and end times of the process. Such graphs may take into account the cyclic nature of realtime applications, resulting in a reduction in the graph size and thus making them more manageable in practical use. The nested subgraphs may model different execution rates of subprocesses. Synchronization graphs are of particular use in identifying the boundaries of recovery schemes in concurrent systems, such as those discussed in Sections 15.8.5–15.8.7.

Mathematically, a synchronization graph is an acyclic bipartite graph with two kinds of vertices: (1) a set of nodes P with each node denoting an instance of a process (a program), and (2) a set of nodes T with each node denoting a time value; see Figure 15.5. The ith instance of a process P_k is denoted by p_k^i, but since it is not important here to distinguish between the generic processes P_k, P_l, etc., the notation p^i refers to an instance of some unspecified process. Symbols such as t_m denote the elements of T and are of the type $\mathbb{T}$ and, therefore, $T \subseteq \mathbb{T}$. Thus, a synchronization graph S is a pair,

$$ S = (V, \overset{s}{<}) $$

where

$$V \subseteq P \cup T$$
$$\overset{s}{<} \subseteq (P \times T) \cup (T \times P)$$

Given $p^i_k \in P$ and $t_m \in T$, the predicate $p^i_k \overset{s}{<} t_m$ means that 'The process instance p^i_k must terminate at or before the time t_m.' On the other hand, the predicate $t_m \overset{s}{<} p^i_k$ means that 'The process instance p^i_k must begin execution at time t_m.'

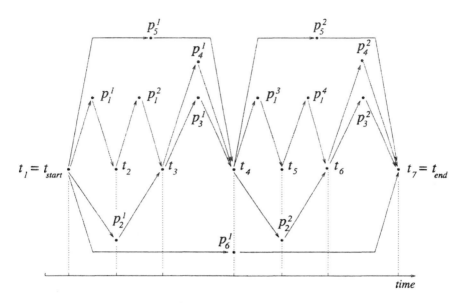

Figure 15.5 A time synchronization graph

Other properties that must be satisfied by the synchronization graph are as follows:

(i) Every process instance has a unique predecessor (i.e. start time) and a unique successor (i.e. end time) related by $\overset{s}{<}$:

$$\forall\, p^i \in P \,\bullet\, p^i \in (\text{fid } \overset{s}{<}) \;\Rightarrow\; \exists_1\, t_m, t_n \in T \bullet t_m \overset{s}{<} p^i \;\wedge\; p^i \overset{s}{<} t_n$$

(ii) If the node labelled by time value $t_n \in T$ is reachable from that labelled by another distinct time value $t_m \in T$ through a series of pairs of processes p^{i_1}, p^{i_2}, $\cdots$, p^{i_j} and time values t_{m_1}, t_{m_2}, $\cdots$, t_{m_j}, for which

$$t_m \overset{s}{<} p^{i_1},\; p^{i_1} \overset{s}{<} t_{m_1},\; t_{m_1} \overset{s}{<} p^{i_2},\; \cdots ,\; t_{m_j} \overset{s}{<} p^{i_j},\; p^{i_j} \overset{s}{<} t_n$$

then $t_n > t_m$. That is, the time values increase with the traversal of the graph.

(iii) There is a unique node $t_{start} \in T$ in S called *start node* with no predecessors related by $\overset{s}{<}$, and another unique node $t_{end} \in T$ called *end node* with no successors related by $\overset{s}{<}$. That is,

$$\exists_1 \, t_{start} \in T \bullet t_{start} \in (\text{dom} \overset{s}{<} - \text{ran} \overset{s}{<})$$
$$\exists_1 \, t_{end} \in T \bullet t_{end} \in (\text{ran} \overset{s}{<} - \text{dom} \overset{s}{<})$$

The interval (t_{start}, t_{end}) is known as the *time frame* of the synchronization graph S.

The elements in T in a synchronization graph are the synchronization times of processes within the graph. The times t_{start} and t_{end}, on the other hand, serve as the interframe synchronization times.

15.8.2   Events in Distributed Systems

The following terminology applies to the discussion below on processes and recovery mechanisms as applicable to recovery in distributed systems.

Events are understood here as significant state transformations of a process or its communications with other processes. The following is a specialized notation used for events of different kinds:

e_i^p — The ith event at the process p. An event e_i^p may be any of the following specialized ones.

s_i^p — The ith state transformation of the process p (or the state immediately after the transformation).

$in_{pq}?m_i$ — The event of the process p receiving a message m_i from the process q.

$out_{pq}!m_i$ — The event of the process p sending the message m_i to the process q.

The *local state* of a process may be defined as the complete historical trace of events starting from the initial state. The trace of a process p up to time t_n^p in its clock is denoted by a sequence of the general form

$$tr^p \overset{def}{=} \langle (t_i^p, e_i^p) \mid i \in 0 .. n \rangle$$

where the notation t_i^p denotes the clock value corresponding to the local time of the process p. By definition,

$$t_i^p = \Omega^p(t_i)$$

where t_i is some external reference time. The notation t_f^p denotes the local failure time of process p. The indices in tr^p orders the time values in ascending order. That is,

$$j > i \Rightarrow t_j^p \geq t_i^p$$

15.8.3 Checkpoints in Distributed Systems

As mentioned earlier, a *checkpoint* is the local state of a process saved at a certain instance of time in stable storage. Mathematically, a checkpoint of the process p is a pair

$$(t_x^p, s_m^p)$$

such that s_m^p is a state transformation with no change to the state. If s_m^p represents the state immediately after the transformation in a trace such as the following:

$$tr^p \overset{def}{=} \langle (t_0^p, s_0^p), (t_1^p, e_1^p), \cdots, (t_i^p, e_i^p), (t_j^p, s_{m-1}^p), (t_x^p, s_m^p), \cdots \rangle$$

then $s_{m-1}^p = s_m^p$. Given a set of processes $p, q, \cdots$, a global checkpoint is a set of checkpoints

$$\{(t_x^p, s_m^p), (t_y^q, s_n^q), \cdots\}$$

Suppose an application is partitioned into a number of tasks which are to be allocated to a number of processing sites. The consistency of the state of the application saved at any time depends on the mutual consistency of the states saved by all sites executing the particular application. A proper definition of consistency of the application invariably involves the conjunction of all state information and its establishment requires the complete and detailed knowledge of these states; see Figure 15.6. The following is a simplified definition based on the correct temporal ordering of inter-process communications, without any reference to the actual contents of states and communications.

Definition:

> A *global checkpoint* of the above form is said to be *consistent* if the saved states are pairwise mutually consistent in the following sense. For every pair of distinct processes p and q, and external reference times t_i and t_j such that $t_i < t_j$, the checkpoints t_x^p and t_y^q are mutually consistent if and only if
>
> $$\neg \exists t_i^p, t_j^q, m_k \bullet \langle (t_i^p, out_{pq}!m_k) \rangle \text{ in } tr^p \wedge$$
> $$\langle (t_j^q, in_{qp}?m_k) \rangle \text{ in } tr^q \wedge (t_i^p > t_x^p) \wedge (t_j^q < t_y^q)$$

That is, if

$$tr^p \overset{def}{=} \langle \cdots, (t_i^p, out_{pq}!m_k), \cdots, (t_{i+m}^p, s_m^p), (t_x^p, s_x^p), \cdots, (t_f^p, \perp) \rangle$$

where $\perp$ signifies an erroneous state, then the checkpoint t_y^q is consistent with t_x^p if q's trace is of the following form,

$$tr^q \overset{def}{=} \langle \cdots, (t_j^q, in_{qp}?m_k), \cdots, (t_{j+n}^q, s_n^q), (t_y^q, s_y^q), \cdots \rangle$$

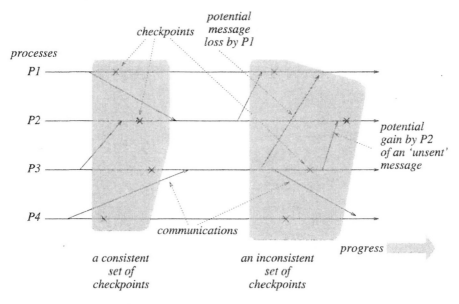

Figure 15.6 Checkpoint consistency

Otherwise, if an error recovery is made from the proposed global checkpoint then q has the record of having received the message m_k at t_j^q, and yet p's state shows that it has not sent the message m_k.

However, there is also the possibility that q would have received the message after time t_f^p if not for p's failure at that time. In this case, the trace is of the form

$$tr^q \overset{def}{=} \langle \cdots , (t_{j-m}^q, s_m^q), (t_y^q, s_y^q), \cdots , (t_j^q, in_{qp}?m_k), \cdots , \rangle$$

with the time of the potential failure t_f^p being such that $t_f^p < t_j^p$. Alternatively, the message could have been lost in the channel linking $out_{pq}!...$ and $in_{qp}?...$, but this possibility can be excluded by adopting an appropriate mechanism for checkpoint creation; see approach (c) in Section 15.8.8.

15.8.4   Failure Modes in Roll-back Recovery

There are two well-known failure modes in roll-back recovery, namely, the *domino effect* and the *livelock*.

The *domino effect* is a scenario in which a set of communicating processes find themselves unable to establish a consistent set of recovery points in the recent history. In the extreme case of inconsistencies between every alternate pair of recovery points, the roll-back may be forced up to the initial state. This is illustrated in Figure 15.7. In the case of the failure shown, the recovery points

$(h, j), (h, g), (e, g), (e, d), (c, d), (c, b)$ and (a, b) are mutually inconsistent, and roll-back to any one of them causes P_1 and P_2 to roll-back to their initial states. This limits the use of roll-back recovery in realtime applications with tight timing constraints.

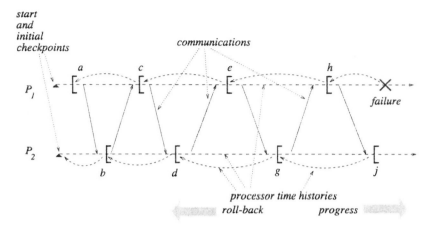

Figure 15.7 Domino effect in roll-back

The second type of failure in roll-back recovery, *livelock* or *unbounded roll-back*, results from not synchronizing the recovery process. In the example illustrated in Figure 15.8, if the process p fails following an exchange of messages with q in the manner given by the trace

$$tr^p \overset{def}{=} \langle \cdots, (t_x^p, s_x^p), \cdots, (t_i^p, out_{pq}!m_k), \cdots, (t_f^p, \bot) \rangle$$
$$tr^q \overset{def}{=} \langle \cdots, (t_y^q, s_y^q), \cdots, (t_j^q, out_{qp}!m_l), \cdots, (t_k^q, in_{qp}?m_k), \cdots, \rangle$$

but without receiving m_l before t_f^p, then the two processes may keep ending up indefinitely in mutually inconsistent states as they attempt recovery. For example, if q remains at, or has progressed in a recovery cycle up to, $in_{qp}?m_k$ when p roll-backs to s_x^p the resulting inconsistency may force q to roll-back to s_y^q. Meanwhile, p might make further progress, and thus not help to resolve the inconsistency.

In view of such potential failures in the recovery process itself, it is essential that roll-back recovery is well designed against them. In this respect, the measures that may be undertaken include:

(a) a disciplined approach to entering and leaving recovery stages;
(b) ensuring consistency of checkpoints at the outset.

Sections 15.8.5–15.8.7 deal with approach (a) above and Section 15.8.8 deals with approach (b).

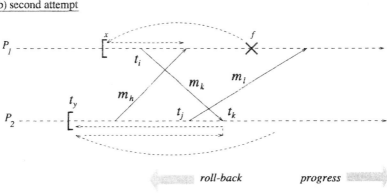

Figure 15.8 Livelock in roll-back

15.8.5   Restricted Communications

In dealing with fault tolerance in concurrent systems, Anderson and Knights [7] propose a certain restriction on communications. In the case of processes which are synchronized in a sequence, communications may be permitted only from processes which terminate earlier to processes which start later. This is a logical necessity. However, in the case of processes terminating at the same time they may be permitted to communicate with each other freely. The above restrictions are captured by two simple rules outlined below. Given that the following holds with respect to a given synchronization graph:

$$t_k \stackrel{s}{<} p^i, \; p^i \stackrel{i}{<} t_l, \; t_m \stackrel{s}{<} p^j, \; p^j \stackrel{s}{<} t_n$$

(a) If the deadlines are such that p^i terminates before p^j begins, that is, $t_l \leq t_m$, then, p^i may be permitted to communicate with p^j.

(b) If $t_l = t_n$, then p^i and p^j are permitted to communicate with each other, provided that the two processes terminate simultaneously.

15.8.6 Conversations

Conversations, illustrated in Figure 15.9, are free communications among the processes of a given set. Processes may join a conversation at any time, but must first establish a recovery point before entry. All processes leave a conversation simultaneously so they can restore their respective recovery points in the event of an error in any one of them. On successful termination, the recovery points may be discarded. Note that in Figure 15.9,

- The lines *ab*, *cd*, *ef* and *gh* represent the environments of the processes concerned at entry, the states of which are automatically backed up in stable storage.
- The lines *aj*, *cb*, *de*, *gf* and *hi* signify absence of interactions between processes delineated by these lines. It must be possible to undo the results of any process interactions taken place within these lines.
- The line *ij* represents the states of the processes at exit satisfying an acceptance test. No internal errors are supposed to propagate beyond *ij*.
- There can be nested conversations such as *klmnop* subject to the same rules, that is, with no communications with processes outside each such conversation.
- Each process may consists of a number of concurrent subprocesses within a conversation. As outlined in Section 15.8.1, the internal structure of such processes may be taken into account using synchronization graphs.

More details of this approach may be found in many sources, including Randell [125].

15.8.7 Exchanges

An exchange is a restricted form of conversation, where the participants p^i, p^j, $\cdots$, p^l have identical termination times, that is,

$$p^i \overset{s}{<} t, \; p^j \overset{s}{<} t, \; \cdots , \; p^l \overset{s}{<} t$$

A conversation may be seen as a generalization of restriction (b) mentioned in subsection 15.8.5 to include any number of processes. Processes join the exchange as soon as they are initiated and all the processes, as well as the exchange itself, terminate simultaneously. Obviously, the exchange is limited to the participants only and, because of this, different exchanges must be completely disjoint. This is a distinguishing feature of exchanges compared to conversations.

The implementation of exchanges is relatively simple in the case of cyclic realtime systems, since the initial state may be set up from some read-only memory if initialization does not involve any inputs. This may still be the case with a limited number of computationally less demanding inputs.

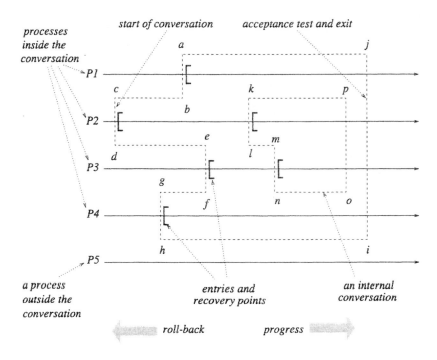

Figure 15.9 A conversation

15.8.8   Checkpoint Creation

The problem of ensuring no failures in the roll-back recovery is closely linked with
how checkpoints are created. Checkpoints are created following positive outcomes
to appropriate *acceptance tests* (see Section 15.7.2), and may be created in a number
of ways. Among them are the following:

(a) Independent Checkpoint Creation

Each process takes checkpoints at different times independently and saves
them in stable storage. In the event of a failure, the processes establish a
consistent global checkpoint for recovery. The checkpoints may be created at
regular intervals.

The disadvantages of this approach are its vulnerability to the domino effect discussed in Section 15.8.4 and excessive storage requirements for saving
checkpoints.

(b) Coordinated Checkpoint Creation

The creation of checkpoints is achieved through coordination and only the
latest checkpoint is saved. Any recovery starts from the global checkpoint

thus established, which is supposed to be consistent by virtue of the process coordination.

This approach generally works, but it may lead to livelock as described in Section 15.8.4.

(c) Coordinated Minimal Checkpoint Creation

The approach due to Koo and Toueg [79] follows the above and is based on the tentative creation of checkpoints and their subsequent confirmation if all processes succeed. It relies on the following assumptions with respect to the behaviour of processes in a distributed environment:

 (i) The system model is such that there is no shared memory between processes and they communicate only through messages transmitted via (communication) channels.

 (ii) The messages are not lost and are eventually delivered to their destinations.

(iii) Processes fail by stopping, but other processes learn about such failures within a finite amount of time.

(iv) Process failures do not result in the partitioning of the communication network.

The checkpoints are created only if they are necessary on the basis of information exchanged between the processes about their mutual communications since the latest checkpoints.

The approach overcomes the problem of potential livelocks and is resilient against process failure during the execution of the roll-back recovery algorithm itself. Furthermore, the processes are assumed to be generally non-deterministic and the events to be not necessarily atomic.

15.9   Software and Hardware Redundancy – A Comparison

15.9.1   Forms of Redundancy

Redundancy is a properly managed set of resources and measures supporting additional computations. It is introduced to any fault tolerant design with respect to time, space and in terms of methods through repetition of computations, concurrent execution of computations in different hardware, and by employing software based on different algorithms and designs. The topic is not totally new in our discussion and the recovery mechanisms discussed in the previous two sections come under the category of multiple computations in time and methods and include the supplementary error handling computations.

15.9.2   Balance between Hardware and Software

The term 'redundancy' frequently refers to that achieved through a mixture of software and hardware. With reference to many components in computer systems, such as watchdog timers, which may be implemented both in software and hardware, this distinction often hardly matters. Despite this high level 'sameness', as discussed in Section 15.4.1, the extent of software and hardware usage does have an important effect on the performance of fault tolerant computer systems. For example, the fault tolerant computer system known as Software Implemented Fault Tolerance (SIFT) described by Wensley *et al.* [168] appeared to spend about 80% of the system throughput on execution of fault tolerant software. According to Hopkins, Smith and Lala [62], the same figure for the Fault Tolerant Multi-Processor (FTMP) using hardware implementation for voting and synchronization was about 60%. There have been a number of other attempts aimed at alleviating the burden of overhead due to software based fault tolerant approaches, namelythe Advanced Information Processing System (AIPS) by Lala *et al.* [85] and Multicomputer Architecture for Fault Tolerance (MAFT) by Kieckhafer *et al.* [75].

Hardware redundancy may also not be increased indiscriminately, because, on the one hand, it places greater responsibility on the system software for its operational management and, on the other, it multiplies the potential sources of unreliability particularly through design faults, thus resulting in higher fault arrival rates. The fault tolerant costs associated with these factors may be as high as 50% and, therefore, the cost-effectiveness of fault tolerance measures by hardware based means must be carefully weighed.

It must also be noted that (unlimited) hardware redundancy may not always be feasible for different reasons. Hardware redundancy may not be economically viable in non-safety critical applications which allow easy replacement of components and in systems operating in corrosive environments requiring frequent replacement of components. There may be other reasons such as spatial or weight restrictions (e.g. redundant hydraulic lanes) and operational reasons (e.g. switching between, for example, hydraulic lanes).

15.10   Software Redundancy

15.10.1   Forms of Software Redundancy

Software redundancy may aim at error detection, error recovery and other error handling measures. Thus, it may involve:

- 'multiple computations' producing the same result or different results meeting the same primary need;

- 'supplementary computations' for error detection, error handling, data validation, redundancy management, time management, etc.

The latter may constitute a significant factor affecting both cost and performance. It is sometimes referred to as *information redundancy*, since the associated computations are not concerned directly with the primary need. Certain forms of information redundancy have already been discussed in Sections 15.7 and 15.8. However, the more general forms of information redundancy addressing error confinement (or fault containment) and error masking are associated with multiple computations, which may be achieved by means of

- execution of identical copies of software on multiple hardware; or
- execution of software which is diverse in design and executed on units of the same or different hardware.

The former may be considered as a special case of the latter, which is known commonly as *N-version programming*. The units of hardware used for the above may in turn be identical or diverse in design, resulting in a number of combinations of different forms of software and hardware. Despite their relevance to our study, these combinations are not considered further in detail.

Multiple computations achieved through the above means may be seen as generalizations of recovery blocks by executing the alternates concurrently. However, there is a characteristic difference between recovery blocks and the multiple computations considered here. This difference lies in the decision algorithm used for establishing the result of the computation. In recovery blocks the role of the decision algorithm is played by the acceptance test designed specifically for the application concerned. On the other hand, multiple computations employ generic fault tolerant algorithms capable of establishing the result on the basis of some form of consensus.

15.10.2   *N*-Version Programming

Multiple computations may, in general, detect both physical and design errors. Naturally, *N*-version programming is effective with respect to physical faults in multiple channel systems, but is primarily intended for detecting design errors. The higher resilience towards design errors is achieved through the use of software which is diverse in design but satisfies the same specification. The software may be executed on the same or several units of hardware. *N*-version programming relies on the hope that, when executed independently or in parallel, alternative algorithms solving the same problem may in consort expose and trap most of the system failures, since different versions are likely to exhibit different capabilities because of the variation in their design. A more formal argument would be that the statistical independence of failures in independently produced software lessens the overall probability of failure.

N-version programming places the greatest emphasis on:

(i) The quality of problem specification

Design faults being its principal concern, *N*-version programming is meaningful only if all algorithms or versions satisfy the same specification, which explains the high emphasis placed on the quality of the problem specification. Most promising in this respect are formal specification techniques.

The problem specification covers, as usual, the specifications of:

(a) the initial state;

(b) the input–output behaviour;

(c) timing constraints on program execution, if applicable; and

(d) exception handling.

(ii) The extent of the diversity of solutions

The design diversity is aimed at minimizing the probability of independently produced different versions of any software developing the same error at the 'decision points' under identical inputs. Therefore, the effectiveness of the approach depends on the degree of diversity among the different versions.

The independence of different versions may be achieved only through careful introduction of some *development diversity* – the diversity of methodologies, the tools and languages being used and the diversity of the professional and academic background of the designers involved. There is also, however, a greater 'diversity' in the sources of error with the employment of multiple teams for developing different versions of any software.

(iii) Specification on how to manage execution of different versions

The execution of different versions of the software has to be coordinated. This takes the form of a decision algorithm checking the results produced by the different versions at predefined intermediate stages in the computation. These stages are referred to as 'decision points'. The clarity and precision of 'decision specification' is vital for the same reason as that in (i) above, that is, to prevent the checks involved causing their own errors.

The decision specification consists of the specifications of:

(a) decision points;

(b) the decision algorithm to be used at each decision point;

(c) data produced by each version for the decision algorithm;

(d) actions in response to the outcome of the decision algorithm; including the case of a negative outcome for all versions requiring higher level error recovery measures.

(iv) A clear separation of application specific and application independent (generic) issues

Application specific issues are covered by (i) and (ii) above. Genericity of the application independent aspects of N-version programming is assured by the genericity of each of the following:

(a) decision algorithms;

(b) means of ensuring input consistency;

(c) inter-version communication;

(d) version synchronization;

(e) local version supervision (e.g. compliance with timing constraints);

(f) global supervision (e.g. faults in different versions);

(g) monitoring, runtime support, performance evaluation and other housekeeping activities.

Another form of diversity is 'data diversity', which relies on the same idea and addresses fault tolerance by re-expression of 'faulty' data and 'retrying' the execution of a failed program. This is not discussed further and the reader is referred to Ammann and Knight [6].

15.10.3 Fault Tolerant Decision Algorithms

Any decision algorithm produces a single result from its inputs which, in the case of N-version programming, are supplied by the different versions of software. In general, these inputs may originate from all kinds of different sources, including clocks, sensors, etc. The decision algorithm, however, may not necessarily use the results from all versions or sources, and may be designed, for example, to use the first m results out of n sources or m computations satisfying the relevant acceptance test.

Fault tolerant decision algorithms are especially designed to shield the effect of invalid data originating from the faulty behaviour of some unit and, thus, to ensure the continued execution of a process. The reader should refer to Section 16.9 of Chapter 16 on clock synchronization algorithms for specific examples on how this may be achieved.

The algorithmic means employed in the above manner for preventing the generation of incorrect results by a processor from the data read from other processors is known as *fault masking*. The simplest algorithm used is the *majority voting*, which is based on a straightforward comparison of results.

Fault masking may be based on the exact or approximate agreement of outputs from different processors, the choice between them being dependent on the reliability requirements of the application and the nature of the data. The criteria on approximate consensus may consist of a range of permitted values. Approximate consensus is applicable commonly to data representing continuous (analog) quantities such as temperatures and velocities; exact consensus applies to situations involving discrete quantities such as event counts and, generally, messages whose values are drawn from discrete domains. Establishing approximate consensus may be more complex if the criteria are dependent on the rapidly changing (dynamical) characteristics of the system (e.g. during take-off, landing, and high speed manoeuvring of aircraft, and shutdown of nuclear installations). It may also result in false alarms if the range of permitted values is relatively narrow (e.g. in realtime patient monitoring systems).

It is interesting to compare the requirements on establishing consensus by majority voting and by algorithms aimed at Byzantine resilience. In majority voting, $(2m+1)$ participants vote in a ratio better than $(m+1):m$ in reaching consensus on a two-way vote (binary issue). If the majority voting is to operate properly with m faulty participants, then a total of $(3m+1)$ participants is required. It turns out that the algorithms based on Byzantine consensus require the same total number of participants for tolerating up to a maximum of m unreliable participants; see Section 16.9 of Chapter 16. However, the important difference between the two approaches is that the former requires the prior knowledge of the identity of the m faulty participants in order to exclude them from the vote, whereas the latter work in the presence of an arbitrary distribution of the unreliable processors with no knowledge of their identity.

15.11   Hardware Redundancy

15.11.1   Fault Containment Regions

Hardware redundancy is the replication of hardware components within a system, commonly used for addressing hardware and operational faults and for supporting various forms of software redundancy. The hardware is replicated in units with independent resources such as processing unit, memory, input/output interfaces, power supply and clock facilities. These units are often referred to as *lanes* or *channels*.

The objective of this organization is to partition the system into a collection of independent *fault containment regions* such that the non-faulty regions operate correctly despite the presence of faulty ones. The fault containment regions may be located physically apart from each other for preventing total potential physical damage, if applicable.

Channels may belong to two different types of operation: asynchronous and synchronized operation. In asynchronous operation, the sampling of sensor data, their processing and generation of control signals are done independently. By contrast, instead of using individually sampled data, synchronous channels work on distributed sensor data. As discussed in Rushby and von Henke [139], the two types are vulnerable to different kinds of errors and failures. Because of the differences in sampling times, the sensor data sampled by different asynchronous channels can be significantly different from one another at critical times. This can result in false alarms as well as in different outcomes at any common decision point. These problems may be overcome in synchronous channels since they are supposed to work on practically the same data, possibly with small margins of error within well-understood tolerances. However, in the presence of failures, this is not sufficient for correct operation, and calls for the resilience of distributed algorithms and protocols being used as well, for example, those used for clock synchronization discussed in Chapter 16.

15.11.2   Management of Fault Containment Regions

The fault containment regions have certain well-defined interfaces, designed for easy identification of faulty lanes, their immediate isolation from the rest of the system and subsequent system reconfiguration for their exclusion. Fault containment comprises the following activities:

(i) Prevention of propagation of erroneous data,

(ii) Isolation and exclusion of faults.

   This is to prevent failures causing incorrect behaviour elsewhere in the system through data corruption in non-faulty processors and through the output of invalid control signals, for example, for request handling and time synchronization.

   Data corruption by faulty processors may be prevented by imposing read-only access to data resident on other processors.

   Improper signals may be prevented by making each unit autonomous in terms of control, and using timeouts for terminating indefinite waiting for responses from the outside world.

(iii) System reconfiguration intended for excluding faulty units

   This may involve either reassignment of tasks from the faulty processors to other non-faulty processors, or the employment of a non-faulty bus, depending on the nature of the fault. Instead of full system reconfiguration, one may temporarily use hardware devices (processor interlocks) operated by the majority of lanes for disabling the outputs from faulty lanes. Such action may retain the fault isolation until a secondary spare can be brought on-line in order to maintain system integrity.

15.11.3   Forms of Replication

The hardware may be replicated in two ways, namely, in the form of active and passive replication. *Active replication (standby redundancy)* is a multiple lane/channel system. One of these lanes is singled out as the *primary lane*, and carries out the primary function of the system at any given moment. The others are called *spares*. Usually one of them, called a *secondary lane*, is maintained either in fully synchronized operation with the primary one, or in a quiescent state, so that it can be brought on-line for taking over the primary lane in the event of the latter's failure. *Passive replication* or *N-modular redundancy* (typically, triple modular redundancy; see Figure 15.10) employs synchronous execution of identical algorithms (code) or tasks on a number of lanes and processes, their outputs using fault tolerant algorithms in order to eliminate the effect of any faulty output among them. In a triple modular redundant (TMR) system, this is achieved typically by accepting the majority result (two agreements) and rejecting the minority.

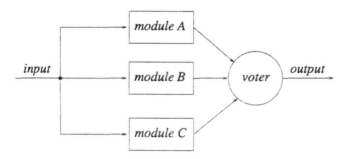

Figure 15.10 Triple modular redundancy (TMR)

15.11.4   Active Replication

When a replica replaces the primary line, it does so from the latest, or the appropriate, checkpoint; a disadvantage of this is the delay in service availability due to switching time and in returning to the checkpoint concerned. It is also important to make sure that the communications made by the primary line before the failure are not repeated or lost. Such communication issues may be dealt with, as mentioned earlier, by establishing recovery points at communication instances in order to eliminate the startup of a replica having to interact with the environment. However, the creation of recovery points for every communication may turn out to be unworkably expensive. In addition to the loss of time in reaching the point of failure, the overhead in establishing recovery points may also adversely affect the system performance, particularly the temporary storage. Such factors restrict the choice of active techniques for fault tolerance purposes, but they may be found more appropriate for application areas such as transaction processing, where some reasonable switching delay may be acceptable.

15.11.5   Passive Replication

Passive replication recognizes the possibility of erroneous data propagating across the boundaries of fault containment regions. Fault masking is really the immediate response to a fault; other provisions for dealing with it must follow, namely, fault diagnosis, fault isolation, system reconfiguration and, finally, repair.

Fault masking is performed at a number of frontiers within a given system, known as *voting planes*. These may additionally perform error detection functions. Typical voting planes are situated at the interfaces between sensors and the control law, inter-lane interfaces and the actuator interfaces. The checks made at these interfaces may include data validity checks, for example, the range of values being exchanged and their rate change with time, etc.; see (v) and (vi) in Section 15.2.1. The sensor and actuator interfaces may not necessarily be limited to, or based on, digital communications, but may involve the conversion or the generation of different forms of stimuli: electrical, mechanical, sonar, radar, etc., requiring the employment of analog-to-digital and digital-to-analog converters as appropriate. In such cases, the voting planes concerned are located inside these converters and the error handling beyond them belong to other specialized disciplines.

Ensuring exact consensus may require a set of so-called *congruent processes*. A set of processes is said to be *congruent* to one another if they are pairwise indistinguishable initially and externally or, more precisely, if they are identical to one other with respect to the initial state, the input–output behaviour and the responses to external events and stimuli. When dealing with exact agreement, any violation of congruency by the processes concerned may be interpreted as a fault, especially in fault detection activities. On the other hand, however, prevalence of congruency does not necessarily ensure the correctness of the agreed output, as the set of all congruent processes may be producing the same incorrect result. Thus, congruency is a necessary condition for exact agreement, but it is not sufficient on its own.

Sufficiency may be assured by requiring additionally the validity or the correctness of the inputs to the set of processors. This is because erroneous output data may be caused not only by a faulty processor, but also by providing incorrect inputs to a perfectly well-functioning processor. Such incorrect inputs may sometimes be traced back to a faulty bus and, for this reason, different copies of each input may have to be obtained from the processors involved via different buses.

15.12   Bibliographical Notes

The sources of material used in this chapter have been cited where it was felt most appropriate. Other relevant sources are Anderson and Lee [8], Jalote [67], Redmill and Anderson [130] and Vytopil [165, 166]. An introduction to reliability metrics and their estimation and to issues specific to a number of important practical applications may be found in Cluley [26]. A more comprehensive exposition of reliability, especially in relation to Sections 15.4 and 15.5, may be found in Siewiorek and Swarz [149]. Another important source is Randell *et al.* [126].

R_F and $MTTF$ mentioned in Section 15.4 are not applicable to gracefully degrading systems since they use redundancy with the twin aims of system reliability and performance and respond to failures by reconfiguration into smaller systems with reduced performance. Beaudry [12] and in Osaki [113] consider the reliability of such systems. Ramanathan and Shin [123] propose an approach to checkpointing and roll-back recovery in distributed systems using a common time base. This is relevant to our discussion in Section 15.8 and aims at the elimination of waiting time incurred by faster processes in a conversation waiting for the slower processes and processes outside it for termination of the conversation. Saglietti [140] is relevant to our discussion in Section 15.10.1, especially regarding various opportunities for introducing software diversity for achieving fault tolerance.

Chapter 16

Systems of Clocks

This chapter is devoted to clock synchronization, namely, to techniques and algorithms intended for maintaining a common time base in an interconnected system with nodes having their own individual clocks. A common time base is essential for ensuring the basic function of any multi-processor realtime system. This may concern recording the time of occurrence of external events at different nodes, timely response to them by generation of stimuli and actions, adaptation to external events and internal evolution.

Some of the terminology and notation used here, especially that applicable to single clocks and different metrics of time, have been explained in Chapter 2.

16.1   Clock Synchronization

All clocks diverge from the ideal behaviour with time. This is inherently due to minute physical imperfections in the devices that make up clocks. Clocks are also sensitive to fluctuations in ambient conditions such as temperature and radiation. Clocks can fail in other ways, too, sometimes directly by stopping and sometimes indirectly because of the failure of the communication medium to deliver clock readings correctly.

Clock synchronization is an intermittent activity undertaken by a clock system in order to rectify the effect of constant drift of clocks and other forms of failure. There are two kinds of clock synchronization:

- Internal Clock Synchronization

  The aim of internal synchronization is the establishment of an approximate global time base among the nodes on the basis of their logical clocks.

  D_{int} denotes the maximum permitted deviation, or permitted skew, between any two clocks. In loosely synchronized systems a value of the order of 50 μs

is considered tolerable. Note that $D_{int} > \Delta$, Δ being the clock granularity.

- External Clock Synchronization

  The aim of the external synchronization is the establishment of an approximate internal time base with respect to the external reference time.

  D_{ext} denotes the maximum permitted deviation between any clock and the external reference time.

The times over which synchronization is performed is referred to as the *synchronization period*, whereas the interval between the end of the last synchronization and the start of the next is referred to as the *synchronization cycle*; see Figure 16.1. The synchronization cycle may be of the order of 10 h in the case of clocks used in advanced avionics with $D_{int} = 50$ μs.

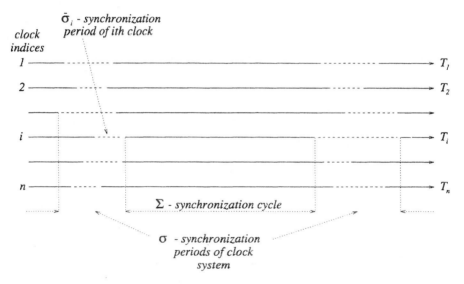

Figure 16.1 Synchronization period and cycle

16.2   Correctness Criteria of Synchronization

Correctness of synchronization involves the correct functioning of individual clocks as well as the correct functioning of the clock system as a whole. Thus, the 'correctness' aspects of synchronization are threefold, namely,

- agreement among the nodal clocks themselves;
- agreement of each nodal clock with the external reference clock; and

- maintenance of the accuracy of the individual clocks over time.

The agreement and accuracy of clocks are based on the following definitions:

(i) *Agreement of Time*

Given that t is an external reference time lying within the synchronization cycle, the criteria on agreement of clock times may be defined as follows:

(a) Internal agreement between every pair of clocks:

$$| \ \Omega_i(t) \ - \ \Omega_j(t) \ | \le \ D_{int}$$

where i and j are clock indices.

(b) External agreement between each clock and the external reference time:

$$| \ \Omega(t) \ - \ \Omega_i(t) \ | \le \ D_{ext}$$

where i is the clock index, and $\Omega(t)$ denotes the time of the external reference clock.

The symbol t in both (a) and (b) above denotes the external reference time over the synchronization cycles.

Being based on approximate global time, the external clock synchronization is less accurate and, therefore, usually $D_{ext} > D_{int}$.

(ii) *Clock Accuracy*

(a) The criterion on clock accuracy is defined by employing a bound γ on the drift rate of the logical clock such that the following is satisfied:

$$(1 - \gamma)t + a \le \Omega_i(t) \le (1 + \gamma)t + b$$

where a and b are some constants dependent on the conditions immediately after synchronization, and representing time offsets of the logical clock from its underlying physical clock; see Figure 16.2. Being an upper bound on drift rate, $\gamma \ge \rho_{\text{physical clock}}$. [Note that a, b and γ in above may be related to Θ_0 and ρ appearing in the definitions given in Sections 2.7.1 and 2.7.2 of Chapter 2.]

(b) The so-called *optimal accuracy* corresponds to the situation where $\gamma = \rho_{\text{physical clock}}$. The use of this term may be justified on the grounds that it is impossible to improve upon the physical clock, except by direct interference or replacement.

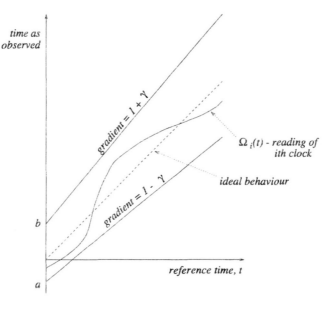

Figure 16.2 Accuracy of clocks

The conditions in (i(a)) and (ii(a)) may be seen as a specification of the behaviour of an ensemble of clocks over the times outside the synchronization periods. Condition (i(a)) is a necessary condition, but is not sufficient since otherwise clocks may be set to the same value and stopped. Condition (ii(a)) excludes such trivial solutions.

Condition (i(b)) has two important practical consequences. Firstly, the clocks maintain a good approximation to real time after the synchronization, provided that they have not exceeded the deviation $\pm D_{ext}$ prior to it. Secondly, the bound may serve as a measure of time determining the idle period for applying the corrections. The bound and the length of the idle period are factors governing the pattern of correction application.

A consequence of (ii) is that if two 'identical' logical clocks are

- in perfect synchrony at t_0, and
- $a = b = 0$

then their displays for $t \geq t_0$ may differ at most by $\pm 2\gamma(t - t_0)$ during the synchronization cycle.

16.3 Pragmatics of Synchronization

Our concern above has been the degree of correctness of clock synchronization, but there are other equally important factors to be considered in synchronization.

These are covered by additional synchronization requirements, which are outlined below:

(i) The process of synchronization must be fault tolerant. That is, it must not be adversely affected beyond well-defined limits by failures of the physical clocks, processor failures, loss of messages and the presence of inconsistent messages resulting from communication failures.

(ii) The execution overheads of the synchronization algorithm must be relatively low in terms of the communications and computations involved, thus avoiding degradation of system performance as a result.

(iii) The process of synchronization must be fast since clock values continually change.

(iv) Synchronization must be chronoscopic, i.e. accurate.

16.4   Message Delay and Reading Error

Message delay is the total time required for sending a message and receiving it at the recipient's end. The messages involved here are concerned with clock synchronization and, therefore, contain clock values, or their differences.

Message delay depends on the physical means of achieving synchronization and, thus, on system configuration. In closely coupled systems the clocks may access one another's clock reading via special channels, whereas in loosely coupled systems the clocks obtain other clock values by exchanging messages. In the latter case, the message delay consists of the following (see Figure 16.3):

1. the time spent by the sender in reading its own time and in composing a message;
2. media access time (accounting for bus contention, token arrival, etc.);
3. message transmission time (dependent on bandwidth, message length, etc.);
4. propagation delay (dependent on distances involved, channel parameters);
5. the time spent by the recipient in receiving and decomposing the message.

Furthermore, message delays incurred by a pair of nodes in reading one another's clocks are, in general, asymmetrical. This is because of the possible information flow restrictions as in the case of unidirectional rings and differences in interrupt handling mechanisms at the two nodes.

It may also be noticed from the above list that the factors contributing to message delay are different in nature. Such terms as message composition and decomposition times and transmission and propagation delays are predictable, whereas the media access time is highly unpredictable. Reading error, denoted by ε here, is the maximum difference between the message delays incurred by clocks in reading one another's clock values. Thus, referring to Figure 16.3,

$$\varepsilon = d_{max} - d_{min}$$

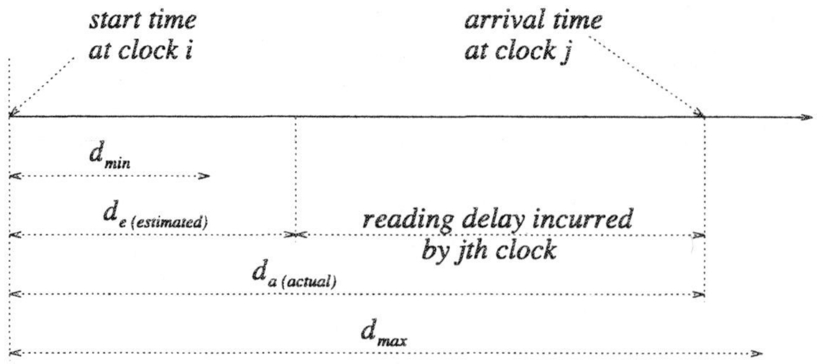

Figure 16.3 Message delay

16.5 Correction of Clocks

The method of application of computed corrections to clock displays depends on the order of magnitude of the message delay.

If the 'typical' message delay σ_i incurred by the node i is such that $\sigma_i \ll \Sigma$ (i.e. the message delay is of second order significance compared to the synchronization cycle) then the correction may be applied as a whole. Otherwise, the correction should be spread out over the synchronization cycle. The time of application is to be chosen from considerations of the significance of the correction to be made in relation to the tasks being executed by the process concerned. If the correction to be made by node i is C_i:

- $C_i > 0$ signifies a loss of C_i time units from the task being executed by the process at the time of correction.
- $C_i < 0$ signifies C_i excess time units spent on the task being executed by the process at the time of correction.

If such a loss of time or excess time is undesirable from the point of view of the application, it may be advisable to apply the correction over a single idling period (one-shot application), or spread the correction gradually over several of them during the synchronization cycle (spread-out application). Note that both these forms violate the properties of monotonicity and uniformity of the clock. A reasonable compromise would be the one-shot application over the synchronization period so that the two properties continue to hold over the clock synchronization cycle.

Alternatively, it may be the case that the precedence constraints among tasks are of greater importance. In this case it is more appropriate to give priority to the maintenance of monotonicity of clocks over uniformity, either by slowing down or by speeding up the clock ticking.

16.6　Computation of Correction

16.6.1　Synchronization Function and Data

In order to ensure correct synchronization of clocks, the nodes must observe the following:

- All nodes must apply the same synchronization function, or at least 'equivalent' functions, for computing the correction.
- The above function must be applied to the same set of data, that is, the clock values (or their differences). This concerns the consistency of the synchronization data.

The first in the above list presents no difficulty, except in relation to timing constraints. However, ensuring the second, that is, ensuring the 'consensus' of all nodes with respect to the data held by them, is extremely difficult if not impossible, especially in the case of loosely coupled systems. It is in this respect that synchronization is regarded as a difficult computational task. This aspect of data is dealt with in greater detail later in the context of certain common system configurations.

16.6.2　Synchronization function

The following illustrates a well-known synchronization function applicable to a set of clock values established by message exchanges. Let the system consist of n_T clocks, with n of them being selected as a preferred subset from the point of view of improving synchronization.

Notations used:

For all clock indices $i, j \in 1 \ldots n$ (see Figure 16.3),

X_j	–	an array of elements x_{ij} denoting the time of arrival of i's message at j in j's metric of time prior to correction.
D_{ij}	–	true clock delay of ith node with respect to jth node.
$d_{e_{ij}}$	–	estimated delivery time of i's message at j.
ϵ_{ij}	–	j's reading delay of i's message relative to $d_{e_{ij}}$. The actual delivery time is thus given by $d_{e_{ij}} + \epsilon_{ij}$.

Assumptions:

1. All x_{ij} as perceived by different nodes are mutually consistent.
2. All messages are time-stamped by the sender just before sending. Note that x_{ii} is measured in i's metric.

Using the above notation and assumptions, each x_{ij} may be represented in terms of constituent terms as

$$x_{ij} = \begin{cases} x_{ii} + D_{ij} + d_{e_{ij}} + \epsilon_{ij}, & \text{if } i \neq j \\ x_{ii}, & \text{if } i = j \end{cases}$$

The above allows the computation of an array Y with terms

$$y_{ij} = \begin{cases} D_{ij} + \epsilon_{ij}, & \text{if } i \neq j \\ 0, & \text{if } i = j \end{cases}$$

where each y_{ij} represents j's view of its clock difference with i but includes j's own reading delay. Obviously, the y_{ij}s may be computed as

$$y_{ij} = x_{ij} - x_{ii} - d_{e_{ij}}$$

The correction may now be computed by averaging Y, if all clock differences are genuine. However, this may not be the case, since certain clocks may unexpectedly turn out be faulty.

In order to allow a maximum of m clocks to be faulty, the array Y may be sorted and then m readings may be left out at each end of the array before taking the average. Thus, j's correction may be computed as

$$C_j = -\frac{1}{n-2m} \sum_{i=m+1}^{n-m} \tilde{y}_{ij}$$

where the $\tilde{y}_{ij}$ are the elements of the sorted array $\tilde{Y}$ of Y.

The expression derived above for clock corrections may account for clock failures due to excessive drift. However, in extreme cases this may also result in the removal of $2m$ non-faulty clocks, particularly in the presence of malicious Byzantine failures; see Section 16.9.2.

16.6.3   Parameters Affecting Synchronization

The parameters affecting the clock difference following a synchronization include:

- the desired level of agreement in internal synchronization, D_{int};
- sample size, n;
- the number of faulty clocks assumed, m (note that this parameter concerns the sample quality);
- maximum reading error, ε (maximum difference between message delays);
- drift rate and synchronization cycle (taken into account through D_{int}).

It is possible to establish an upper bound Π on clock differences immediately after synchronization in the form

$$\Pi = \Pi_0(D_{int}, n, m) + \epsilon$$

where $\Pi_0(...)$ essentially accounts for the faulty clocks. Although, as mentioned above, C_j has already made an allowance for drift failures, it does not account for other failures such as the loss of messages and Byzantine failures. If such failures exist, a single faulty clock contributes at most

$$\frac{D_{int}}{n-2m}$$

Therefore, the total contribution due to m still remaining faulty clocks is

$$\Pi_0(D_{int}, n, m) = \frac{mD_{int}}{n-2m}$$

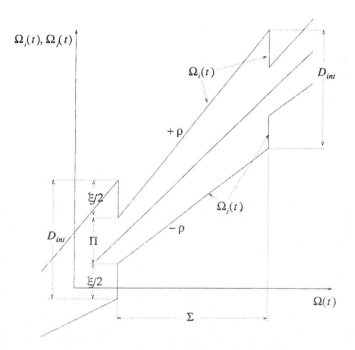

Figure 16.4 Extreme clock drifts

In order to avoid any two clocks reaching D_{int} within any synchronization cycle, the following must be ensured in the worst case at the time of synchronization; see Figure 16.4:

$$\Pi \leq D_{int} - \xi$$

where ξ represents the worst total clock deviation, possible only in the event of two clocks drifting apart from each other at the maximum rate ρ. That is,

$$\xi = 2 \rho \Sigma$$

The above relationships lead to

$$\frac{mD_{int}}{n-2m} + \epsilon \leq D_{int} - \xi$$

or

$$\frac{D_{int}}{\epsilon + \xi} \geq \frac{n-2m}{n-3m}$$

Finally, letting the right hand side of the above be denoted by $U(n, m)$, we arrive at

$$D_{int} \geq (\epsilon + \xi) U(n, m)$$

where

$\epsilon + \xi$ –   is the worst non fault-tolerant disagreement, and
$U(n, m) = \frac{n-2m}{n-3m}$ –   is the penalty for tolerating m faulty clocks. Note that $U(n, m) \geq 1$.

The above lower bound for D_{int} provides for a way to compute a suitable value for D_{int} for a specific clock system using:

- a representative (or worst case) clock drift rate ρ;
- a desired clock synchronization cycle Σ;
- an acceptable reading error ϵ; and
- a maximum allowance of m faulty clocks among a total of n clocks.

A similar analysis of penalty factors may be made in the case of other synchronization functions.

16.7   Clocks in Distributed Systems

Clocks in distributed systems fall into three major categories outlined below:

1. Central Clock Systems

    In these systems a central clock maintains the time for the whole system and the processors read its value directly, usually via special channels. Such clock systems are expensive in terms of hardware, but cheap in terms of communication costs. Fault tolerance is provided by standby clocks.

    The computations involved are straight forward and, therefore, these systems are not dealt with here further.

2. Centrally Controlled Clock Systems

These are master–slave configurations where a single clock (the master) is designated for computing the correction for all clocks in the system. The master first obtains the values of the subordinate (slave) and own clocks, computes the correction and then tells them the correction to be made. The slave clocks implement the corresponding corrections according to a prescribed discipline (one-shot or spread out).

3. Distributed Clock Systems

Clocks located at the site of each processor are autonomous and are responsible for the complete task of synchronization. A common time base is maintained by exchanging messages containing clock values. This form of establishing common network time is costly in terms of communications. Fault tolerance is dealt with by communication protocols and algorithms.

16.8   Centrally Controlled Clocks

A typical configuration for a centrally controlled clock system would be a set of processors communicating via a local area network, each with its own clock. One of these clocks acts as the master clock with the responsibility for maintaining the network time.

16.8.1   Algorithm of Synchronization

At the beginning of each synchronization period, the master clock exchanges time-stamped messages with slave clocks, each message containing the times of its dispatch and delivery as applicable. Using the information in these messages, the master then computes a mean network time. For fault tolerance, the computation may exclude, for example, all known faulty clocks (i.e. those with excessive drift rates) and clock values outside a prescribed deviation (which may again be dependent on drift rates). The master also computes the clock differences for all clocks, including self and the faulty clocks. The master clock then instructs all clocks to apply the computed difference as a correction. The slave clocks obey the instruction according to a predefined discipline. For example, as mentioned in Section 16.5, this may involve slowing down or speeding up the clock ticking.

Changes to the system configuration may be accommodated easily. Newly joining processors obtain the network time from the master clock prior to any processing. In the event of failure of the processor hosting the master clock, or network partition, a new master is elected.

The computations are based on clock differences, and this eliminates the dependence of synchronization on transmission delays associated with the instruction delivery. On the other hand, a disadvantage of master–slave configurations is that fault tolerance measures exclude the possibility of faults with the master clock.

16.8.2   Notations and Definitions

Let us present the notations and definitions applicable to our discussion on centralized clock systems.

S –   The set of indices identifying distinctly each and every clock in the system.

Q –   A non-empty subset of the above identifying all non-faulty clocks.

A –   The index of master clock; $A \in Q$.

$B, C, \cdots$ –   Clock indices (mainly used for slave clocks);
$$B, C, \cdots \in S$$

D_{AB} –   True clock difference between A and B, that is,
$$D_{AB} = \Omega_A(t) - \Omega_B(t) .$$
Note that $D_{AB} > 0$ signifies a delay of B with respect to A or, in other words, that A is ahead of B.

d_{AB} –   Apparent clock delay of B with respect to A, derived directly from the exchanged clock values.

E_{AB} –   Apparent clock delay based on the round trip, but otherwise as above.

E, D –   System-wide averages of E_{AB}s and D_{AB}s, respectively, over non-faulty clocks. For example,
$$E = \tfrac{1}{\#Q} \sum_{B \in Q} E_{AB}$$

T_{AB} –   Propagation time of a time-stamped message from A to B (includes transmission and delivery).
Note the superscripts '*max*' and '*min*' denote the possible maximum and minimum values.

T_{AB}^{R} –   A bound on propagation time for a round trip from A to itself via B. By definition,
$$T_{AB}^{R} \geq 2max(T_{AB}^{min}, T_{BA}^{min})$$

ε –   A bound on the deviation of clock agreement.
By definition,
$$\varepsilon = \frac{T_{AB}^{R} - 2 \times min(T_{AB}^{min}, T_{BA}^{min})}{2}$$
and,
$$\varepsilon \geq 0$$

C_B –   The correction to be applied on B (applicable also to master).

t_1, t_2, t_3 –   External reference times, respectively, of dispatching a time-stamped message by A, its receipt and response by a slave clock, and the receipt of slave clock's reply by A.

16.8.3 Other Preliminaries

Immediate Observations:

(i) $D_{AB} = -D_{BA}$ –   This signifies the reciprocity of true clock differences.
(ii) $T_{AB} \neq T_{BA}$ –   This is true in general due to asymmetry of the network architecture and interrupt mechanisms.

Assumptions:

1. $d_{AB} = -d_{BA}$
2. Slave clocks attend to the master clock's request immediately with no other intervening tasks. However, this is not an absolutely necessary condition.

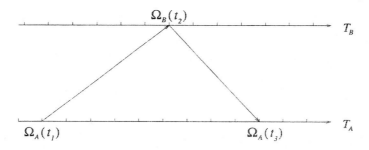

Figure 16.5 Exchange of clock values between master and slave

16.8.4 Accuracy of Clock Agreement

On the basis of the preliminaries introduced so far, it is possible to establish a number of observations theoretically. These express relationships involving parameters of the system configurations and, therefore, give certain means for achieving the desired level of clock agreement.

Observation 16.1

$$| E_{AB} - D_{AB} | \leq \varepsilon$$

Proof:

The master clock's apparent delay with respect to B is

$$d_{BA} = \Omega_B(t_2) - \Omega_A(t_1) = D_{BA} + T_{AB}$$

see Figure 16.5, while B's apparent delay with respect to the master clock is

$$d_{AB} = \Omega_A(t_3) - \Omega_B(t_2) = D_{AB} + T_{BA}$$

The above leads to the following round trip average of B's apparent delay with respect to the master clock:

$$E_{AB} = \frac{d_{AB}-d_{BA}}{2} = D_{AB} + \frac{T_{BA}-T_{AB}}{2}$$

Therefore,

$$E_{AB} - D_{AB} = \frac{T_{BA}-T_{AB}}{2}$$

Let us now examine the bounds on the above.

Case 1: $E_{AB} - D_{AB} \geq 0$

In this case,

$$2(E_{AB} - D_{AB}) \leq T_{BA}^{max} - T_{AB}^{min}$$
$$\leq T_{BA}^{R} - 2T_{AB}^{min} \leq 2\varepsilon$$

Case 2: $E_{AB} - D_{AB} \leq 0$

In this case,

$$2(E_{AB} - D_{AB}) \geq T_{BA}^{min} - T_{AB}^{max}$$
$$\geq -T_{BA}^{R} + 2T_{AB}^{min} \geq -2\varepsilon$$

The above case analysis constitutes the proof.

The significance of the observation lies in the fact that it is possible to achieve a tolerance level of $\pm\varepsilon$ in B's agreement with A by using E_{AB} for synchronization. Even greater reliance may be placed on this result by using several values of E_{AB} based on different computations.

Observation 16.2 For any two non-faulty clocks B and C,

$$| D_{BC} | \leq 4\varepsilon$$

immediately after synchronization.

Proof:

Consider the inequalities given below expressing the result in Observation 16.1 for an arbitrary clock $j \in Q$:

$$-\varepsilon \leq E_{Aj} - D_{Aj} \leq \varepsilon$$

Summation of these inequalities over all $j \in Q$ and averaging each term in the resulting inequality leads to

$$| E - D | \leq \varepsilon \qquad\qquad (i)$$

Furthermore, the correction applicable to any clock $j \in Q$ is

$$
\begin{aligned}
C_j &= E - E_{Aj} &\text{definition of } C_j \\
C_j + D_{Aj} - D &= E - D + D_{Aj} - E_{Aj} \\
&\leq | E - D | + | D_{Aj} - E_{Aj} | \\
&\leq 2\varepsilon &\text{Observation 16.1 and from (i)} \quad (ii)
\end{aligned}
$$

Let D_{AB} and D'_{AB}, etc., respectively, represent the clock differences immediately before and after synchronization. Then

$$
\begin{aligned}
D'_{BC} &= D'_{AC} - D'_{AB} \\
&= (C_C + D_{AC}) - (C_B + D_{AB}) \\
&= (C_C + D_{AC} - D) - (C_B + D_{AB} - D) \\
&\leq | (C_C + D_{AC} - D) | + | (C_B + D_{AB} - D) | \\
&\leq 2\varepsilon + 2\varepsilon = 4\varepsilon &\text{from (ii)}
\end{aligned}
$$

Hence, the proof.

A consequence of this observation is that all non-faulty clocks are within the limit $(4\varepsilon + 2\rho t)$ at any time t within any synchronization cycle. Its significance lies in the fact that it is possible to achieve, within the physical constraints of a given architecture, any desired accuracy by controlling ε, that is, by choosing the design parameters affecting the message propagation time.

16.9 Distributed Autonomous Clock Systems

It may be worth noting that the ideas discussed in this section are not restricted to clock synchronization, but belong also to techniques on fault tolerance (see Section 15.10.1 of Chapter 15) and, in particular, to the problem of establishing consensus among autonomous systems vulnerable to different kinds of failures.

This section discusses three separate algorithms. They have the following assumptions in common:

- Clocks are initially synchronized. In other words, let us treat initialization as a separate problem.
- Non-faulty clocks display the desired accuracy.

16.9.1   Configuration Features

Each node in the system has its own clock or, in the case of relatively large sites, a local internal clock system. The network is loosely coupled and, therefore, the knowledge about time at other remote sites may be acquired only by means of message passing. As a result, each node must attend to all aspects of synchronization independently and locally. In a well-designed system, synchronization should not be affected by failures at other sites and network failures or, at least, the extent to which failures prevent proper synchronization must be known in advance.

Heavy communication traffic imposed by the synchronization process is potentially a major problem in this type of clock system.

16.9.2   Consensus in Distributed Systems

Section 16.6.1 mentioned, in passing, the importance of consensus about clock values used in synchronization. Underlying this is a generic problem applicable to a multitude of different problems in computing, particularly in distributed systems. This is referred to as the *Byzantine generals' problem* [89].

The Byzantine generals' problem is set in a hypothetical historical context and concerns an army preparing for a battle. The generals in charge of the battle cannot communicate with one another directly. The technology at their disposal is modest and is limited to messengers. The problem is whether the generals can work out a sensible battle plan in the presence of potential betrayals, either on the part of one or more generals or the messengers involved.

Consider, for example, a scenario involving three generals and a betrayal involving only one of them. Suppose that the other two generals come to different conclusions. One of them concludes to 'attack' and the other to 'retreat' and, accordingly, they both inform each other as well as the third general of their independently reached decisions. The third, however, communicates conflicting information about his conclusion. He communicates to the first general 'attack' and to the second 'retreat'. As a result, the two perfectly 'loyal' generals see no reason to change their views, although the three together could have arrived at a mutually consistent decision had there not been a betrayal.

Sections 16.10–16.13 discuss three different approaches to establishing consensus in the context of clock synchronization.

16.10   Interactive Convergence Algorithm CNV

16.10.1   Description of Algorithm

The algorithm is called the *interactive convergence algorithm* because each synchronization brings about a convergence of non-faulty clocks. At the beginning of synchronization, each processor reads every other processor's clock reading and its own. If any clock value differs from its own by more than D_{int}, then the processor replaces the offending clock value with its own clock value. The processor then sets its clock to the average of the resulting array of clock values. The degree of convergence depends on a number of factors:

- proportion of faulty clocks;
- predominant mode of failure;
- extent of agreement prior to synchronization.

The types of clock failure tolerated are:

- Failure of a processor to receive/transmit messages, thus preventing the exchange of clock values.
- Failures of clocks in generating correct clock values.
- Sending conflicting clock values to different processors/sites. A typical failure of this form is 'multi-faced' clocks (clocks showing different clock values to its different users) caused usually by communication failures. Figure 16.6 illustrates a typical situation involving a 'two-faced' clock C, where the clocks A and B are unable to agree on a mutually consistent common time despite the fact that they themselves are not faulty.

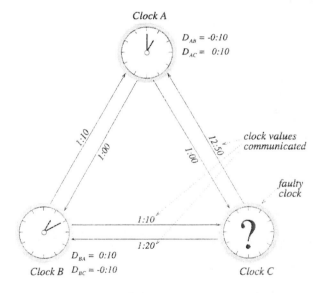

Figure 16.6 A clock failure preventing synchronization

16.10.2   Assumptions and Notations

The working of the algorithm may be shown relatively easily on the basis of a simplification, namely by ignoring read error completely and assuming that all processors execute the algorithm simultaneously and instantaneously.

The following is a summary of the notations being used.

n	–	The total number of clocks in the system (elsewhere in this chapter as well).
m	–	The number of faulty clocks, $m \leq n$ (elsewhere in this chapter as well).
$1, 2, \cdots, n$	–	Indices of arbitrary clocks.
$A, B, \cdots$	–	Indices of specific non-faulty clocks.
$\Omega_i(t),\ \Omega'_i(t)$	–	Reading of the non-faulty clock indexed by i immediately before and after synchronization, respectively, at external reference time t. [Note that, whenever there is no room for confusion, Ω_i is written instead of $\Omega_i(t)$ for brevity.]
$\Omega_i^A(t),\ \Omega_i^B(t)$	–	Reading of the faulty clock indexed by i as read by clocks A and B, respectively, at external reference time t.
Ω_{av}	–	The average of non-faulty clock values.

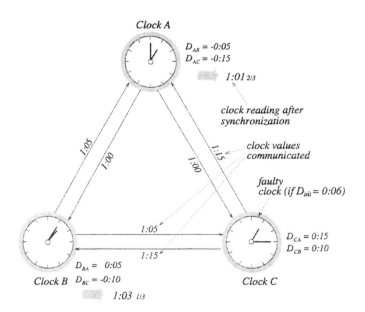

Figure 16.7 Synchronization under drift failure ($D_{int} = 0{:}06$)

16.10.3   Clock Agreement

In understanding the effectiveness of the algorithm let us examine two extreme forms of malfunctioning of faulty clocks.

Extreme Fault Form 1: Drift Failure of Clocks

Let us assume here that all faulty clocks show incorrect readings, that is, for all clock indices i such that $(n - m) < i \leq n$ the following hold:

$$| \Omega_i^A(t) - \Omega_A(t) | > D_{int}$$
$$| \Omega_i^B(t) - \Omega_B(t) | > D_{int}$$

The table below shows the clock values being used by the clocks A and B depending on the fault status of the clock concerned.

Originator		Actual value as read by		Value used by	
Index	Fault status	A	B	A	B
1	non-faulty	Ω_1	Ω_1	Ω_1	Ω_1
⋮	⋮	⋮	⋮	⋮	⋮
B	non-faulty	Ω_B	Ω_B	Ω_B	Ω_B
⋮	⋮	⋮	⋮	⋮	⋮
A	non-faulty	Ω_A	Ω_A	Ω_A	Ω_A
⋮	⋮	⋮	⋮	⋮	⋮
$n - m$	non-faulty	Ω_{n-m}	Ω_{n-m}	Ω_{n-m}	Ω_{n-m}
$n - m + 1$	faulty	Ω_{n-m+1}^A	Ω_{n-m+1}^B	Ω_A	Ω_B
⋮	⋮	⋮	⋮	⋮	⋮
n	faulty	Ω_n^A	Ω_n^B	Ω_A	Ω_B

Assuming here that the clock readings of A and B after synchronization are the averages of the values that have been read by them, or adopted in the case of values communicated by faulty clocks, the following may be obtained:

$$\Omega'_A = \frac{m\Omega_A + (n-m)\Omega_{av}}{n}$$
$$\Omega'_B = \frac{m\Omega_B + (n-m)\Omega_{av}}{n}$$

where Ω'_A, for example, denotes the value of $\Omega_A(t)$ soon after synchronization at time t. The above leads to

$$| \Omega'_A - \Omega'_B | = \frac{m}{n} | \Omega_A - \Omega_B | \leq \frac{m}{n} D_{int}$$

That is, clock readings of A and B converge towards each other provided that $m < n$.

Extreme Fault Form 2: Presence of 'Multi-Faced' Clocks

Let us assume here that all faulty clocks are 'multi-faced' and that the values communicated by them to either A or B do not compensate for one another's inconsistencies. In other words, the clock values received by either A or B from faulty clocks show a consistent bias towards either low values or high values but within the agreement tolerance D_{int}. Thus, one of the two conditions:

(i) $\Omega_i^A(t) < \Omega_i^B(t)$
(ii) $\Omega_i^A(t) > \Omega_i^B(t)$

must be true of all clock indices i in the range $(n - m) < i \le n$, and the other condition false. Considering the worst case of one of these two possible scenarios, let the readings of the faulty clocks as perceived by A and B be

$$\Omega_i^A(t) = \Omega_A(t) + D_{int} ,$$
$$\Omega_i^B(t) = \Omega_B(t) - D_{int} ,$$

for all clock indices $i \in (n - m) .. n$.

In this particular case, clock values of the faulty clocks as perceived by A and B being within the required tolerance, the clocks A and B do not substitute their own clock values for those of the faulty clocks. The table below shows the clock values being used by the clocks A and B depending on the fault status of each clock.

Originator		Actual value as read by		Value used by	
Index	Fault status	A	B	A	B
1	non-faulty	Ω_1	Ω_1	Ω_1	Ω_1
$\vdots$	$\vdots$	$\vdots$	$\vdots$	$\vdots$	$\vdots$
B	non-faulty	Ω_B	Ω_B	Ω_B	Ω_B
$\vdots$	$\vdots$	$\vdots$	$\vdots$	$\vdots$	$\vdots$
A	non-faulty	Ω_A	Ω_A	Ω_A	Ω_A
$\vdots$	$\vdots$	$\vdots$	$\vdots$	$\vdots$	$\vdots$
$n - m$	non-faulty	Ω_{n-m}	Ω_{n-m}	Ω_{n-m}	Ω_{n-m}
$n - m + 1$	faulty	Ω_{n-m+1}^A	Ω_{n-m+1}^B	$\Omega_A + D_{int}$	$\Omega_B - D_{int}$
$\vdots$	$\vdots$	$\vdots$	$\vdots$	$\vdots$	$\vdots$
n	faulty	Ω_n^A	Ω_n^B	$\Omega_A + D_{int}$	$\Omega_B - D_{int}$

Analogous to the previous case, the clock values after the synchronization may be found as the mean values,

$$\Omega'_A = \frac{m(\Omega_A + D_{int}) + (n-m)\Omega_{av}}{n}$$

$$\Omega'_B = \frac{m(\Omega_B - D_{int}) + (n-m)\Omega_{av}}{n}$$

which leads to

$$\Omega'_A - \Omega'_B = \frac{m}{n}(\Omega_A - \Omega_B + 2D_{int})$$

Therefore,

$$|\Omega'_A - \Omega'_B| \leq \frac{3m}{n} D_{int}$$

That is, clock values of A and B converge towards each other provided that $3m < n$.

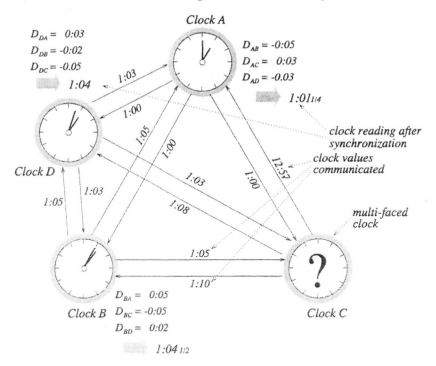

Figure 16.8 Synchronization in the presence of multi-faced clocks ($D_{int} = 0{:}06$)

On the basis of the above two extreme forms of failure of faulty clocks, it may thus be concluded that the actual convergence of the clock values of any two clocks A and B is bounded by two possible extremes:

$$| \Omega'_A - \Omega'_B | \leq \frac{m}{n} D_{int}$$

$$| \Omega'_A - \Omega'_B | \leq \frac{3m}{n} D_{int}$$

but subject to the margins of error due to our simplifications. The variation of the upper bound on clock differences between these two extreme fault forms is linear; see Figure 16.9. If a fraction α of clock failures is due to multi-faced clocks and the rest is purely due to drift failures, then the actual clock differences are bounded by

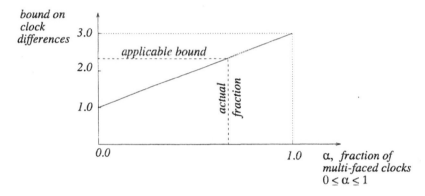

Figure 16.9 The effect of failure mode on synchronization accuracy by CNV

$$| \Omega'_A - \Omega'_B | \leq \frac{(1+2\alpha)m}{n} D_{int}$$

where α is a rational number in the range $0 \leq \alpha \leq 1$. Therefore, real applications may exhibit a bias towards either the lower or the greater bound due to the prevalent mode of failure among the faulty clocks.

16.11 Interactive Consistency Algorithms

The synchronization functions introduced so far are based on averaging clock values, but with modifications for ensuring fault tolerance. However, are there alternatives to averaging? For example, are the following acceptable?

- The choice of the median (that is, the middle element of the sorted array of clock values)

  This is especially suitable in situations where the histogram of observations is skewed due to the presence of a minority of particularly 'bad' values.

- The choice of the largest value.

- The choice of the message which has travelled fastest.

All the above are acceptable choices. The right choice would depend on the particular predominant form of failure addressed by the fault tolerant design. Synchronization functions based on such ideas are likely to return approximately the same value for different processors, provided that:

(i) All non-faulty clocks <u>obtain</u> approximately the <u>same</u> value for every clock, including the faulty ones.

   This is effectively a condition on the extent of differences between values communicated by different clocks, as in the case of 'multi-faced' clocks.

(ii) All non-faulty clocks obtain approximately the <u>correct</u> value for every non-faulty clock.

   The choice of one such value automatically ensures the correctness of synchronization. This is a condition on non-faulty 'correct' clocks. The two conditions exclude the failure of the network.

The two conditions are very close to the assumptions made in the Byzantine generals' problems, referred to in Section 16.9.2 of this chapter and in Section 15.10.3 of Chapter 15, on how to establish consensus among a number of distributed processors with inconsistencies in information held by them. These assumptions are:

(i) All non-faulty processors obtain the same message (value) from every other processor.

(ii) If processor r is non-faulty, then every non-faulty processor obtains the message (value) that r sends.

The algorithm about to be discussed and that discussed in Section 16.13 are based on these general assumptions, but on different synchronization functions.

16.12   Interactive Consistency Algorithm COM

On similar grounds to those in the Byzantine generals' problem, the algorithm works for $n > 3m$ only, m and n being, respectively, the number of faulty clocks and the total number of clocks. The algorithm may be described as follows:

Begin Algorithm *COM*

Step 1. Every processor sends its clock value to every other processor. Every processor also uses its own clock value.

Step 2. Every processor relays to others the messages it receives.

Step 3. Every recipient of a message establishes the clock value sent by the originator by picking the median of the copies it received.

Step 4. Repeat Step 3 for messages from all processors.

End Algorithm *COM*

This may be seen as a recursive algorithm, requiring $(m + 1)$ rounds of message exchanges in order to tolerate m faults. Termination is bounded by the number of clocks involved.

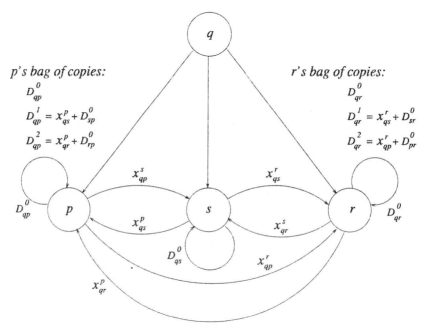

p's bag of copies:

$$D_{qp}^0$$
$$D_{qp}^1 = x_{qs}^p + D_{sp}^0$$
$$D_{qp}^2 = x_{qr}^p + D_{rp}^0$$

r's bag of copies:

$$D_{qr}^0$$
$$D_{qr}^1 = x_{qs}^r + D_{sr}^0$$
$$D_{qr}^2 = x_{qp}^r + D_{pr}^0$$

Figure 16.10 Exchange of clock values in COM

16.12.1   Notations

The following is a summary of the notations being used (see Figure 16.10).

ϵ	–	An error tolerance limit.
ϵ_i	–	An error term of the same order of magnitude as ϵ (subscripts for distinguishing between different terms).
D_{ij}^l	–	j's lth copy of j's supposed delay with respect to i. A positive value corresponds to i being ahead of j.

Note that j may compute these values knowing third party information, say k's, as follows:

$$D_{ij}^l = D_{ik}^m + D_{kj}^n$$

for some m, n. Since these values are assumed reliable, j may further infer that,

$$D_{ij}^l = D_{ij}^0 \pm \epsilon_i$$

where D_{ij}^0 is the first value j obtained directly from i.

x_{ik}^j —   The value communicated by k to j as k's supposed delay with respect to i. Note that a positive value signifies that i is ahead of k.

$\perp$ —   The symbol used herein for suspicious values. The only law in our 'algebra of suspicious values' is

$$\perp + a = \perp$$

where a represents a numerical quantity, or $a = \perp$.

16.12.2   Clock Agreement

It follows from the above definitions that, for any given l,

$$D_{ij}^l = x_{ik}^j + D_{kj}^0$$

for some k. Our reasoning about the above, and not its actual algorithmic processing, depends on the nature of x_{ik}^j:

$$x_{ik}^j = \begin{cases} D_{ik}^l \pm \epsilon_i, & \text{for some } l \text{ provided that } k \text{ is non-faulty,} \\ \perp, & \text{otherwise.} \end{cases}$$

That is, x_{ik}^j represents a genuine (lth) copy of delay D_{ik}, provided that k is not faulty. It may also be noted that, for some ϵ_i,

$$D_{ij}^0 + D_{jk}^0 = D_{ik}^0 \pm \epsilon_i$$

In order to appreciate the underlying reasoning behind this algorithm, let us consider four processors p, q, r and s, with at most one faulty clock among them. Notice in this case that $n = 4$ and $m \le 1$ and, therefore, $n > 3m$.

Let us single out one of them, for example q, and examine how q's clock value (or clock difference) is relayed under two different situations:

<u>*Case A*</u>: q is not faulty; see Figure 16.11.

Let another processor, say s (a relaying processor), be the faulty one, and let us examine the form of different views p and r may have about q's clock values.

Case A   Case B

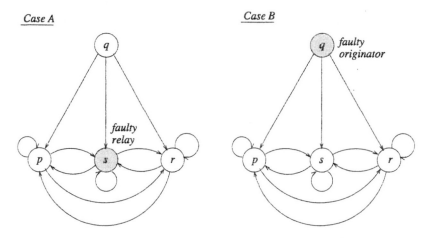

Figure 16.11 Faulty relay (Case A) and faulty originator (Case B)

Mathematically speaking, each such view of clock values is a *multi-set* or a *bag*. This is because certain clock values may repeat themselves in any given view. Thus, p's view about q's clock values is the bag of clock values

$$[\![D^0_{qp},\ D^1_{qp},\ D^2_{qp}]\!] \ =\ [\![D^0_{qp},\ x^p_{qr} + D^0_{rp},\ x^p_{qs} + D^0_{sp}]\!]$$
$$=\ [\![D^0_{qp},\ D^0_{qr} + D^0_{rp},\ \bot + D^0_{sp}]\!]$$
$$=\ [\![D^0_{qp},\ D^0_{qp} \pm \epsilon_1,\ \bot\,]\!]$$

It is clear from the above that there are at least two reasonable (reliable) clock values among the three which p would be able to establish from the exchanged values. Therefore, the median among them must correspond to the delay of a non-faulty clock. By picking the median clock value among them, p is bound to make a right choice as to its delay with q.

Similarly, r's view of q's values is a bag of clock values of the form

$$[\![D^0_{qr},\ D^1_{qr},\ D^2_{qr}]\!] \ =\ [\![D^0_{qr},\ x^r_{qp} + D^0_{pr},\ x^r_{qs} + D^0_{sr}]\!]$$
$$=\ [\![D^0_{qr},\ D^0_{qr} \pm \epsilon_2,\ \bot\,]\!]$$

By a similar argument as that given above, it may be concluded that the median value that r would pick among its values would be an acceptable value. Thus, both p and r each have at least two consistent values about q's clock value and, as a result, are able to arrive at a consensus about q's clock reading, irrespective of what s communicates to p and r about q.

Case B: q (the originator) is faulty; see Figure 16.11.

In this case, the other three processors are non-faulty. And, p's view of q's clock values is,

$$[\![D^0_{qp}, D^1_{qp}, D^2_{qp}]\!] = [\![D^0_{qp}, x^p_{qr} + D^0_{rp}, x^p_{qs} + D^0_{sp}]\!]$$
$$= [\![D^0_{qp}, D^0_{qr} + D^0_{rp}, D^0_{qs} + D^0_{sp}]\!]$$
$$= [\![D^0_{qp}, D^0_{qp} \pm \epsilon_3, D^0_{qp} \pm \epsilon_4]\!]$$

Similarly, r's view of q's values is

$$[\![D^0_{qr}, D^1_{qr}, D^2_{qr}]\!] = [\![D^0_{qr}, D^0_{qp} + D^0_{pr}, D^0_{qs} + D^0_{sr}]\!]$$
$$= [\![D^0_{qr}, D^0_{qr} \pm \epsilon_5, D^0_{qr} \pm \epsilon_6]\!]$$

Likewise, s's view of q's values is

$$[\![D^0_{qs}, D^1_{qs}, D^2_{qs}]\!] = [\![D^0_{qs}, D^0_{qp} + D^0_{ps}, D^0_{qr} + D^0_{rs}]\!]$$
$$= [\![D^0_{qs}, D^0_{qs} \pm \epsilon_7, D^0_{qs} \pm \epsilon_8]\!]$$

In this case, although q is faulty, the other three processors thus have a consistent view about q's clock value to the accuracy of a certain ϵ. Needless to say, the clocks p, r and s do not face any difficulty in establishing one another's readings.

It should be noted that the two cases just considered obey the conditions on 'two-sidedness' and 'correctness'. In either case, picking the median clock value leads to 'correct' synchronization.

The argument behind the two cases given above can be extended to any number of clocks and would enable every non-faulty clock to establish an array of consistent clock delays with respect to other clocks, provided that $n > 3m$. This array of clock values may then be used as the data for an appropriate synchronization function.

16.13   Interactive Consistency Algorithm CSM

What is distinctive about the algorithm CSM is the use of signed messages and their authentication before computations are performed. The reason for adopting this approach is that it allows the recipient clocks to rely on the messages content if they detect no tampering.

16.13.1   Message Corruption

In the absence of measures proposed as part of this algorithm, potential forms of undesirable, but perfectly possible, forms of interference with messages are:

(i)   interference with the list of signatories;
(ii) direct interference with the message content;
(iii) indirect interference with the message content;
      this may be due to malicious or unavoidable propagation (including trans-
      mission) delays.

One may combat the above by taking a number of measures. What is advocated in the case of (i) is the use of digital signatures as used in cryptography. This technology allows:

- validation of the message by the recipient;
- unique signature generation and, thus, the elimination of forgery;
- third party authentication.

The form of interference (ii) may be prevented by imposing copyright and restricting modifications only to add new signatures at the end. The form of interference under (iii) is not preventable. It could be a consequence of reading errors or malicious failures, requiring the provision of some fault tolerance measures.

16.13.2   The Preliminaries

Notations and Definitions:

The following is a summary of the notations being used:

ε	–	Maximum reading error.
δ	–	Maximum true difference between clocks.
D_{qp}	–	Clock difference between p and q as obtained by p.

By definition, D_{qp} corresponds to the following. Let the clock (representation) value, as read by q at an external reference time t_1, be T_0, that is,

$$\Omega_q(t_1) = T_0$$

D_{qp} is established by p using q's clock value at an external reference time t_2 such that $t_2 > t_1$ and $t_2 - t_1 < \epsilon$ as

$$\Omega_p(t_2) = T_0 + D_{qp}$$

$\overline{D}_{qp}$	–	Clock difference as above but with the provision of a special 'NULL' value.
γ	–	'Normal' or average message propagation delay; may include message generation.

Notation of Messages:
A signed message is a pair

$$(T, s)$$

Here s is a sequence of counter-signed processor identifiers and T is the message 'dispatch' time by its initiator, i.e. the first signatory as found in $s(1)$. Given a processor p, let $signature(p)$ denote its unique signature.

Assumptions:

(a) On Message Transmission

(i) A message dispatched at t_0 by a non-faulty processor arrives at time t_1 at its non-faulty destination within $\gamma \pm \epsilon$ time units, that is,

$$| t_1 - t_0 - \gamma | < \epsilon$$

(ii) A message from a faulty processor arrives at t_1 at its destination $(\gamma - \epsilon)$ time units after its dispatch:

$$t_1 - t_0 > \gamma - \epsilon$$

That is, faulty processors may only cause delays.

(b) On Message Transmission Time

(iii) The message propagation delays are insignificant compared to the synchronization cycle, that is, $\gamma \ll \Sigma$.

(iv) Usually, $\epsilon \leq \gamma$.

(v) As a simplification γ is assumed to be constant.

Note that γ depends on a number of factors, among them, on transmission lines, processors involved, message length, etc. This assumption does not affect the generality.

(vi) Clock drift during the maximum possible relay time (potentially over n processors) is much smaller than the message delay, that is,

$$n \, \gamma \, \rho \ll \epsilon$$

16.13.3   Description of Algorithm

Preamble Algorithm *CSM*

The algorithm is executed once during the synchronization period. t, t_1 and t_2 are variables ranging over this period such that $t < t_1 < t_2$.

Step 1. Each processor q initializes the vector $[\overline{D}_{qp}]$ setting each clock difference $\overline{D}_{qp}$ with respect to each p to ∞.

Step 2. Each processor p dispatches at time t a message

$$(\Omega_p(t), \langle (p, signature(p)) \rangle)$$

to every other process. Strictly speaking, $t \in \Omega^{-1}(\{T_p\})$, T_p being an agreed local time for synchronization. A more specific solution is $t = \omega^{-1}(T_p)$, where ω is the clock tick time function; see Section 2.4 in Chapter 2.

Step 3. Each processor q, upon receiving a message in the above at t_1, or one of its relays from a third party in the form,

$$(T, s)$$

with p being the originator and $q \neq p$, first checks whether the message is authentic, and if so it sets $\overline{D}_{qp}$ to the minimum given by

$$min \ (\overline{D}_{qp}, \ (\Omega_q(t_1) - T - \#s \times \gamma))$$

and sends the message

$$(T, s \frown \langle (q, signature(q)) \rangle)$$

to all other non signatories r of the message ($r \notin$ ran s), if $\#s < m$.

Step 4. At time t_2, where

$$t_2 = t + (m + 1)(\gamma + \delta + \epsilon) \ ,$$

all processors finalize the vector $[\overline{D}_{qp}]$ by setting all elements with values of ∞ to 'NULL'. The resulting vector of each processor contains its view of clock differences with others.

The comment made in (ii) with respect to t applies also to t_2. That is, $t_2 = \omega^{-1}(T + (m + 1)(\gamma + \delta + \epsilon))$.

End of algorithm *CSM*

The following observations may be made with respect to this algorithm.

- The vector that each processor establishes by the above algorithm forms the data for an appropriate synchronization function.
- q's view of p's clock value is established using the message travelling fastest in q's pile of messages.
- Faulty processors cannot change the clock values in messages, sign on behalf of others or reduce the apparent clock difference by more than ϵ. These failures are detectable in the message, thanks to the technology being used.
- Delay failures are handled by timeouts.
- Error in CSM is of the order $m \times \epsilon$.

EXAMPLE

Consider the collection of clocks shown in Figure 16.12. Let γ be $0:03$ time units and let us ignore the contribution to the reading error due to other factors. Consider the attempt by H to establish its clock difference with the clock A. At different times H receives messages from A about its clock reading, but relayed to H via different routes. By examining them, H can establish an approximation to its clock difference with A in the manner given below:

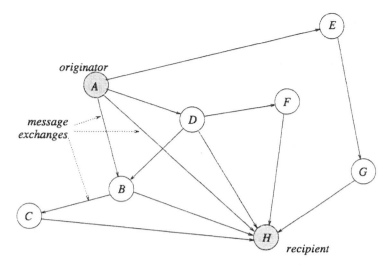

Figure 16.12 Message exchanges in algorithm CSM

Time of receipt by H	Received via	Message	D_{HA}	Authenticity
1:05	A	$(1:00,\langle A\rangle)$	0:02	
1:06	A, B	$(1:00,\langle A, B\rangle)$	0:00	
1:07	A, D, F	$(1:00,\langle A, B, F\rangle)$	-0:02	violated
1:08	A, E, G	$(1:00,\langle A, E, G\rangle)$	-0:01	
1:09	A, D	$(1:00,\langle A, D\rangle)$	0:03	
1:10	A, B, C	$(1:02,\langle A, B, C\rangle)$	-0:01	violated
clock difference of H with A as estimated by H			-0:01	

16.14 General Notes on the Algorithms

This is a brief comparison of the algorithms CNV, COM and CSM used for the synchronization of distributed systems consisting of autonomous clocks. These were discussed in Sections 16.10, 16.12 and 16.13 respectively.

1. The criteria for judging the suitability of the algorithms for any particular environment may include:

   - accuracy;
   - number of message exchanges required;
   - number of message generations required;
   - degree of fault tolerance achievable with each additional allowance made towards the possible number of faulty clocks.

Note that a reduction in the extent of message generation may be achieved at the expense of higher message exchanges and vice versa. However, each additional round of message exchanges contributes a further error of the order ε.

2. The interactive convergence algorithm CNV requires the least number of message exchanges. Interactive consistency algorithms COM and CSM require $(m + 1)$ rounds of message exchanges in order to handle m faults, a figure which makes COM, and CSM superior to other known algorithms based on the Byzantine generals' solutions.

3. COM generates about n^{m+1} messages and CSM a similar number. These can be reduced by eliminating redundant messages, that is, those containing approximately the same clock difference or clock differences corresponding to clock readings delivered faster than others.

4. On the assumption that the clock drift during the synchronization period is much smaller compared to the maximum reading error ε in obtaining clock differences, the maximum true difference between any pair of clocks $\tilde{\delta}$ is shown to be

$$
\begin{aligned}
\tilde{\delta} &= (6m + 2)\varepsilon + (3m + 1)\rho\Sigma & \text{for CNV} \\
\tilde{\delta} &= (6m + 4)\varepsilon + \rho\Sigma & \text{for COM} \\
\tilde{\delta} &= (m + 6)\varepsilon + \rho\Sigma & \text{for CSM}
\end{aligned}
$$

Note that, since ε depends on how clocks are being read, ε in CSM is incomparable with that in CNV and COM, both of which employ the same method of clock reading. Therefore, any comparison of CSM with the other two algorithms using the above formulae must take into account the difference in ε.

5. With the knowledge of ε applicable to each algorithm, one may use the above formulae for selecting the design parameters of any clock system:

   • the desired quality of clocks as represented by ρ;

   • the frequency of synchronization as represented by Σ;

   • the desired clock agreement as represented by $\tilde{\delta}$;

   • the acceptable level of faults as represented by the ratio $m : n$;

   as appropriate to the application.

6. The greatest strength of CSM is its superiority in terms of fault tolerance that is, $n > m$, whereas it is $n > 3m$ for CNV and COM.

7. CNV and COM are based on purely algorithmic strategies for achieving faul tolerance. CSM is technology based, especially on the reliable implementa tion of digital signatures and authentication in cryptography.

16.15 Bibliographical Notes

The basic issues related to clock synchronization may be found in [80, 81, 86, 153]. The algorithms presented in this chapter are due to Kopetz and Ochsenreiter [81], Gusella and Zatti [51] and Lamport and Melliar-Smith [88]. The latter caters for various forms of 'faults' in clocks. Some of these faults may be due to physical failures and such factors as radiation (see Rushby *et al.* [115, 139]); others may be attributed to other factors such as communication failures and network traffic (see Roberts [136]). Because of the heavy overhead on system performance imposed by software based fault tolerant algorithms such as those due to Lamport and Melliar-Smith [88], Kopetz and Ochsenreiter [81] and Shin and Ramanathan [148] propose hardware based solutions. Clock synchronization has received considerable attention in the scientific literature, including Dolev *et al.* [39] and Lamport *et al.* [87, 89, 118].

16.16 Exercises

1. The rows of the following table represent clock values obtained by clocks D and G from nodal clocks $A, B, \cdots, L$ in a distributed system. Assume that the clock values have already been adjusted in order to take discrepancies due to reading delays and other factors into account.

Recipient	Clock readings (in hours:minutes) of					
	A	B	C	D	E	F
D	12:01	12:04	12:00	11:58	11:59	12:00
G	12:01	12:04	12:00	11:58	11:59	12:02
(contd.)	G	H	I	J	K	L
D	12:00	12:01	11:54	11:59	11:54	12:02
G	12:00	12:01	11.54	11:59	12:03	12:02

Identify the nature of the faults, if any, as evident from the clock data. Assuming the maximum permissible deviation D_{int} between any two clocks to be 3 minutes, compute the new clock values of D and G after synchronization to the nearest minute.

Assuming the pattern of faulty clocks remains unchanged, that is, any 'multi-faced' clock remains multi-faced and any clock with excessive drift continues to show the same, compute the maximum possible difference between clock values of D and G.

2. Consider the synchronization of a system of seven clocks: A, B, C, D, E, F and G. The table below presents the clock differences that clock A has been able to establish from message exchanges at the end of the synchronization period.

Recipient	Clock difference originally communicated by:						
	A	B	C	D	E	F	G
A	0	-2	4	30	-5	-6	6
Relaying clock	Relayed clock difference with respect to:						
	A	B	C	D	E	F	G
B	2	–	2	28	4	3	-4
C	-4	-6	–	20	4	3	2
D	-30	2	6	–	3	0	1
E	5	6	1	25	–	3	-2
F	16	23	-30	24	-12	–	22
G	-6	-4	-3	18	-4	-2	–

The row against A represents the clock differences that A has established using clock values it obtained directly from all clocks, including itself. Other rows represent clock differences between pairs of clocks as relayed to A by other clocks. For example, the row against E shows the values E has relayed to A as E's delay with respect to other clocks. A positive value x_{ij} signifies that clock i is ahead of clock j, i and j being, respectively, the labels of the corresponding <u>column</u> and <u>row</u> in the table. Hyphens denote nil entries.

Identify the nature of the faults, if any, as evident from the clock data. Compute first the estimates of the clock delays that A is able to adduce from the data and, hence, the clock differences A should choose from among them for the purpose of clock synchronization. Determine by how much A advances or delays its reading.

3. During the clock synchronization period, the clocks $A, B, \cdots, M$ in a fully interconnected distributed system establish the readings of other clocks by exchanging messages. The authenticity of a message is guaranteed by the inclusion within it of the unique digital signatures of the originating node and of any nodes that forward it. Assume a uniform propagation delay of 0.03 time units between any pair of clocks. The clocks have a granularity of 0.01 time units and a maximum reading error of 0.01 time units. The maximum difference between the reading of any pair of clocks is 0.04 time units. Clock times are given in real number format with two decimal digits after the decimal point.

The table below is a summary of information on messages received by the clock G during the synchronization period originating from A. The agreed time for the synchronization concerned is 3.00 in local clock time. The second column of the table contains the nodes of the route in the order each message arrived at G. Although this information is not at its disposal, G can detect, as can all other clocks, any interference with the message content.

Recipient	Time of receipt	Actual route of delivery	Message content	
			Originator's clock reading	Signatures of the forwarding nodes and their order
G	3.01	A, D, G	3.00	A, C
G	3.06	A, C, G	3.03	A, C
G	3.09	A, G	3.00	A
G	3.13	A, F, C, G	3.00	A, F, C
G	3.14	A, B, D, G	3.00	A, B, D
G	3.15	A, B, D, E, G	3.00	A, B, D, E
G	3.33	$A, C, B, E, L, D,$ F, J, M, I, K, G	3.00	$A, C, B, E, L, D,$ F, J, M, I, K

(i) Identify the messages that G would not use in computations of the clock difference with A according to CSM.

(ii) Give in chronological order the calculations that clock G needs to make in order to establish the difference between it and clock A according to CSM.

Realtime Scenarios

This appendix provides a number of realtime scenarios as extended open ended exercises. They are suitable for a variety of purposes, in particular analysis, modelling and design. Because of the nature of the applications in real life, some of these scenarios are quite complex and tend to be quite large in size. The descriptions given are obviously brief, but are sufficiently detailed for the purpose of most academic exercises.

We deliberately avoid being prescriptive with respect to the specific task intended by each case study. We encourage the reader to formulate a smaller task in relation to any particular aspect or a complete project in the development of a computerized system for automated management of a given scenario.

It is to be noted that the material presented in this book is not sufficient to address all design issues raised by a complete project. In the case of such a project which, for example, ranges from the requirements analysis to an implementation, it is essential that the reader consult other appropriate text books and publications and undertake further research. In this connection, the reader may find the bibliographical references cited in Section 1.6 of Chapter 1 useful. More application specific references on some of the scenarios are given at the end of the relevant sections below.

As elsewhere in this book, some of the timing parameters given in the various exercises are hypothetical. Symbols such as T_i denote unknown time values. Any specific figures given for timing parameters and distances are rough guides and do not necessarily conform with figures used in real life.

A.1 An Intruder Alarm

An intruder alarm system receives information about the state of the monitored building from a number of sensors located at every possible entrance and exit. Sensors function basically as switches, indicating whether a given sensor has detected an intruder or not. The alarm is located inside the building. It is set (armed) and reset (disarmed) from inside the building. A digital code of fixed length is required for both setting and resetting the alarm. One of the entrances, which also functions as an exit, is nominated as the entrance and the exit after the alarm has been set.

Timing information is crucial for proper functioning of an intruder alarm. When the alarm is initially set, a specific time delay is allowed for the user to leave the building through the nominated exit. When the alarm is set, the use of any of the entrances other than the nominated one for re-entry activates the alarm instantly or, at most, within a matter of a few seconds. The sensors monitoring the entrance nominated for re-entry and the route to the alarm control point do not activate the alarm until a set time has elapsed. This set time allows the user to enter the building and disarm the alarm by entering the correct digital code. If this is not done successfully, the alarm is activated at the end of the set time.

The alarm system has a siren and a strobe and these are located outside the building. If an intruder is detected or the alarm is not disarmed by the person entering the building through the nominated entrance during the required time, the siren begins to sound and the strobe begins to flash immediately, as mentioned above. In this event, the siren continues to sound for a specified time, usually for a few minutes, and then stops, but the strobe continues to flash. The alarm can be reset by the user only by entering the correct code. If the alarm has already been triggered, this would turn the alarm off. The correct code is the most up to date code entered when arming the system.

When entering the code for disarming the alarm, the user is allowed a maximum period to complete the task. If the user fails to complete this within the given time, the system discards the partial entry and awaits for the next attempt. The user is allowed as many attempts as possible to enter the correct code within the allocated time. If the alarm has already been set off, after this period it cannot be reset except by an appointed independent authority.

Some reasonable limiting values for the timing parameters involved are:

Time allowed for setting the alarm and leaving the building	– 30 seconds
Time between detecting an intruder and triggering the alarm off	– 5 seconds
Time allowed for re-entry through the nominated entrance and start resetting the alarm	– 2 minutes
Duration for resetting the alarm after re-entry	– 1 minute
Maximum duration for entering the code at each attempt	– 20 seconds
Duration of the siren sound	– 5 minutes

A.2   Postal Address Recognition System

Postal address recognition systems are used for automatic sorting of small postal packages such as letters. Sorting is done using a post-code (zip-code, in the USA) given as part of the destination address. Sorting involves recognition of the post-code in the address given on the envelope, establishing the address catchment area by consulting a postal address database according to the recognized post-code and verifying the catchment area using other features such as the street name detected in the address. Packages failing this verification are rejected and are directed for manual sorting.

Automatic post-code and address feature recognition use an image of the address produced by a camera. It is a computationally complex task, not only because of the complexity of image processing tasks in general, but also because of the significant variations in handwritten scripts. As a result, the algorithms concerned involve a significant element of heuristics.

Timing of automated sorting is constrained by such requirements as the number of packages processed by each machine per unit time and the capacity of the associated mechanical pipeline. Cuhadar and Downton [31] cite a figure of ten envelopes per second for the processing rate and 90 envelopes for the maximum capacity of the mechanical pipeline. Downton [40] gives the following statistics for the execution times of the computational tasks and the size of data.

Processing function	Time sec/image	Approx. execution time ratios	Data packet size (bytes)
Preprocessing (feature extraction)	4.48	3	2144
Classification (postcode identification)	4.45	3	54
Dictionary (database search)	1.50	1	202
Complete processing	10.43		

A.2.1   Bibliographical Notes

The above description is based on the works due to Cuhadar and Downton [31] and Downton *et al.* [40], which also provide interesting solutions and related research.

A.3   An Automatic Flight Landing System

A.3.1   Terminology

Table A.1 presents some standard terminology used in aviation that can be explained briefly. Further clarification of some of these terms may be found in Figure A.1. Other terminology requiring more detailed descriptions is as follows.

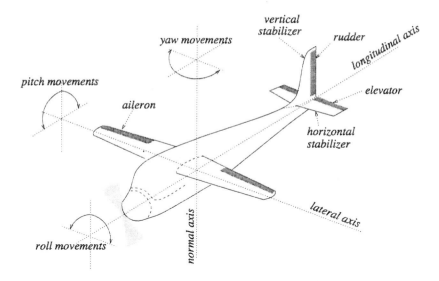

Figure A.1 Flight control surfaces

Localizer Beam

The localizer beam is a radio beam aligned with the extended centre line of the runway giving horizontal guidance to aircraft approaching the airport for landing. As shown in Figure A.2, the beam consists of two separate radio signals transmitted at different frequencies by a transmitter located at the far end of the runway. Both signals overlap each other slightly along the runway centre line but, otherwise, each lies on either side of it and both fade away beyond a certain angle from it. The different frequencies of the signals enable an approaching aircraft to establish its location (azimuth) with respect to the centre line in the horizontal plane, namely, whether the aircraft is on the left or the right of the localizer.

Glide Path

The glide path, see Figure A.3, is a radio beam aligned with the extended centre line of the runway. It provides vertical guidance to approaching aircraft by indicating the desired approach path though a plane inclined to the horizontal. This beam also consists of two separate radio signals transmitted by a transmitter located near the threshold of the glide path and the runway. The signals peak at the centre line of the glide path and both signals slightly overlap each other along it. Otherwise, one signal lies above the glide path and the other one below it. Signals are transmitted on separate frequencies so that an approaching aircraft

Table A.1 Some terminology used in aviation

Term	The meaning
Pitch	– Aircraft position in the longitudinal vertical plane (across the nose and the tail)
Roll	– Aircraft position in the lateral vertical plane (across the wings)
Yaw	– Aircraft position in the (horizontal) plane across the wings, the nose and the tail
Attitude	– The values of pitch, roll and yaw individually or as a triple
Coupling	– Provision of raw data to an appropriate flight path controller (subsystem)
Hold and Lock	– Setting of control panel switches for holding the relevant flight path parameter (altitude or height) constant
Capture	– Setting of control panel switches until the aircraft intercepts a given signal generated by a ground based aid
Heading	– The direction of the aircraft as established by sensing the earth's magnetic field directly
Heading Error	– The difference of the heading set by the pilot and the actual heading
Rudder	– The vertical control surface located at the back end of the tail 'fin' for bringing about yawing movements
Elevator	– The horizontal control surfaces located at the back end of the tail plane for bringing about pitching movements
Ailerons	– The horizontal control surfaces located at the back end of the wings for bringing about roll movements
Flight Director	– An automatic flight control system operable in all phases of flight rationalizing data processing and actuator control functions
GS	– Abbreviation for 'Glide Slope' (see below)
Markers	– Markers are ground based beacons transmitting radio signals vertically into the descent path
ILS	– Abbreviation for 'Instrument Landing System' (see below)

can establish whether it is below or above the glide path.

Instrument Landing System (ILS)

The instrument landing system is a short range navigational aid, consisting of instruments located both on ground and on board the aircraft. It supports an

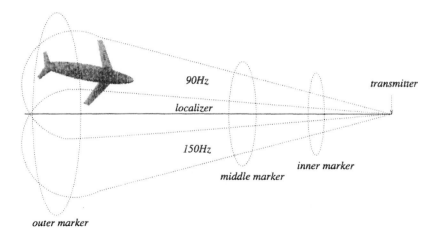

Figure A.2 Localizer beam

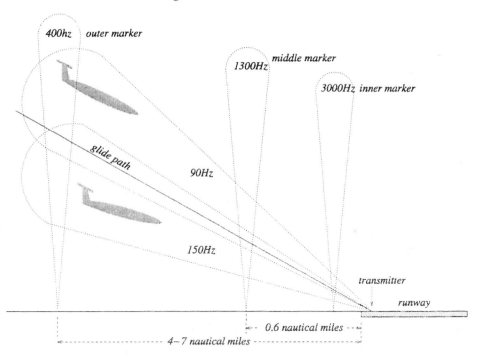

Figure A.3 Glide path beam

approach path for correct alignment of the aircraft in terms of altitude and course for landing and for its descent onto a runway with sufficient accuracy. The ground equipment consists of those supporting the localizer and gliding path and three markers. The *outer marker* is located at 4–7 nautical miles from the runway threshold, the *middle marker* at 0.6 nautical mile from it and a third *inner marker* near the runway (see Figure A.3).

The airborne equipment includes the receivers for the localizer, glide path and markers and a display of the approach parameters in relation to those due to the ground equipment. The localizer and glide path receivers are capable of receiving the signals transmitted by the ground equipment, decoding them and computing the localizer and glide path beams. ILS guides the aircraft on the basis of the difference in strength of 90 Hz and 150 Hz signals of the two beams. These signal levels are roughly equal along the centre line of the runway. The marker beacon receiver produces from the marker signals audio tones and visual output that indicate the passage of the aircraft over the marker beacons. Detection of the marker beacons along the glide path enables the aircraft to determine its range from the runway. The marker beacons also serve as holding points for aircraft waiting for authorization to land. Self-checking circuits in the receivers establish the validity of the processed information and, in the event of failures, produce appropriate warning messages.

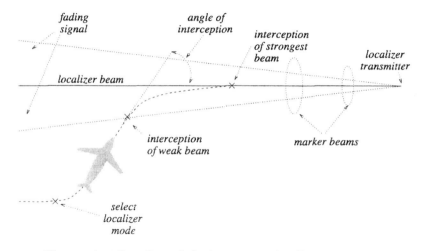

Figure A.4 Coupling of the instrument landing system

A.3.2   How does it work?

The flight control system receives data from sensors and receivers about the air speed, altitude, actual heading and interception of signals generated by ground based equipments. It processes these data, computes the necessary responses and affects the activators such as throttle, rudder, elevator and ailerons to position aircraft on an optimum flight path within the ILS beams.

The automatic landing system is operable only when the aircraft is under auto-

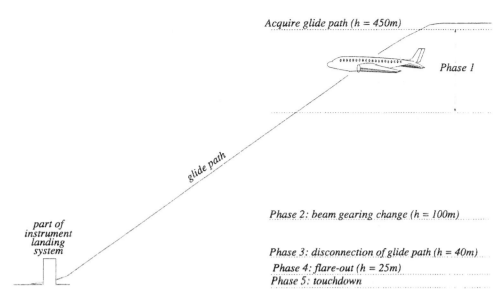

Figure A.5 Phases in aircraft descent

matic control in the heading mode of operation and the aircraft is at an altitude between about 450 metres (~1500 feet) and touchdown, but may not be invoked below a certain minimum altitude. The automatic landing is invoked by the pilot by selecting this mode via a switch. An immediate consequence is the coupling of the ILS within T_1 time units. Furthermore, the system responds to the pilot action by:

Stage 1 Setting the localizer mode immediately and capturing the localizer while flying at constant altitude (see Figure A.4).

Stage 2 Setting the GS mode within T_2 time units of intercepting the centre of the localizer beam but T_3 time units (estimated on the basis of the current aircraft speed) before intercepting the glide path, whichever is the lesser. This is followed by capturing the glide path before descending down the glide path (see Figure A.5).

The descent of the aircraft consists of four different phases (see Figure A.5).

Phase 1 'Glide acquire' at an altitude of approximately 450 metres (~1500 feet), but not later than T_4 time units after intercepting the glide path. At this point, the flight director and the automatic landing system begin to work in conjunction. The flight director performs its usual functions of signal processing, monitoring, actuator control and the display of flight attitude with respect to the glide path. At an altitude of about 300 metres (~1000 feet), the system selects a switch intended for compensation of the aerodynamic effects due to wind if this causes deviations from the glide path.

Phase 2 'Beam gearing change' at an altitude of approximately 100 metres ($\sim$350 feet) in order to reduce the intensity of signals resulting from the narrowing down of beams with increased proximity to the ground.

Phase 3 Disconnection of glide path signals from the 'control servo system' operating on the actuators. This occurs at an altitude of approximately 40 metres ($\sim$140 feet). Instead, the system begins to use a mean glide path computed from past pitch rates. This is done in order to affect a smoother descent since the glide path signals tend to vary abruptly at low levels.

Phase 4 'Flare' at an altitude of approximately 25 metres ($\sim$65 feet) in order to reduce the rate of descent in proportion to height. Also, auto-throttle terminates in this phase. At a height of around 4 metres ($\sim$12 feet), the system begins to utilize the rudder control channels for aligning the heading with the runway.

Phase 5 'Touchdown' – the pilot disconnects the automatic flight control system.

The pilot must be able to intervene and launch a recovery immediately in the event of a sensor indicating the malfunction of any of the actuators and a 'runaway' condition resulting from malfunctions of all kinds. Sensors monitoring actuators function at a frequency of f Hz (i.e. f cycles per second) and the pilot is informed of any malfunction within T_5 time units of receipt of sensor data. [Note: If a sensor works at a frequency of f Hz, then it means that the sensor samples the environment and produces the relevant data once in every $1/f$ seconds.] The 'approximate altitudes' given in relation to various events mean that each such event takes place within T_0 time units of reaching the given altitude.

A.3.3   Bibliographical Notes

The above is a brief description of the requirements for an automatic landing system and is based on the book by Pallett [117] (Chapter 9) and the instruction guide [137] by Rockwell Collins Avionics.

A.4   Railway Signalling

Railway signalling systems detect the presence of trains on the track and facilitate the correct movement of trains. Any such system consists of two major components. The first is the *permanent way*, which comprises the tracks, the points and the signals on the ground (see Figures A.8 and A.9). The second component is the *interlocking*, which is a safety mechanism designed to prevent system operation resulting in hazardous circumstances or danger. It also monitors the permanent way in order to ensure that it is in a safe state.

A.4.1 The Permanent Way

Tracks

The physical tracks include the rails, the sleepers and the ballast. However, from the point of view of signalling, the most important feature of tracks is how they detect trains on the rails. This is achieved by dividing them into physically separate and electrically insulated sections called *track circuits*, each around 180 metres (~200 yards) long. Each track circuit has its own power supply, called a *feed*, and a relay. A standard relay is essentially a switch with two possible states up and down:

State	*Description*
up or picked	The relay is electrically connected.
	In this state, the relay is up. This state is possible only when there is no train on the track, that is, the track circuit is *clear*. This is shown in Figure A.6.
down or dropped	The relay is electrically disconnected.
	This state takes place when a train moves to the given track circuit. The wheels and axle of the train short the circuit and, as a result, the relay *drops*, indicating that the track circuit is *occupied*.

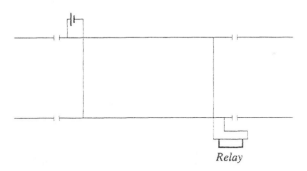

Relay

Figure A.6 A relay of a clear track circuit

It can be observed that relays operate in a failsafe manner. That is, in the event of an electrical failure, namely, in the case of a power failure or a broken circuit, the relay drops under its own weight due to gravity, and thus brings its state to occupied, which is a safer assumption to make, although the track concerned may itself be unoccupied at the time.

At any location, tracks are assumed to be running in two mutually opposite primary directions which, in British Rail practice, are referred to as *up* and *down* directions.

Signals

Signals are the standard means for giving instructions to drivers on train movements. A signal typically displays three possible aspects with obvious meanings. In appearance and basic operations, rail signals are similar to road traffic signals. However, different *aspects* shown by rail signals carry a different meaning and, as a result, rail signals perform a different function. Rail signals are intended to both maintain safety and give advanced warning to train drivers. Because of the high operational speeds of trains, normally around 160 km/hour (~100 miles per hour), trains require about 1500-3400 metres (~1600-3700 yards) to stop. Therefore, train drivers require plenty of warning to respond to changing circumstances on the tracks, namely, when trains need to be stopped or slowed down.

This is achieved by *aspect sequencing*, whereby signals along a certain stretch of tracks convey, using the following code, a consistent message to train drivers:

Aspect		*Intended meaning*
red	–	Do not proceed beyond this signal.
yellow	–	Expect the next signal to be at red.
green	–	Expect the next signal to be at yellow or green.

As part of safety, all signals are normally at red, unless instructed otherwise. This state is referred to as the normal state for signals. The signals consist of local sensors for detecting the state of the signal, that is, whether its current aspect is alight or not, and informing the controlling system of the current state of the signals. It is up to the controlling system then to prevent trains entering a track section with a failed signal.

Points

Points are a device for routing trains in a desired direction at a junction with multiple directions for train movement. There are several different types of points, two most common among them being: single ended and double ended (see Figure A.7).

The controlling system issues control signals to the points for moving a given point to one of the possible two states: normal or reverse. Usually, the normal state is the initial state and it is also the state chosen as the failsafe state. Sensors located at points are able to detect the current position of points and pass that information to the controlling system.

A third possible state is undetected, which is an intermediate state when a given point is in transition between normal and reverse. If this does not take place within a prescribed time interval after issuing the control signal, the point is to be regarded as broken. Once the points are moved to the desired position, they may be locked

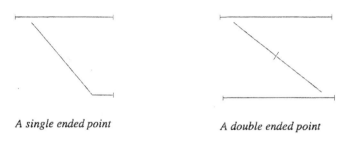

A single ended point   *A double ended point*

Figure A.7 Point types: single ended and double ended points

to prevent any change in position. The points are also equipped with sensors for enabling the controlling system to know about the current positions of points.

Subroutes and Routes

Subroutes and *routes* are abstract (logical) entities founded on components of the permanent way supporting the management of safe movement of trains on tracks. Safety is ensured by keeping track of the states of subroutes and routes in one of the two distinct lock states: **locked** and **free**. *Subroutes* are pairs of track sections reachable in a given direction via a third intermediate track section.

A *route* is a section of a track in a given direction lying between two adjacent signals. It also includes all other ground equipment lying within its boundary, namely, the signals and points, as well as the subroutes.

A.4.2   The Interlocking

As mentioned earlier, *interlocking* is the means by which certain undesirable events are prevented from happening. Until recent times, major railways relied on mechanical interlocking devices, implemented physically as a suitably arranged rack of levers and associated rods with precise and well-understood sequences of permitted movements. The modern-day systems of interlocking consist instead of racks of relays that perform the requests made by the signal-person if it is safe to do so, otherwise doing nothing in the interest of overall safety.

Granting Routes

Route requests are made by the signal-person in order to secure a section of the track for a particular train. On safety grounds, the request is granted and the route is set only when:

(a) the points are not locked against the route; and
(b) no opposing route is set or in use.

Aspect Control

Even if a route is set, trains are not permitted to enter it, unless the signal protecting the section concerned displays a proceed aspect. The interlocking must therefore ensure that signals clear from their most restrictive aspect, i.e. from red, only when it is required and safe to do so. The aspect of any signal is determined by the conditions ahead of it, including the aspect displayed by the next signal down the track.

For safety reasons, each signal capable of displaying red is so equipped that it can be individually controlled to red, if required.

The conditions determining *safety* for a signal to clear are as follows:

(a) The signal ahead is alight, that is, the lamp in the signal head is working.
(b) The line ahead is clear, that is, all the track circuits on the route are clear.
(c) The points on the route are all detected in their correct position.

It is also important in signalling to make sure that trains approach a junction at the right speed. For example, it may be the case that the train speed over a given point is less than a certain limiting speed. This may be ensured by requiring the train to occupy the track just prior to the route concerned for a certain length of time. This may be worked out knowing the limiting speed over the point, the time taken by a train to clear the track ahead of the route.

A.4.3   Example

Figure A.8 presents a simple example of a railway junction. A more elaborate example is shown in Figure A.9. The two signals in Figure A.8 control trains moving from left to right and the junction contains a double ended set of points.

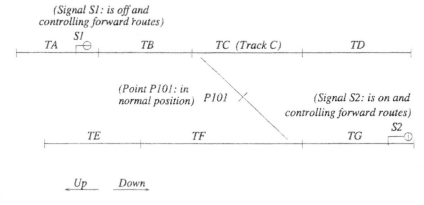

Figure A.8 Sketch of a simple junction

The junction contains no opposing routes. Setting of the route involves the signals $S1$ to $S2$ and the point $P100$. For this, the point must already be in the reverse position or must be free to move to that position. The options for signal sequencing are as follows:

S1	S2
yellow	red
green	yellow or green

Signals may be set as above provided that:

1. All tracks in the route, namely, *TB*, *TC* and *TF* must be clear.
2. The point *P*100 must be in the **reverse** position.
3. The signal *S*2 must be alight.

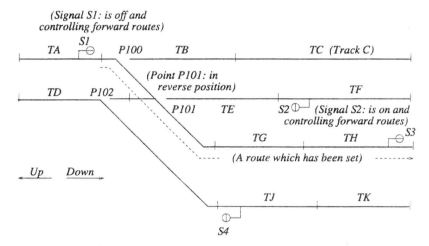

Figure A.9 Sketch of a junction

A.4.4   Bibliographical Notes

More details about railway signalling may be found in Standard Signalling Principles [112], Barnard [11] and Cribbens [30]. The examples given above and some work related to the specification of safety features in railway signalling may be found in Nissanke and Robinson [111] and Nissanke [109]. Another relevant publication is Simpson [150], dealing with the specification of an automatic train protection system in CSP.

A.5   A Submarine Sonar System

A.5.1   Introduction

Sonar employs acoustic waves to detect and identify underwater objects. There are two kinds of sonar: *active* and *passive* sonar. In active sonar, the submarine emits an acoustic wave and then analyses the reflected waves from either known or unknown objects. In passive sonar the submarine simply listens to sound emanating from the objects themselves. The analysis of the acoustic wave received helps to establish the physical characteristics of the wave such as the frequency content and enables the identification of other underwater vessels and life-forms. This description concerns only passive sonar.

Submarines receive underwater sound through an array of on-board hydrophones, which convert sound waves into electrical signals. The hydrophones are spatially separated so that the signal from each can be analyzed and compared with each other in working out the bearing and the velocity of the target object, usually another submarine in the locality of the given area, relative to the hydrophone array. This enables, among other things, establishment of the direction of the acoustic waves.

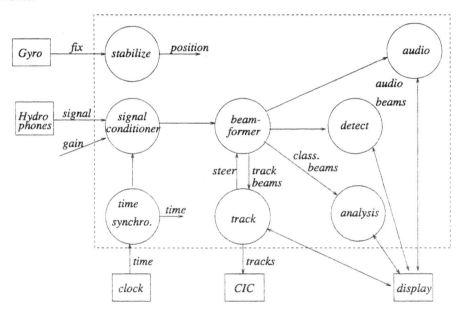

Figure A.10 A data flow diagram for submarine sonar system

A.5.2   Individual Processes

The general arrangement of the sonar processing system is shown as a data-flow diagram in Figure A.10. Arrows in the diagram which point to no specific entity represent data that is broadcast to all processes.

In relation to submarine sonar, Molini *et al.* [102] identify the following tasks and associated processes: signal conditioner (SC), beam former (BF), tracking (TR), detection (DET), analysis (SC), audio (AU), display (DIS), stabilization (PK) and time synchronization (TS). These computational processes are based on the different tasks involved. These are shown in Figure A.11 and are described below.

Signal Conditioner (SC)

The *signal conditioner* receives the signals from the hydrophones, samples them, amplifies them and filters them. The amplification is controlled by the *gain* which usually stays constant after initialization. The resulting data, *Samples*, are output to the beamformer.

Beamformer (BF)

The *beamformer* receives the data *Samples* from the SC. It contains time-stamped samples from each hydrophone. The beamformer gathers these samples until there are enough to form 'beams' which can be sent on to its successor processes. A 'beam' is formed by applying weighted delays to the output from each hydrophone. Due to the fact that they are spatially separated, the sound from a target reaches the various hydrophones at different times. Application of weighted delays to the samples has the effect of forming a 'beam' which emphasizes the sound from a particular direction.

The beamformer calculates several beams from one set of hydrophone data. There are different kinds of beams. Detect beams are intended to locate new objects and, therefore, are evenly spaced in all directions. Audio beams are intended for the operator and contain the sound from a given direction. Track beams are intended to follow objects which have already been detected. Analysis beams provide detailed information for identifying objects. The size of the problem depends on the number of hydrophones and the total number of the different kinds of beam intended for the above-mentioned different purposes.

The beamformer receives *steer* information from the tracking which is used to change the weights of the track beams so that they follow their targets. It is possible in a given implementation that the audio and analysis beams are subsets of the fixed detect beams or the moving track beams. This reduces the number of beams that the beamformer has to produce.

Detection (DET)

The process *detect* receives the data *DetectBeams* from the BF, manipulates the waves above a certain threshold by filtering and integrating over time and presents them appropriately formatted to the operator. This enables the operator to request more detailed information, if required.

Tracking (TR)

The process *track* receives *TrackBeams* from the beamformer. These are used to 'follow' targets of interest. The track process analyses track beams to work out the bearing of the target and its velocity. The beam must be 'steered' to keep pointing at the target. The track process calculates the required change in bearing for each track beam and sends this *Steer* message to the beamformer. The track process keeps a log of each target and sends it to a database. It also sends information about the targets to the operator displays.

Analysis (CL)

The process intended for *analysis* receives *ClassBeams* from the BF. Each of the beams is automatically analyzed for frequency distribution and dynamics. The resulting data is compared against those corresponding to known targets in order to identify the objects. The results enable the annotation of the displayed *track* and *detect* results.

Audio (AU)

The *audio* process inputs *AudioBeams* from the BF. These are converted into high fidelity analog sound and fed to the operator's headphones. The operator may select beams for audio reconstruction.

Display (DIS)

As indicated in the Figure A.11, the *display* provides the operator with the results from various computational processes and enables the operator to interact with the system by selecting tracks for audio reconstruction, analysis and tracking targets, etc.

Stabilization (PK)

The *stabilize* function receives a *Fix* from the submarine gyroscope and uses it to compute the attitude and location vector of the hydrophone array. These are broadcast as *Position* data to all other processes.

Synchronization (TS)

The *time synchronization* function receives the GMT from the clock and superimposes the resulting time and date information onto the sampling pulse. This message is broadcast to all other processes.

Table A.2 Characteristics of sonar signal processing

Signal	Description	Source	Destination	Rate	Size (bytes)
Samples	Processed electrical signals from hydrophones	SC	BF	512 Hz	$3k$
Detect Beams	Acoustic time samples	BF	DET	512 Samples/beam/sec	
Track Beams	(As above)	BF	TR	(As above)	
Class Beams	(As above)	BF	CL	(As above)	
Audio Beams	(As above)	BF	AU	(As above)	
Detect Display	Detection data	DET	Display	4 Hz	$2N_d$
Steer	Updated weights for track beams	TR	BF		$2kN_t$
Tracks	Status of targets being tracked	TR	CIC	> 1	$64N_t$
Class Display	Status of targets being tracked	CL	Display	> 4	
Fix	Gyroscope reading	Gyro	PK	16	24
Position	Location and velocity of submarine	PK	all processes	< 16	32
Inputs	4 Inputs by the operator	Display	relevant processes	$\sim$1–10 HZ	8–34

A.5.3 The Data

As indicated in Figures A.10 and A.11, the above processes exchange various kinds of data in performing the overall function. The data flow is labelled appropriately in the diagrams. More detailed characteristics are given in Table A.2. Note that k is the number of hydrophones and N_d and N_t are the numbers of detect beams and track beams respectively.

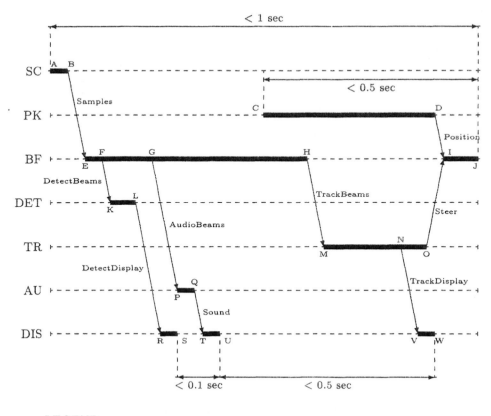

Figure A.11 Diagrammatic view of sonar system timing requirements

A.5.4   Timing Requirements

Figure A.11 shows the data flows and general timing requirements for the system. Points of interest in the execution are labelled with letters. The timings apply to the lifetime of one set of samples in the system, that is, from the time a set of samples is taken by the signal conditioner to the time the data from those samples has been computed, displayed and used to compute new steering weights. It should be noted that each of the main processes has several threads of execution running concurrently.

Some of the specific timing requirements are as follows:

1. The signal conditioner produces samples from each hydrophone at 512 Hz.
2. The beamformer must keep up with the signal conditioning and block samples into messages sufficiently frequently to keep up with detection, track and audio reconstruction. The position data used must be less than 0.5 seconds old.
3. Detection display data is sent at least four times a second and is synchronized to within 100 milliseconds of the audio data.
4. Track beam directions must be updated sufficiently frequently to prevent targets being lost. The time between taking a beam sample and using the information derived must be less than one second.
5. Automatic comparisons of selected beams against known targets made by the Analysis module must be presented to the operator within 1 second of selection.
6. Position information must reach the relevant modules within 200 milliseconds of the time when the fix is taken.
7. The timing pulse must reach the signal conditioner and the beamformer at 512+0.005 Hz.
8. The synthesized audio must be presented to the operator within 100 milliseconds of the corresponding display data.

A.5.5 Bibliographical Notes

This description is based on Molini *et al.* [102], which is intended as a source of realistic realtime scenarios for academic research. Curtis and Ward [32], Knight *et al.* [78] and Winder [170] are concise and general sources on sonar.

Appendix B

Selected Proofs

This appendix contains proofs of some selected observations made in several chapters.

B.1   Proofs of Observations in Chapter 2

Proof of Observation 2.12

Observation 2.12: Tick times are the real time values for which ω is defined. For any given $t \in \tilde{\Theta}$, t is related to its tick time $\tilde{t}$ as

$$t \in \text{dom } \omega \Rightarrow t = \tilde{t}$$

The above observation may be proved as follows:

1.	$t \in \text{dom } \omega$	assumption
2.	$\omega(t) = \tilde{\Omega}(t)$	from 1; def. of ω (ω and $\tilde{\Omega}$ being functions and $\omega \subset \tilde{\Omega}$)
3.	$\omega^{-1}(\omega(t)) = \omega^{-1}(\tilde{\Omega}(t))$	from 2; function application to equals
4.	$t = \tilde{t}$	from 3; definition of $\tilde{t}$ and since ω is an injective function
5.	$t \in \text{dom } \omega \Rightarrow t = \tilde{t}$	from 1, 4; introduction of $\Rightarrow$

Proof of Observation 2.13

Observation 2.13: The relationship between real time values and their tick times. For every $t \in \text{dom } \tilde{\Omega}$

$$\tilde{t} \leq t < \tilde{t} + \Delta$$

The proof may be based on two subgoals as expressed in the following observations:

Observation B.1 Tick times always precede or coincide with the corresponding real time values. That is, for every $t \in \text{dom } \tilde{\Omega}$

$$\tilde{t} \leq t$$

Observation B.2 Real time values always precede their corresponding next tick time values. That is, for every $t \in \text{dom } \tilde{\Omega}$

$$t < \tilde{t} + \Delta$$

Observation B.1 may be proved as follows:

1.	$(t, \tilde{t}) \in \omega^{-1} \circ \tilde{\Omega}$	def. of $\tilde{t}$
2.	$\exists x \bullet (t, x) \in \tilde{\Omega} \wedge (x, \tilde{t}) \in \omega^{-1}$	from 1; def. of composition
3.	$(t, x) \in \tilde{\Omega} \wedge (x, \tilde{t}) \in \omega^{-1}$	from 2; elimination of $\exists$
4.	$(t, x) \in \tilde{\Omega}$	from 3; elimination of $\wedge$
5.	$x = \tilde{\Omega}(t)$	from 4; $\tilde{\Omega}$ being a function
6.	$(x, \tilde{t}) \in \omega^{-1}$	from 3; elimination of $\wedge$
7.	$(\tilde{t}, x) \in \omega$	from 6; def. of ω^{-1}
8.	$(\tilde{t}, \tilde{\Omega}(t)) \in \omega$	from 5, 7; substitution of an equal
9.	$\tilde{t} = min((\tilde{\Omega}^{-1} \circ \tilde{\Omega})(\{t\}))$	from 8; def. of ω
10.	$\tilde{t} \in ((\tilde{\Omega}^{-1} \circ \tilde{\Omega})(\{t\}))$	from 9; $\tilde{t}$ being the minimum of the set concerned
11.	$t \in ((\tilde{\Omega}^{-1} \circ \tilde{\Omega})(\{t\}))$	from 4; since id(dom $\tilde{\Omega}) \subseteq \tilde{\Omega}^{-1} \circ \tilde{\Omega}$; 'id' being the identity relation
12.	$t \geq \tilde{t}$	from 9, 10, 11; def. of min

Below is a proof by contradiction for Observation B.2.

1.	$t \geq \tilde{t} + \Delta$	assumption
2.	$\tilde{\Omega}(t) \geq \tilde{\Omega}(\tilde{t} + \Delta)$	from 1; monotonicity of $\tilde{\Omega}$ (Observation 2.3 of Chapter 2)
3.	$\tilde{\Omega}(t) = \tilde{\Omega}(\tilde{t} + \Delta)$	assumption
4.	$\omega^{-1}(\tilde{\Omega}(t)) = \omega^{-1}(\tilde{\Omega}(\tilde{t} + \Delta))$	from 3; function application to equals
5.	$\tilde{t} = \tilde{t} + \Delta$	from 4; def. of $\tilde{t}$ and Observation 2.12 proved earlier ($\tilde{t} + \Delta$ is a tick time by definition)
6.	false	from 5; contradiction since $\Delta \neq 0$
7.	$\tilde{\Omega}(t) = \tilde{\Omega}(\tilde{t} + \Delta) \Rightarrow$ false	from 3, 6; introduction of $\Rightarrow$
8.	$\tilde{\Omega}(t) > \tilde{\Omega}(\tilde{t} + \Delta)$	assumption
9.	$\omega^{-1}(\tilde{\Omega}(t)) > \omega^{-1}(\tilde{\Omega}(\tilde{t} + \Delta))$	from 8; monotonicity of ω based on Observation 2.3 of Chapter 2
10.	$\tilde{t} > \tilde{t} + \Delta$	from 9; def. of $\tilde{t}$ and Observation 2.12 proved earlier ($\tilde{t} + \Delta$ is a tick time by definition)
11.	false	from 10; contradiction since $\Delta \neq 0$
12.	$\tilde{\Omega}(t) > \tilde{\Omega}(\tilde{t} + \Delta) \Rightarrow$ false	from 8, 11; introduction of $\Rightarrow$

13. false   from 2, 7, 12; constructive dilemma
14. $t < \tilde{t} + \Delta$ from 1, 13; contradiction and intro-
                                   duction of $\neg$

Proof of Observation 2.14

Observation 2.14: For any given t_1 and t_2 in $\tilde{\Theta}$ such that $t_1 \in$ dom $\tilde{\Omega}$ and $t_2 \in$ dom $\tilde{\Omega}$,

$$\tilde{\Omega}t_1 = \tilde{\Omega}t_2 \vdash \tilde{t}_1 \leq t_2 < \tilde{t}_1 + \Delta$$

where, as has already been mentioned, $\Gamma \vdash \phi$ states that the formula ϕ is *provable* from the formulae Γ. The above observation may be proved as follows:

1. $\tilde{\Omega}t_1 = \tilde{\Omega}t_2$ assumption
2. $\omega^{-1}(\tilde{\Omega}t_1) = \omega^{-1}(\tilde{\Omega}t_2)$ from 1; function application to equals
3. $\tilde{t}_1 = \tilde{t}_2$ from 2; def. of $\tilde{t}$s
4. $\tilde{t}_2 \leq t_2 < \tilde{t}_2 + \Delta$ Observation 2.13 proved earlier
5. $\tilde{t}_1 \leq t_2 < \tilde{t}_1 + \Delta$ from 3, 4; substitution of equals

Proof of Observation 2.15

Observation 2.15: Given any t_1 and t_2 in $\tilde{\Theta}$ such that $t_1 \in$ dom $\tilde{\Omega}$ and $t_2 \in$ dom $\tilde{\Omega}$,

$$\tilde{\Omega}t_1 = \tilde{\Omega}t_2 \vdash 0 \leq |\, t_2 - t_1 \,| < \Delta$$

The fact that $|\, t_2 - t_1 \,| \geq 0$ in the above follows immediately from the definition of $|\, t_2 - t_1 \,|$ given on page 28. Below is a proof just for $t_1 - t_2 < \Delta$.

1. $\tilde{\Omega}t_1 = \tilde{\Omega}t_2$ assumption
2. $\omega^{-1}(\tilde{\Omega}t_1) = \omega^{-1}(\tilde{\Omega}t_2)$ from 1; function application to equals
3. $\tilde{t}_1 = \tilde{t}_2$ from 2; def. of $\tilde{t}$s
4. $t_1 - \tilde{t}_1 < \Delta$ Observation B.2 proved earlier for t_1
5. $t_1 - \tilde{t}_1 - (t_2 - \tilde{t}_2) < \Delta - (t_2 - \tilde{t}_2)$ from 4
6. $0 \leq t_2 - \tilde{t}_2 < \Delta$ Observation 2.13 proved earlier for t_2
7. $t_1 - \tilde{t}_1 - (t_2 - \tilde{t}_2) < \Delta$ from 5, 6
8. $t_1 - t_2 < \Delta$ from 3, 7

Proof of Observation 2.16

Observation 2.16: Given any t_1 and t_2 in $\tilde{\Theta}$ such that $t_1 \in$ dom $\tilde{\Omega}$ and $t_2 \in$ dom $\tilde{\Omega}$,

$$\tilde{\Omega}t_1 < \tilde{\Omega}t_2 \vdash \tilde{t}_1 < \tilde{t}_2$$

The above may be proved as follows:

1.	$\tilde{\Omega}t_1 < \tilde{\Omega}t_2$	assumption
2.	$\omega^{-1}(\tilde{\Omega}t_1) < \omega^{-1}(\tilde{\Omega}t_2)$	from 1; monotonicity of ω based on Observation 2.3 of Chapter 2
3.	$\tilde{t}_1 < \tilde{t}_2$	from 2; def. of $\tilde{t}$s
4.	$\tilde{t}_1 + \Delta \leq \tilde{t}_2$	from 3; since tick times constitute a discrete domain
5.	$t_1 < \tilde{t}_1 + \Delta$	Observation B.2 proved earlier
6.	$\tilde{t}_1 + \Delta < \tilde{t}_2$	assumption
7.	$t_1 < \tilde{t}_2$	from 5, 6; transitivity of $<$
8.	$\tilde{t}_1 + \Delta < \tilde{t}_2 \Rightarrow t_1 < \tilde{t}_2$	from 6, 7; introduction of $\Rightarrow$
9.	$\tilde{t}_1 + \Delta = \tilde{t}_2$	assumption
10.	$t_1 < \tilde{t}_2$	from 5, 9
11.	$\tilde{t}_1 + \Delta = \tilde{t}_2 \Rightarrow t_1 < \tilde{t}_2$	from 9, 10; introduction of $\Rightarrow$
12.	$t_1 < \tilde{t}_2$	from 4, 8, 11; constructive dilemma

B.2   Proofs of Observations in Chapter 3

Proof of Observation 3.2

Let us prove here only the last claim of Observation 3.2, namely, the following:

Observation B.3 The relationship of time in clock time intervals with real time:

$$\tilde{\Omega}t \in [\tilde{\Omega}t_1, \tilde{\Omega}t_2) \Rightarrow t \in [\tilde{t}_1, \tilde{t}_2)$$

Its proof is as follows:

1.	$\tilde{\Omega}t \in [\tilde{\Omega}t_1, \tilde{\Omega}t_2)$	assumption
2.	$\tilde{\Omega}t_1 \leq \tilde{\Omega}t \wedge \tilde{\Omega}t < \tilde{\Omega}t_2$	from 1; def. of $[\_, \_)$
3.	$\tilde{\Omega}t < \tilde{\Omega}t_2$	from 2; elimination of $\wedge$
4.	$t < \tilde{t}_2$	from 3; Observation 2.16 proved earlier
5.	$\tilde{\Omega}t_1 < \tilde{\Omega}t \vee \tilde{\Omega}t_1 = \tilde{\Omega}t$	from 2; elimination of $\wedge$
6.	$\tilde{\Omega}t_1 < \tilde{\Omega}t$	assumption
7.	$t_1 < \tilde{t}$	from 6; Observation 2.16 proved earlier
8.	$\tilde{t}_1 \leq t_1$	Observation B.1 proved earlier for t_1
9.	$\tilde{t} \leq t$	Observation B.1 proved earlier for t
10.	$\tilde{t}_1 < t$	from 7, 8, 9; transitivity of $<$
11.	$\tilde{\Omega}t_1 < \tilde{\Omega}t \Rightarrow \tilde{t}_1 < t$	from 6, 10; introduction of $\Rightarrow$
12.	$\tilde{\Omega}t_1 = \tilde{\Omega}t$	assumption
13.	$\tilde{t}_1 \leq t < \tilde{t}_1 + \Delta$	from 12; Observation 2.14 proved earlier

14. $\tilde{t}_1 \leq t$	from 13; elimination of $\wedge$
15. $\tilde{\Omega}t_1 = \tilde{\Omega}t \Rightarrow \tilde{t}_1 \leq t$	from 12, 14; introduction of $\Rightarrow$
16. $\tilde{t}_1 < t \vee \tilde{t}_1 \leq t$	from 5, 11, 15; constructive dilemma
17. $\tilde{t}_1 \leq t$	from 16; a notational simplification
18. $\tilde{t}_1 \leq t \wedge t < \tilde{t}_2$	from 4, 17; introduction of $\wedge$
19. $t \in [\tilde{t}_1, \tilde{t}_2)$	from 18; def. of $(\_,\_)$
20. $\tilde{\Omega}t \in [\tilde{\Omega}t_1, \tilde{\Omega}t_2) \Rightarrow t \in [\tilde{t}_1, \tilde{t}_2)$	from 1, 19; introduction of $\Rightarrow$

Proof of Observation 3.3

Observation 3.3:

$$\theta \text{ before } \theta' \vdash \theta_c \text{ before}_c \ \theta'_c \vee \theta_c \text{ meets}_c \ \theta'_c$$

The above may be proved as follows:

1. $\theta \text{ before } \theta'$	assumption
2. $right(\theta) < left(\theta')$	from 1; def. of *before* on Γ
3. $\tilde{\Omega}(right(\theta)) \leq \tilde{\Omega}(left(\theta'))$	from 2; monotonicity of $\tilde{\Omega}$
4. $right(\theta) \in \text{dom } \omega$	assumption
5. $right(\tilde{\Omega}(\!(\theta)\!)) \leq left(\tilde{\Omega}(\!(\theta')\!))$	from 3, 4; Observation 3.1 of Chapter 3
6. $right(\theta_c) \leq left(\theta'_c)$	from 5; def. of θ_c and θ'_c
7. $right(\theta_c) < left(\theta'_c) \vee$ $right(\theta_c) = left(\theta'_c)$	from 6; def. of $\leq$
8. $\theta_c \text{ before}_c \ \theta'_c \vee \theta_c \text{ meets}_c \ \theta'_c$	from 7; def. of *before*$_c$ and *meets*$_c$
9. $right(\theta) \notin \text{dom } \omega$	assumption
10. $prev(right(\tilde{\Omega}(\!(\theta)\!))) \leq left(\tilde{\Omega}(\!(\theta')\!))$	from 3, 9; Observation 3.1 of Chapter 3
11. $prev(right(\theta_c)) \leq left(\theta'_c)$	from 10; def. of θ_c and θ'_c
12. $right(\theta_c) < left(\theta'_c) \vee$ $right(\theta_c) = left(\theta'_c) \vee$ $right(\theta_c) = next(left(\theta'_c))$	from 11; def. of $\leq$ and domain of clock time being discrete
13. $\theta_c \text{ before}_c \ \theta'_c \vee \theta_c \text{ meets}_c \ \theta'_c$	from 12; def. of *before*$_c$ and *meets*$_c$
14. $\theta_c \text{ before}_c \ \theta'_c \vee \theta_c \text{ meets}_c \ \theta'_c$	from 4, 8, 9, 13; constructive dilemma

Proof of Observation 3.4

Observation 3.4:

$$\theta \approx \theta_c, \theta' \approx \theta'_c, \theta_c \text{ before}_c \ \theta'_c \vdash \theta \text{ before } \theta'$$

The above may be proved as:

1. $\theta_c \ before_c \ \theta'_c$ — assumption
2. $right(\theta_c) < left(\theta'_c)$ — from 1; def. of $before_c$ on Γ_c
3. $\theta \approx \theta_c$ — assumption
4. $\theta' \approx \theta'_c$ — assumption
5. $right(\theta) \in dom \ \omega$ — assumption
6. $\tilde{\Omega}(right(\theta)) < \tilde{\Omega}(left(\theta'))$ — from 2, 3, 4, 5; Observation 3.1 of Chapter 3
7. $right(\theta) < left(\theta')$ — from 6; monotonicity of $\tilde{\Omega}$
8. $\theta \ before \ \theta'$ — from 7; def. of $before$
9. $right(\theta) \notin dom \ \omega$ — assumption
10. $next(\tilde{\Omega}(right(\theta))) < \tilde{\Omega}(left(\theta'))$ — from 2, 3, 4, 9; Observation 3.1 of Chapter 3
11. $\tilde{\Omega}(right(\theta)) < \tilde{\Omega}(left(\theta'))$ — from 10; Observation 2.1 of Chapter 2
12. $right(\theta) < left(\theta')$ — from 11; monotonicity of $\tilde{\Omega}$
13. $\theta \ before \ \theta'$ — from 12; def. of $before$
14. $\theta \ before \ \theta'$ — from 5, 8, 9, 13; constructive dilemma

Proof of Observation 3.7

Observation 3.7:

$$\theta \approx \theta_c, \theta' \approx \theta'_c,$$
$$left(\theta) < left(\theta'), right(\theta) < right(\theta'),$$
$$\theta_c \ meets_c \ \theta'_c \ \vdash \ \theta \ before \ \theta' \lor \theta \ meets \ \theta' \lor \theta \ overlaps \ \theta'$$

As mentioned in Chapter 3, the derivation of the above relies on the simplifying assumption:

$$left(\theta) < left(\theta') \land right(\theta) < right(\theta')$$

The proof is as follows:

1. $\theta_c \ meets_c \ \theta'_c$ — assumption
2. $right(\theta_c) = left(\theta'_c) \lor prev(right(\theta_c)) = left(\theta'_c)$ — from 1; def. of $meets_c$ on Γ_c
3. $\theta \approx \theta_c \land \theta' \approx \theta'_c$ — essential assumption
4. $left(\theta) < left(\theta') \land right(\theta) < right(\theta')$ — simplifying assumption
5. $right(\theta_c) = left(\theta'_c)$ — assumption
6. $right(\theta) \in dom \ \omega$ — assumption
7. $\tilde{\Omega}(right(\theta)) = \tilde{\Omega}(left(\theta'))$ — from 3, 5, 6; Observation 3.1 of Chapter 3

8. $right(\theta) \leq left(\theta') < right(\theta) + \Delta$ — from 7; Observation 2.14 proved earlier; note that according to line 6 $right(\theta)$ is a tick time.

9. $right(\theta) \leq left(\theta')$ — from 8; elimination of $\wedge$

10. θ *before* $\theta' \vee \theta$ *meets* θ' — from 9; def. of *before* and *meets*

11. $right(\theta) \notin \operatorname{dom} \omega$ — assumption

12. $next(\tilde{\Omega}(right(\theta))) = \tilde{\Omega}(left(\theta'))$ — from 3, 5, 11; Observation 3.1 of Chapter 3

13. $\tilde{\Omega}(right(\theta)) < \tilde{\Omega}(left(\theta'))$ — from 12; Observation 2.1 of Chapter 2

14. $right(\theta) < left(\theta')$ — from 13; monotonicity of $\tilde{\Omega}$

15. θ *before* θ' — from 14; def. of *before*

16. $right(\theta_c) = left(\theta'_c) \Rightarrow$ θ *before* $\theta' \vee \theta$ *meets* θ' — from 5, 6, 10, 11, 15; constructive dilemma and introduction of $\Rightarrow$

17. $prev(right(\theta_c)) = left(\theta'_c)$ — assumption

18. $right(\theta) \in \operatorname{dom} \omega$ — assumption

19. $prev(\tilde{\Omega}(right(\theta))) = \tilde{\Omega}(left(\theta'))$ — from 3, 17, 18; Observation 3.1 of Chapter 3

20. $\tilde{\Omega}(right(\theta)) > \tilde{\Omega}(left(\theta'))$ — from 19; Observation 2.1 of Chapter 2

21. $left(\theta') < right(\theta)$ — from 20; monotonicity of $\tilde{\Omega}$

22. θ *overlaps* θ' — from 4, 21; def. of *overlaps*

23. $right(\theta) \notin \operatorname{dom} \omega$ — assumption

24. $\tilde{\Omega}(right(\theta)) = \tilde{\Omega}(left(\theta'))$ — from 3, 17, 23; Observation 3.1 of Chapter 3

25. $0 \leq |\, right(\theta) - left(\theta')\,| < \Delta$ — from 24; Observation 2.15, proof of which is outlined earlier

26. $right(\theta) < left(\theta') \cdot \vee$ $right(\theta) = left(\theta') \vee$ $right(\theta) > left(\theta')$ — from 25; elimination of $\wedge$ and def. of $|\cdots|$ (absolute value); also a tautology

27. θ *before* $\theta' \vee \theta$ *meets* $\theta' \vee$ θ *overlaps* θ' — from 4, 26; def. of. *before*, *meets* and *overlaps*

28. $prev(right(\theta_c)) = left(\theta'_c) \Rightarrow$ θ *before* $\theta' \vee \theta$ *meets* θ' θ *overlaps* θ' — from 17, 18, 22, 23, 27; constructive dilemma and introduction of $\Rightarrow$

29. θ *before* $\theta' \vee \theta$ *meets* $\theta' \vee$ θ *overlaps* θ' — from 2, 16, 28; constructive dilemma

30. θ_c *meets*$_c \theta'_c \wedge \theta \approx \theta_c \wedge \theta' \approx \theta'_c \wedge$ $left(\theta) < left(\theta') \wedge$ $right(\theta) < right(\theta') \Rightarrow$ θ *before* $\theta' \vee \theta$ *meets* $\theta' \vee$ θ *overlaps* θ' — from 1, 3, 4, 29; introduction of $\Rightarrow$

The above general conclusion holds anyway because of our simplifying assumption.

However, the proof has enabled us to focus attention on consequences under all possible sets of circumstances but taken in isolation.

B.3   Proofs of Observations in Chapter 12

Proof of Observation 12.16

> Observation 12.16: Deadline driven scheduling of a set of tasks is feasible if and only if $U \leq 1$. That is,
>
> $$feasible_{\text{DDS}}(S) \Leftrightarrow U \leq 1 \,,$$

Note that $feasible_{\text{DDS}}(S)$ is true if and only if S may be scheduled by DDS; see Section 12.2.3 of Chapter 12. The above may be substantiated with the following proof. [Note that despite its appearance, the proof is presented semi-formally because of its length, and is intended to convey the reasoning behind Observation 12.16.]

Proof of Forward Implication:

Necessity of $U \leq 1$ for DDS feasibility, that is,

$$feasible_{\text{DDS}}(S) \Rightarrow U \leq 1$$

follows immediately from Observation 12.2 in Section 12.2.3 of Chapter 12.

Proof of Backward Implication: Sufficiency of $U \leq 1$ for DDS feasibility

Let us attempt a proof by contradiction. The first line of this proof is motivated by the following observation:

$$U \leq 1 \Rightarrow feasible_{\text{DDS}}(S) \quad \Leftrightarrow \quad U > 1 \vee feasible_{\text{DDS}}(S)$$
$$\Leftrightarrow \quad \neg\,(U \leq 1 \wedge \neg\,feasible_{\text{DDS}}(S))$$

1.	$U \leq 1 \wedge \neg\,feasible_{\text{DDS}}(S)$	assumption
2.	$U \leq 1$	A conjunct of (1)
3.	$\neg\,feasible_{\text{DDS}}(S)$	A conjunct of (1)
4.	$\exists t \bullet 0 < t \leq T_1 T_2 \cdots T_m \wedge$ $overflow_{\text{DDS}}(S, t)$	From (3); def. of feasibility
5.	$0 < t \leq T_1 T_2 \cdots T_m \wedge overflow_{\text{DDS}}(S, t)$	From (4); elimination of $\exists$
6.	$overflow_{\text{DDS}}(S, t)$	From (5); a conjunct of (5)
7.	$\exists\,\tau : Task \bullet \tau \in S \wedge \tau.d = t$	From (6) using def. of overflow
8.	$\neg\,idle_{\text{DDS}}(S, t)$	As above.
9.	$S' = \varnothing \Rightarrow P_0(S, t) > t$	As above.
10.	$S' \neq \varnothing \Rightarrow (\exists\,t' : \mathbb{T} \bullet t' < t \wedge$ $P_{\text{DDS}}(S - S', (t', t)) = P_{\text{DDS}}(S, (t', t)) \wedge$ $P_0(S, (t', t)) > t - t')$	As above.

Case 1: There are no partially computed tasks, i.e. $S' = \varnothing$:

11.1 $S' = \varnothing$	Assumption
11.2 $P_0(S, t) = \sum_{\tau_i \in S} \lfloor t/T_i \rfloor \times c_i > t$	From (9), (11.1); eliminating the implication in (9) and using def. $P_0(S, t)$.
11.3 $\sum_{\tau_i \in S} (t/T_i) \times c_i > t$	From (11.2); since $x \geq \lfloor x \rfloor$.
11.4 $U = \sum_{\tau_i \in S} (c_i/T_i) > 1$	From (11.3) and def. of U.
11.5 $\neg\,(U \leq 1 \wedge \neg\,feasible_{\text{DDS}}(S))$	From (1), (2), and (11.4); by negating the assumption (1)

Case 2: There are partially computed tasks, i.e. $S' \neq \varnothing$:

12.1 $S' \neq \varnothing$	Assumption
12.2 $\exists\, t' : \mathbf{T} \bullet t' < t \,\wedge$ $\quad P_{\text{DDS}}(S - S', (t', t)) = P_{\text{DDS}}(S, (t', t)) \,\wedge$ $\quad P_0(S, (t', t)) > t - t'$	From (10) and (12.1); eliminating the implication in (10).
12.3 $t' < t \wedge P_0(S, (t', t)) > t - t' \,\wedge$ $\quad P_{\text{DDS}}(S - S', (t', t)) = P_{\text{DDS}}(S, (t', t))$	From (12.2); eliminating $\exists$.
12.4 $P_0(S, (t', t)) = \sum_{\tau_i \in S} \lfloor (t - t')/T_i \rfloor \times c_i$ $\qquad\qquad\qquad\qquad\quad\; > t - t'$	Eliminating a conjunction in (12.3) and using def. $P_0(S, (t', t))$
12.5 $\sum_{\tau_i \in S} ((t - t')/T_i) \times c_i > t - t'$	From (12.4); since $x \geq \lfloor x \rfloor$.
12.6 $U = \sum_{\tau_i \in S} (c_i/T_i) > 1$	From (12.5) and def. of U.
12.7 $\neg\,(U \leq 1 \wedge \neg\,feasible_{\text{DDS}}(S))$	From (1), (2), and (12.6); by negating the assumption (1)

The end of the case analysis:

13. $U \leq 1 \Rightarrow feasible_{\text{DDS}}(S)$	From (11.1), (11.5), (12.1) and (12.7)
14. $feasible_{\text{DDS}}(S) \Leftrightarrow U \leq 1$	From forward implication and (13); introducing the equivalence.

Appendix C

The Basic Mathematical Notation

On the Notation

This work relies on the Z notation for most of the basic mathematics. The reader should consult Spivey [152] for a full definition of the Z notation. The reader may benefit from reading the material presented in Appendix D, since it provides an appreciation of the wider practical context of the Z notation.

The notations which are outside the Z notation are those in common use in mathematics. Therefore, more information on them may be found in many standard textbooks in mathematics.

The Glossary of Mathematical Notation

General:

$x : X$	A typical type declaration (to be read as 'x has the type X')
$\stackrel{def}{=}$ and $\widehat{=}$	Syntactic equality of objects such as sets
$\stackrel{def}{\Leftrightarrow}$	Syntactic equivalence of propositions and predicates

On Logic:

true	A proposition which is true by definition
false	A proposition which is false by definition
$\neg$	Negation
$\wedge$	Conjunction
$\vee$	Disjunction
$\Rightarrow$	Implication
$\Rrightarrow$	Logical implication
$\Leftrightarrow$	Material equivalence
$\Lleftrightarrow$	Logical equivalence
$\bullet$	Delimiter between declarations and an associated predicate (see below)

|	Delimiter between declarations and a constraint (see below)
∀	Universal quantifier.

$$\forall x : X \mid p(x) \bullet q(x) \overset{\text{def}}{\Leftrightarrow} \forall x : X \bullet p(x) \Rightarrow q(x)$$

∃	Existential quantifier

$$\exists x : X \mid p(x) \bullet q(x) \overset{\text{def}}{\Leftrightarrow} \exists x : X \bullet p(x) \wedge q(x)$$

$\exists_1 x \bullet \cdots$	Existential quantifier quantifying a unique occurrence of x
⊢	Provability. For a formula ϕ and a set of formulae Γ, $\Gamma \vdash \phi$ states that ϕ is *provable* from Γ.

On Sets:

$\{\cdots\}$	Set definition
	Applicable to set comprehension as shown below:

$$\{t(x) \bullet x : X \mid p(x)\}$$

The above represents the set of elements defined by the term $t(x)$, x being of type X and satisfying the predicate $p(x)$.

$\{a, b, ..\}$	Set enumeration
∅	Empty set
#S	Size (cardinality) of set S
∪	Set union
∩	Set intersection
−	Set difference ($S - T$ – the difference between the set S and the set T)
S'	Complement of the set S (i.e. set difference between the universal set and the set S)
×	Cartesian product
$a \mapsto b$	Enumeration of a pair of elements consisting of a and b in that order. Note that $a \mapsto b \overset{\text{def}}{=} (a, b)$ and '$a \mapsto b$' is read as 'a maps to b.
ℙ	Power set (set of all subsets of its operand set; e.g. ℙ S for the power set of the set S)
𝔽	Set of finite subsets of its operand set (e.g. 𝔽 S)
μ	Choice operator for choosing an element arbitrarily from a set

On Numbers:

N	The set of natural numbers including zero
N_1	The set of natural numbers excluding zero

div, mod	Operators of modular arithmetic
$m .. n$	The set of numbers from m to n inclusive
$\mathbb{R}$	The set of real numbers
$\mathbb{Z}$	The set of integers
$\mathbb{Q}$	The set of rational numbers
$\lfloor x \rfloor$	The largest integer smaller than or equal to x. $\lfloor x \rfloor$ is to be read as '*floor of x*'
$\lceil x \rceil$	The smallest integer greater than or equal to x. $\lceil x \rceil$ is to be read as '*ceiling of x*'
$x \ll y$	x is much smaller than y
∞	Infinity (a fictitious value)
$\displaystyle\sum_{i=m}^{n} f(i)$	The sum of numbers $f(i)$ for $i \in m .. n$, f being a function from $\mathbb{N}$ or $\mathbb{Z}$ to any set of numbers
$\displaystyle\sum_{i \in S} f(i)$	The sum of numbers $f(i)$ for $i \in S$, f being a function as above
$\displaystyle\prod_{i=m}^{n} f(i)$	The product of numbers $f(i)$ for $i \in m .. n$, f being a function as above
$\displaystyle\prod_{i \in S} f(i)$	The product of numbers $f(i)$ for $i \in S$, f being a function as above

On Relations:

$\leftrightarrow$	Relational type (in type declarations)
dom	Domain of a relation
ran	Range of a relation
id	Identity relation
$(\!(\ )\!)$	Relational image ($R (\!(\ S \ )\!)$ – the image of the relation R thorough the set S)
$\circ$	Relational (function) composition (the standard mathematical notation)
$\S$	Forward relational (function) composition (an alternative to the above in Z)
	(Note that $R \,\S\, S \stackrel{def}{=} S \circ R$)
$\lhd$	Restriction of the domain of a relation R (the right operand) to a set S (the left operand). It is written as $S \lhd R$
$\rhd$	Restriction of the range of a relation R (the left operand) to a set S (the right operand). It is written as $R \rhd S$
$\mathbin{\lhd\!\!\!-}$	Co-restriction of the domain of a relation R (the right operand) to a set S (the left operand); also known as domain subtraction. It is written as $S \mathbin{\lhd\!\!\!-} R$
$\mathbin{-\!\!\!\rhd}$	Co-restriction of the range of a relation R (the left operand) to a set S the right operand); also known as range subtraction. It is written as $R \mathbin{-\!\!\!\rhd} S$

S^{-1}	Inverse of the relation S
$\oplus$	Relational overriding, $(S \oplus R \overset{def}{=} (\text{dom } R \lhd S) \cup R)$
$/$	Quotient operator (A/R – the quotient of A induced by R and R being a relation on A)
R^n	nth iteration of relation R defined on a set
R^*	Reflexive transitive closure of relation R
R^+	Irreflexive transitive closure of relation R

On Functions:

$f(x)$, $f\ x$	Function application (of the function f to argument x)
$\rightarrow$	Total functions (in type declarations)
$\nrightarrow$	Partial functions (in type declarations)
$\rightarrowtail\!\!\!\!\rightarrow$	Partial injective (one-to-one) functions (in type declarations)
$\rightarrowtail$	Total injective (one-to-one) functions (in type declarations)
$\twoheadrightarrow\!\!\!\!\!$	Partial surjective (onto) functions (in type declarations)
$\twoheadrightarrow$	Total surjective (onto) functions (in type declarations)
λ	Prefix indicating anonymous functions (Lambda function notation)
$f : A \rightarrow B \rightarrow C$	

The syntax of a form of function abstraction known as *curried functions*. The function f takes each of its arguments one at a time in the order indicated by arrows and parentheses. It allows the application of f to its arguments partially. For example, for an $x \in A$, $f(x)$ denotes the function space $B \rightarrow C$. For a further $y \in B$, the function f may be applied fully to both its arguments as in $f(x, y)$, in which case f returns an appropriate element of C as the final result. This kind of function abstraction is due, among others, to H. B. Curry

On Sequences: Given that s and t are sequences,

seq	Sequences (in type declarations)
$\langle a,\ b,\ \cdots \rangle$	shows a sequence containing the elements a, b, etc.
$s(i)$	ith element of sequence s (since sequences are mathematical functions)
head	Function returning the first element (head) of a given sequence
tail	Function returning the tail end of a sequence (without its first element)
last	Function returning the last element of a given sequence
front	Function returning the front end of a sequence (without its last element)
$s \frown t$	Concatenation of the sequences s and t

↾	Filtering ($U \upharpoonright s$ denotes the sequence obtained by retaining the elements occurring in s and given in the set U but in the order they appear in s)
squash	Function compacting any mapping f from N_1 to an arbitrary type X into a sequence s of elements of X such that: (1) for each pair in f there is exactly one corresponding pair in s and vice versa, and (2) the indices of the corresponding pairs in f and s are in the same relative order
#s	Length of the sequence s (since sequences are also sets)
in	Subsequence relation (s in t if and only if s is a contiguous subsequence anywhere in t. Given that s is singleton sequence of the form $s = \langle a \rangle$, we may write a in t instead of $\langle a \rangle$ in t.)
ran s	The elements in the sequence s as a set (since sequences are also relations)

On Bags (Multi-sets)

bag	Bags (in type declarations)
⟦ ⟧	Definition of elements in a bag
⟦ $a, b, c, \cdots$ ⟧	Enumeration of elements $a, b, \cdots$, etc., in a bag
count	Function returning multiplicity of an element in a bag (e.g. '*count a x*' denoting the number of occurrences of the element a in the bag x)
⊎	Bag union (a binary operator)

On Time: (see Chapter 2 for definitions)

$\tilde{\Theta}$	A set, the elements of which denote real time (objective time)
Θ	A set, the elements of which approximate the above, for example the external standard physical time
$\mathbb{T}$	Set of clock (representation) time values
Δ	Actual or target granularity
∇	Calibrated granularity
$\tilde{\Omega}$	Clock function; $\tilde{\Omega} : \tilde{\Theta} \twoheadrightarrow \mathbb{T}$
Ω	Clock function; $\Omega : \Theta \twoheadrightarrow \mathbb{T}$

On Probabilities and Reliability: Given random variables X and T and values x and t,

$Pr[pred]$	Probability that the predicate *pred* holds
$F(x)$	Probability that X is less than or equal to x,

$$F(x) = Pr[X \leq x]$$

$f(x)$ Probability density function,

$$f(x) = \frac{dF}{dx}$$

$E[X]$ The expected value of X,

$$E[X] = \int_{-\infty}^{\infty} xf(x)$$

$R(t)$ Reliability function,

$$R(t) = 1 - F(t) = Pr[T > t]$$

T being a random temporal variable and t a time value.

An Appreciation of Schema Language

This appendix is a basic introduction to the *Schema Language* – an extended mathematical language of Z. The introduction is necessarily superficial and is intended to enable the reader to understand the limited number of definitions written in the Schema Language and appearing in Chapter 2. The interested reader may refer to [152] for a full definition of the Z notation. What follows is a short informal introduction to the language using a small example.

D.1 What is Schema Language?

Z is a formal specification language intended for the precise expression of software (or system) requirements. Bearing in mind the primary concern of any specification language, it is also designed for better communication of such requirements among professionals. Z notation consists of two basic components:

- A standard notation for traditional mathematics.
  The standard notation covers two branches of mathematics used in the formal specification of requirements, namely, predicate logic and set theory. A glossary of notation applicable to logic and sets is given in Appendix C.
- An extended notation known as the *Schema Language* for structuring specifications.
  This is the subject of the present appendix. The schema language is intended to facilitate the communication of large pieces of mathematical text among requirement analysts, specifiers, software designers and customers in an easily comprehensible manner.

D.2 Type Definitions in Z

The basic types of values may be introduced into a specification in a number of different ways. Two basic ways among them are:

1. *Generic Types*

   Generic types introduce types of values without giving any formal definition. For example, two sets called PERSON and ROOM, which are to be used as types, may be introduced as follows:

   [PERSON, ROOM]

   Informally, PERSON and ROOM are supposed to consist of all possible persons and rooms of interest to a given application.

2. Enumerated (Free) Types

   Quite often it is necessary to introduce types with explicitly named values. The names of such values are reserved for denoting those values only and, therefore, they may not be used for any other purpose.

   An example is.

   STATUS ::= In | Out | Absent

D.3   Schemas

A specification written in Z is a collection of mathematical definitions, which may be presented in a number of ways. Some of these definitions are called *schemas*. For better comprehension and ease of mathematical manipulation, schemas are organized in the following manner. Each schema consists of:

- *Schema Name*

  Naming a schema introduces a syntactic equality of the schema name with the mathematical text enclosed in the schema. Given a need, the schema name may be replaced with the content of the schema, and vice versa.

- *Signature Part*

  The signature part introduces components (identifiers) and declares their types (mathematical data structures such as sets, relations, functions and sequences).

- *Predicate Part*

  The predicate part introduces constraints on the values that the components in the signature part may take. These predicates may be referred to as data invariants (in data abstraction) or state invariants (in system specifications).

In visual presentations, schemas are presented in two forms:

- Vertical layout

  This takes the form of a box subdivided by a horizontal line.

  Example: A specification for an office may be presented as follows.

  ```
  ┌─ Office ──────────────────────────────────────────
  │   staff : ℙ PERSON                  ⎫
  │   place : PERSON ↔ ROOM             ⎬  . . . . . . . . . . . . .    Signature
  │   availability : PERSON ⇸ STATUS    ⎭                               Part
  ├───────────────────────────────────────────────────
  │   staff = dom place                 ⎫                               Predicate
  │   staff = dom availability          ⎬  . . . . . . . . . . . . .    Part
  └───────────────────────────────────────────────────
  ```

The intention of the above is to capture the state of an office with respect to its workers, their offices and their availability. The mathematical structures such as sets, relations and functions may be chosen in such a way that some of the system requirements are satisfied by their choice automatically.

In this layout several conventions apply, namely,

- Implicit between type declarations on two successive lines is a semicolon, which signifies the continuation of the type declaration. Thus, type declarations may be broken at a semicolon and the semicolon may be omitted.

- Likewise, implicit between predicates on two successive lines is a conjunction, signifying the continuation of the predicate. A lengthy predicate may therefore be broken at a conjunction and the connective ∧ may be omitted.

- Horizontal Layout (not covered here)

A schema may be extended in various ways to include new components and new predicates.

D.4 Specification of Systems

A specification of any system requires the specification of:

(i) the general state of the system;
(ii) its initial and, where applicable, terminal states;
(iii) state transformations under an agreed set of operations.

Specifications of the general state mentioned in (i) above may be captured through a schema by using it in the following manner:

(a) schema components representing the *state variables*;

(b) schema predicates representing the *state invariant*.

The earlier specification *Office* illustrates the use of schemas in the context of (a) and (b) above. In order to describe the system evolution proper, we need the specifications for (ii) and (iii) listed above. This requires some additional notation, which is outlined below.

Our description below uses the term 'decoration'. An identifier is said to have been 'decorated' by post-fixing a dash (a quotation mark) at the end. This results in a new identifier with a matching name. A decorated identifier may be used as an identifier, which is distinct from the original one.

Utility	Convention
For identifying the state before the operation	Use the schema representing the given state in the original (undecorated) form. Let the undecorated schema components refer to the individual state variables of the before state
For identifying the state after the operation	Decorate the schema representing the given state with a dash (quote). This is equivalent to decorating each state variable within the scope of the given schema with a dash as well. Use these implicitly dashed names for referring to after state variables
For identifying the initial state (a unique operation with only an 'after state')	Use the schema name with the subscript '*init*' to identify the initial state and define the initialization with the dashed schema name, dashed component names and, where applicable, any inputs
For identifying the terminal state	Use the schema as in 'before state'
For identifying the inputs	Postfix the identifier representing the input with a question mark '?'
For identifying the outputs	Postfix the identifier representing the output with an exclamation mark '!'

Of particular interest in the specification of operations is the Δ *notation*. In relation to our example, $\Delta\textit{Office}$ is defined as

$$\Delta\textit{Office} \;\hat{=}\; \textit{Office} \;\wedge\; \textit{Office}'$$

which is a conjunction of two states. This is syntactically equivalent to a new schema, containing state variables and predicates as they appear in *Office* and another corresponding set of state variables and predicates as in *Office* but with all variables being decorated.

The intention is that the notation Δ *Office* identifies two adjacent states of the system. *Office* describes here the before state of the system concerned, and *Office'* its immediate after state. The two states may in general be different, the difference signifying the expected transformation from the before state to the after state. The task of operation specification is then to describe this transformation by relating the dashed and non-dashed variables with appropriate predicates.

Example: In order to illustrate the notation and the conventions outlined above, let us define an operation *Leave* on *Office*. This will formalize the situation where a person leaves the office premises.

$$
\begin{array}{|l}
\hline
\text{\textit{Leave}} \\
\hline
\Delta\,\textit{Office} \\
\textit{identity}? : \text{PERSON} \\
\hline
\textit{identity}? \in \textit{staff} \\
\textit{identity}? \in \text{dom } \textit{availability} \rhd \{\text{In}\} \\[4pt]
\textit{staff}' = \textit{staff} \\
\textit{place}' = \textit{place} \\
\textit{availability}' = \{\textit{identity}?\} \lhd \textit{availability} \\
\hline
\end{array}
$$

$\left.\begin{array}{}\\\\\end{array}\right\}$ . . . . pre condition

$\left.\begin{array}{}\\\\\\\end{array}\right\}$ . . . . . . post condition

Obviously, the above is a partial operation since it might not succeed in the event of the value provided as the input *identity?* not satisfying the precondition stated in the specification. This requires the specification of additional exception handling operations and their integration with the above in order to produce a total operation.

Although it has not been used in this text, an initialization of a system (i.e. its initial state) may be specified using a schema decorated with a dash.

Example: The initial state of the system represented by *Office* may be specified as

$$
\textit{Office}_{\textit{init}} \,\hat{=}\, \textit{Office}' \mid \textit{staff}' = \varnothing \wedge \textit{place}' = \varnothing \wedge \textit{availability}' = \varnothing
$$

where, using the notation |, we have extended the after state *Office'* with some additional predicates. The predicates being used signify that every component of the specification is initially empty.

References

[1] M. Abadi and L. Lamport. An old-fashioned recipe for real time. In J. W. de Bakker, C. Huizing, W. P. de Roever, and G. Rozenberg, editors, *Real-Time: Theory and Practice*, volume 600 of *Lecture Notes in Computer Science*. Springer-Verlag, 1991.

[2] W. B. Ackerman. Data flow languages. *Computer*, 15, February 1982.

[3] T. Agerwala. Putting Petri nets to work. *IEEE Computer*, December 1979.

[4] J. F. Allen. Towards a general theory of action and time. *Artificial Intelligence*, 23, 1984.

[5] R. Alur and T. A. Henzinger. Logics and models of real time: A survey. In J. W. de Bakker, C. Huizing, W. P. de Roever, and G. Rozenberg, editors, *Real-Time: Theory and Practice*, volume 600 of *Lecture Notes in Computer Science*. Springer-Verlag, 1991.

[6] P. E. Ammann and J. C. Knight. Data diversity: An approach to software fault tolerance. *IEEE Trans. on Computers*, 37(4), 1988.

[7] T. Anderson and J. C. Knight. A framework for software fault tolerance in real-time systems. *IEEE Trans. on Software Engineering*, 9(3), 1983.

[8] T. Anderson and P. A. Lee. *Fault Tolerance – Principles and Practice*. Prentice-Hall International, 1981.

[9] B. Banieqbal, H. Barringer, and A. Pnueli, editors. *Temporal Logic in Specification*, volume 398 of *Lecture Notes in Computer Science*. Springer-Verlag, 1987.

[10] J. A. Bannister and K. S. Trivedi. Task allocation in fault-tolerant distributed systems. *Acta Informatica*, 20:261–281, 1983. (appears also in [157]).

[11] R. E. B. Barnard. Electronic interlockings, a survey of approaches to safety-critical signalling systems. IEE Vacation School on Railway Signalling and Control Systems, University of Bermingham, 19–23 September, IEE, 1994.

[12] M. D. Beaudry. Performance-related reliability measures for computing systems. *IEEE Trans. on Computers*, 27(6), 1978.

[13] S. Bennett. *Real-Time Computer Control*. Prentice Hall, 1994.

[14] B. Berthomieu and M. Diaz. Modeling and verification of time dependent systems using time Petri nets. *IEEE Trans. on Software Engineering*, 17, March 1991.

[15] S. H. Bokhari. Partitioning problems in parallel, pipelined and distributed computing. *IEEE Trans. on Computers*, pages 48–57, June 1988.

[16] S. D. Brookes. *A Model for Communicating Sequential Processes*. PhD thesis, Oxford University, 1983.

[17] G. Bucci and E Vicario. Compositional validation of time-critical systems using communicating time Petri nets. *IEEE Trans. on Software Engineering*, 21(12), 1995.

[18] A. Burns and A. Wellings. *Real-Time Systems and Programming Languages*. Addison-Wesley, 1991.

[19] J. P. Calvez. *Embedded Real-Time Systems – A Specification and Design Methodology*. Wiley, 1993.

[20] T. L. Casavant and J.G. Kuhl. A taxonomy of scheduling in general-purpose distributed computing systems. *IEEE Trans. on Software Engineering*, 14(2), February 1988.

[21] Z. Chaochen, C. Hoare, and A. Ravn. A calculus of durations. *Information Processing Letters*, 40(5), 1991.

[22] Z. Chaochen, A. Ravn, and M. Hansen. An extended duration calculus for hybrid real-time systems. In R. Grossman et al., editors, *Hybrid Systems*, volume 736 of *LNCS*, pages 36–59. Springer-Verlag, 1993.

[23] S. Cheng and J.A Stankovic. Scheduling algorithms for hard real-time systems – a brief survey. In J.A. Stankovic and Ramamritham, editors, *Hard Real-Time Systems – Tutorial*. IEEE Computer Society, 1988.

[24] W. W. Chu, L. J. Holloway, M. Lan, and K. Efe. Task allocation in distributed data processing. *IEEE Computer*, November 1980.

[25] W. W. Chu and L. M. Lan. Task allocation and precedence relations for distributed real-time systems. *IEEE Trans. on Computers*, June 1987.

[26] J. C. Cluley. *Reliability in Instrumentation and Control*. Butterworth–Heineman Ltd, 1993.

[27] J. E. Coolahan and Roussopoulos. Timing requirements for time-driven systems using augmented Petri nets. *IEEE Trans. on Software Engineering*, 9(5), 1983. (appears also in [157]).

[28] E. Corsetti, A. Montanari, and E. Ratto. Dealing with different time granularities in formal specifications of real-time systems. *The Journal of Real-Time Systems*, (3):191–215, 1991.

[29] P. Coveney and R. Highfield. *The Arrow of Time*. Flamingo, 1991.

[30] A. H. Cribbens. Solid-state interlocking (ssi): An integrated electronic signalling system in mainline railways. *IEE Proceedings*, 134, Part B(3), May 1987.

[31] A. Cuhadar and A. C. Downton. Structured parallel design for embedded vision systems: An application case study. 5th International Conference on Image Processing and its Applications, 4–6 July. IEE, 1995.

[32] T. E. Curtis and R. J. Ward. Digital beam forming for sonar system technology. *IEE Proceedings*, 127, Part F(4), 1980.

[33] B. Dasarathy. Timing constraints of real-time systems: Constructs for expressing them, methods for validating them. *IEEE Trans. on Software Engineering*, 11(1), January 1985. (appears also in [157]).

[34] J. Davies. *Specification and Proof in Real-Time Systems*. Cambridge University Press, 1993.

[35] J. Davies and S. A. Schneider. Making things happen in timed CSP. Technical Report PRG-TR-2-90, Oxford University Computing Laboratory, 1990.

[36] J. Davies and S. A. Schneider. Real-time CSP. In T. Rus and C. Rattray, editors, *Theories and Experiences for Real-Time System Development*. World Scientific, 1994.

[37] J. B. Dennis. Data flow supercomputers. *Computer*, 13, November 1980.

[38] M. L. Dertouzos and A.K. Mok. Multi-processor on-line scheduling of hard real-time systems. *IEEE Trans. on Software Engineering*, 15(12), December 1989.

[39] D. Dolev, C. Dwork, and L. Stockmeyer. On the minimal synchronization needed for distributed consensus. *Journal of the ACM*, 34(1), July 1987.

[40] A. C. Downton, Tregidgo R. W. S., and A. Cuhadar. Top-down structured parallelisation of embedded image processing applications. *IEE Proceedings – Vision, Image and Signal Processing*, 141(6):431–437, December 1994.

[41] K. Edwards. *Real-Time Structured Methods – Systems Analysis*. Wiley, 1993.

[42] K. Efe. Heuristic models of task assignment scheduling in distributed systems. *IEEE Computer*, June 1982.

[43] B. Furht, D. Grostick, D. Gluch, G. Rabbat, J. Parker, and M. McRoberts. *Real-Time Unix Systems*. Kluwer Academic Publishers, 1991.

[44] D. M. Gabbay, I Hodkinson, and M. Reynolds. *Temporal Logic, Mathematical Foundations and Computational Aspects*, volume 1 of *Oxford Logic Guides 28*. Clarendon Press, Oxford, 1994.

[45] R. Gale. *The Philosophy of Time*. Macmillan, 1968.

[46] A. Galton. *The Logic of Aspect, An Axiomatic Approach*. Clarendon Press Oxford, 1984.

[47] A. Galton. *Temporal Logics and Their Applications*. Academic Press, 1987.

[48] C. Ghezzi, D. Mandrioli, S. Morasca, and M. Pezze. A general way to put time in Petri nets. In *Proc. of Int. Workshop on Software Specification and Design*. IEEE Computer Society, 1989.

[49] C. Ghezzi, D. Mandrioli, S. Morasca, and M. Pezze. A unified high-level Petri net formalism for time-critical systems. *IEEE Trans. on Software Engineering*, 17(2), 1991.

[50] M. J. Gonzalez. Deterministic processor scheduling. *Computing Surveys, ACM*, 9(3), September 1977.

[51] R. Gusella and S. Zatti. The Accuracy of Clock Synchronization Achieved by TEMPO in Berkeley UNIX 4.3BSD. *IEEE Trans. on Software Engineering*, 15(7), July 1989.

[52] W. A. Halang and A. D. Stoyenko. *Constructing Predictable Real-Time Systems*. Kluwer Academic Publishers, 1991.

[53] N. Halbwachs. *Synchronous Programming of Reactive Systems*. Kluwer Academic Publishers, 1993.

[54] R. Hale. Using temporal logic for prototyping: The design of a lift controller. In H. Zedan, editor, *Real-Time Systems – Theory and Applications*. Elsevier Science Publishers, 1990.

[55] D.A. Harrison. A real-time language based on explicit timeouts. In P.J. Fleming and D.I Jones, editors, *Algorithms and Architectures for Real-Time Control*, number 4 in IFAC Workshop Series, pages 129–134, Bangor, Wales, 1992. Pergamon Press.

[56] H. Hecht. Fault-tolerant software. *IEEE Trans. on Reliability*, 28(3), 1979.

[57] C. Heitmeyer and D. Mandrioli, editors. *Formal Methods for Real-Time Computing*. Wiley, 1996.

[58] M. Hennessy. *Algebraic Theory of Processes*. The MIT Press, 1988.

[59] C. A. R. Hoare. *Communicating Sequential Processes*. Prentice Hall, 1985.

[60] B. Hoogeboom and W. A. Halang. The concept of time in the specification of real time systems. In K. M Kavi, editor, *Real-Time Systems – Abstractions, Languages and Design Methodologies*. IEEE Computer Society Press, 1992.

[61] J. Hooman. Compositional verification of distributed real-time systems. In H. Zedan, editor, *Real-Time Systems – Theory and Applications*. Elsevier Science Publishers, 1990.

[62] A. L. Hopkins, T. B. Smith, and J. H. Lala. FTMP – a highly reliable fault tolerant computer for aircraft control. *IEEE Proceedings*, 66(10), 1978.

[63] C. Houstis. Module allocation of real-time applications to distributed systems. *IEEE Trans. on Software Engineering*, 16(7), 1990.

[64] J. P. Huang. Modeling software partition for distributed real-time applications. *IEEE Trans. on Software Engineering*, 11(10), 1985.

[65] B. Indurkhya, H. S. Stone, and L. Xi-Cheng. Optimal partitioning of randomly generated distributed programs. *IEEE Trans. on Software Engineering*, 12(3), 1986.

[66] F. Jahanian and A.K. Mok. Safety analysis of timing properties in real-time systems. *IEEE Trans. on Software Engineering*, 12(9), 1986. (appears also in [157]).

[67] P. Jalote. *Fault Tolerance in Distributed Systems*. Prentice Hall, 1994.

[68] K. Jensen. *Coloured Petri Nets – Basic Concepts, Analysis, Methods and Practical Use*, volume 1. Springer-Verlag, 1996.

[69] K. Jensen. *Coloured Petri Nets – Basic Concepts, Analysis, Methods and Practical Use*, volume 2. Springer-Verlag, 1996.

[70] M Joseph, editor. *Real-Time Systems – Specification, Verification and Analysis*. Prentice Hall, 1996.

[71] *Journal of Real-Time Systems*. Kluwer Academic Publishers, from 1989.

[72] K. M Kavi, editor. *Real-Time Systems – Abstractions, Languages and Design Methodologies*. IEEE Computer Society Press, 1992.

[73] A. Kay and J. N Reed. Using rely and guarantee method for TCSP: A specification and design of a telephone exchange. Technical Report PRG-TR-11-91, Oxford University Computing Laboratory, 1991.

[74] A. Kay and J. N. Reed. A rely and guarantee method for timed CSP: A specification and design of a telephone exchange. *IEEE Trans. on Software Engineering*, 19(6), June 1993.

[75] R. M. Kieckhafer, C. J. Walter, A. M. Finn, and P. M. Thambidurai. The MAFT architecture for distributed fault tolerance. *IEEE Trans. on Computers*, 37(4):398–405, 1988.

[76] M. Klein, T. Ralya, B. Pollak, R. Obenza, and M. G. Harbour. *A Practitioners' Handbook for Real-Time Analysis – Guide to Rate Monotonic Analysis of Real-Time Systems*. Kluwer Academic Publishers, 1994.

[77] M. H. Klein, J. P. Lehoczky, and R. Rajkumar. Rate-monotonic analysis for real-time industrial computing. *IEEE Computer*, January 1994.

[78] W. C. Knight, R. G. Pridham, and S. M. Kay. Digital signal processing for sonar. *Proceedings of the IEEE*, 69(11), 1981.

[79] R. Koo and S. Toueg. Checkpointing and rollback-recovery for distributed systems. *IEEE Trans. on Software Engineering*, 13(1), 1987.

[80] H. Kopetz. Clock Synchronization. In B. Randell, editor, *Real-Time Systems*, The Joint University of Newcastle Upon Tyne / International Computers Ltd Seminar, 6–9 September 1989. Computing Laboratory, University of Newcastle Upon Tyne, UK, 1989.

[81] H. Kopetz and W. Ochsenreiter. Clock synchronization in distributed real-time systems. *IEEE Trans. on Computers*, 36(8), August 1987. (appears also in [157]).

[82] R. Koymans. (real) time: A philosophical perspective. In J. W. de Bakker et al., editors, *Real-Time: Theory and Practice*, volume 600 of *LNCS*. Springer-Verlag, 1991.

[83] S. T. Kuhn. Tense and time. In D. Gabbay and F. Guenthner, editors, *Handbook of Philosophical Logic*, volume IV, chapter IV.8, pages 513–552. 1968.

[84] R. Kurki-Suonio. Real time: Further misconceptions (or half-truths). *IEEE Computer*, June 1994.

[85] J. H. Lala, R. E. Harper, and L. S. Alger. A design approach for ultra-reliable real-time systems. *IEEE Computer*, pages 12–22, May 1991.

[86] L. Lamport. Time, clocks, and the ordering of events in a distributed system. *Communication of the ACM*, 21(7), July 1978.

[87] L. Lamport. Using time instead of timeout for fault-tolerant distributed systems. *ACM Transactions on Programming Languages and Systems*, 6(2), April 1984.

[88] L. Lamport and P. M. Melliar-Smith. Synchronizing clocks in the presence of faults. *Journal of the ACM*, 32(1), January 1985.

[89] L. Lamport, R. Shostak, and M. Pearse. The Byzantine Generals' Problem. *ACM Transactions on Programming Languages and Systems*, 4(3), July 1982.

[90] E. A. Lee and D. G. Messerschmitt. Static scheduling of synchronous data flow programs for digital signal processing. *IEEE Trans. on Computers*, 36(1), January 1987. (appears also in [157]).

[91] J. Lehoczky, L. Sha, and Y. Ding. The rate monotonic scheduling algorithm: Exact characterization and average case behaviour. In *6th IEEE Real-Time Systems Symposium*, pages 166–171, Williamsburg, Va., 1989.

[92] S. Levi and A. K. Agrawala. *Real-Time System Design*. McGraw-Hill, 1990.

[93] B. Littlewood. Software reliability model for modular program structure. *IEEE Trans. on Reliability*, 28(3), 1979.

[94] C.L. Liu and J.W. Layland. Scheduling Algorithms for Multiprogramming in a Hard Real-Time Environment. *Journal of the ACM*, 20(1), 1973. (appears also in [157]).

[95] L.Y. Liu and R.K. Shyamasundar. Static analysis of real-time distributed systems. *IEEE Trans. on Software Engineering*, 16(4), 1990.

[96] J.R. Lucas. *A Treatise on Time and Space*. Methuen & Co. Ltd, 1973.

[97] P. R. Ma, E. Y. S. Lee, and M. Tsuchiya. A task allocation model for distributed computing systems. *IEEE Trans. on Computers*, 31(1), 1982. (appears also in [157]).

[98] T Maibaum. A logic for formal requirements specification of real-time embedded systems. Technical report, Imperial College of Science and Technology, 1987.

[99] P. Mataga and P. Zave. Formal specification of telephone features. In J. P. Bowen and J. A. Hall, editors, *Z User Workshop*, Cambridge, 1994. Springer-Verlag.

[100] P. M. Merlin and D. J. Farber. Recoverability of communication protocols – implications of a theoretical study. *IEEE Trans. on Communications*, 24, September 1976.

[101] R. Milner. *Communications and Concurrency*. Prentice Hall, 1989.

[102] J.J. Molini, S.K. Maimon, and P.H. Watson. Real-time system scenarios. In *Proceedings of 11th Real-Time Systems Symposium*. IEEE Computer Society, 1990.

[103] L. Motus and M. G. Rodd. *Timing Analysis of Real-Time Software*. Pergamon, 1994.

[104] R. R. Muntz and E. G. Coffman. Preemptive scheduling of real-time tasks in multiprocessor systems. *Journal of the ACM*, 17(2), April 1970. (appears also in [157]).

[105] T. Murata. Petri nets: Properties, analysis and applications. *Proceedings of the IEEE*, 77(4), April 1989.

[106] W.H. Newton-Smith. *The Structure of Time*. Routledge & Kegan Paul, 1980.

[107] D. Niehaus, K. Ramamritham, J. A. Stankovic, G. Wallace, and C. Weems. The spring scheduling co-processor: Design, use and performance. In *Proceedings of Real-Time Systems Symposium*. IEEE Computer Society, 1993.

[108] N. Nissanke. A tutorial on the logic of aspect. Technical Report SEG/RTS/93/1, Department. of Computer Science, University of Reading, 1993.

[109] N. Nissanke. Safety specification in deontic logic. In *Proceedings*, 2nd IMA Conference on the mathematics of Dependable Systems, York, England. The Institute of Mathematics and its Applications, 1995.

[110] N Nissanke and R. J. Loader. Reactive scheduler for realtime systems. In *Proceedings*, 20th IFAC/IFIP Workshop on Realtime Programming, pages 107–114. Elsevier Press, 1996.

[111] N. Nissanke and R. Robinson. Formal methods in safety analysis. In V. Maggioli, editor, *SAFECOMP'94*, International Conference on Computer Safety, Reliability and Security, pages 239–248, Anaheim, California, 1994. Instrument Society of America.

[112] Director of S & T Engineering and Director of Operations. *Standard Signalling Principles*. British Railways Board.

[113] S. Osaki. Performance/reliability measures for fault-tolerant computing systems. *IEEE Trans. on Reliability*, 33(4), October 1984.

[114] J.S. Ostroff. *Temporal Logic for Real-Time Systems*. John Wiley and Sons, 1989.

[115] S. Owre, J. M. Rushby, N. Shankar, and F. von Henke. Formal verification for fault-tolerant architectures: Prolegomena to the design of pvs. *IEEE Trans. on Software Engineering*, 21(2), February 1995.

[116] M. A. Palis, J-C. Liou, and D. S. L. Wei. Task clustering and scheduling for distributed memory parallel architectures. *IEEE Trans. on Parallel and Distributed Systems*, 7(1), 1996.

[117] E. H. J. Pallett. *Automatic Flight Control*. Granada Publishing Ltd, London, 1979.

[118] M. Pearse, R. Shostak, and L. Lamport. Reaching agreement in the presence of faults. *Journal of the ACM*, 27(2), April 1980.

[119] J. L. Peterson. Petri nets. *Computing Surveys*, 9(3), September 1977.

[120] J. L. Peterson. *Petri Net Theory and the Modeling of Systems*. Prentice Hall, 1981.

[121] I. Pyle, P. Hruschka, M. Lissandre, and K. Jackson. *Real-Time Systems – Investigating Industrial Practice*. Wiley, 1993.

[122] R. Rajkumar. *Synchronization in Real-Time Systems – A Priority Inheritance Approach*. Kluwer Academic Publishers, 1991.

[123] P. Ramanathan and K. G. Shin. Use of common time base for checkpointing and rollback recovery in a distributed system. *IEEE Trans. on Software Engineering*, 19(6), June 1993.

[124] C. Ramchandani. Analysis of asynchronous concurrent systems by Petri nets. Technical Report Project MAC, TR-120, MIT, Cambridge, MA, 1974.

[125] B. Randell. System structure for software fault tolerance. *IEEE Trans. on Software Engineering*, 1(2), June 1975.

[126] B. Randell, P. A. Lee, and P. C. Treleaven. Reliability issues in computing system design. *ACM Computing Surveys*, 10(2):123–165, June 1978.

[127] G. S. Rao, H. S. Stone, and T. C. Hu. Assignment of tasks in a distributed processor system with limited memory. *IEEE Trans. on Computers*, 28(4), 1979.

[128] A. P. Ravn, H. Rischel, and K. M. Hansen. Specifying and verifying requirements of real-time systems. *IEEE Trans. on Software Engineering*, 19(1):41–55, 1993.

[129] *Real-Time Systems Symposium, Proceedings*. IEEE Computer Society (Annually).

[130] F. Redmill and T. Anderson. *Safety-Critical Systems: Current Issues, Techniques and Standards*. Chapman & Hall, 1993.

[131] G. M. Reed. *A Uniform Mathematical Theory for Real-Time Distributed Computing*. PhD thesis, Oxford University, 1988.

[132] G.M. Reed and A.W. Roscoe. A timed model for communicating sequential processes. volume 226 of *LNCS*. Springer-Verlag, 1986.

[133] W. Reisig. *Petri Nets – An Introduction*. Springer-Verlag, 1985.

[134] N. Rescher. On the logic of chronological propositions. *Mind*, 75, 1966.

[135] C. Reutenauer. *The Mathematics of Petri Nets*. Prentice Hall, 1990.

[136] D.J. Roberts and P.M. Sharkey. Clock Synchronization for Distributed Virtual Reality. Technical report, Department. of Cybernetics, University of Reading, UK, 1994.

[137] Rockwell Collins, Collins Air Transport Division, Rockwell International Corporation, Cedar Rapids, Iowa 52498, USA. *What is VOR/ILS? – Instruction Guide*, 1985.

[138] T. Rus and C. Rattray. *Theories and Experiences for Real-Time System Development*. World Scientific, 1994.

[139] J. M. Rushby and F. von Henke. Formal verification of algorithms for critical systems. *IEEE Trans. on Software Engineering*, 19(1), January 1993.

[140] F Saglietti. Fault tolerance by software diversity: How and when? In V. Maggioli, editor, *SAFECOMP'94*, International Conference on Computer Safety, Reliability and Security, pages 239–248, Anaheim, California, 1994. Instrument Society of America.

[141] M. Schiebe and S. Pferrer. *Real-Time Systems Engineering and Applications*. Kluwer Academic Publishers, 1992.

[142] S. A. Schneider. *An Operational Semantics for Timed CSP*. PhD thesis, Oxford University, 1991.

[143] W. Schutz. *The Testability of Distributed Real-Time Systems*. Kluwer Academic Publishers, 1993.

[144] P. Senac and M. Diaz. Un modele formel pour la specification et la verification des sytemes temps reels (time stream Petri nets). In *RTS'94*, Real-Time System Conference, pages 141–154, Paris, 1994. Teknea Toulouse.

[145] L. Sha and J. B. Goodenough. Real-time scheduling theory and ada. *IEEE Computer*, April 1990.

[146] L. Sha, R. Rajkumar, and J. P. Lehoczky. Priority inheritance protocols: An approach to real-time synchronization. *IEEE Trans. on Computers*, 39(9), September 1990.

[147] L. Sha and S.S. Stahaye. A systematic approach to designing distributed real-time systems. In S. H. Son, editor, *Advances in Real-Time Systems*. Prentice Hall, 1995.

[148] K. G. Shin and P. Ramanathan. Clock synchronization of a large multiprocessor system in the presence of faults. *IEEE Trans. on Computers*, 36(1), January 1987.

[149] D.P Siewiorek and R. S. Swarz. *The Theory and Practice of Reliable System Design*. Digital Press, 1982.

[150] A. Simpson. A formal specification of an automatic train protection system. In M. Naftalin, T. Denvir, and M. Bertran, editors, *FME '94: Industrial Benefit of Formal Methods: Proceedings of the Second International Symposium of Formal Methods Europe, Barcelona, Spain, October 1994*, volume 873 of *LNCS*. Springer-Verlag, 1994.

[151] S. H. Son, editor. *Advances in Real-Time Systems*. Prentice Hall, 1995.

[152] M. Spivey. *The Z Notation*. Prentice Hall, 1992.

[153] T. K. Srikanth and S. Toueg. Optimal clock synchronization. *Journal of the ACM*, 34(3), July 1987.

[154] J. A. Stankovic and K. Ramamritham. The design of the spring kernel. Real-Time Systems Symposium, pages 146–157. IEEE, 1987. (appears also in [157]).

[155] J. A. Stankovic and K. Ramamritham. The spring kernel: A new paradigm for real-time systems. *IEEE Computer*, May 1991.

[156] J. A. Stankovic, M. Spuri, M. Di Natale, and C. Buttazzo. Implications of classical scheduling results for real-time systems. *IEEE Computer*, pages 16–25, June 1995.

[157] J.A. Stankovic and K. Ramamritham. *Hard Real-Time Systems - A Tutorial*. IEEE Computer Society Press, 1988.

[158] J.A. Stankovic, K. Ramamritham, and P. Shiah. Efficient scheduling algorithms for real-time multi-processor systems. *IEEE Trans. on Parallel and Distributed Systems*, 1(2), April 1990.

[159] H. S. Stone. Multiprocessor scheduling with the aid of network flow algorithms. *IEEE Trans. on Software Engineering*, 3(1), 1977.

[160] J. J. P. Tsai, B. Yi, S. J. M. Yang, and R. A. W. Smith. *Distributed Real-Time Systems - Monitoring, Visualization, Debugging and Analysis*. Wiley-Interscience, 1996.

[161] K. Turner. *Using Formal Description Techniques*. Wiley, 1993.

[162] K. Vairavan and R. A. DeMillo. On the computational complexity of a generalized scheduling problem. *IEEE Trans. on Computers*, 25(11), November 1976.

[163] A. M. van Tilborg and G. M. Knob. *Foundations of Real-Time Computing – Formal Specifications and Methods*. Kluwer Academic Publishers, 1991.

[164] A. M. van Tilborg and G. M. Knob. *Foundations of Real-Time Computing – Scheduling and Resource Management*. Kluwer Academic Publishers, 1991.

[165] J. Vytopil. *Formal Techniques in Real-Time and Fault Tolerant Systems*, volume 571 of *LNCS*. Springer-Verlag, 1992.

[166] J. Vytopil. *Formal Techniques in Real-Time and Fault Tolerant Systems*. Kluwer Academic Publishers, 1993.

[167] I. Watson and J. Gurd. A practical data flow computer. *Computer*, 15, February 1982.

[168] J. H. Wensley, L. Lamport, J. Goldberg, M. W. Green, K. V. Levitt, P. M. Melliar-Smith, R. E. Shostak, and C. B. Weinstock. SIFT: Design and analysis of a fault-tolerant computer for aircraft control. *IEEE Proceedings*, 66(10):1240–1255, 1978. (appears also in [157]).

[169] G. J. Whitrow. *The Natural Philosophy of Time*. Thomas Nelson & Sons Ltd, 1961.

[170] A. A. Winder. Sonar system technology. *IEEE Trans. on Sonics and Ultrasonics*, 22(5), 1975.

[171] J. Xu. Multiprocessor scheduling processes with release times, deadlines, precedence and exclusion relations. *IEEE Trans. on Software Engineering*, 19(2), February 1993.

[172] J. Xu and D. L. Parnas. Scheduling processes with release times, deadlines, precedence and exclusion relations. *IEEE Trans. on Software Engineering*, 16(3), March 1990.

[173] J. Xu and D. L. Parnas. On satisfying timing constraints in hard real-time systems. *IEEE Trans. on Software Engineering*, 19(1), January 1993.

Index

RABHI, F.A., and LAPALME, G., *Designing Algorithms with Functional Languages* (forthcoming)

ROSCOE, A.W. (ed.), *A Classical Mind: Essays in honour of C.A.R. Hoare*

ROZENBERG, G., and SALOMAA, A., *Cornerstones of Undecidability*

SHARP, R., *Principles of Protocol Design*

SLOMAN, M. and KRAMER, J., *Distributed Systems and Computer Networks*

SPIVEY, J.M., *An Introduction to Logic Programming through Prolog*

SPIVEY, J.M., *The Z. Notation: A reference manual (2nd edn)*

TENNENT, R.D., *Semantics of Programming Languages*

WATT, D.A., *Programming Language Concepts and Paradigms*

WATT, D.A., *Programming Language Processors*

WATT, D.A., *Programming Language Syntax and Semantics*

WATT, D.A., WICHMANN, B.A. and FINDLAY, W., *ADA: Language and methodology*

WELSH, J. and ELDER, J., *Introduction to Modula-2*

WELSH, J. and ELDER, J., *Introduction to Pascal (3rd edn)*

WIKSTRÖM, Å., *Functional Programming Using Standard ML*

WOODCOCK, J. and DAVIES, J., *Using Z: Specification, refinement, and proof*